2108 $10

SECESSION TO SIEGE 1860 / 1865

THE CHARLESTON ENGRAVINGS

BY
DOUGLAS W. BOSTICK

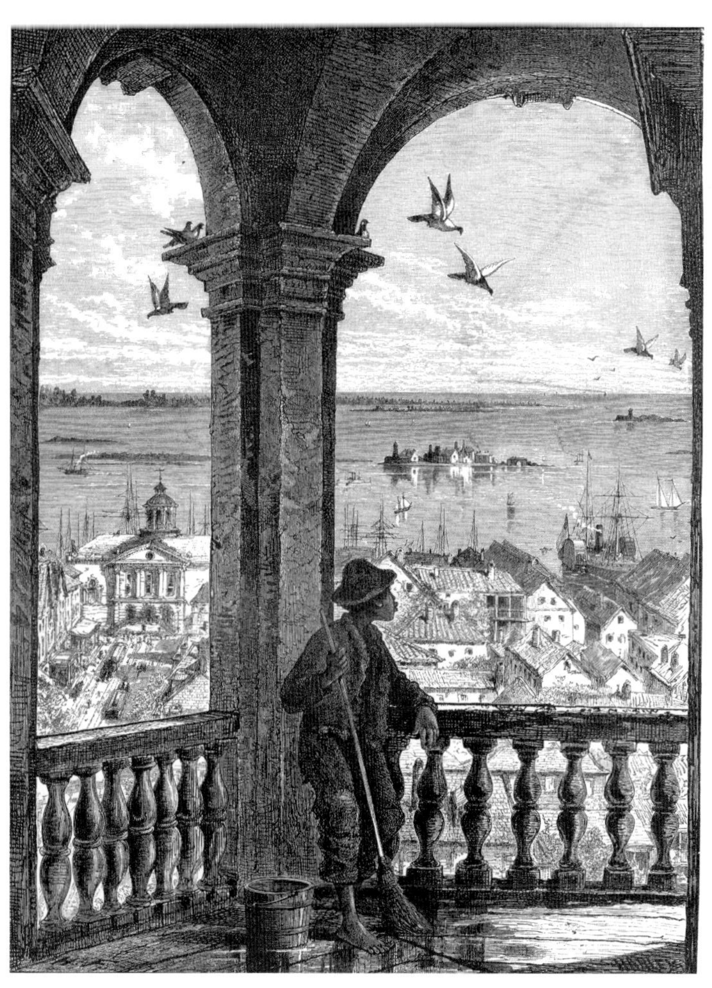

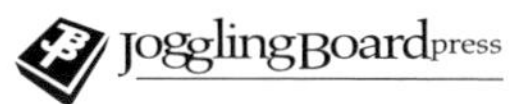

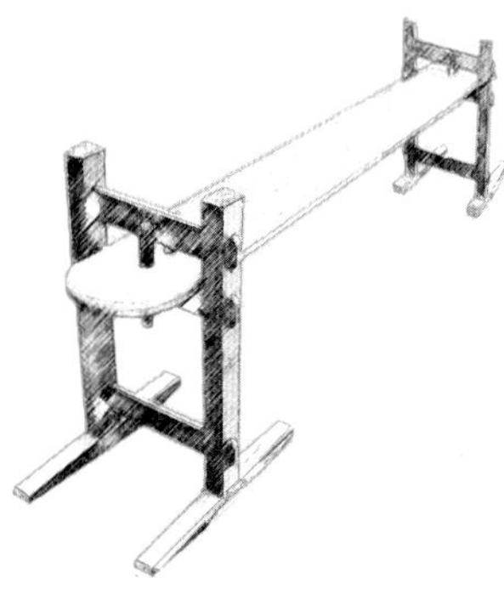

THE JOGGLING BOARD

Legend has it the idea for the joggling board came to South Carolina from Scotland in the early 1800s. The long board supported by rockers at each end allows for several persons to joggle and rock together. This playful outdoor furniture became a common site in the 19th century, gracing Southern porches, yards and piazzas. It is said that no daughter went unmarried in any antebellum home that was host to a joggling board.

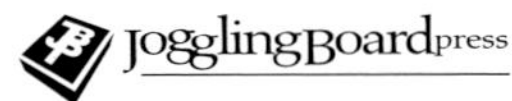

Published by Joggling Board Press
Joggling Board Press, LLC
P.O. Box 13029
Charleston, S.C. 29422

Copyright © 2004 by Douglas W. Bostick and Susan Kammeraad-Campbell
Printed and bound in the United States of America.
All rights reserved.
First edition

All illustrations are from the author's collection.
Design by Damon Simmons

No part of this book may be reproduced or transmitted in any form or by any means, electronic or mechanical, including photocopying, recording, or by information storage and retrieval system – except by a reviewer who may quote brief passages in a review to be printed in a magazine, newspaper, or on the Web – without permission in writing from the publisher. For information, please contact the publisher.

First printing April 2004.

A CIP catalog record for this book has been applied for from the Library of Congress.
ISBN 0-9753498-0-5

Attention corporations, universities, colleges and professional organizations: Quantity discounts are available for bulk purchases of this book for educational or gift purposes and as premiums for increasing magazine subscriptions or renewals. For information, please contact Joggling Board Press, LLC, P.O.Box 13029, Charleston, S.C., 29422. Ph. (843) 225-6009, www.jogglingboardpress.com.

TABLE OF CONTENTS

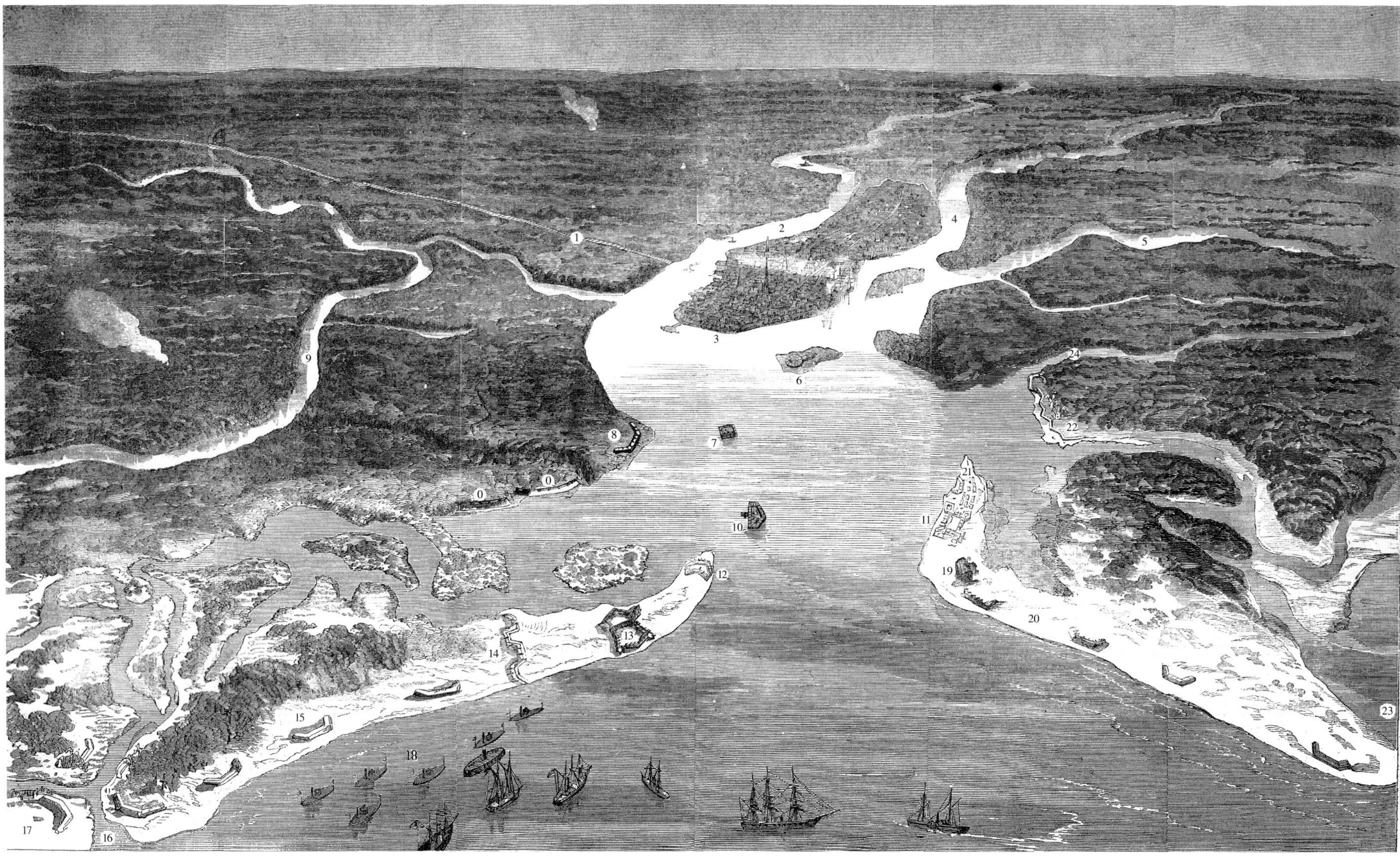

Bird's-Eye View of Charleston

Artist: unknown
Harper's Weekly

This *Harper's Weekly* illustration provides an excellent bird's-eye view of the harbor defenses, the Union Army and fleet, and the significance of them all to the harbor of Charleston during the long siege and blockade.

1– Charleston & Savannah Railroad
2– Ashley River
3– Charleston
4– Cooper River
5– Wando River
6– Castle Pinckney
7– Fort Ripley
8- Fort Johnson (James Island)
9– Stono River
10– Fort Sumter
11– Fort Moultrie
12– Battery Gregg (Cummings Point)
13– Fort Wagner
14– General Gillmore's advanced batteries
15– Captured works–Morris Island
16– Lighthouse Inlet
17– Union Battery–Folly Island
18– Ironclads and wooden ships
19– Hotel
20– Sullivan's Island and rebel batteries
21– Moultrieville
22– Mount Pleasant
23– Breach Inlet
24– Shem Creek
0,0– Rebel batteries on James Island

PREFACE

Like many Charlestonians, I became interested in history at an early age. My grandfather, J. Frank Taylor, shared many stories of our ancestors with me. I learned about the Revolutionary-era Sons of Liberty. He riveted me with tales of my great-great-grandfather, George Flagg Trescot, a daring blockade runner during the siege of Charleston, who finished the war in New York's Elmira Prison.

My grandfather owned a water drilling company, and he often took me where his work took him – Fort Sumter, Sheldon Church ruins, Magnolia Cemetery, Hell Hole Swamp, Kiawah Island, Fort Moultrie. So I became familiar with all sorts of lowcountry gems.

A decade ago, I began studying historic newspapers, first on microfilm, later as a collector. At first, I sought the various printed stories for research on other projects. It quickly became obvious that the method and manner in which the stories were told in the newspapers of the day was a story in itself. This is particularly so for the illustrated newspapers, which convey the story with both narrative and illustrations.

This book is not intended to offer a comprehensive story of the Civil War in Charleston. Nor is it my purpose to offer a detailed explanation of the political events leading to secession. These issues have been taken up effectively in other works. In writing and compiling this book, my intent is to provide readers an opportunity to see the images of the war that were presented to 19th-century readers and, through the text, help to illuminate highlights of the war in Charleston.

Some of the illustrations published here may be familiar. Others have rarely been seen. Many were sketched by war correspondents or military officers on the scene as the action occurred. Some of the illustrations published were simply drawn in New York from descriptions of war events arriving by telegraph. All were used to tell the story of the Civil War in Charleston to readers in the 19th century.

Two notable events in Charleston were not covered by illustrations. The first was the capture of the Union gunship *Isaac P. Smith* in January 1863. The story is a fascinating one and may be the only time an enemy naval vessel was captured from land batteries alone. The second event was the sinking of the *U.S.S. Housatonic* by the Confederate submersible, the *Hunley*, in February 1864. At the time of the sinking, Union Adm. John Dahlgren assumed the attack was made by a torpedo boat much like the *David*, which attacked the *New Ironsides* in October 1863. Both events occurred during a lull of war activity in Charleston, and, at the time, none of the illustrated newspapers had a correspondent in the area.

These illustrations were not intended to be works of art but to serve an informational purpose. Very quickly, though, illustrations from *Harper's Weekly* and *Frank Leslie's Illustrated Newspaper* were recognized for their artistic value and often were displayed in homes during the 19th century. Not only did the illustrators provide effective visuals of the war but their work also influenced American perceptions and culture. From the many political cartoons, to the evolution of the manner in which blacks were depicted, to the depiction of Thomas Nast's Santa Claus in a December 1862 issue of *Harper's Weekly* (the first appearance of the jolly man as we know him today), the 19th-century illustrated newspapers had a profound impact.

I want to thank Susan Kammeraad-Campbell of Joggling Board Press for her editorial work and her prodding, curious inquisitions and her fresh perspective on this project. This book would not have been possible without her; she always elevates my work.

I also want to thank Damon Simmons of Nomad Designz for his creative input and suggestions in layout and design creation. The staffs at the Charleston Library Society, South Carolina Room at the Charleston County Public Library and the South Carolina Historical Society have always been a great help in my research. Many thanks go to Timothy Hughes Rare and Early Newspapers and Danny Petterson with Petterson Antiques for their help in acquiring additional illustrations needed for this project.

I want to thank my daughter Katey and my two sons Brooks and Taylor for their support and patience while I spent many hours researching and writing, as well as for their many enthusiastic hours at the dinner table and on family trips playing "Bostick family history trivia." Finally, I want to thank my wife Karen. Her support, encouragement and love have allowed me to pursue my passion for history. Every writer needs an angel to guide him.

Milby Burton stated in his notable work, *The Siege of Charleston,* "History cannot be changed; it can only be clarified." I hope, in some small way, *Secession to Siege* clarifies the Civil War in Charleston for you.

Douglas W. Bostick

P R O L O G U E

Images of War

At the time of the American Civil War, newspapers that carried illustrations were rare. Only a handful of publishers had the technology to print images quickly – among them *Frank Leslie's Illustrated News, Harper's Weekly*, the *Illustrated London News* and *New York Illustrated News*. Artists and journalists in the field became the eyes and ears of the war, bringing the conflict into the homes of Americans in a way never before possible.

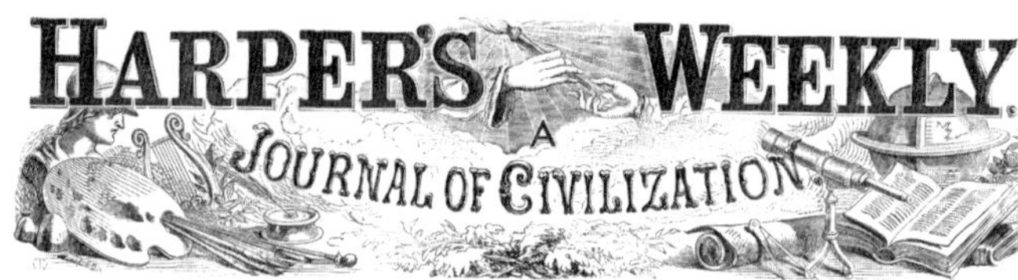

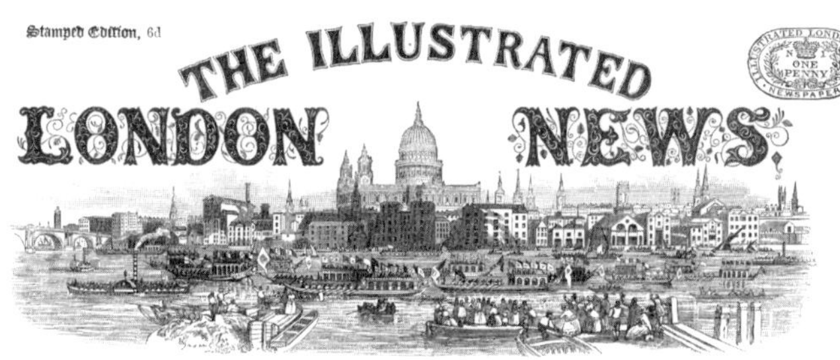

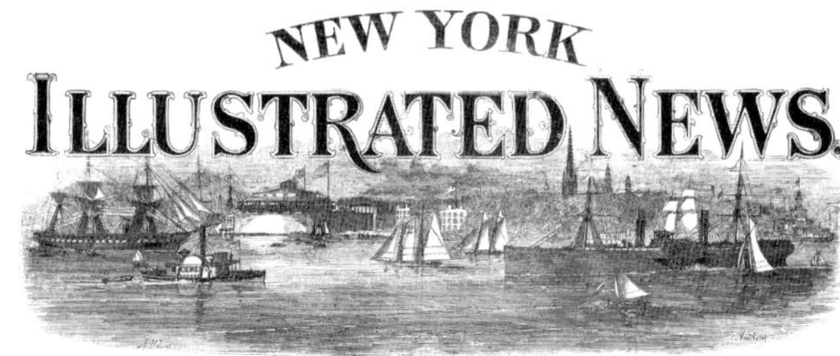

The engravings that make up *Secession to Siege, 1860-65: The Charleston Engravings* are the same images seen by 19th-century readers from Britain to Boston, from Chattanooga to Charleston, some of them experiencing the war at arm's length, some right in the thick of it. In crucial ways, the impact of these engravings on Americans at that time was of the magnitude television coverage had on Americans a century later during the Vietnam War.

By 1860, there were more than 50,000 miles of telegraph wire criss-crossing the nation and more than 2,500 newspapers distributing news to Americans. And, while photography was becoming prevalent, the process of translating a photograph onto a printing-plate would not develop for another decade.

The engravings that ran in the illustrated papers during the Civil War had tremendous influence, shaping readers' views of and responses to the conflict. The illustrated newspapers put a face on the war.

The Beginning

Woodcuts were developed in ancient Egypt and Babylonia and used by the Romans for stamping letters and symbols. In the early 15th century, woodcut engravings were used to make religious pictures. After the invention of the printing press, woodcuts were used throughout Europe and, later, in Colonial America's early newspapers. The process was slow and tedious, sometimes taking as long as 30-60 days to make one woodcut.

In 1842, Herbert Ingram, a young news agent, moved from Nottingham to London. In his business, he noticed that any time the newspapers published engravings on the front page, sales were higher. He conceived of a weekly newspaper that would make liberal use of engraved images. The first issue of the *Illustrated London News* was published on May 14, 1842, and sold 26,000 copies. The paper's format each week was 16 pages and 32 engravings. Herbert recognized that "visual appeal is the essence of drama," and his paper was an instant success.

One artist engraver employed by Ingram was a young man named Henry Carter. Carter used the *nom de plume* of Frank Leslie when signing his drawings. It wasn't long before Carter was in charge of the engraving department for the *Illustrated London News*.

Coming to America

Carter came to America in 1848 as Frank Leslie, opening an engraving shop in New York at 98 Broadway, where he met Phineas T. Barnum. Leslie and Barnum began a mutually beneficial relationship in which Barnum promoted Leslie's work and Leslie illustrated the program for P.T. Barnum's Jenny Lind Tour, which traveled the country in 1850-51.

Upon his return to New York, Leslie worked with Frederick Gleason to create America's first illustrated paper, *Gleason's Pictorial Drawing-Room Companion*. Leslie quickly moved on and began the *Illustrated News* with Barnum in 1853. After only 11 months, though, the paper ceased publication and was sold to *Gleason's Pictorial*.

By 1855, Leslie founded *Frank Leslie's Illustrated Newspaper*. The weekly paper was an enormous success, using a format similar to his former London employer. The paper was 16 pages in length and contained engravings on eight of the pages. By 1858, *Leslie's* circulation was 90,000 copies per issue with some special editions as large as 130,000.

Leslie soon encountered competitors, the most notable being Fletcher Harper. J & J Harper & Co. began as a small printing firm in 1817. By 1825, the growing company was the largest book publisher in the United States. After studying Leslie's craft, Harper and Brothers launched *Harper's Weekly Journal of Civilization* in 1857, also based in New York.

In November 1859, a third illustrated newspaper began, called the *New York Illustrated News*. While this new venture published news through 1864, the paper was in constant financial trouble and had four editors and three ownership changes in its four years.

From Sketch to Reader

Reader response made it clear the public wanted illustrations of current events. Leslie was at the forefront, creating innovations in centralizing, subdividing and speeding production.

The sketch was only the first step in printing the engraving. When the field sketch was delivered to the paper's offices, it was re-worked to provide greater detail. After much experimentation, the Turkish boxwood tree became the wood of choice. An outline drawing was created, then rubbed down in reverse on a plank of polished and whitewashed Turkish boxwood.

The engravings were cut across the grain so the wood could handle fine detail. The fibers in the boxwood ran vertically rather than horizontally, providing a surface which would not splinter.

Once carved, the wood could hold fine lines to produce detailed drawings. The Turkish tree, however, presented some challenges. At full maturity, it was only 6 ins. in diameter. To use this preferred wood, Leslie bolted small blocks together to accommodate the larger engravings.

When the sketch was rubbed on the wood, the image was reinforced with India ink and pencil, then sent to the engraving department. Leslie created a system of work division to decrease the time required to produce an engraving. The engraving would then be unbolted and the pieces distributed to some 15 engravers. A double-page engraving could require up to 40 engravers. Each engraver, wearing eyeshades and looking through a watchmaker's lens, carved his block of wood, placing it securely on a small sandbag. The engraver carved out the spaces between the lines, referred to as "cutting out the negative."

Using this "divisible wood block" system reduced the time for the completion of an engraving from one week to as short as eight hours. Over time, engravers took on specialties. One man might be more skilled at carving clouds and sky, while another at people or ships. Once a block was completed, the large image was reassembled, and a master engraver cut in the lines running from one wood block to another.

This block was then "electrotyped," a process that involved the making of a beeswax mold of the entire page, then immersing it in an electro-charged bath with copper particles. This created a thin copper plate to be used on the printing press. Given that the plates had a limited life, multiple plates were made from each engraving in order to maintain quality and extend the print runs.

Leslie's purchase of the Taylor Perfecting Press in 1858 greatly increased the speed of his operation. *Frank Leslie's Illustrated Newspaper*, at 16 pages, was printed on two sides of a large sheet of paper. One side was eight pages of text and illustrations; the second side was eight pages of text. The large printed sheets were delivered to a packing room where the issues were folded then mailed or delivered to newsagents.

Each engraving cost the publisher as much as $30 to have it drawn and cut. A double-page illustration ran as high as $130. In 1860, Leslie's expenditures for his paper included $7,000 for ink and $160,000 for paper. He employed 130 editors, artists, engravers.

Once Leslie had refined the process, he could put out copies of his paper within 48 hours of receiving the rough sketch.

Part of Leslie's strength as a publisher was his experience in the newspaper business, starting out as a simple engraver. This detailed knowledge helped him to design a system that worked. Throughout his career, he continued to supervise the preparation of each illustration from sketch to printing press.

The Coming Conflict

In the years leading up to the war, both *Leslie's* and *Harper's* opposed abolition. Because of its moderate stance on slavery, critics called the illustrated paper "Harper's Weakly." Even though their positions on slavery might have been questioned by abolitionists, the struggle over slavery and the depictions of blacks in the illustrated papers, though often buffoonish and minstrel-like, brought many new readers to the weekly papers.

Both papers enjoyed a substantial readership in the South, and neither would put itself at financial risk by taking controversial editorial positions. Politically, both *Harper's* and *Leslie's* preferred William Seward or Stephen Douglas for U.S. president in 1860, which appeased Southern readers. But then, after Abraham Lincoln's election to the presidency, *Harper's* published a series of controversial editorials that offended many Southerners. As a result, Charleston bookstores cancelled their orders for *Harper's Weekly* and many Southern postmasters refused to deliver the paper.

Leslie's, by contrast, had gained the confidence of Southerners through its cautious coverage of the presidential elections.

Leslie sent journalist William Waud, an Englishman, to Charleston in November 1860. Given England's leanings in support of the Southern states, Waud's accent and manner opened many doors for him in Charleston. Leslie was specific in his instructions to Waud, telling him to be careful not to offend Carolinians with his reports or sketches.

When Union Major Robert Anderson moved his small garrison from Fort Moultrie to Fort Sumter, both illustrated newspapers scrambled to provide "on-site" coverage. Fletcher Harper personally traveled to Charleston in January 1861 and arranged with Capt. Truman Seymour, an officer in Anderson's command, to cover developments at Fort Sumter. Seymour was formerly a drawing instructor at West Point and capable of providing competent sketches to *Harper's Weekly*. With the Charleston authorities unwilling to host a *Harper's* correspondent, illustrations outside of Fort Sumter were created based on reading telegraph reports.

By February 1861, both *Harper's* and *Leslie's* accepted that the Southern states would form a nation, and called for the U.S. government to reach a compromise to avoid a conflict.

Waud was granted permission to sketch the Confederate batteries around Charleston and to cover the significant news events. Gov. Francis W. Pickens, though, barred him from Fort Sumter. Waud drew a total of 35 sketches for *Leslie's* in Charleston prior to the firing on Fort Sumter.

He then traveled to Montgomery, Ala., to cover Jefferson Davis' inauguration, returning to Charleston in time to cover the events leading to the firing on Fort Sumter. Leslie also sent Eugene Benson to Charleston just before the firing on Fort Sumter. The young artist sketched several scenes of excited crowds during the bombardment.

On March 29, 1861, Confederate Gen. P. G. T. Beauregard terminated mail delivery to and from Fort Sumter. This effectively eliminated *Harper's* access to firsthand sketches on the scene in Charleston. As telegraph reports of the bombardment of Sumter reached New York, *Harper's* illustrated two unlikely scenes, an obvious mistake resulting from not having a reporter on site. The cover of the May 4, 1861, issue (see page 61) of *Harper's Weekly* showed the spectators on the Charleston housetops watching and weeping over the bombardment of Sumter. Given the great cheering and celebrations covered by *Leslie's*, the despair shown on the *Harper's* cover was unlikely.

A second questionable illustration was published in the April 27, 1861, issue (see page 62) depicting Union soldiers on the parade ground at Sumter calmly watching as incoming shells exploded. Apparently, *Harper's* simply altered an earlier illustration from its Feb. 16 issue (see page 52) to depict action in the fort. The men at Fort Sumter would not have been standing in the open during this intense engagement.

A New Demeanor

After the bombardment of Fort Sumter, all three New York illustrated papers adopted strong positions in support of the Union. Initially cool toward Lincoln, the New York papers became ardent supporters of the president and his policies.

In July 1861, *Leslie's* and *Harper's* claimed to have 50 artists/correspondents in the field traveling with the Union army. By September, *Leslie's* circulation was more than

100,000. Both papers' strong Union stance outraged Southerners, who saw the papers as sharply biased. Eliza Francis Andrews of Georgia writes in her journal:

> *The pictures in* Harper's Weekly *and* Frank Leslie's *tell more lies than Satan himself was the father of. I get in such a rage when I look at them that sometimes I take off my slipper and beat the senseless paper with it.*

Carlton McCarthy, a Confederate private with the Richmond Howitzers, writes:

> *The Confederate soldier fought bounties and regular monthly pay; the "Stars and Stripes," the "Star Spangled Banner," "Hail Columbia," "Tramp, Tramp, Tramp"... He fought good wagons, fat horses and tons of quartermasters stores; pontoon trains, of splendid material and construction, by the mile; gunboats, wooden and iron, and man-of-war; illustrated papers, to cheer the "Boys In Blue" with sketches of the glorious deeds they did not do.*

Even Lincoln paid a clear compliment to the impact of the illustrated papers. He writes:

> *Thomas Nast [with* Harper's Weekly*] has been our best recruiting sergeant... His emblematic cartoons have never failed to arouse enthusiasm and patriotism, and have always seemed to come just when these articles were getting scarce.*

'Not a luxury, but a necessity'

In response to the partisan reporting of the New York illustrated papers, Ayers and Wade, a Richmond publishing company, launched the *Southern Illustrated News* in September 1862. The newspaper sought to be the voice for the Southern cause. But the paper was besieged with problems from the outset.

Most of the Southern illustrators at the outbreak of the war were in New Orleans and Baltimore. Baltimore was behind enemy lines, and New Orleans fell in 1862. The few engravers who could be pressed into service were busy engraving currency and stamps for the new Southern nation. Often, counterfeit Confederate money spread through the South from sources in the North and was easily detectable because the quality of the engravings was simply too high.

An ad in the *Southern Illustrated News* read, "Engravers Wanted. Desirous, if possible, of illustrating the *News* in a style not inferior to the *Illustrated London News*, We offer the highest salaries ever paid in the country for good engravers."

The first issue of the *Southern Illustrated News* was published on Sept. 13, 1862. Under the paper's name, the masthead reads, "Not a luxury, but a necessity." The paper announced, "We shall present engravings of battles as they actually occurred, and not from sketches originating only in the brains of our artists."

Constant shortages of paper, ink and personnel plagued the Southern paper, which was never able to employ competent engravers. As a result, the paper never presented a battle-scene engraving. The eight-page issues typically featured a crude engraving of a Confederate general on the cover drawn from a portrait and a cartoon on the back page.

At its peak, the *Southern Illustrated News* had a circulation of 20,000, but that was short-lived. Beyond all of its production problems, the paper was also beset with problems of credibility. The paper printed inaccuracies. On the cover of the Jan. 17, 1863, issue, the paper published its first engraving of the beloved Confederate commander Robert E. Lee. The copy identified Lee with his full name but listed his middle name as Edmund rather than Edward. In a more grave error, the *Southern Illustrated News* first reported the battle of Gettysburg as a Confederate victory.

The last issue of the *Southern Illustrated News* was published on Oct. 29, 1864. Two other attempts to publish illustrated newspapers with a Southern perspective, were *Southern Punch* and the *Raleigh Illustrated Mercury*, but both ventures quickly fizzled.

The South, however, was not without a voice. At the outbreak of the war, the *Illustrated London News* sent Frank Vizetelly to cover the war. One of the first battles he covered was the Confederate victory at Bull Run. In reviewing the resulting sketches, U.S. Secretary of War Edwin M. Stanton was incensed at the depiction of the fleeing Union soldiers. Stanton subsequently rejected a request by Vizetelly to travel with Gen. George McClellan's army into Virginia.

Vizetelly ultimately joined the Confederate troops covering Vicksburg, the siege of Charleston and Chattanooga. The *Illustrated London News* published 133 of his engravings during the course of the war. Few of the issues of the *Illustrated London News* that carried Vizetelly's engravings, however, ever made it to the South due to the blockade. In fact, a number of Vizetelly's engravings bound for London by blockade runner were absconded by Union sailors and sold to *Harper's Weekly*, where they appeared in print.

Through his coverage of the war, Vizetelly became an ardent supporter of the Confederate cause and of Southern culture. He was rewarded with the honorary rank of captain in the Confederate army after he served as a messenger for Gen. James Longstreet during the Battle of Chickamauga.

Covering the Siege

Harper's and *Leslie's* provided intense coverage of the siege of Charleston. Northern readers harbored great resentment for Charleston; the illustrated papers were eager to provide coverage that bolstered that resentment. By 1863, neither paper was in good stead with the Confederates, making it difficult for them to report developments within the Southern army.

Leslie sent W. T. Crane to Charleston in 1863 as a correspondent. He was familiar with South Carolina, having covered the Union Army and Navy at Port Royal. His illustrations of the Port Royal Experiment, portraying the government's work with former slaves on the South Carolina sea islands, fed readers' appetites in 1862.

Gen. Quincy Gillmore, Union commander in Charleston, was so impressed with Crane's illustrations and his attention to detail that he included Crane's sketches in his official reports. This, of course, only served to boost the credibility and enhance the image of the newspaper. Crane fell ill in 1865 and died just after the end of the war.

Harper's sent Theodore "Theo" Russell Davis to Charleston. Davis had covered Gen. Ulysses S. Grant at Vicksburg in the spring of 1863 and arrived in Charleston in July just after the fateful charge of the 54th Massachusetts on Battery Wagner. Davis often traveled with British journalist William H. Russell, pretending he was with the *Illustrated London News*. This ruse was effective in occasionally getting him behind Confederate lines. He became a spy for the North, detailing the weaponry in the Southern arsenal.

Davis proved an intrepid reporter, always trying to catch the best vantage point while action was under way. He was wounded twice during the war and at least once had his horse shot out from under him. Davis was highly regarded for the detailed sketches and notes he took during battle, covering more battles and engagements than any other Civil War correspondent.

In 1864 when the siege of Charleston hit a lull, Davis joined William T. Sherman for the "March To The Sea."

Authenticity, Accessibility and Immediacy

The illustrated newspapers and their war coverage evolved during the four years of the conflict. Early in the war, illustrations were more romantic in their depictions. The public and the press did not expect the war to last as long as it did. Romantic notions about the pageantry of marching off to war soon gave way to more realistic images of pain, suffering and death.

War photographers often charged that the illustrations lacked authenticity. The illustrated papers responded by attributing sketches to their artists and authors, a practice also adopted by the daily papers by 1863. *Leslie's* issued pre-stamped drawing pads to their artists stating, "An actual sketch, made on the spot by one of the special Artists of *Frank Leslie's Illustrated Newspaper*. Mr. Leslie holds the copyright and reserves the exclusive rights of publication."

Photographs had their own limitations. The technology of photography had not evolved to capture the action of a battle as it unfolded. Most pictures were taken of battle scenes after the fight was over. Some battlefield photographers were known to move corpses to heighten the drama in a specific picture. The New York illustrated newspapers published close to 6,000 war illustrations. The chief advantage they held over photographs was their "accessibility and immediacy" compared to photograph albums or the expensive New York photographic parlors that were the purview of the elite.

In the field, commanders on both sides followed the illustrated papers. In late 1861, Sherman charged, "You fellows make the best spies that can be bought. Jeff Davis owes more to you newspapermen than to his army." A Union officer stationed in Port Royal, S.C., had his brother mail copies of *Leslie's* to him. He writes, "His map of this place is very correct; we went by it altogether on our last reconnaissance and found it entirely correct."

Grant, anxiously following the developments in Charleston, bypassed the Union command and requested sketches directly from Davis regarding harbor operations. Grant responded, "These [sketches] clear up the situation far better than printed descriptions that have reached us."

Accurate or not, authentic or not, the illustrated papers conveyed powerful images that had a profound impact on readers in the North and South. Early in the war, the artists drew predictable illustrations of camps and battlefields. By the war's end, they had evolved to illustrate scenes and events that interpreted the larger military, political and social issues of the war.

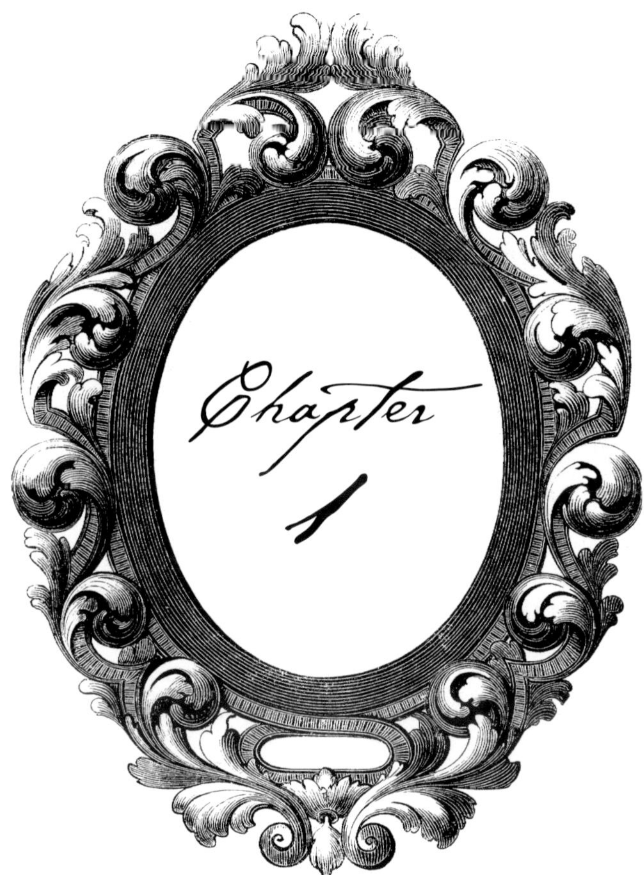

South Carolina Secedes

The seeds of secession were planted long before 1860. As early as the 1820s, John C. Calhoun, South Carolina's native son, espoused the doctrine of nullification, essentially believing that all states had a right to "nullify" any federal law which was contrary to its best interest or in conflict with its own sovereign laws. Calhoun was the leading proponent of the political philosophy that came to be called states' rights. Even after his death in 1850, it was Calhoun's philosophy that guided South Carolina down the path to secession a decade later.

Biographer Carl Sandburg points out in his works on Abraham Lincoln that before the Civil War the common reference was "the United States are," but after 1865 it became proper to say "the United States is." Even officers of the U.S. Army, when taking their oath stated, "these United States," not "the United States."

The expansion of slavery into the Western territories was argued in newspapers and debated in political circles, conventions and elections as the nation edged toward war. But there were other compelling issues fueling the fire of secession. Industrial factions were in an economic and political struggle with agricultural factions to control government and public policy. The South perceived it was being exploited by the commercial interests of the North.

By 1860, raw cotton was the nation's leading export commodity. Southern raw goods and agricultural products were essential to the success of manufacturing in the North and in Europe. Southerners preferred direct trade with Europe, but the Northern-controlled Congress imposed tariffs, making the import of European goods exorbitant. Through the imposition of these trade tariffs, Northern manufacturers sought to retain their Southern markets for finished goods just barely undercutting the European tariffs.

Author Charles Dickens, who closely followed the sectional conflict in America, writes in a published letter:

> *... the North having gradually got to itself the making of the laws and the settlement of the Tariffs, and having taxed the South most abominably for its own advantage, began to see, as the country grew, that unless it advocated the laying down of a geographical line beyond which slavery should not extend, the South would necessarily recover*

its old political power, and be able to help itself a little in the adjustment of commercial affairs.

Further, Southerners feared the election of a Republican to the White House was a precursor to the adoption of high-tariff policies. The confluence of these divisive issues contributed to the growing movement for Southern nationalism.

At the 1860 Democratic Convention, Southern delegates were determined to preserve the sovereignty of the new Western territories on the issue of slavery. Despite the party's conciliatory move to hold the convention in the South, the proceedings and the resulting deadlock proved a fiasco.

Believing that Lincoln would be elected president, South Carolina Gov. W. H. Gist began corresponding with other Southern governors, hoping to garner support for secession. He strongly preferred that another state take the lead in secession, fearing that South Carolina's reputation for political extremism might deter other states from joining the movement.

South Carolina leaders, increasingly concerned over being perceived as hot-headed and arrogant, courted Georgia to lead the secession movement. William Henry Trescot, a South Carolinian and former assistant secretary of state for the Buchanan administration, wrote to South Carolina Congressman William Porcher Miles that Georgia must lead this movement to secure support among the Southern states: "Give her [Georgia] all the glory... We must cut up by the roots some home ambitions and much home selfishness." Meanwhile, others suggested South Carolina try to co-opt Alabama, to which S.C. Congressman Lawrence Keitt issued this rejoinder: "If we wait for Alabama, we will wait eternally."

Robert Barnwell Rhett and his son, editor of the *Charleston Mercury*, had long held that if any one state were bold enough to secede, the rest of the South would surely follow. By the time Lincoln was elected, South Carolina was losing patience. Representatives from Mississippi and Alabama indicated their respective states would follow South Carolina in secession.

In the presidential election, the Democratic votes were split between Stephen Douglas, candidate for the Northern Democrats, and John C. Breckinridge, candidate for the Southern Democrats. Lincoln was elected president with only 40 percent of the popular vote.

After the election, the secession movement gained momentum. On Nov. 7, Charleston federal Judge Andrew Magrath resigned his position, to be followed three days later by U.S. Senator James Chesnut. Initially, fellow Senator James Hammond opposed secession. Hammond, in a 34-page letter, suggested Lincoln's election alone was not sufficient to merit withdrawal from the Union. Three days later, Hammond reversed himself and resigned.

In a letter to a family member, he writes:

I thought Magrath and all those fellows were great apes for resigning and have done it myself. It is an epidemic and very foolish. It reminds me of the Japanese who when insulted rip open their own bowels... People are wild.

In December, Francis W. Pickens was elected governor of South Carolina. In his inaugural speech, he pledged the state would "open her ports free to the tonnage and trade of all nations" once secession occurred. The Northern newspapers were quick to react. The *Chicago Times*, in an editorial echoing the sentiments of most of the Northern press, writes:

In one single blow our foreign commerce must be reduced to less than one-half what it now is. Our coastwise trade would pass into other hands. One-half of our shipping would lie idle at our wharves. We should lose out trade with our South, with its immense profits. Our manufactories would be in utter ruins. Let the South adopt the free-trade system, or that of a tariff for revenue, and these results would likely follow. If protection be wholly withdrawn from our labor, it could not compete, with all the prejudices against it, with the labor of Europe. We should be driven from the market, and millions of our people would be compelled to go out of employment.

South Carolina moved to select a quick date for the convention to consider secession. On Dec. 20, 1860, South Carolina became the first state to secede from the Union.

Charleston Episcopal priest the Rev. A. Toomer Porter, in his 1898 autobiography, recalls the vote on the Ordinance of Secession:

The ordinance of secession was read, and a stillness that could be felt prevailed... Yea after yea, was answered until every name was called, and the vote was unanimous.

Then each went up and signed the paper, and the deed was done, which cost millions and millions of money, tens of thousands of lives, destruction of cities and villages, plantations and farms, the emancipation of five millions of African slaves, the entire upheaval of society, the impoverishment of a nation; and let loose a demoralization which has left its impress on the whole land, North and South. It was a deed which made the North rich and the South poor, and has made Southern life one great struggle from that day to this.

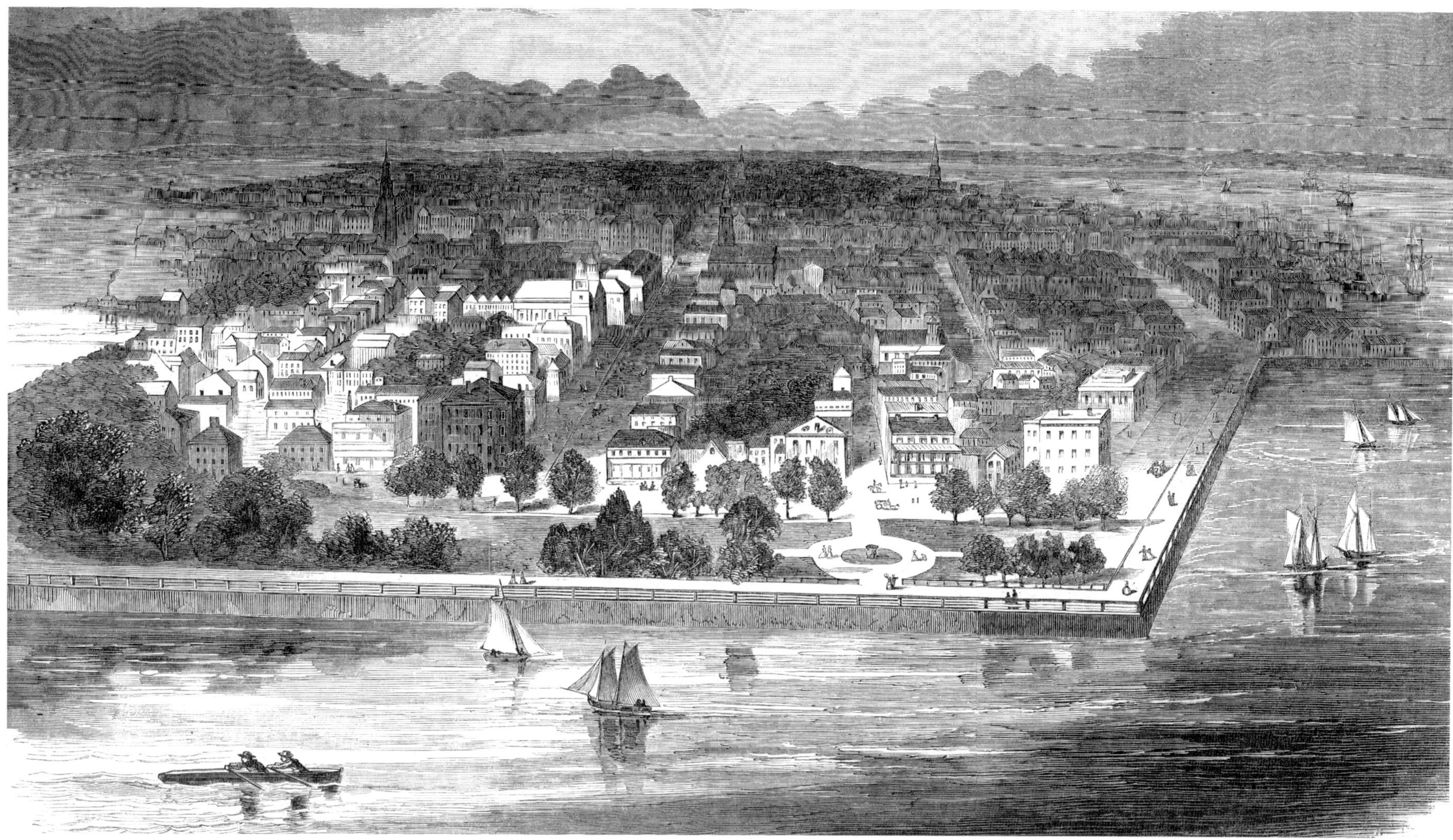

Rising Like Venice from the Ocean

Artist: unknown
Harper's Weekly

The nation was focused anxiously on the coming National Democratic Convention, knowing the fate of the Union might well rest in the hands of the delegates who would assemble in Charleston.

The decision was made to convene the convention in Charleston in hopes the selection of a Southern site might bring some measure of unity and harmony. As the Convention delegates arrived, the city was a welter of spring color.

Harper's Weekly reintroduced readers to Charleston with the printing of an illustration previously published in 1857. The editor writes:

> *It [Charleston] is, we need hardly add, one of the oldest, noblest, and most beautiful cities of the South... As you enter from the sea, between the Islands of Sullivan and Morris, the city opens before you in the fore-ground, five miles distant – rising, like another Venice, from the ocean.*

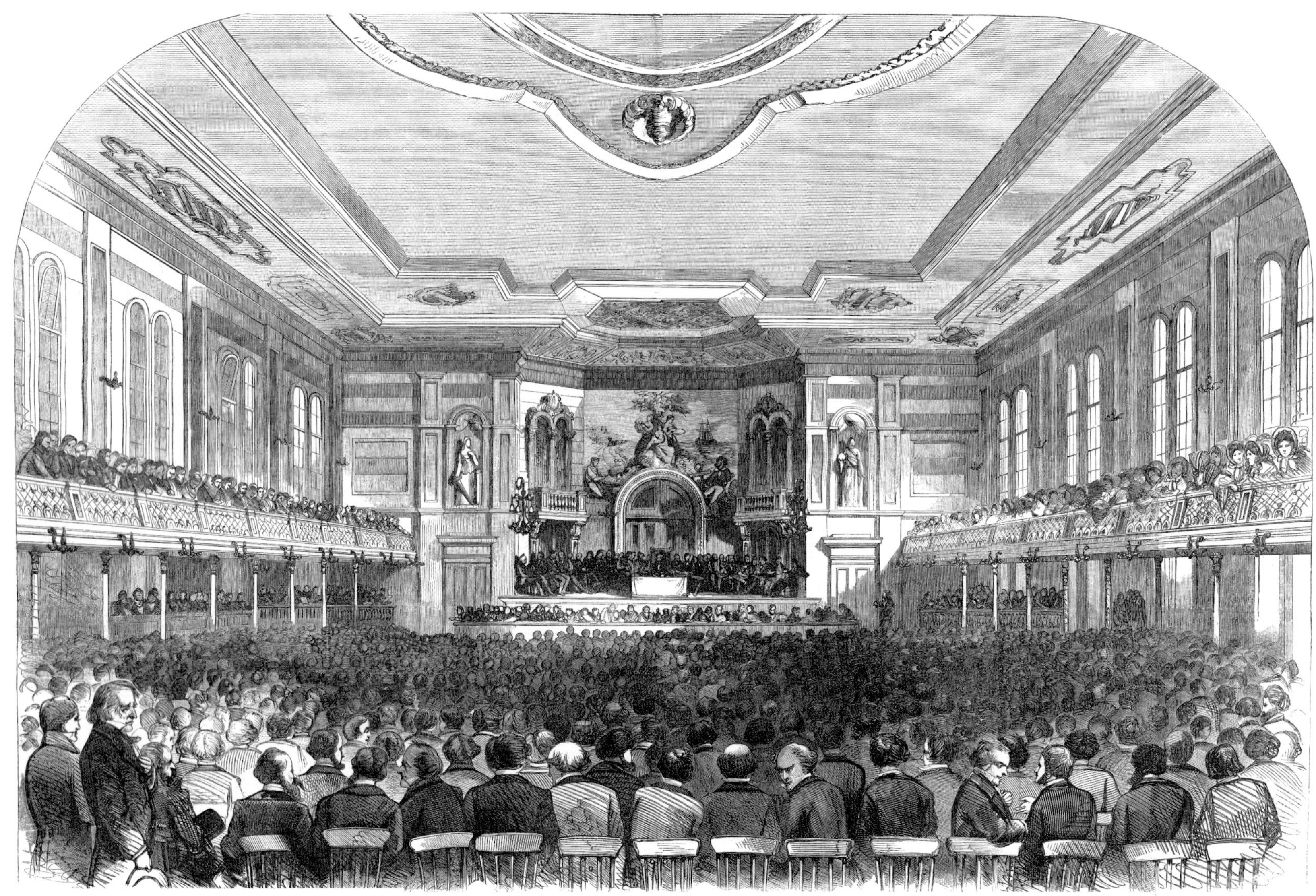

1860 Democratic Convention

Artist: unknown
Harper's Weekly

The National Democratic Party Convention of 1860 was a key event leading to secession and the beginning of the Civil War. While no one in the Democratic Party wanted the Republicans to win the presidency, there were serious divisions within the party.

This illustration is of the convention in session, located at South Carolina Institute Hall at 134 Meeting Street. More than 3,000 people crowded into the hall to witness the 606 delegates at work. Ironically, eight months later, the hall would be the site of the signing of the Ordinance of Secession.

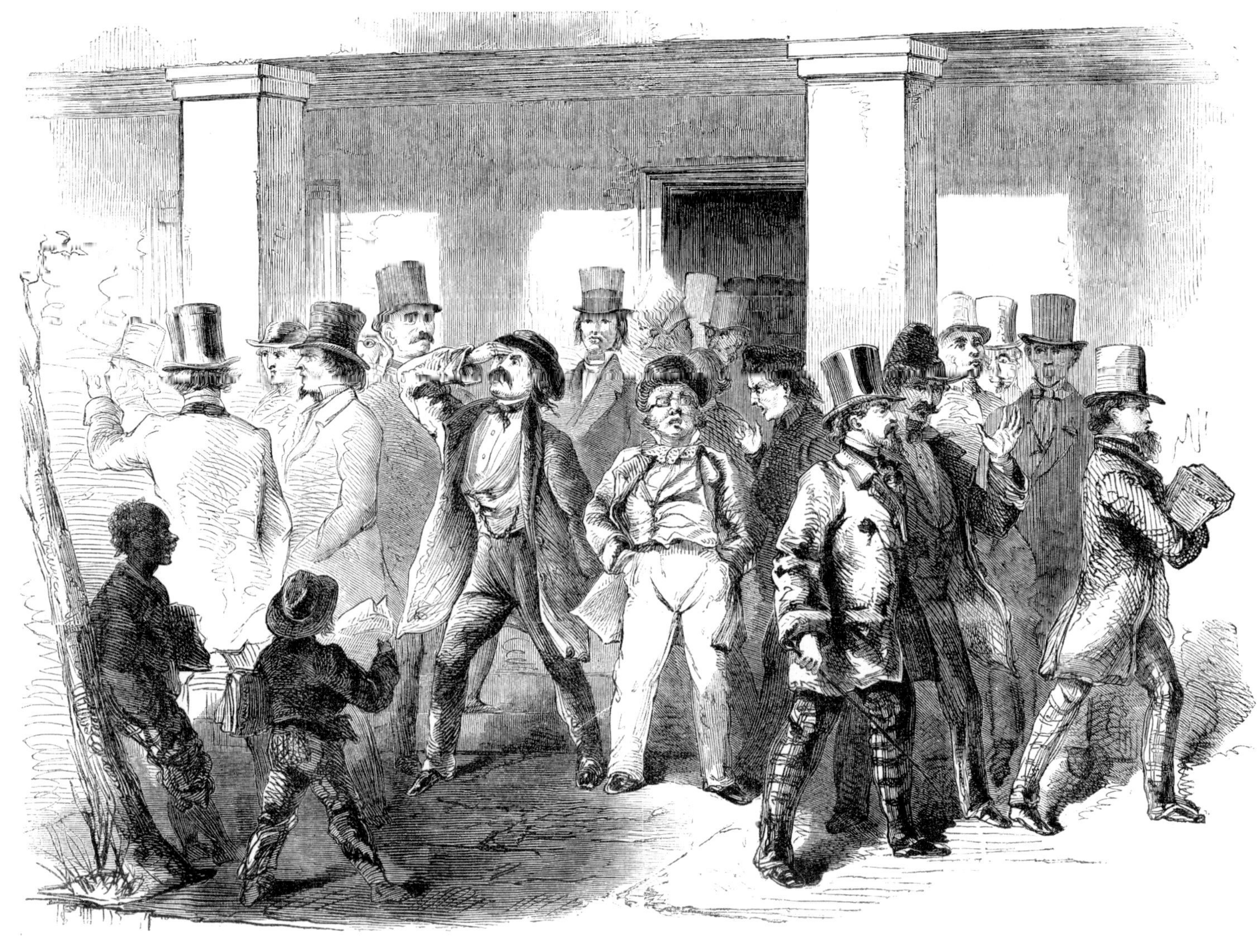

Delegates to the Democratic Convention

Artist: unknown
Harper's Weekly

Charleston was too small to host a convention of this magnitude. The city lacked sufficient hotel and boarding rooms to accommodate the many delegates and spectators in attendance. Delegates began arriving as early as April 18, 1860, for the convention, which began on April 23.

Harper's Weekly describes the convention as "momentous... and upon the fruit of whose labors the destiny of the Union may depend." As the convention unfolded, the party split between Northern and Southern factions over the issue of slavery in the Western territories. The factions deadlocked.

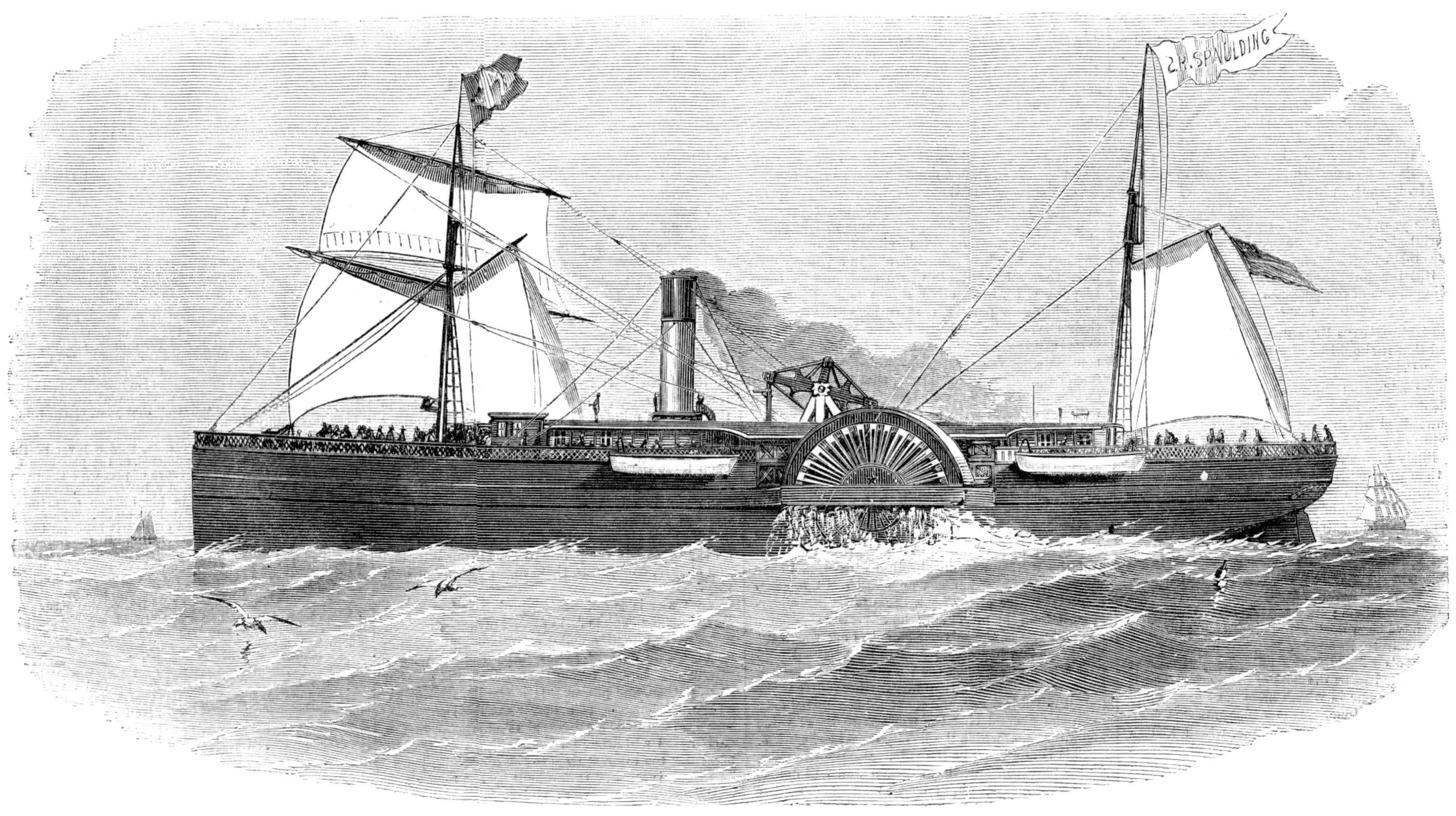

S. R. Spaulding

Artist: unknown
Harper's Weekly

With hotel space in Charleston limited, many delegations made other arrangements. The delegates from Boston arrived in Charleston by boat and lived aboard while attending the 1860 Democratic Convention.

The *S. R. Spaulding*, the steamship housing the Bostonians, was a new iron steamer built in Wilmington, Del. At 1,500 tons and 218-ft. long, the *Spaulding* carried three brass guns, two of which were used in the Battle of Bunker Hill and the third was taken from the wreck of a Spanish ship sunk in 1815.

The New England delegates chartered the steamship for 18 days for $10,000. *Harper's Weekly* claimed the delegates lived on board "more cheaply, and probably more comfortably, and certainly more healthily, than in the over-crowded hotels of Charleston." Caleb Cushing, the convention chairman, was among the delegates living aboard the *Spaulding*.

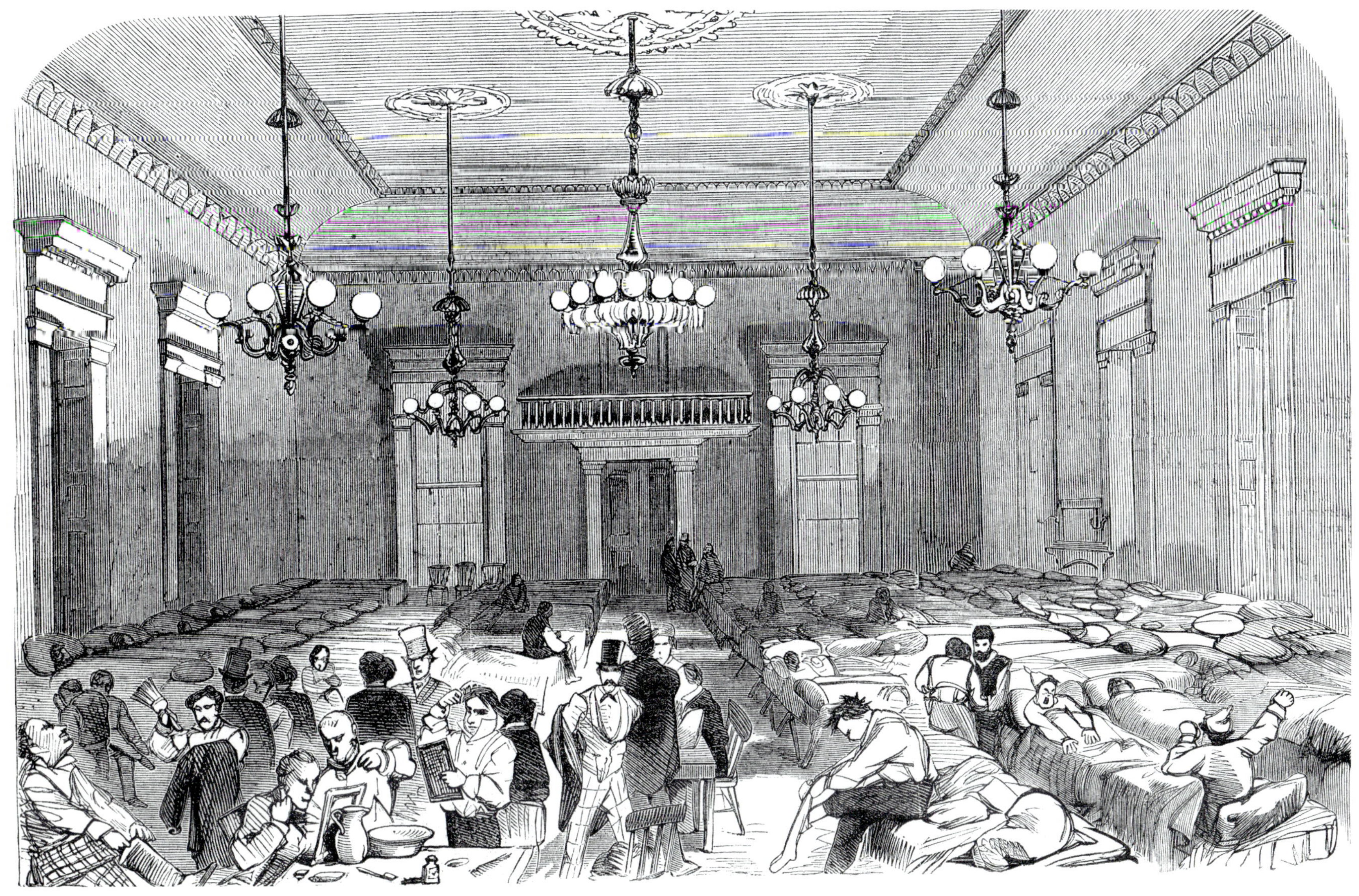

Sleeping Room of the Northwest Delegation

Artist: unknown
Harper's Weekly

As delegates spread out in the various hotels in Charleston, they booked accommodations with liked-minded delegates. This illustration depicts the second floor of the Hibernian Hall set up dormitory-style for the "Douglas delegates." The first floor was used for strategy meetings throughout the long convention. Most of the "Buchanan delegates" were located in one King Street hotel. The secessionists were headquartered at the Charleston Hotel.

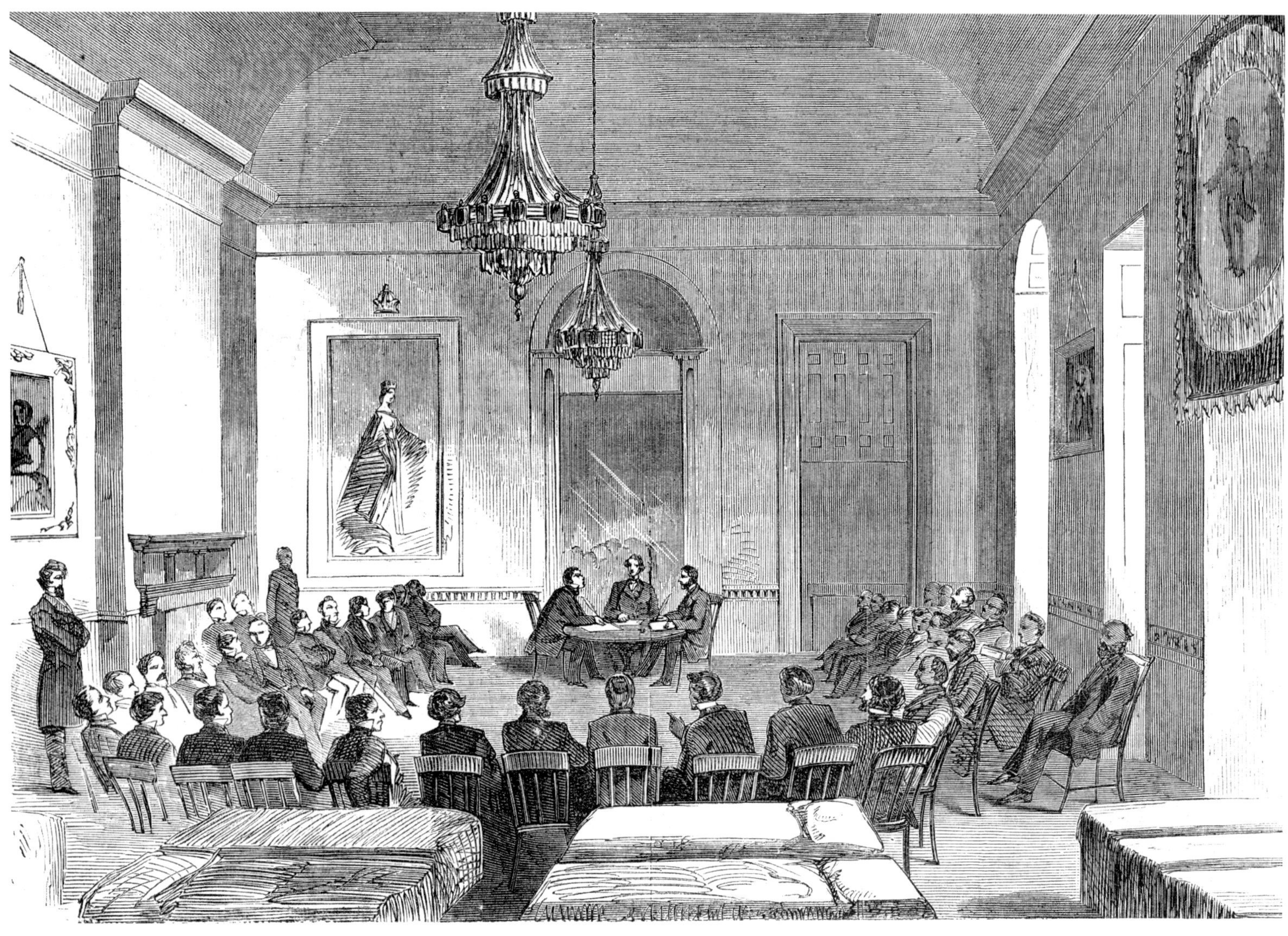

Meeting at the St. Andrews Hall

Artist: unknown
Harper's Weekly

The Southern delegates wanted a party platform guaranteeing the unconditional extension of slavery into the Western territories. The Northern delegates favored a doctrine endorsing the right of each territory to adopt or abolish slavery. After failing to win the platform vote on April 30, 1860, the Southern delegates walked out of the convention. With no resolution in hand, the convention adjourned on the seventh day. As each Southern delegation left the South Carolina Institute Hall, they met as a group at St. Andrews Hall. The Democrats would reconvene in Baltimore and nominate Stephen Douglas for the presidency.

The Secession Convention would be held in St. Andrews Hall in December 1860. St. Andrews Hall and the South Carolina Institute Hall would ultimately be destroyed in the great Charleston fire of 1861.

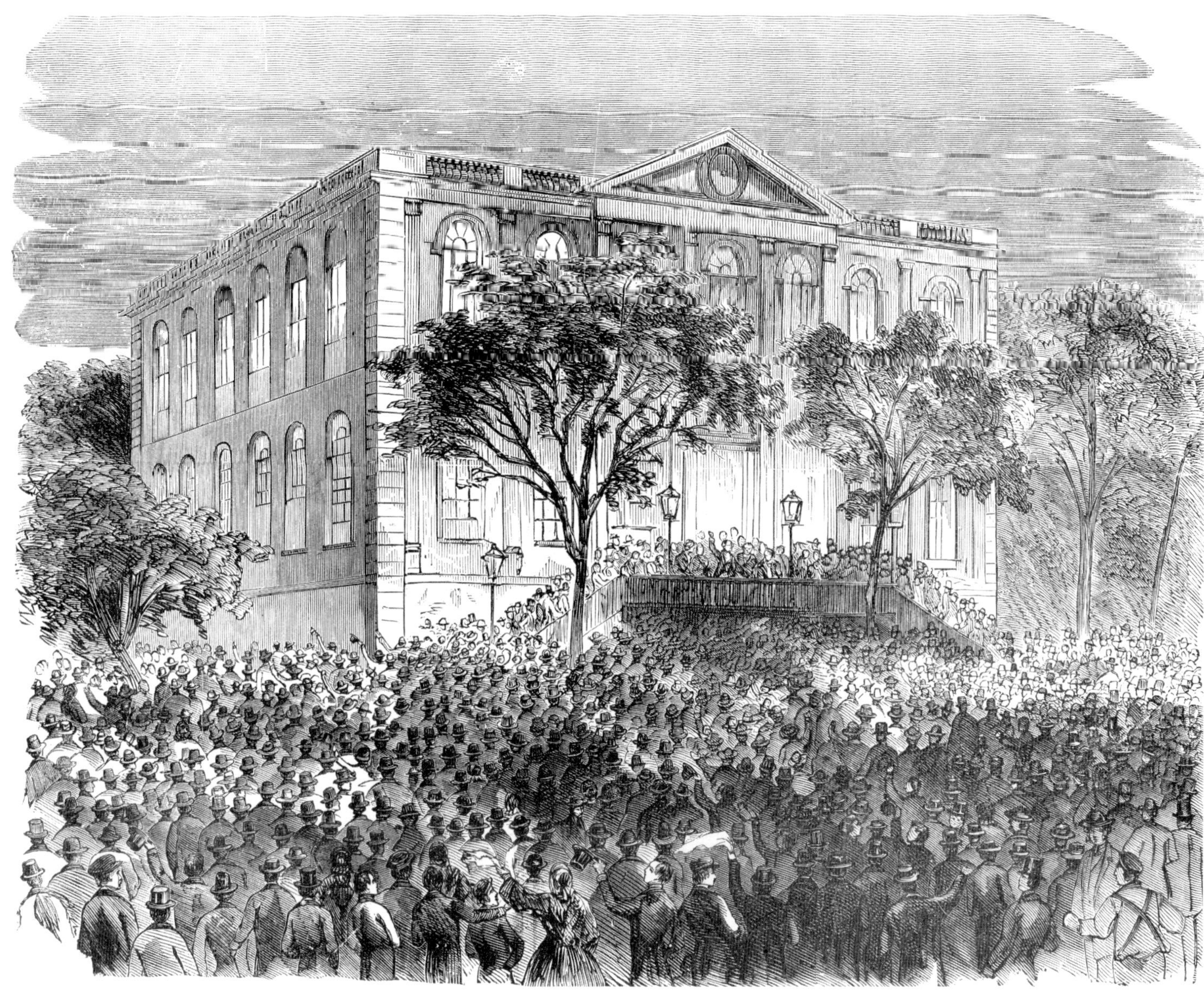

Charleston at the News of the Election of Lincoln and Hamlin

Artist: William Waud
Frank Leslie's Illustrated Newspaper

South Carolinians received the news of Abraham Lincoln's election to the presidency on Nov. 7, 1860, at Charleston City Hall, a day after the election. That same day, the Palmetto Flag was raised in Charleston. The governor and the Council of South Carolina went into secret session. When their deliberations were complete, Gov. Francis W. Pickens announced the decision to raise and equip 10,000 volunteers and to convene a state convention to address the question of South Carolina's secession from the Union.

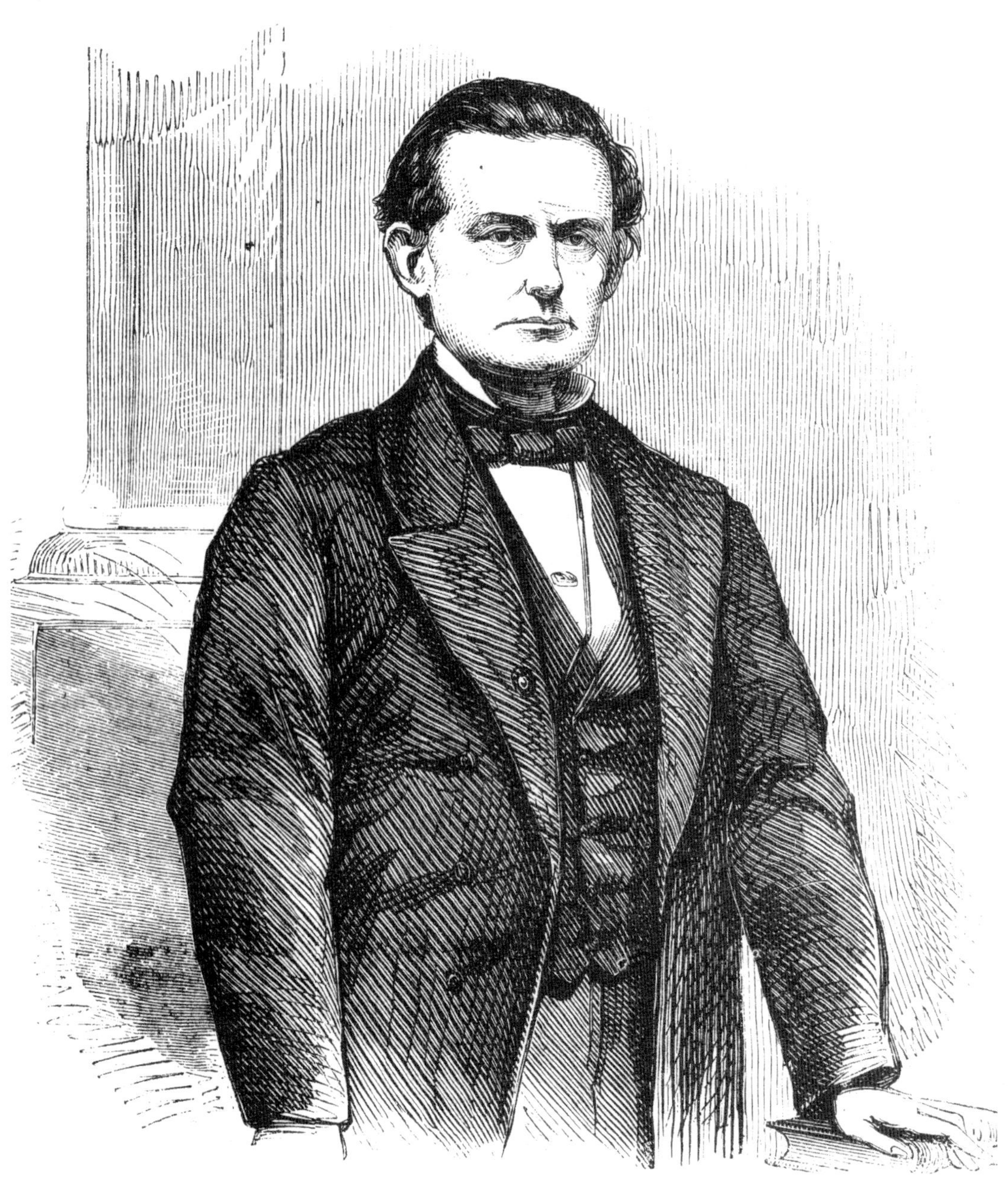

Judge Andrew G. Magrath

Artist: unknown
Harper's Weekly

Judge Andrew Magrath served as judge for the U. S. District Court at Charleston. With secession looming, Magrath addressed the Grand Jury at the conclusion of its business on Nov. 7, 1860.

> *In the political history of the United States an event has happened of ominous import to the 15 slave-holding states. The State of which we are citizens has always been understood to have deliberately fixed its purpose, whenever that event shall happen. Feeling an assurance of what will be the action of the state, I consider it my duty, without delay, to prepare to obey its wishes. That preparation is made by the resignation of the office I have held. For the last time I have, as a Judge of the United States, administered the laws of the United States, within the limits of the State of South Carolina.*

Magrath thanked the jury, the members of the bar and the officers of the court. He rose from the bench, laid aside his robe and retired.

His early act in support of secession earned him the admiration of the people of South Carolina. After the state seceded, Magrath served, first as secretary of state for the Republic of South Carolina and later as a Confederate judge. In 1864, he was elected governor of South Carolina.

South Carolina's Congressional Delegation

Artist: unknown
Harper's Weekly

Harper's Weekly published the images of the South Carolina congressmen and senators on the cover of its Dec. 22, 1860, issue. The two senators did not take their seats for the fall session. The six congressmen were in Washington until the secession convention, but provided notice they too would resign their seats as soon as the business of the convention was completed.

In a tribute to the eight South Carolinians, *Harper's Weekly* writes:

> *Personally, as well as politically, this exodus from the national halls of legislation will be felt; although for* [sic] *some of the Palmetto delegation have, at times, used harsh words in debate, they leave no enemies behind them. Gallant gentlemen, with high endowments, manly attributes and an integrity upon which suspicion has never even dared to glance, they carry with them kind wishes and sincere regrets, even of those who go so far to believe that 'secession is treason.'*

The delegation members were: *(from top left)* U.S. Rep. Lawrence M. Keitt; U.S. Rep. John McQueen; U.S. Rep. Milledge L. Bonham *(from middle left)* Sen. James Chesnut; Sen. James Hammond *(from bottom left)* U.S. Rep. William W. Boyce; U.S. Rep. John D. Ashmore; and U.S. Rep. William Porcher Miles.

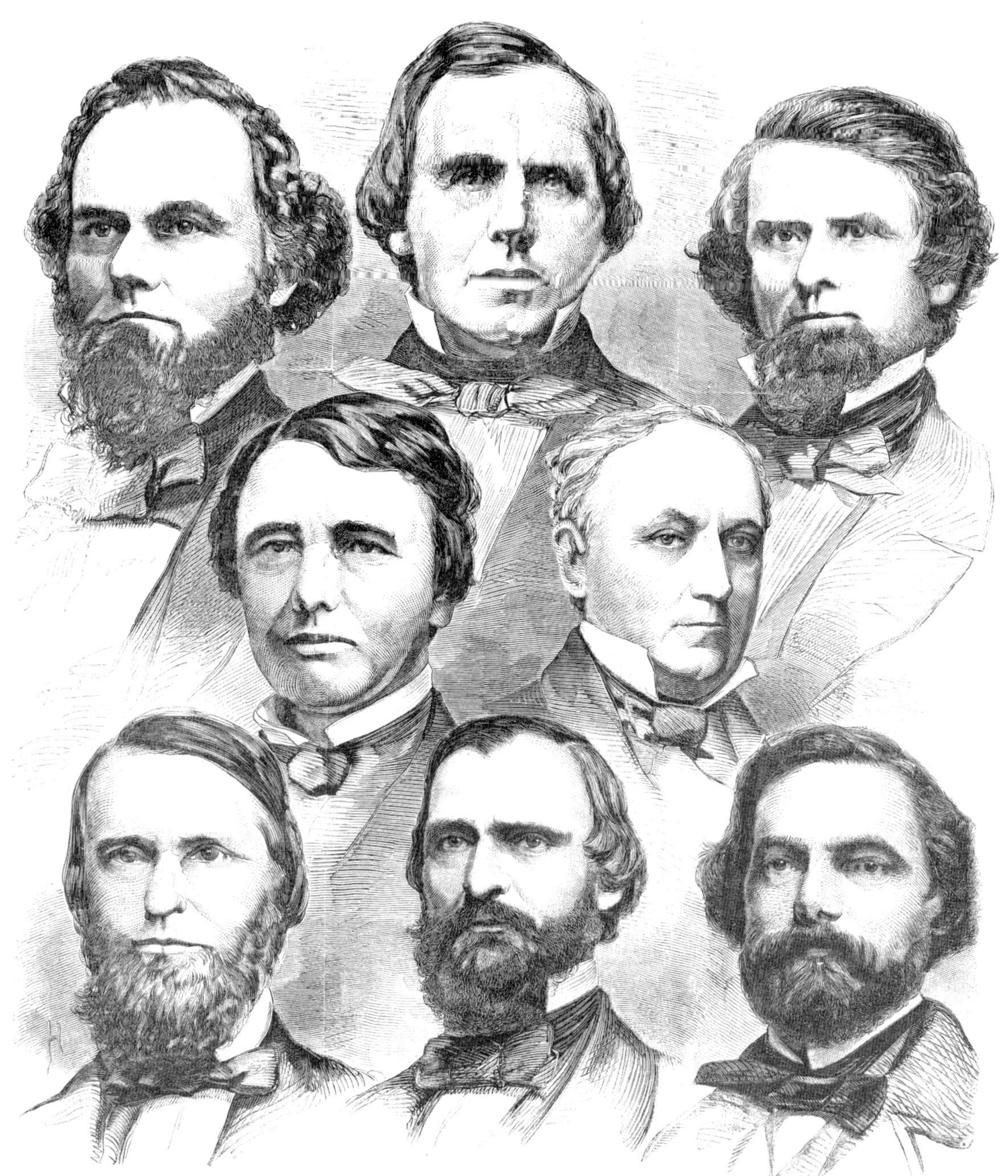

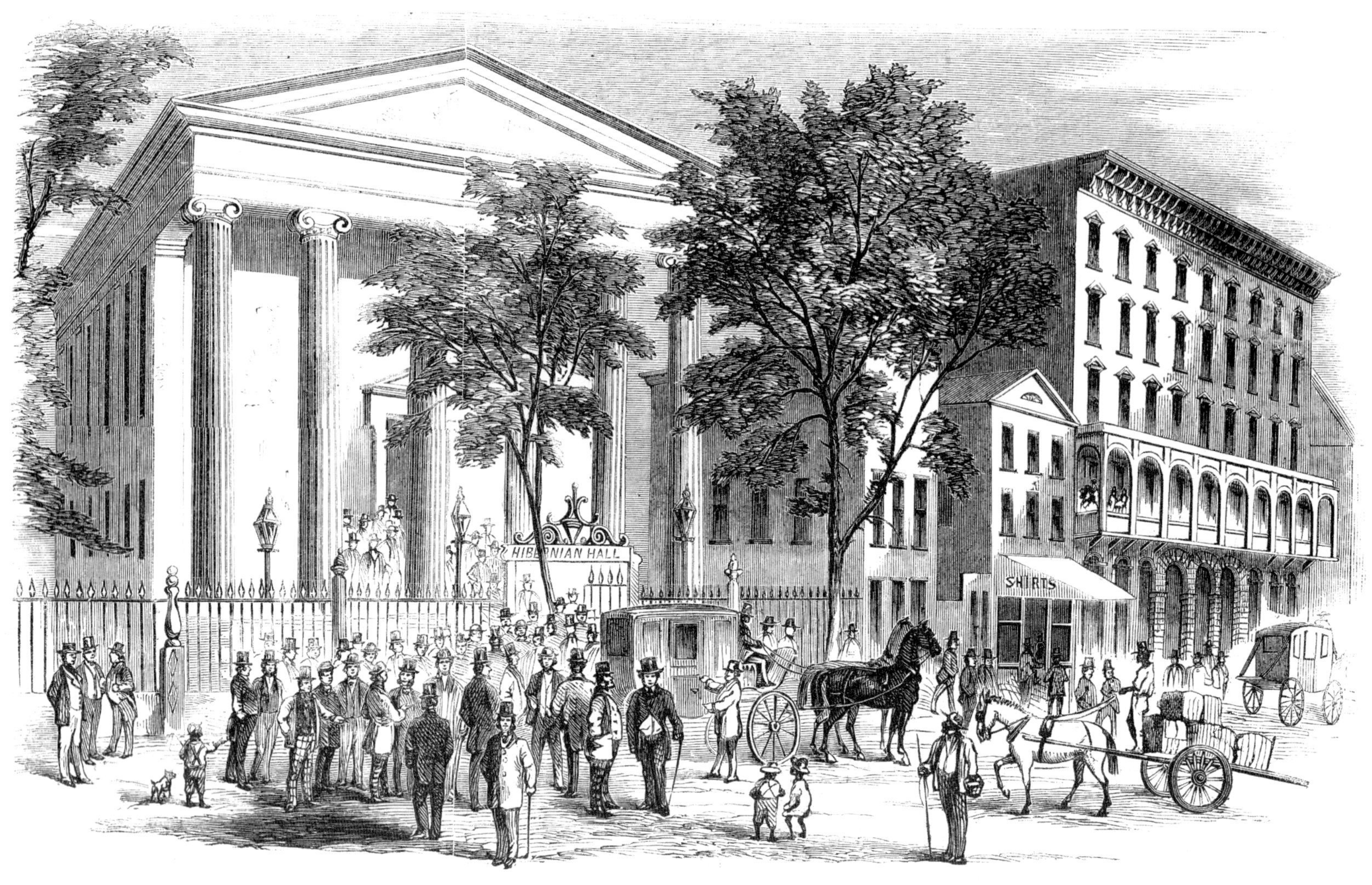

Street Views in Charleston

Artist: William Waud
Frank Leslie's Illustrated Newspaper

With secession of the Southern states looming, the illustrated newspapers dedicated more space to printing scenes and articles about the South, particularly Charleston. In the Dec. 1, 1860, issue, Frank Leslie provided readers a view of Meeting Street in Charleston:

> *The Mills House [right] is a commodious and beautiful hotel, and is kept in very popular style by Major Nickerson, who is known and respected by everyone. It was built a few years ago by Otis Mills, Esq., one of the merchant princes of the 'Queen City of the South'... It is four stories in height, and interiorly it is decidedly the most handsome hotel in the city, and is generally esteemed the favorite stopping-place of Northern sojourners.*
>
> *Hibernian Hall is situated a few doors below the Mills House. Its architectural style being of the Ionic Order, it is a neat, plain and impressive structure, and in size is next to the largest hall in the city. It is the property of the Hibernian Society, and the favorite resort of our Celtic friends for holding anniversary suppers, balls and festivals.*

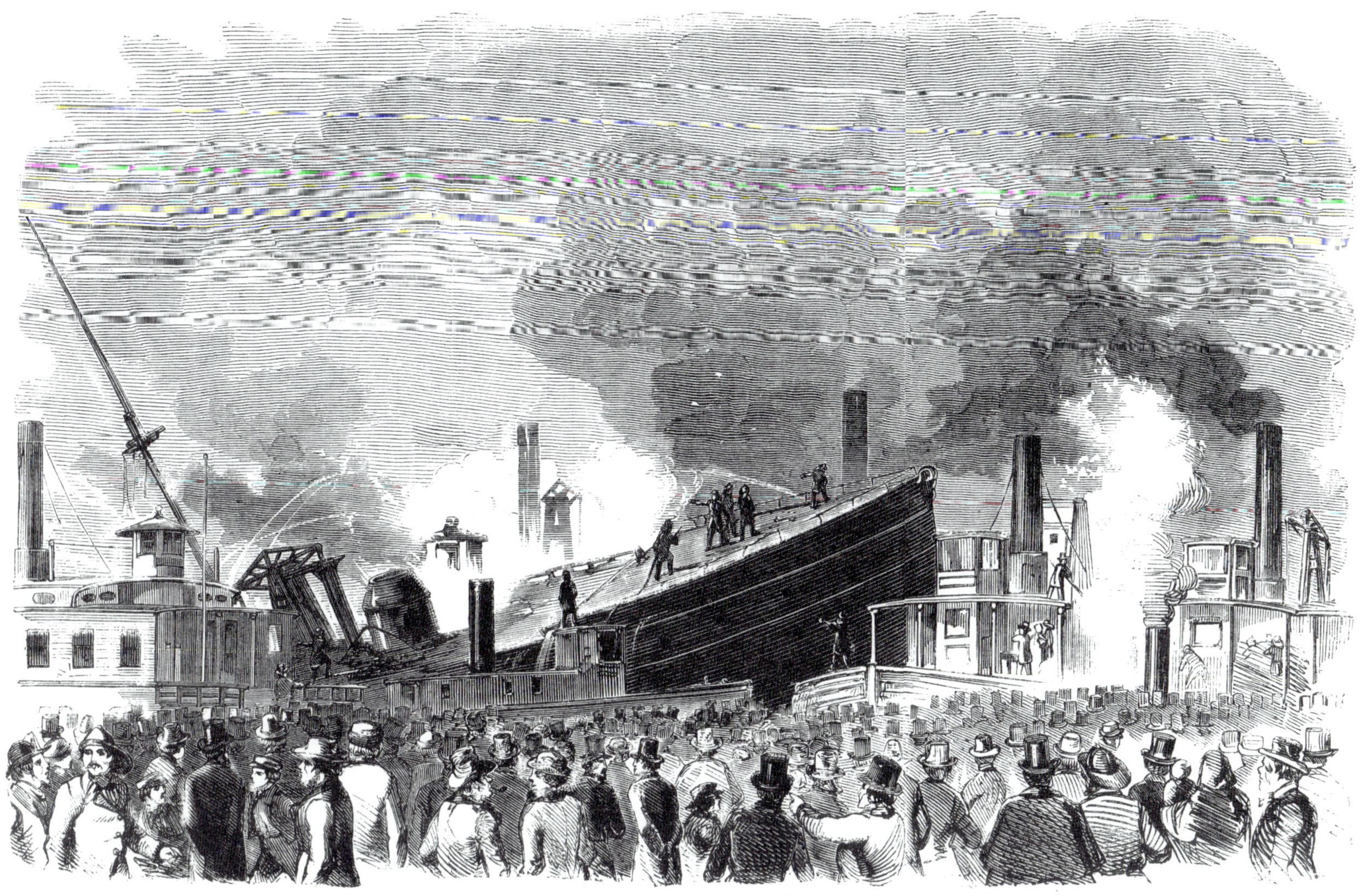

Burning of the *John P. King*

Artist: unknown
Harper's Weekly

The steamship *John P. King* was a 1,600-ton ship built for passenger trade between Charleston and New York. In December 1860, she embarked on her maiden voyage, a trial run leaving Charleston and arriving in New York in mid-December.

Early on Dec. 18, as the *John P. King* was tied to the docks, a fire broke out aboard the steamer. Quickly, the flames spread out of control, engulfing the new passenger ship. Efforts to control the fire failed. The steamer was towed to deep water to prevent the flames from spreading to the docks and other ships tied up at Pier 4. Built at a cost of $160,000, she was only insured for $76,000.

Harper's Weekly reported rumors in New York asserting that the *John P. King* would fly the Palmetto Flag upon her return to Charleston. Many believed the fire that destroyed the steamer may have been deliberately set.

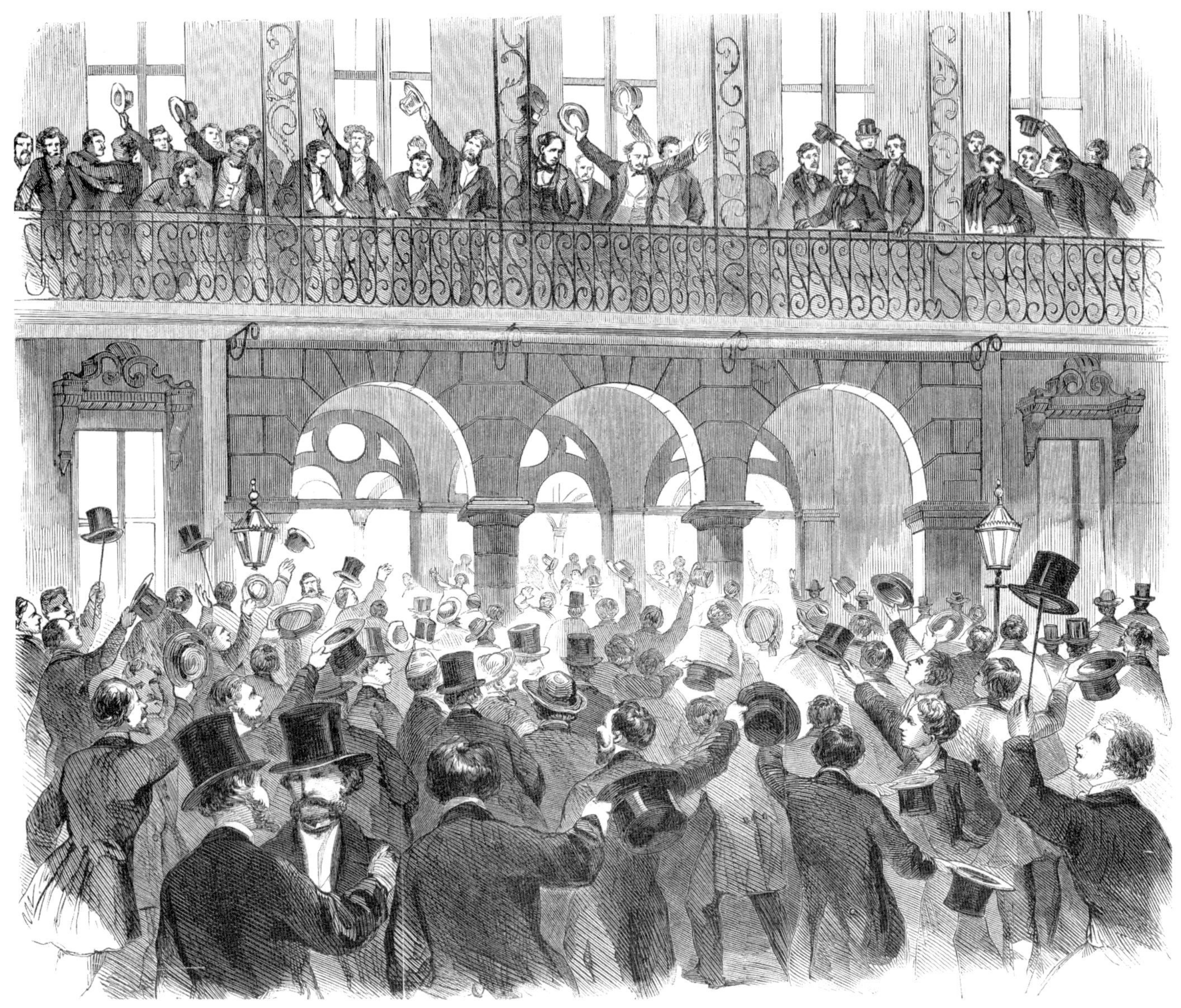

Secession Celebration

Artist: William Waud
Frank Leslie's Illustrated Newspaper

On Nov. 10, 1860, the S.C. General Assembly enacted a bill calling for a Secession Convention. The convention opened in Columbia, S.C., on Dec. 17. Fears about an outbreak of smallpox brought the convention to an abrupt end, and the much-anticipated meeting moved to Charleston, reconvening the next day. The political elite of the Palmetto State made up the 169 delegates at the convention.

On Dec. 20, the convention, by unanimous vote, seceded from the United States, establishing the Republic of South Carolina. The Ordinance of Secession was signed that same night at the South Carolina Institute Hall, allowing the public to witness the historic occasion. After the two-hour ceremonial signing of the ordinance, the convention adjourned. Throughout the night, South Carolinians celebrated.

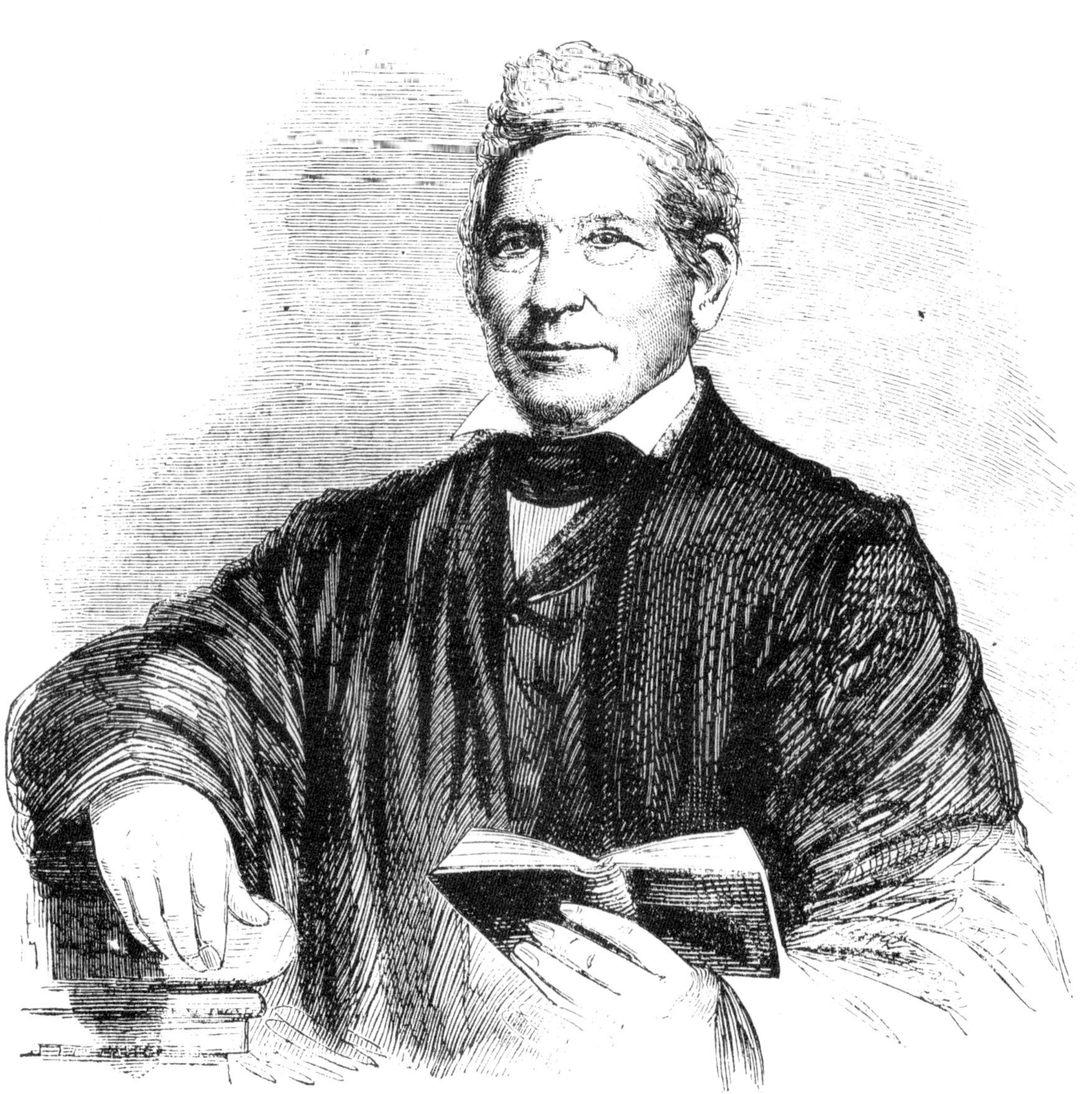

Rev. Dr. John Bachman

Drawn from a portrait
Harper's Weekly

The Rev. Dr. John Bachman, pastor of St. John's Lutheran Church, was often referred to as the "chief religious spokesman for slavery." In addition to his reputation as a biblical scholar, Bachman was a noted naturalist, enjoying a long-standing and close friendship with John James Audubon. Politically, he was known for his strong views favoring secession.

Bachman was selected by the Secession Convention to offer a prayer on the ratification of the ordinance. The *Mercury* reported the events at the ordinance signing:

> *In the midst of deep silence, an old man, with bowed form and hair as white as snow, the Rev. Dr. Bachman, advanced forward, with upraised hands, in prayer to the Almighty God, for His blessings and favor in this great act of his people about to be consummated. The whole assembly at once rose to its feet, and, with hats off, listened to the touching and eloquent appeal to the All-Wise Dispenser of events.*

As the president of the convention read the final document, the entire hall of delegates and spectators rose to its feet with shouts and cheers when he read the word "dissolved."

Honorable D. F. Jamieson

Drawn from a portrait
Harper's Weekly

D. F. Jamieson was a cotton planter with more than 2,000 acres under cultivation in South Carolina. He was highly regarded for his skills as a planter and as a writer. He often contributed articles to publications such as *Southern Quarterly, Southern & Western,* and *Russell's Magazine*. He further distinguished himself in service to the state, commanding a brigade in the S.C. Cavalry, rising to the rank of brigadier general.

In 1860, Jamieson was elected president of the Sovereign Convention of South Carolina during which the state seceded from the Union. After the secession, he continued in service as secretary of war for the Republic of South Carolina.

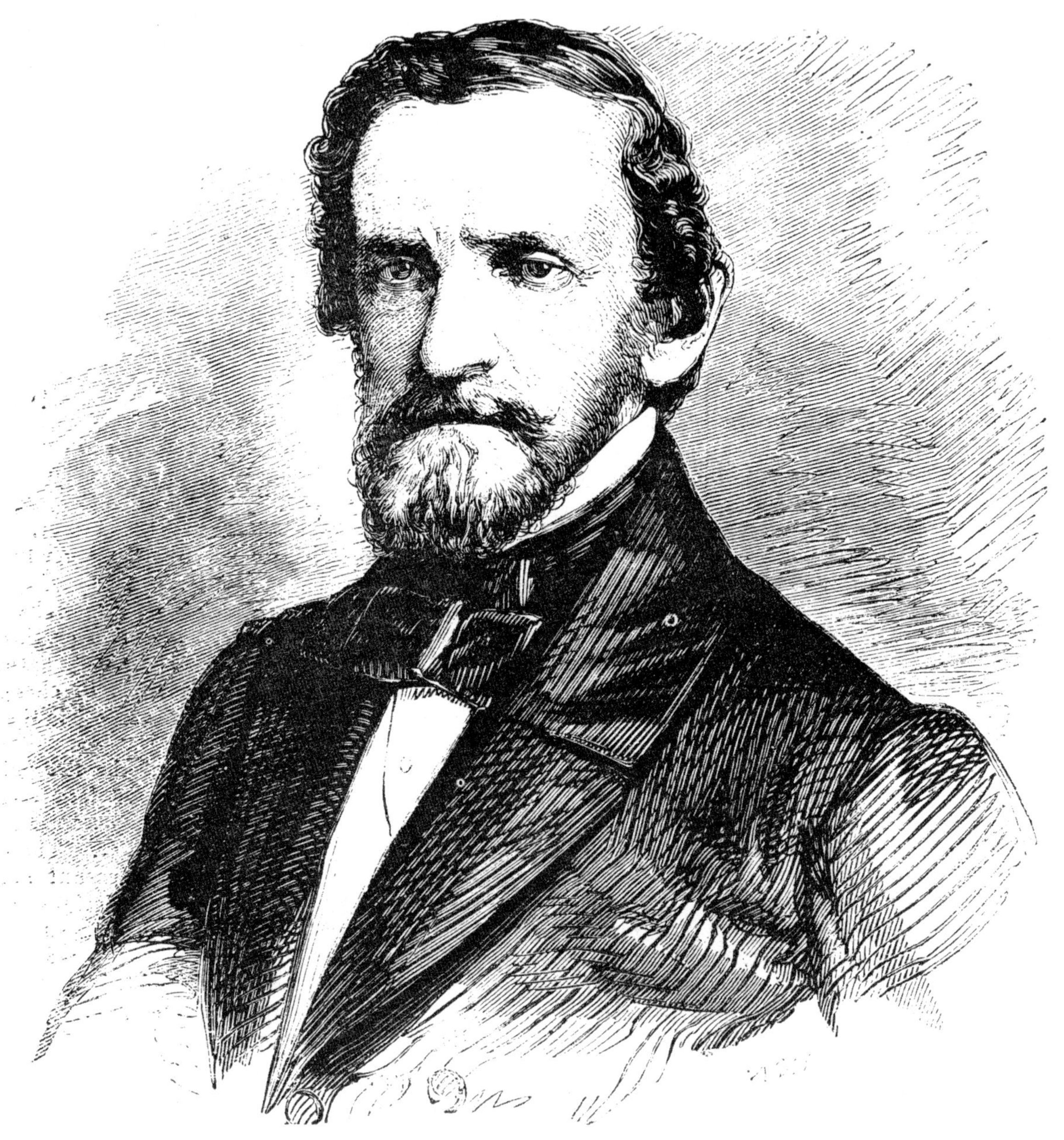

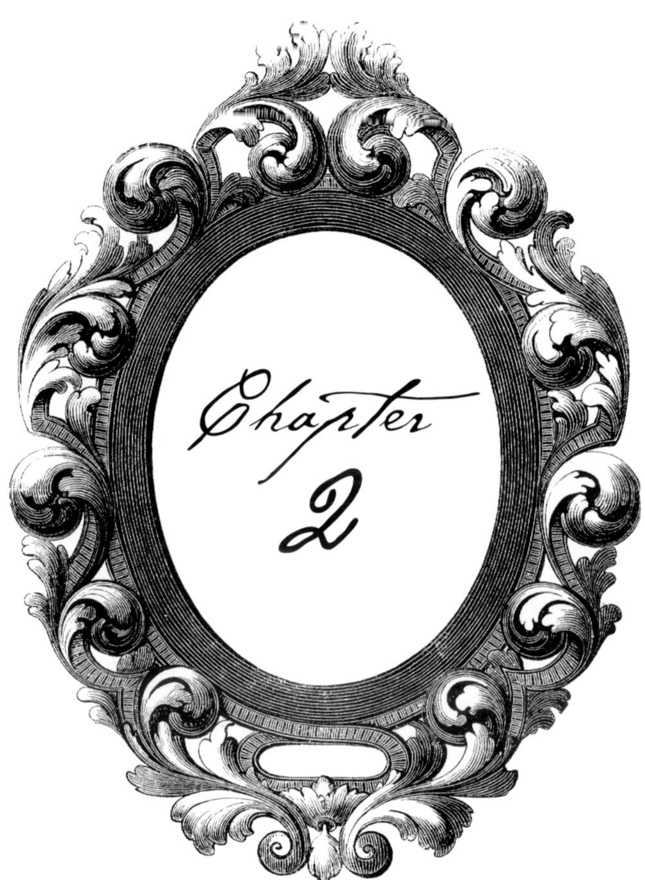

The First Shot

Fort Moultrie was considered a plum assignment for an officer in the Union army. The fortification's proximity to Charleston gave easy access to this social and cultural mecca of the South. Charlestonians had long been hospitable to the officers at Moultrie. William T. Sherman had been stationed there and was said to have found love with a young woman on a James Island cotton plantation, enjoying many a Sunday dinner with her family.

But in December 1860, the climate in Charleston was markedly different. South Carolina had seceded from the Union, declaring itself a Republic, and was poised for other Southern states to join the movement. The federals were no longer welcome in town.

Robert Anderson was familiar with Fort Moultrie and Charleston – his father had served at Fort Moultrie during the Revolutionary War. Anderson himself served a short tour there years before. But when Anderson arrived to accept command of the federal garrison in Charleston, tensions were high. In 1860, as Anderson moved his garrison from Fort Moultrie to Fort Sumter, his former stronghold was precarious.

Many in Charleston thought the federal government might simply withdraw from Fort Sumter, abandoning the vulnerable site that was surrounded by Carolina batteries. On Jan. 31, 1861, the attorney general for the Republic of South Carolina even offered to purchase Fort Sumter from the federal government. Although South Carolinians believed they held the destiny of the United States in their hands, they could not have predicted the long and tortuous war ahead.

The Rev. A. Toomer Porter, in his reminiscences about the first months of 1861, recalls a conversation with Col. James Chesnut, former U.S. senator from South Carolina and the officer who later ordered the first shot over Fort Sumter:

> *I remarked to him, 'These are troubled times, Colonel; we are at the beginning of a terrible war.' 'Not at all,' he said. 'There will be no war, it will all be arranged. I will drink all the blood shed in the war.' So little did some of our leaders realize the awful import of what we were doing.*

Many Northern newspapers questioned the wisdom of going to war simply over allowing the expansion of slavery. *Frank Leslie's Illustrated Newspaper*, in a February 1861 editorial, suggests, "The destruction of our Union, merely to rescue a runaway nigger, would be as absurd as the Chinaman who set fire to his house merely to roast a little pig."

As the firing on Fort Sumter commenced, the *New York Herald* offered an editorial in its April 12 issue: "Oceans of blood and millions of treasure will be wasted, with no other imaginable end than to leave the country exhausted, impoverished and wretched, and worse than all, despoiled of the freedom purchased at such cost by our forefathers."

The small garrison at Fort Sumter was in no position successfully to resist the concentrated attack by the Confederate batteries, particularly without support and reinforcements. After 36 hours of steady fire and depleted food and munitions, Major Robert Anderson had but one option – the evacuation of his post.

With the exception of Anderson, the major players in the brewing conflict got what they wanted. South Carolina got the federal troops out of her "front door," and Pres. Abraham Lincoln finally had the event that galvanized support for his political policies in defense of the Union.

Once Anderson vacated Fort Sumter, S.C. Gov. Francis W. Pickens was forthright in declaring the accomplishments of the short confrontation:

> *We have defeated their twenty millions. We have humbled the flag of the United States before the Palmetto and Confederate, and so long as I have the honor to preside as your chief magistrate, so help me God, there is no power on earth shall ever lower from that fortress those flags, unless they be lowered and trailed in a sea of blood. I can here say to you it is the first time in the history of this country that the stars and stripes have been humbled. That flag has never before been lowered before any nation on this earth. But today it has been humbled and humbled before the glorious little State of South Carolina.*

Major Robert Anderson

Drawn from a photograph
Frank Leslie's Illustated Newspaper

Robert Anderson was an unlikely commander to lead the Union into war. He was a Southerner, born in Kentucky, and married to the daughter of one of Georgia's wealthiest rice planters and politicians, Gen. Duncan Clinch.

Anderson was graduated from West Point in 1825 and distinguished himself in both the Black Hawk War and Mexican War. He also served for a period as professor of artillery at West Point, instructing some of the nation's brightest military students, several of whom would later lead the Southern armies. In November 1860, he was appointed to command the forts in Charleston harbor.

Calm and dignified, Anderson had a reputation as a scholar and a war hero. He was a Southern sympathizer, yet he opposed secession. He was also friends with Jefferson Davis – who would be named president of the Confederacy on Feb. 22, 1862. In a letter to the federal government, Anderson offers, "I need not say how anxious I am – indeed determined, so far as honor will permit, – to avoid collision with the citizens of South Carolina."

After the fall of Fort Sumter, Anderson was promoted to brevet major general and given command of the Department of Kentucky and the Cumberland, where he served until his retirement in October 1863.

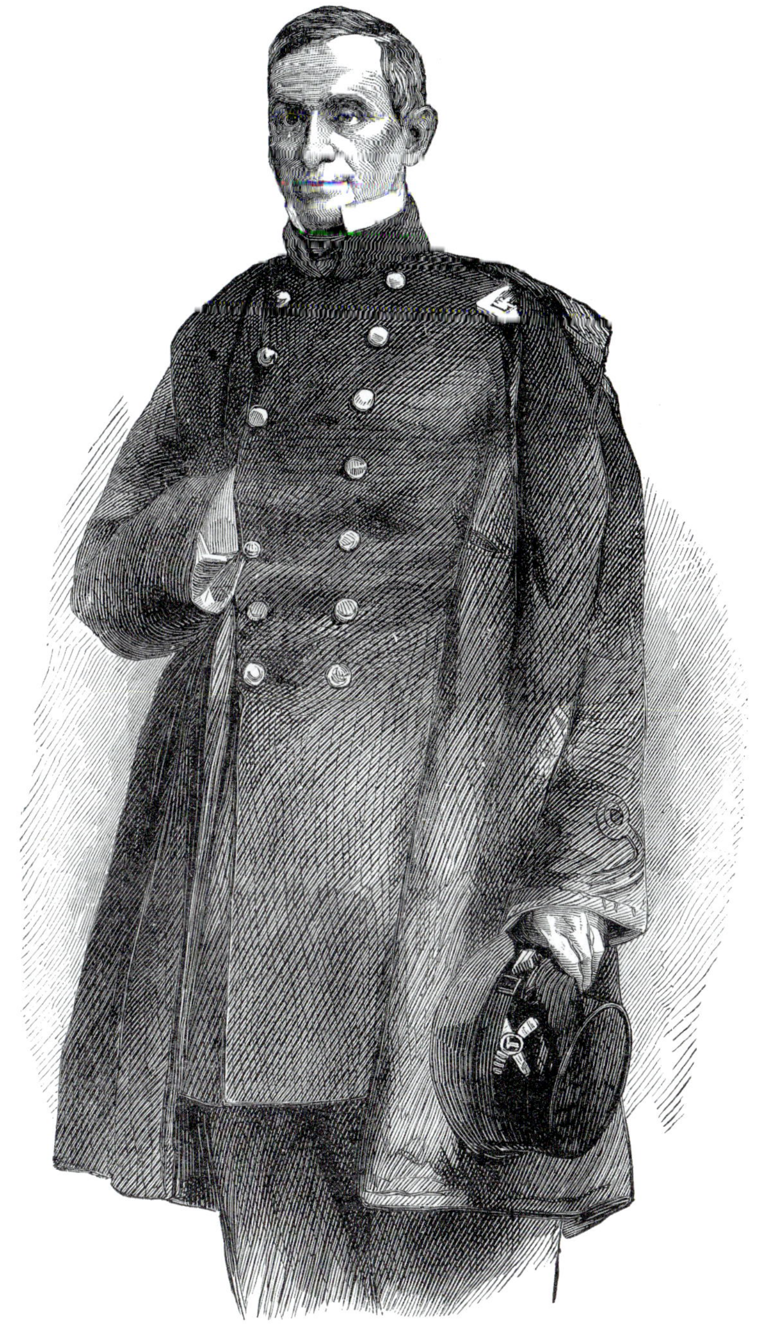

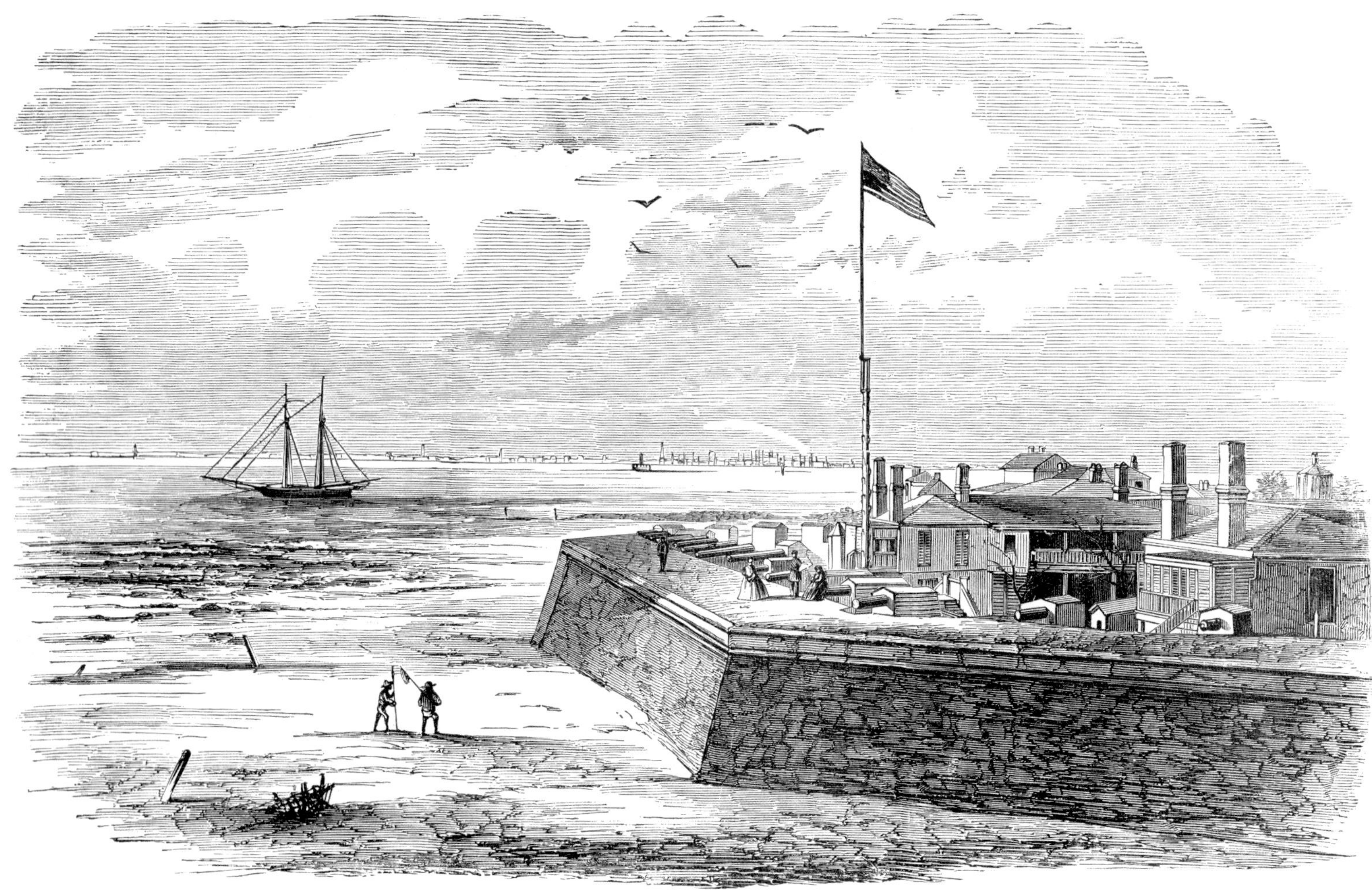

Exterior of Fort Moultrie

Astist: William Waud
Frank Leslie's Illustrated Newspaper

When Major Robert Anderson assumed command in November 1860, Castle Pinckney and Fort Sumter had no garrison. The federal troops, two incomplete companies of regular artillery totaling 61 men, seven officers and a regimental band of 13 musicians, were headquartered at Fort Moultrie on Sullivan's Island. Facing the prospect of war, this garrison should have been at least 300 men strong.

An experienced officer, Anderson recognized that Fort Moultrie was not a good defensive position for his troops. The fort was constructed to protect Charleston Harbor from a naval attack but was vulnerable to ground assault.

In a report to the federal government, Anderson notes:

> *We have, within 160 yards of our walls, sand hills which command our works, and which afford admirable sites for batteries, and the finest cover for sharpshooters; and that, besides this, there are numerous houses, some of them within pistol-shot, you will at once see that, if attacked in force, headed by any one but a simpleton, there is a scarce possibility of our being able to hold out...*

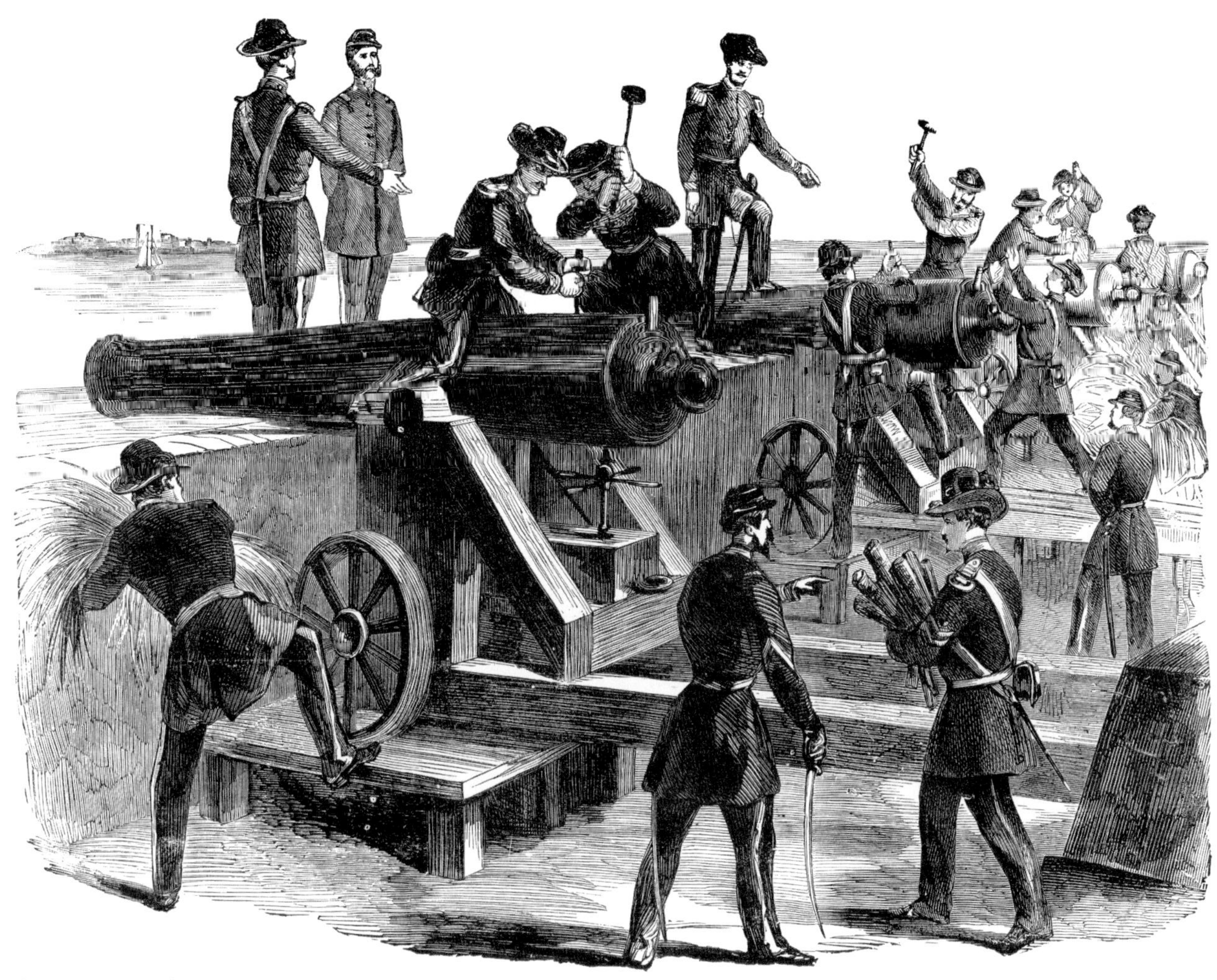

Spiking the Guns of Fort Moultrie

Artist: William Waud
Frank Leslie's Illustrated Newspaper

Concerned that Major Robert Anderson might send his garrison to Fort Sumter, Gov. Francis W. Pickens ordered a gun boat to patrol the harbor between Fort Moultrie and Fort Sumter just two days before the Secession Convention.

Anderson, in a calculated deception, informed the civilian authorities he was moving the women and children of his troops to Fort Johnson. A schooner picked up the families on the afternoon of Dec. 26 to make the short trip across the harbor. Anderson, however, smuggled supplies he'd need at Fort Sumter aboard the ship as well. The loaded schooner, escorted by Lt. Norman Hall, pulled away from Sullivan's Island, then anchored just off James Island.

The removal of the women and children was only the first step in Anderson's plan to move his troops out of the vulnerable Fort Moultrie into Fort Sumter where he could exercise more control over his fate.

Anderson and his men spiked the guns at Fort Moultrie, rendering them useless. The gun carriages and other property were then set afire as the troops evacuated.

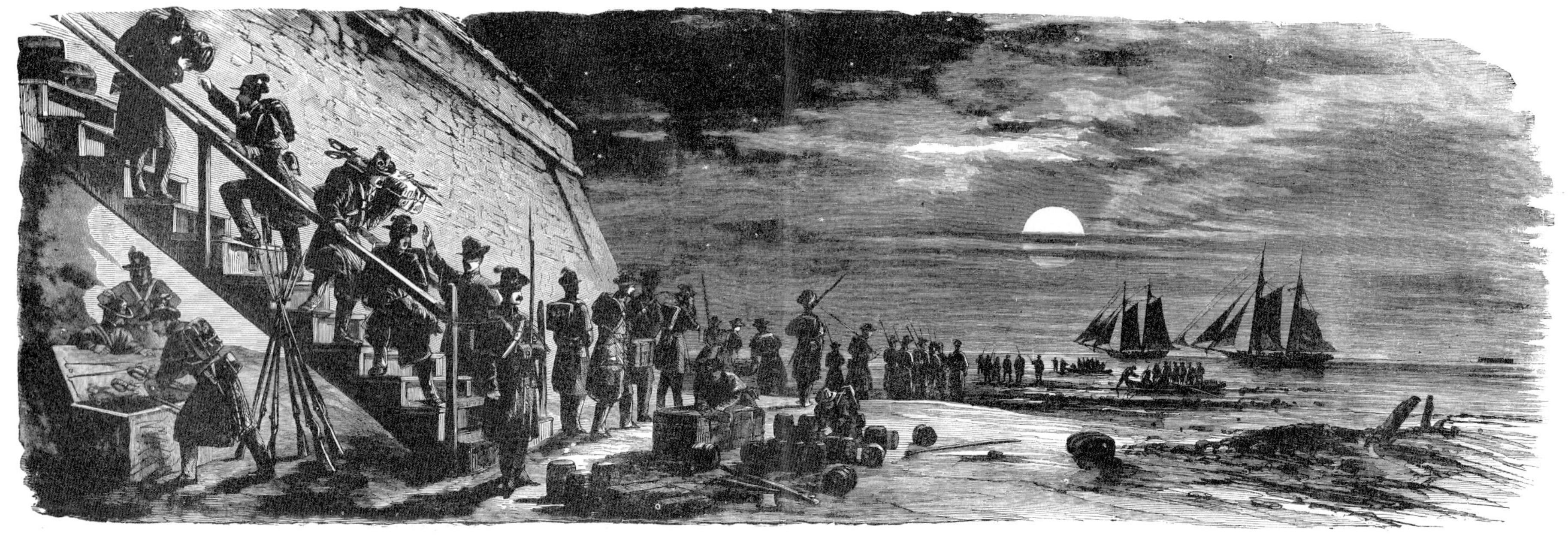

Evacuation of Fort Moultrie

Artist: William Waud
Frank Leslie's Illustrated Newspaper

Major Robert Anderson's decision to leave Fort Moultrie for Fort Sumter was kept secret, even from his officers, until 20 minutes before his departure. Only Lt. Norman Hall, who escorted the women and children, and Capt. John Foster, who was to bring up a number of small vessels for the troops, knew of Anderson's bold plan.

As the federal troops set out for Sumter, Anderson left a few men to defend the moving troops with Moultrie's guns if necessary. Showing no weapons or uniforms and covered in the approaching darkness, Anderson's men had the appearance of workmen moving to and from Sumter, rather than a garrison on the move.

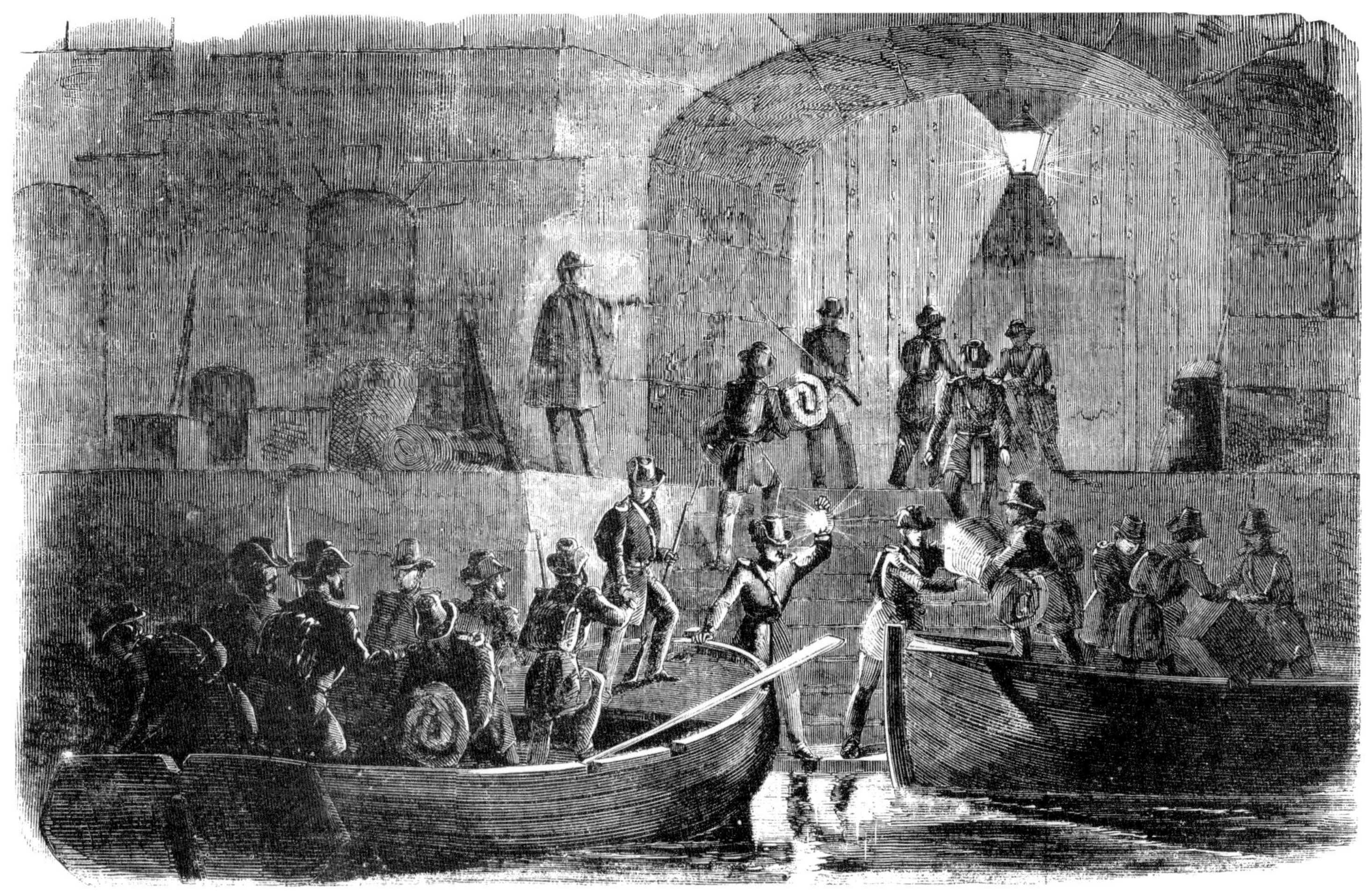

Entry into Fort Sumter

Artist: unknown
Harper's Weekly

As soon as the garrison was safely in Fort Sumter, two shots were fired to signal Lt. Norman Hall to bring his schooner to Fort Sumter as well. The schooner arrived safely, unloading women, children, and four months of rations, supplies and munitions that had been on hand at Fort Moultrie.

At daybreak on the morning of Dec. 27, smoke rose from Fort Moultrie. The first assumption was that a fire had erupted at the fort. Just as two Charleston fire companies were en route to "rescue" Major Robert Anderson, word arrived that the federal garrison had moved to Fort Sumter and the fires had been deliberately set.

Anderson's strategic move caught everyone – from the president of the United States to the governor of South Carolina – by surprise. While Pres. James Buchanan condemned the move to Sumter, he did not order Anderson and his garrison to return to Sullivan's Island. The authorities in Charleston denounced Anderson, declaring the move to Sumter the first act of war.

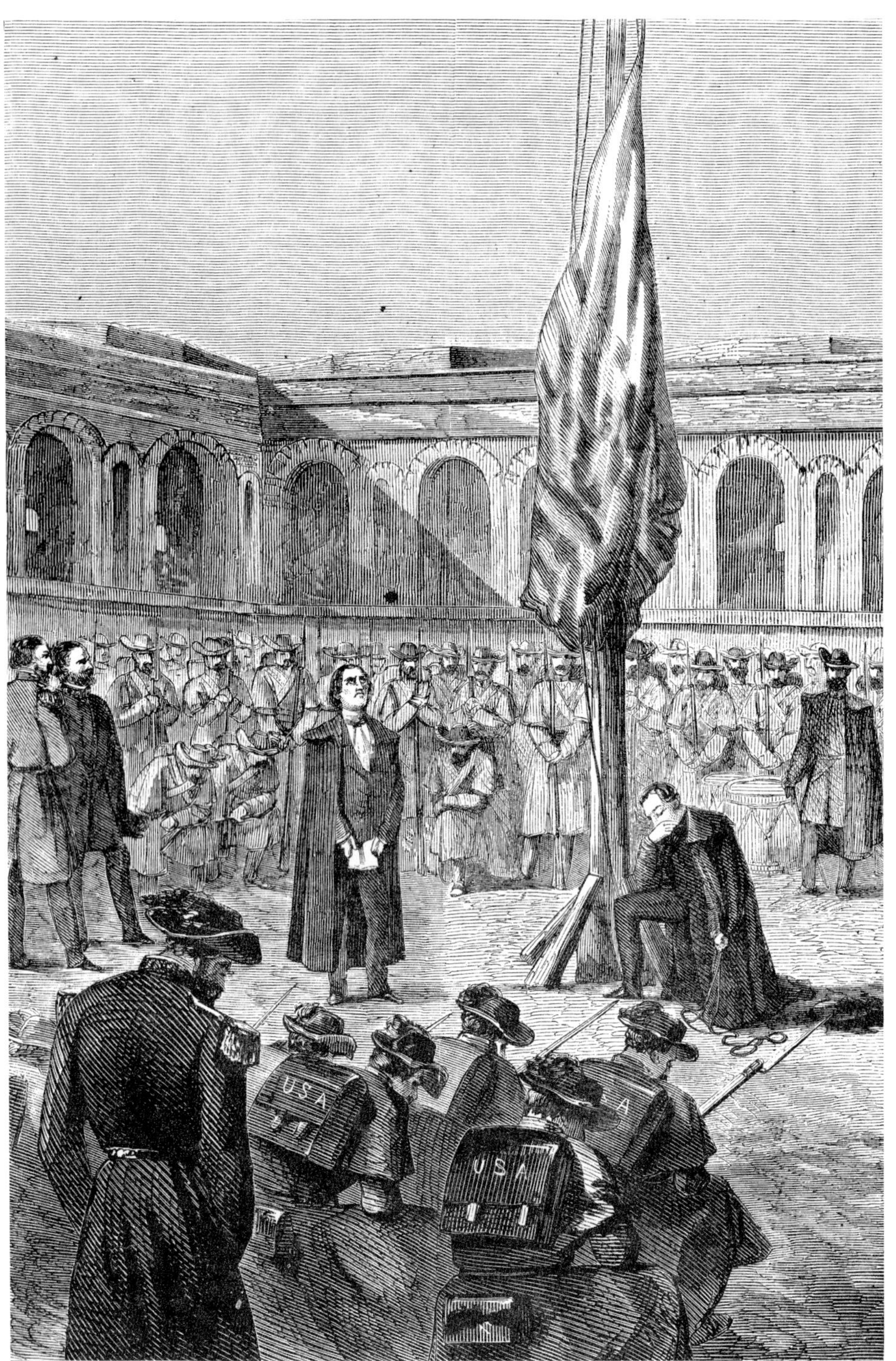

Prayer at Sumter

Drawn by an officer in Major Anderson's command
Harper's Weekly

Under cover of darkness, Major Robert Anderson and his troops moved into Fort Sumter on the evening of Dec. 26. At noon the following day, he assembled the Union troops to hoist the garrison flag brought from Fort Moultrie. The words of an eyewitness were published in *Harper's Weekly:*

> *A short time before noon, Major Anderson assembled the whole of his little force, with the workmen employed on the fort, around the foot of the flag-staff. The national ensign was attached to the cord, and Major Anderson, holding the end of the lines in his hands, knelt reverently down. The officers, soldiers, and men clustered around, many of them on their knees, all deeply impressed with the solemnity of the scene. The chaplain made an earnest prayer – such an appeal for support, encouragement, and mercy, as one would make who felt that 'Man's extremity is God's opportunity.' As the earnest, solemn words of the speaker ceased, the men responded Amen with a fervency that perhaps they had never before experienced, Major Anderson drew the 'Star Spangled Banner' up to the top of the staff, the band broke out with the national air of 'Hail Columbia' and loud and exultant cheers, repeated again and again were given by the officers, soldiers and workmen.*

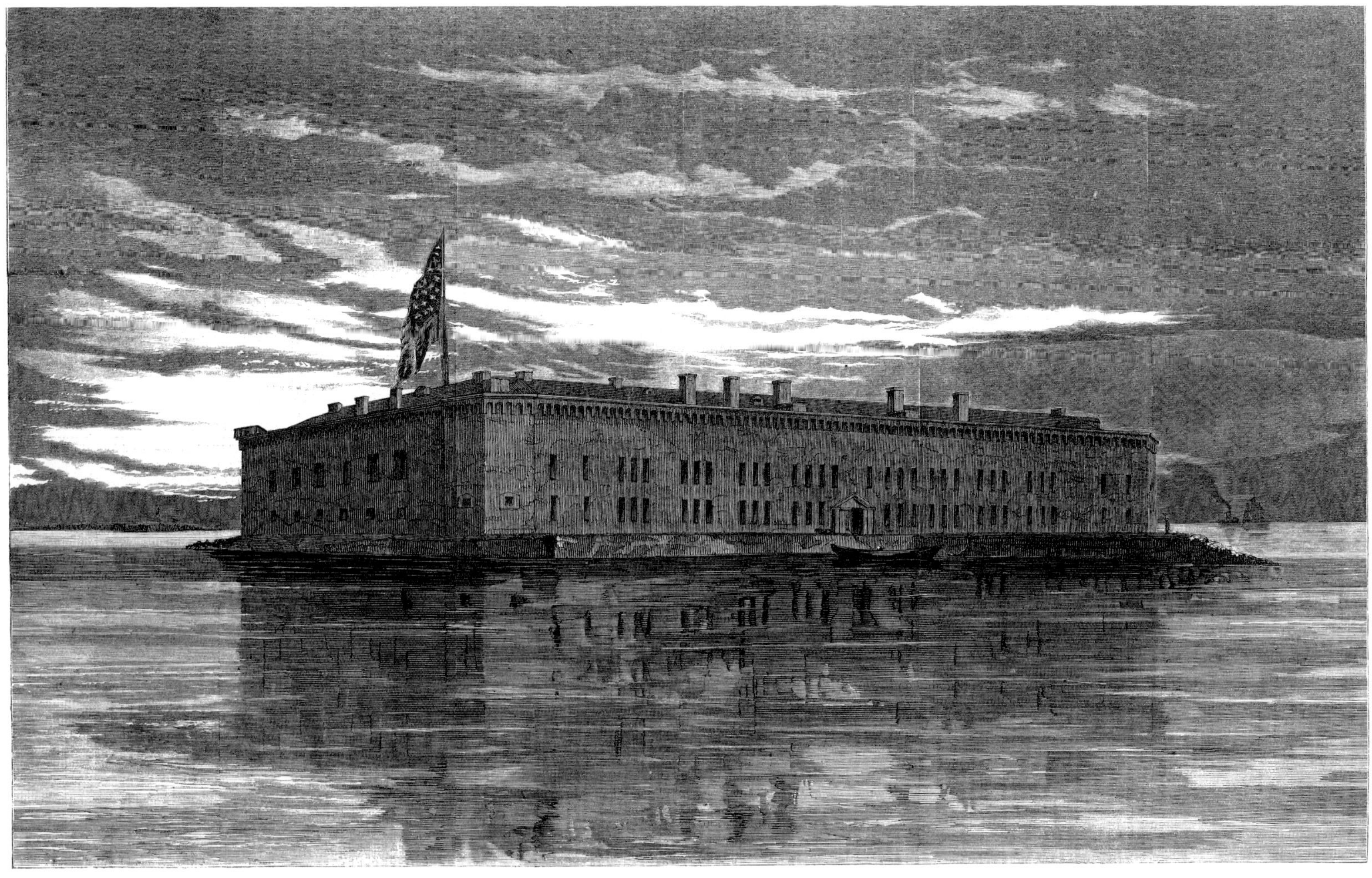

Fort Sumter

Drawn by an officer of Major Anderson's command
Harper's Weekly

Major Robert Anderson moved his troops from Fort Moultrie to Fort Sumter, seeking the best defensive position for his men. He desperately wanted to avoid the impending conflict but knew that taking Fort Sumter might be viewed as an act of aggression by the South Carolina governor. As was always the case in his career, he was guided by his sense of duty to his country and to the men in his command.

Fort Sumter, named for South Carolina Revolutionary War hero Gen. Thomas Sumter, was planned as part of a system of coastal defenses determined to be built after the War of 1812. The fort was built on a mud and sand bank known as Middle Ground.

The island was created with Northern granite, principally from Maine, taking 10 years and $500,000 to build. The fort, which required another $500,000 to construct, was built of brick and concrete masonry. The walls, built in three tiers, were 60-ft. high and 8- to 12-ft. thick.

The lower tier was designed for 42-lb. Paixhan guns, the second tier for 8- to 10-in. Columbiads firing solid or hollow shot, the third and final tier for mortars and 24-lb. guns. When Anderson took the fort, many of the guns for the fort were not in position.

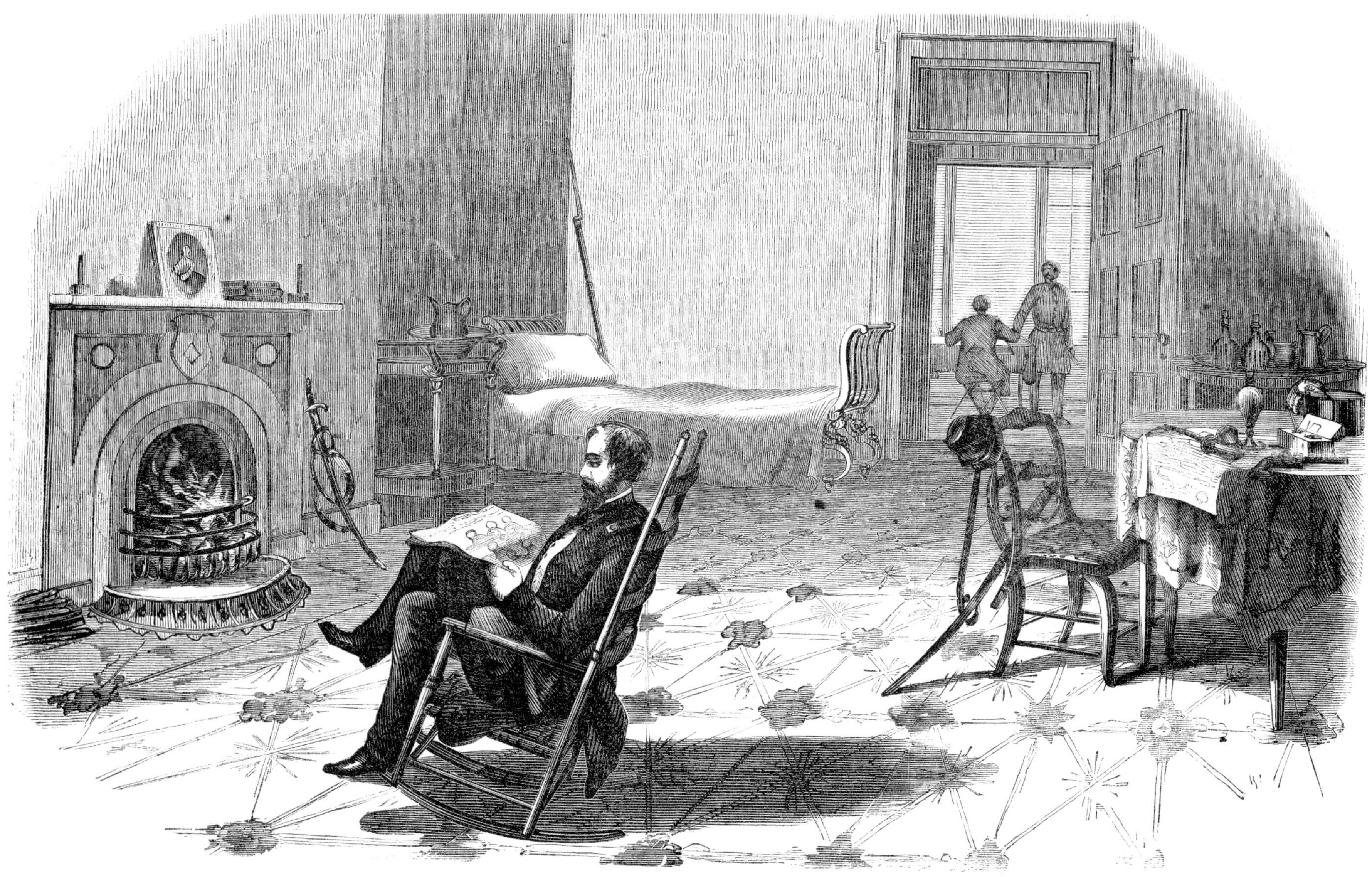

Officer's Quarters at Fort Sumter

From a sketch by an officer of Major Robert Anderson's command
Harper's Weekly

Within the confines of Fort Sumter were, of course, the many gun emplacements, barracks, a one-acre parade ground and the powder magazine. Yet Fort Sumter also was designed to provide adequate living quarters for the officers and their families. In this engraving, the quarters for this officer appear to be both spacious and comfortable.

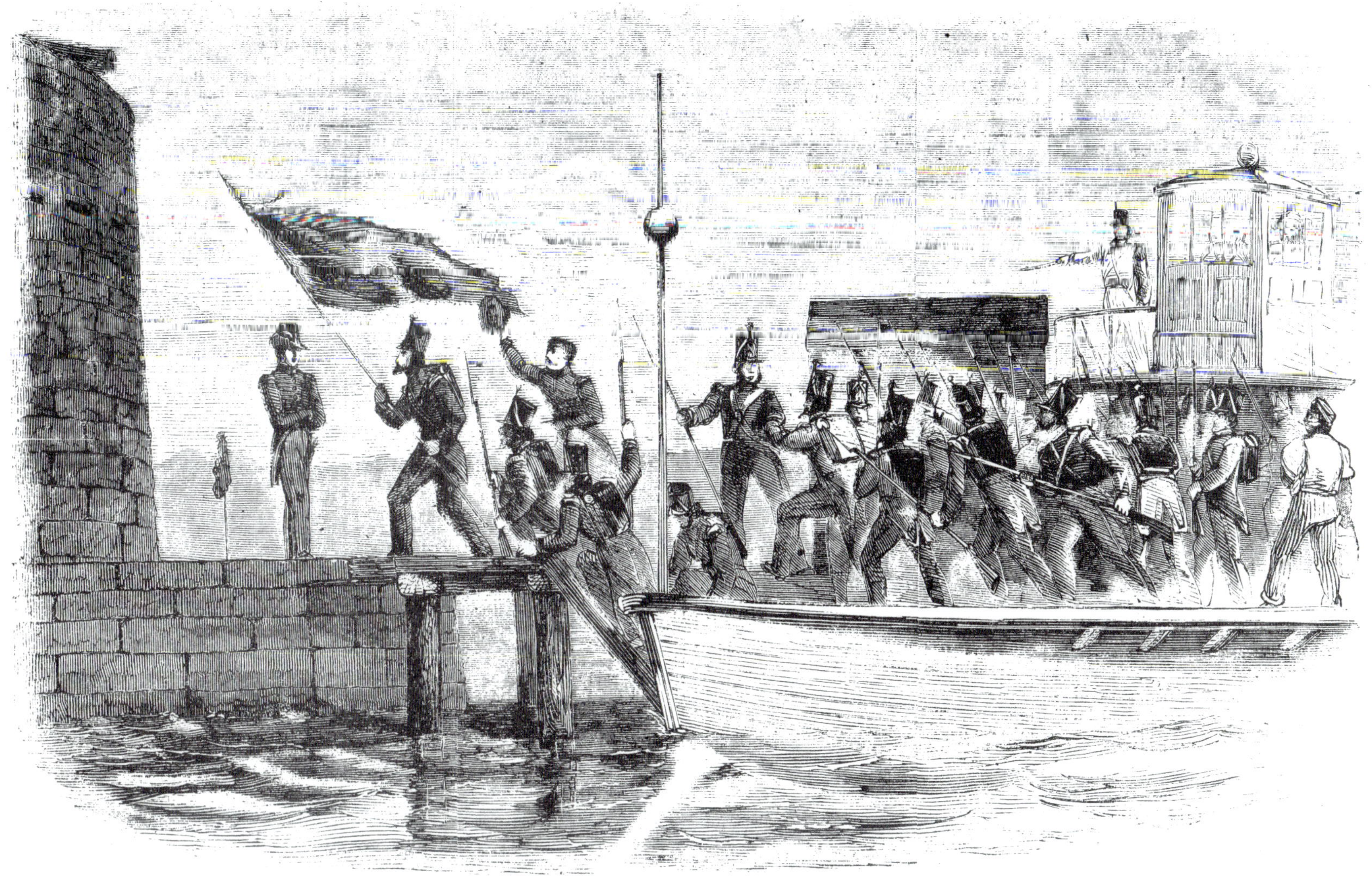

Occupation of Castle Pinckney

Artist: unknown
Harper's Weekly

When word of Major Robert Anderson's move to Sumter reached Gov. Francis W. Pickens, he immediately ordered the Charleston Militia to take Forts Moultrie, Johnson and Castle Pinkney. Col. J. J. Pettigrew, commanding three companies, boarded the guard boat *Nina* and made the short trip from Charleston to Castle Pinckney, located on Shute's Folly in the middle of the harbor. Concerned they would face a fight, Pettigrew and his men were surprised to find only Lt. Richard Meade and his family with a few workmen at Castle Pinkney. Meade and his family were allowed to leave.

Pettigrew found the guns at Castle Pinckney spiked and the ammunition removed. He raised the flag of the *Nina*, a red flag with a white star, over the Castle to the cheers of the thousands of onlookers in Charleston. This was the first secessionist flag raised over a United States fortification.

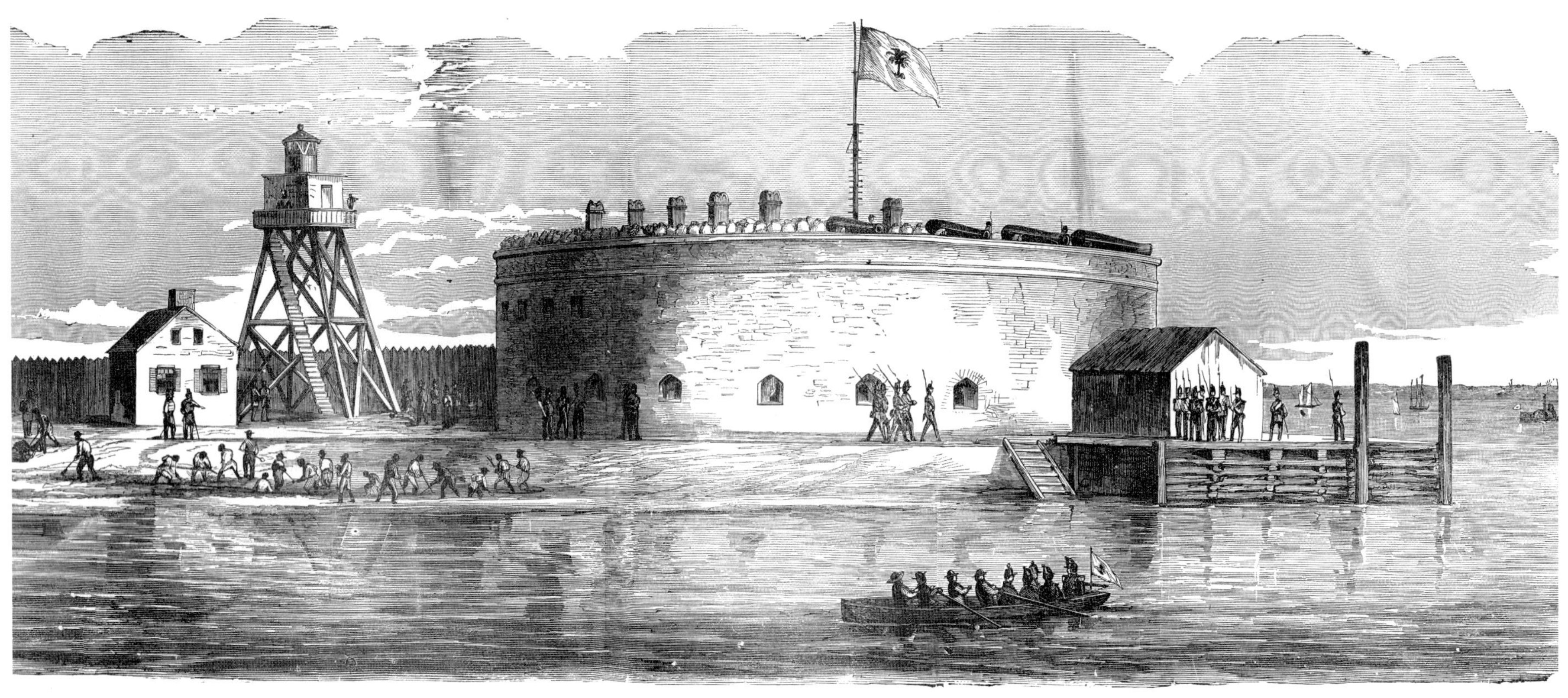

Castle Pinckney, Charleston Harbor

Artist: William Waud
Frank Leslie's Illustrated Newspaper

Castle Pinckney was the first fortification taken by the Confederacy, but this inner harbor location actually played a fairly insignificant role in the defense of Charleston. So far interior to the harbor, the Castle, while taken with great pride, had marginal strategic importance. Many of the 28 guns at Castle Pickney were removed and used in the Confederate batteries on Morris Island. The fortification was used during the course of the war as a location to hold Union prisoners taken during the lengthy siege of Charleston.

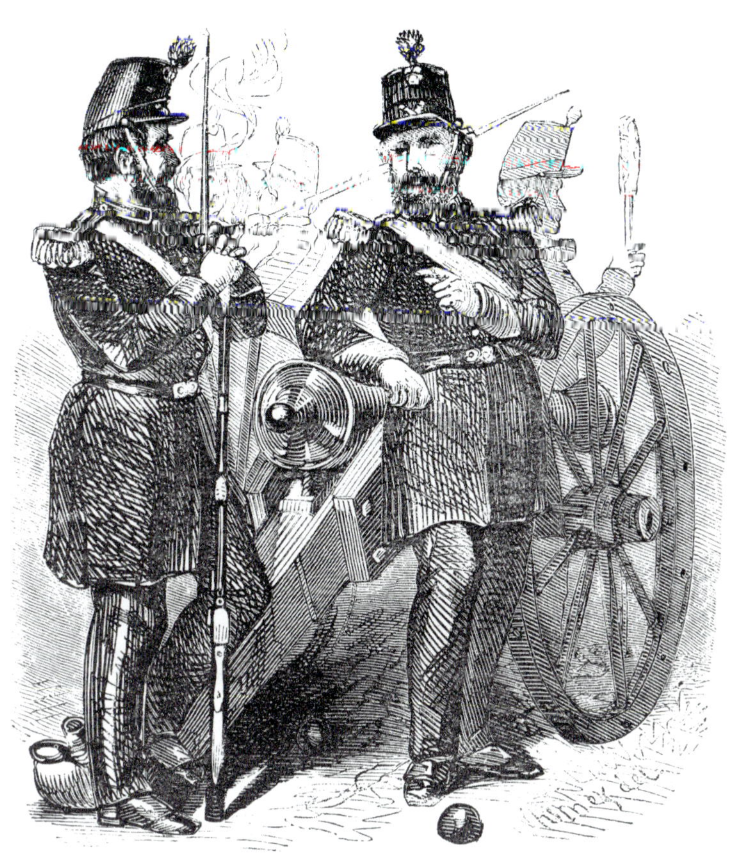

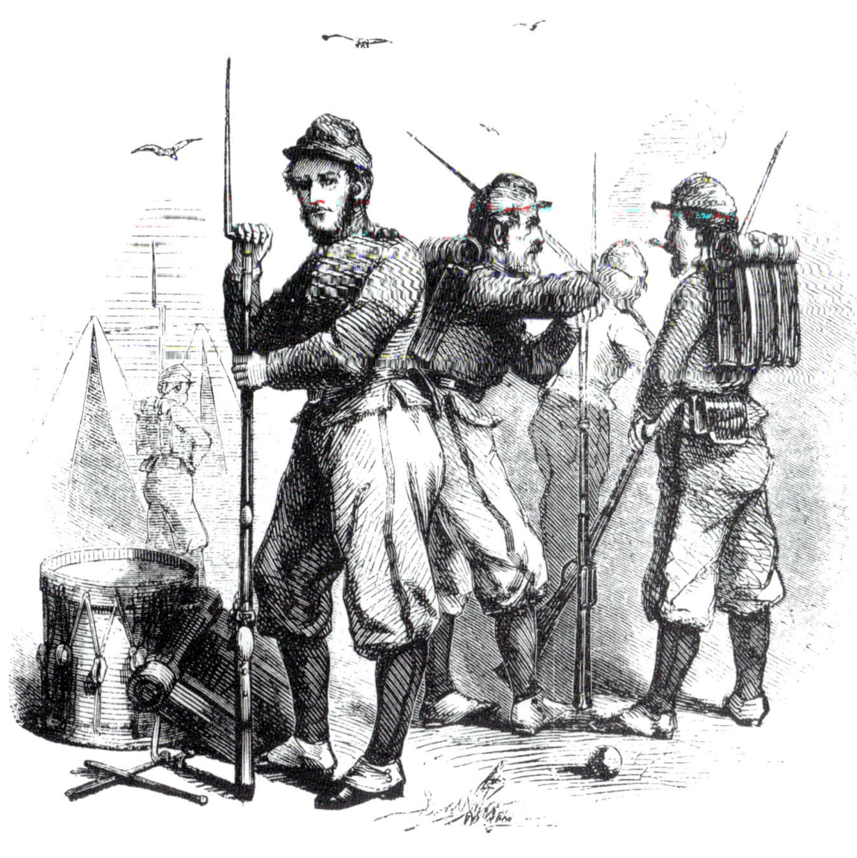

Charleston Militia Units

Artist: unknown
Harper's Weekly

Prior to the war, many militia units existed in Charleston. Operating like the volunteer fire companies, these units served as social organizations as much as they did military units. *Harper's Weekly* published illustrations of two Charleston units – the Washington Artillery (*left*) and the Charleston Zouaves (*right*).

The Washington Artillery was the first militia unit to offer its services to the state after South Carolina seceded from the Union. The unit was 150 men strong and had a reputation for efficiency and thorough training. After Major Robert Anderson moved the federal garrison to Fort Sumter, the Washington Artillery was among the first units to be placed at Fort Moultrie.

Referring to the Charleston Zouaves, *Harper's* writes: "The uniform, it cannot be denied, is very handsome; and the men who wear it are gallant and brave."

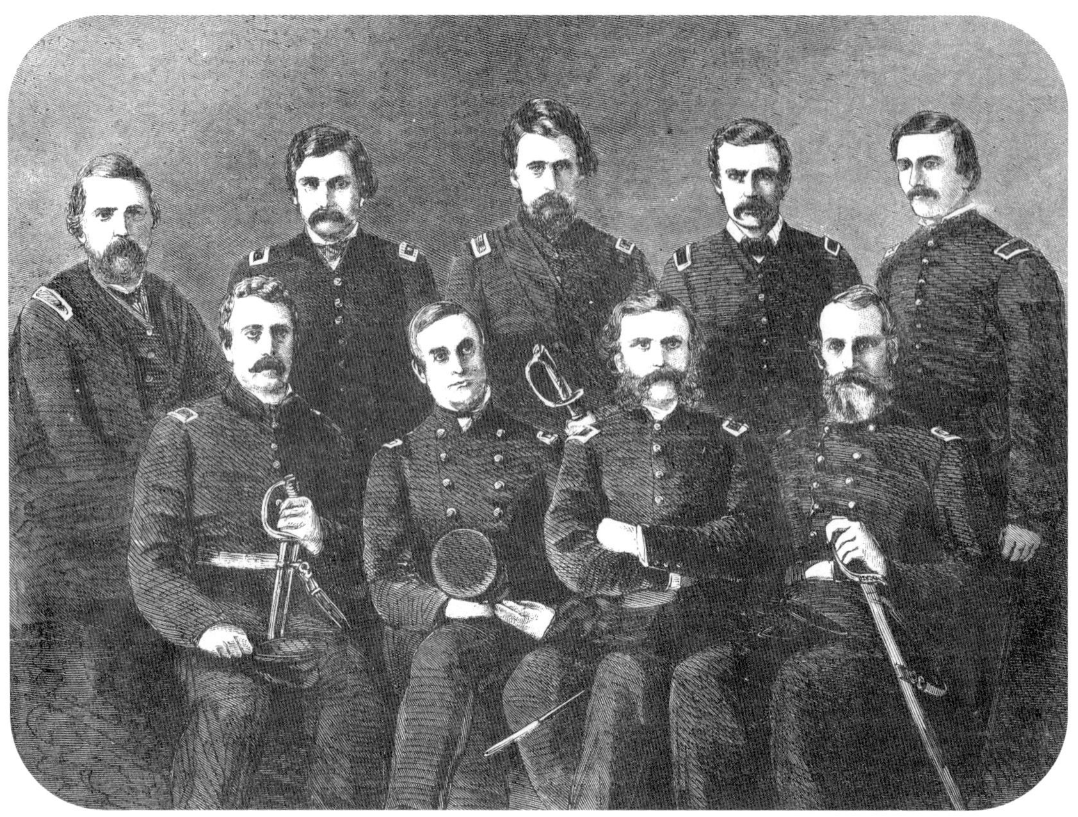

The Defenders at Fort Sumter

Drawn from a photograph taken at the fort
Harper's Weekly

A total of nine officers served in the small garrison at Fort Sumter in early 1861. In the front row are (*left to right*): Capt. Abner Doubleday, Major Robert Anderson, Asst. Surgeon Samuel W. Crawford and Capt. John G. Foster.

Doubleday was later promoted to major general and saw action at Bull Run, Fredericksburg and Gettysburg. He was long credited with inventing baseball, though earlier references have been discovered.

Anderson was promoted to brevet major general and transferred to command the armies in Kentucky. He participated in the flag raising at Fort Sumter in 1865, fours years to the day of his withdrawal in 1861.

Crawford would be promoted to brigadier general and serve at Bull Run, Gettysburg, the Wilderness and Petersburg. In 1864, Foster returned as major general to participate in the siege of Charleston.

In the back row are (*left to right*): Capt. Truman Seymour, 1st Lt. George W. Snyder, 1st Lt. Jefferson C. Davis, 2nd Lt. Richard K. Meade, and 1st Lt. Theodore Talbot.

Seymour, promoted to brigadier general, led an unsuccessful charge against Battery Wagner in 1863. During the siege of Charleston, he was captured and held in Charleston until its fall. Snyder died in Washington in November. Davis, promoted to brigadier general, served with Gen. William T. Sherman in his march to the sea. Meade resigned his commission and joined the Confederate army. While stationed in Richmond, he became ill, dying in 1861. Talbot was known for his participation in John C. Freemont's first expedition to cross the Rockies. After Sumter, he was promoted to assistant adjutant general and was killed less than a year later.

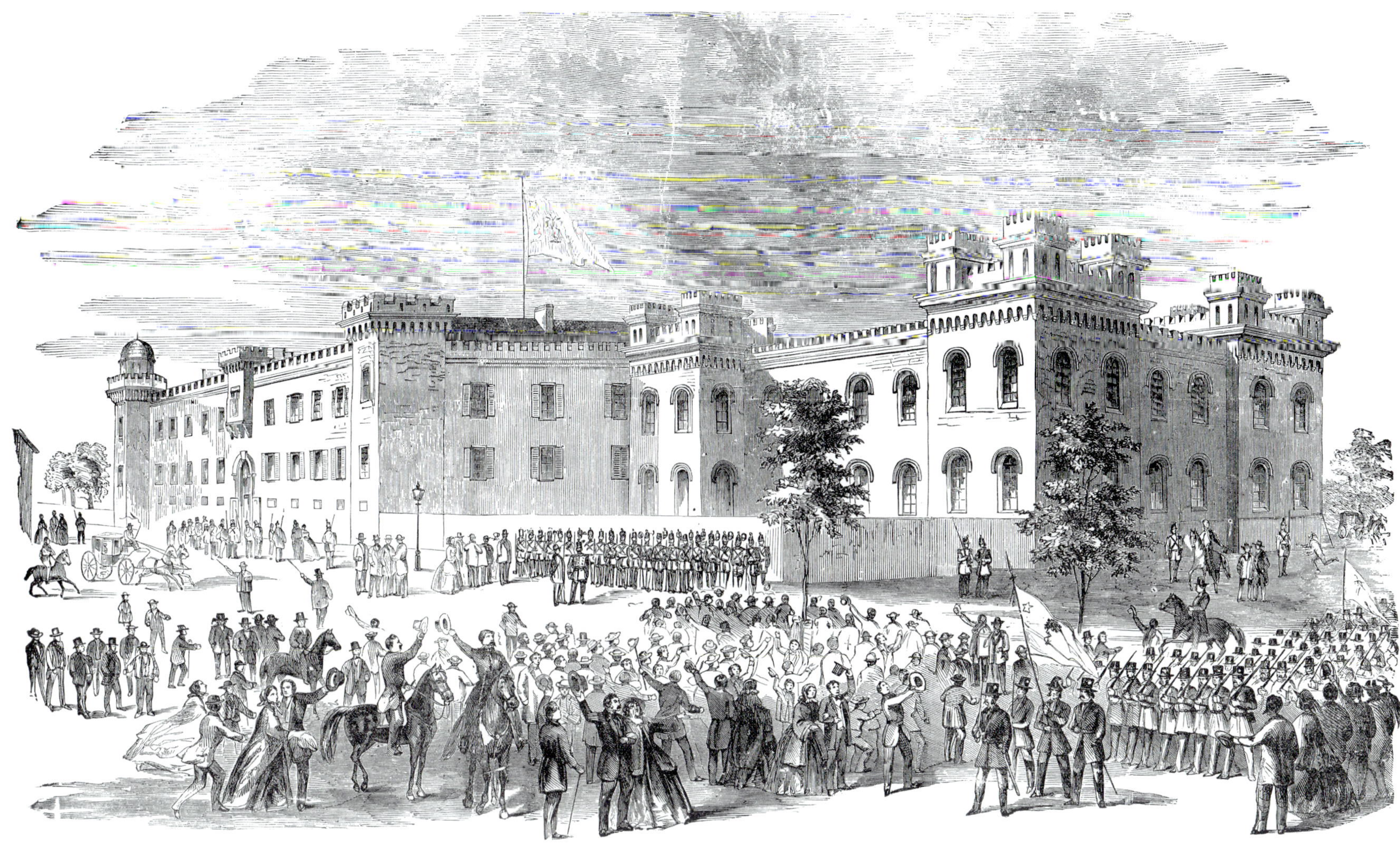

Seizing the U.S. Arsenal

Artist: William Waud
Frank Leslie's Illustrated Newspaper

As a result of Gen. Robert Anderson's attempt to withdraw munitions from the U.S. arsenal in early November 1860, Gov. Francis W. Pickens stationed a detachment of troops there to ensure no such transfer was attempted again. This action effectively left the 14 federal troops and the arsenal storekeeper, F. C. Humphreys, confined to the large structure.

Following Anderson's move to Fort Sumter and the state's seizure of Forts Moultrie, Johnson and Castle Pinckney, Pickens ordered state troops to seize the arsenal on Dec. 30. The seizure, led by Col. John Cunningham, was orderly and proceeded without incident. Humphreys and the small federal detachment fired a salute as the United States flag was lowered. The seizure not only kept these munitions from reaching Anderson but gave South Carolina enough muskets, rifles and ordinance to outfit three divisions. While a handsome engraving, this illustration was titled incorrectly by *Leslie's* as the U.S. Arsenal. William Waud had forwarded a fine illustration of The Citadel at Marion Square.

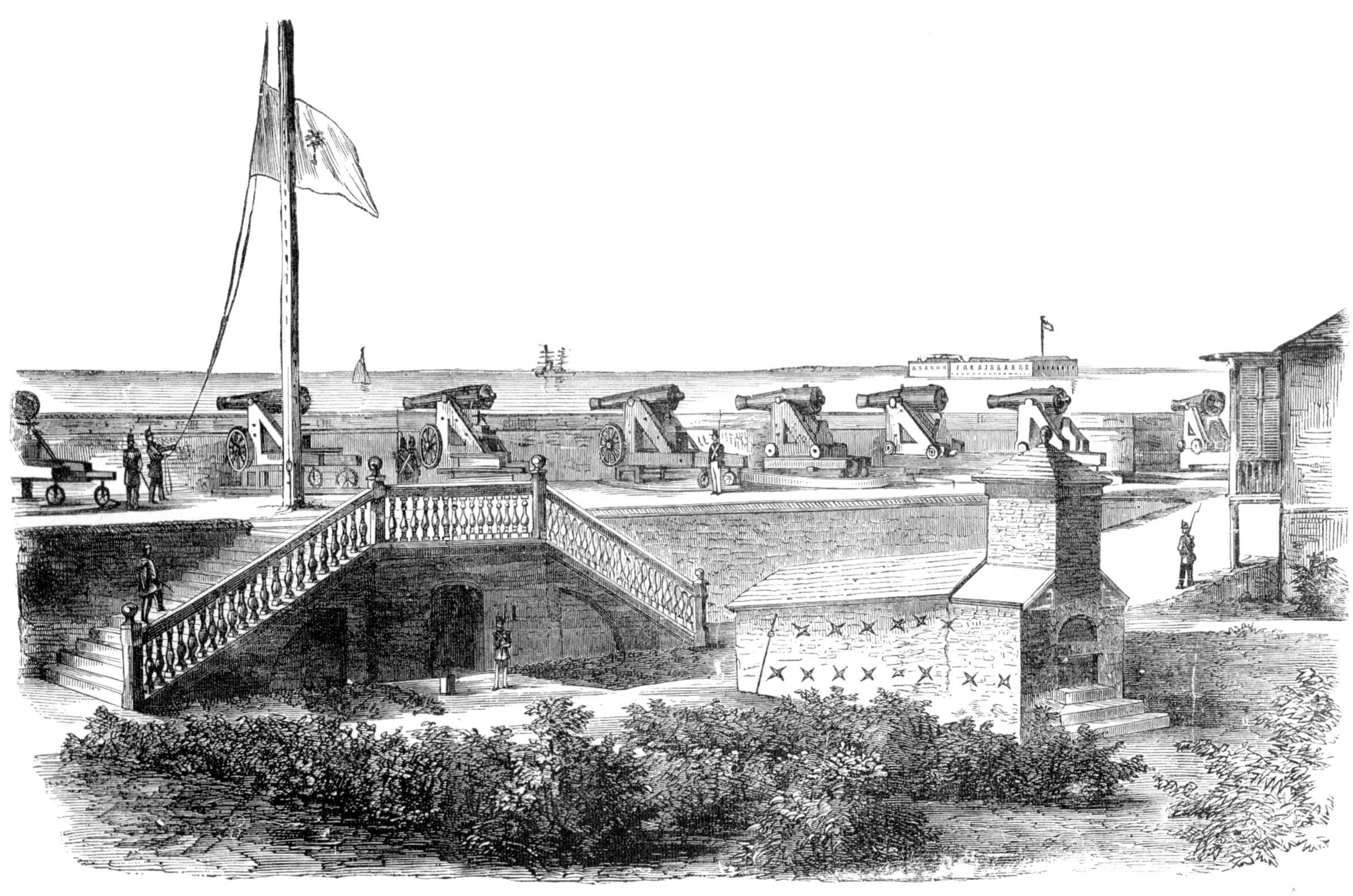

Interior View of Fort Moultrie

Artist: William Waud
Frank Leslie's Illustrated Newspaper

The citizens of South Carolina had a strong emotional attachment to Fort Moultrie. As Abner Doubleday noted in his *Reminiscences of Forts Sumter and Moultrie:*

> *To the South Carolinians Fort Moultrie was almost a sacred spot, endeared by many precious historical associations; for the ancestors of most of the principal families had fought there in the Revolutionary War behind their hastily improvised ramparts of palmetto logs, and had gained a glorious victory over the British fleet in its first attempt to enter the harbor and capture the city.*

Fort Moultrie was 1.8 miles from Sumter, well within range for the two fortifications to exchange fire. The design had 11 heavy caliber guns and mortars. The construction consisted of inner and outer walls of brick filled with sand, creating a wall approximately 15-ft. thick. As noted by Doubleday, part of the Civil War fortification included the site of the Revolutionary War fort.

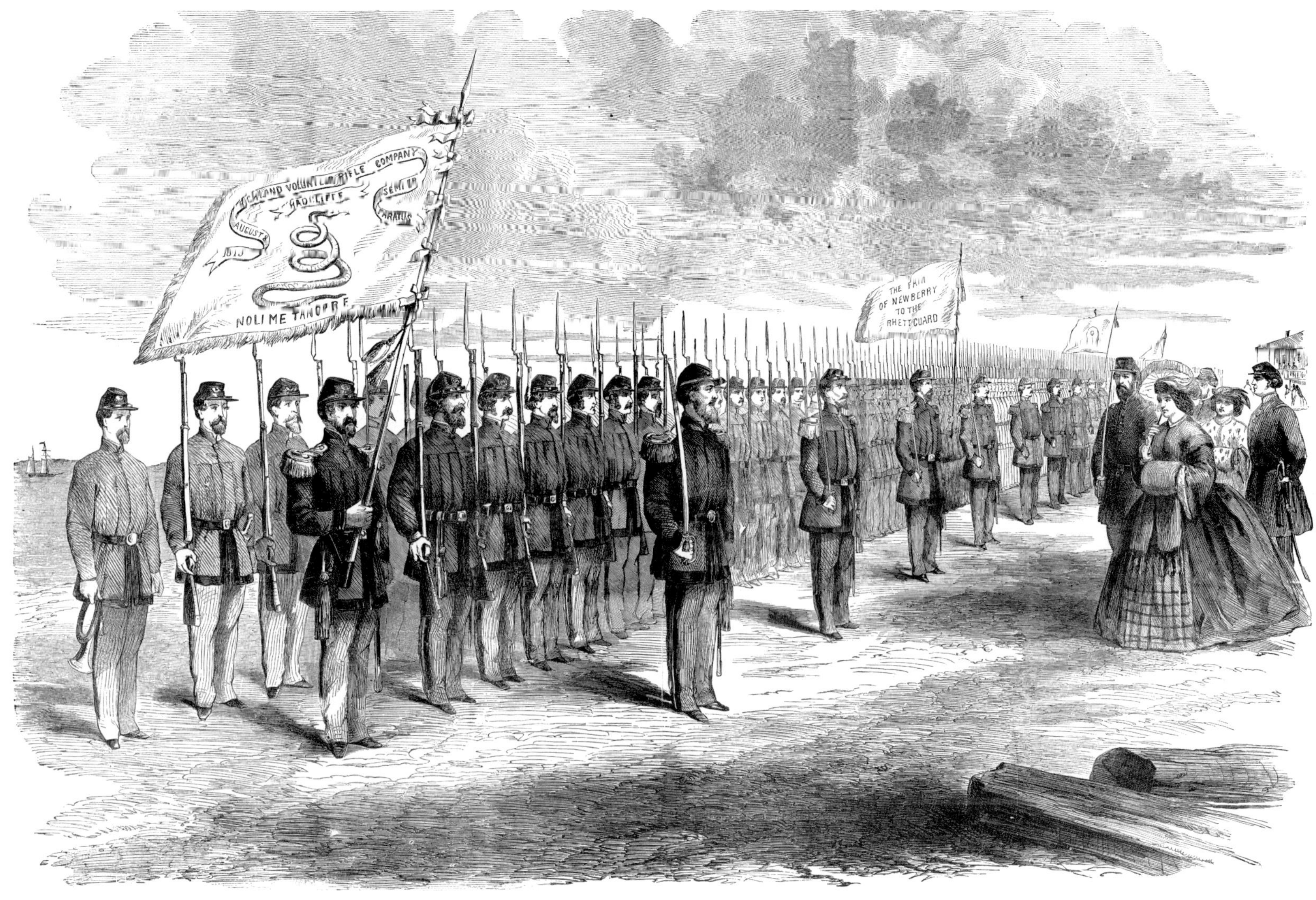

Review of S.C. Volunteer Troops

Artist: William Waud
Frank Leslie's Illustrated Newspaper

After the militia occupied Castle Pinckney, additional troops were formed from the city militia units. They were transported to Fort Moultrie by the *Nina* and the *General Clinch*, a paddle-wheel steamship named for Major Robert Anderson's highly regarded father-in-law, a Georgia planter, politician and general. The militia found the fort unoccupied, save for a few workmen, and claimed the fortification for South Carolina. The militia transferred the Palmetto flag from the *General Clinch* and placed it over Fort Moultrie.

Shortly after, volunteer militia from the upstate were added to the garrison at Fort Moultrie. This engraving shows the wife and daughter of Gov. Francis W. Pickens in review of the South Carolina Volunteer Troops assembled at the fort. The artist noted in the newspaper that the Richland Guards were a "gentlemenly and hospitable group... well uniformed, well drilled, and well officered."

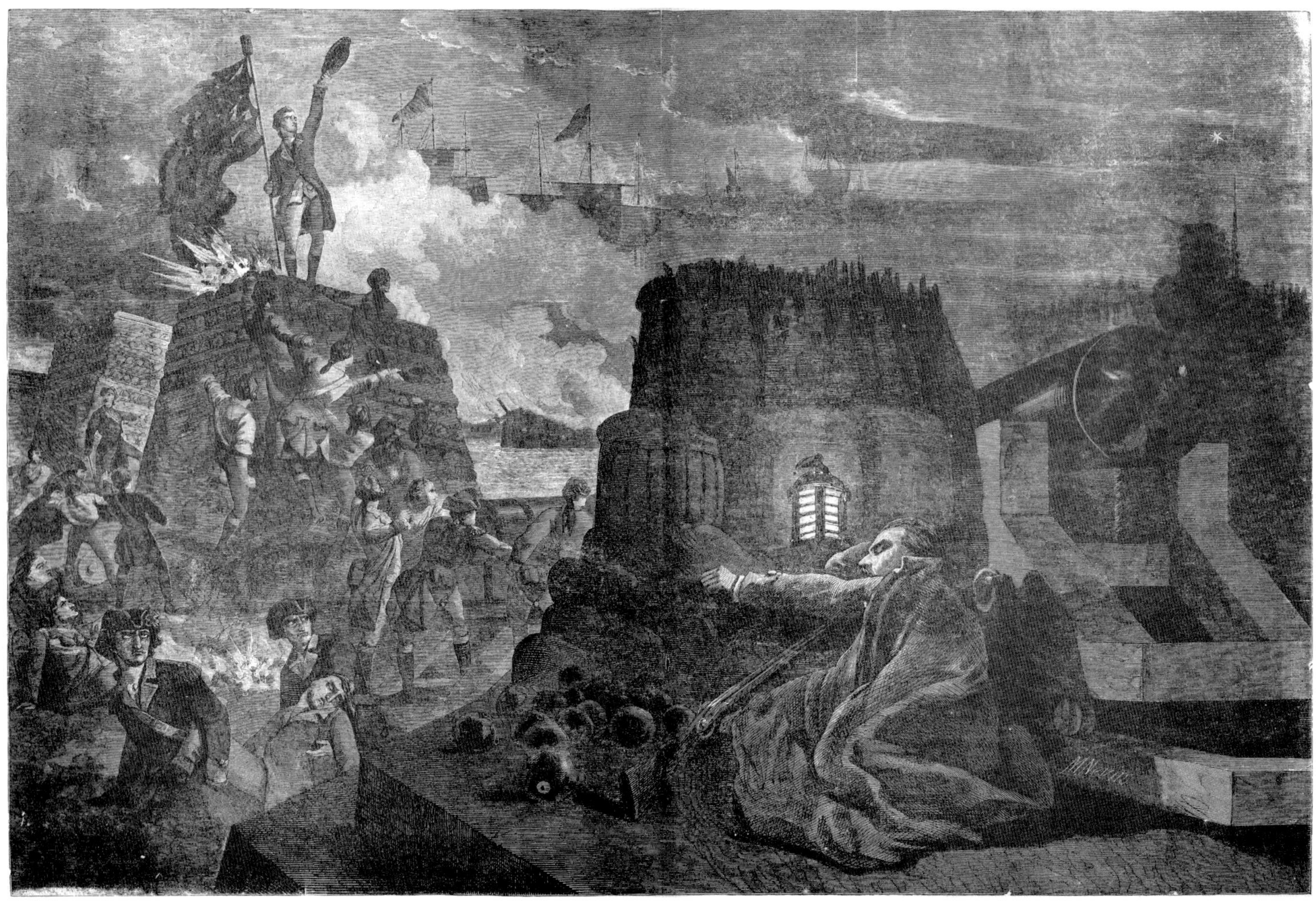

Moultrie Dreamer

Artist: unknown
Harper's Weekly

In January 1861, *Harper's Weekly* published a provocative illustration entitled, "Moultrie Dreamer." It appeared just after Maj. Robert Anderson had moved his federal garrison from Fort Moultrie to Fort Sumter. Fort Moultrie was then occupied by troops from the Republic of South Carolina flying the Palmetto Flag. The illustration depicts a South Carolina soldier asleep on the wall at Fort Moultrie remembering the valiant stance of the patriots there who turned back the British fleet in 1776.

The two patriots carrying the wounded comrade appear disturbed, taking in the scene of the fort now being used as an instrument of secession. Pro-Unionists would have viewed the occupation of Fort Moultrie as the desecration of a sacred place given its pivotal role in the creation of the Union. Ironically, Anderson's own father, Major Richard Anderson, served in 1780 at Fort Moultrie where he was wounded and captured by the British.

But symbolism serves the eye of the beholder. Many Southerners saw secession and the pending conflict as the second War for Independence. To them, it was fitting to launch that war from a site that played such a key role in 1776, a place that embodied the courage and determination of South Carolinians in their quest for freedom.

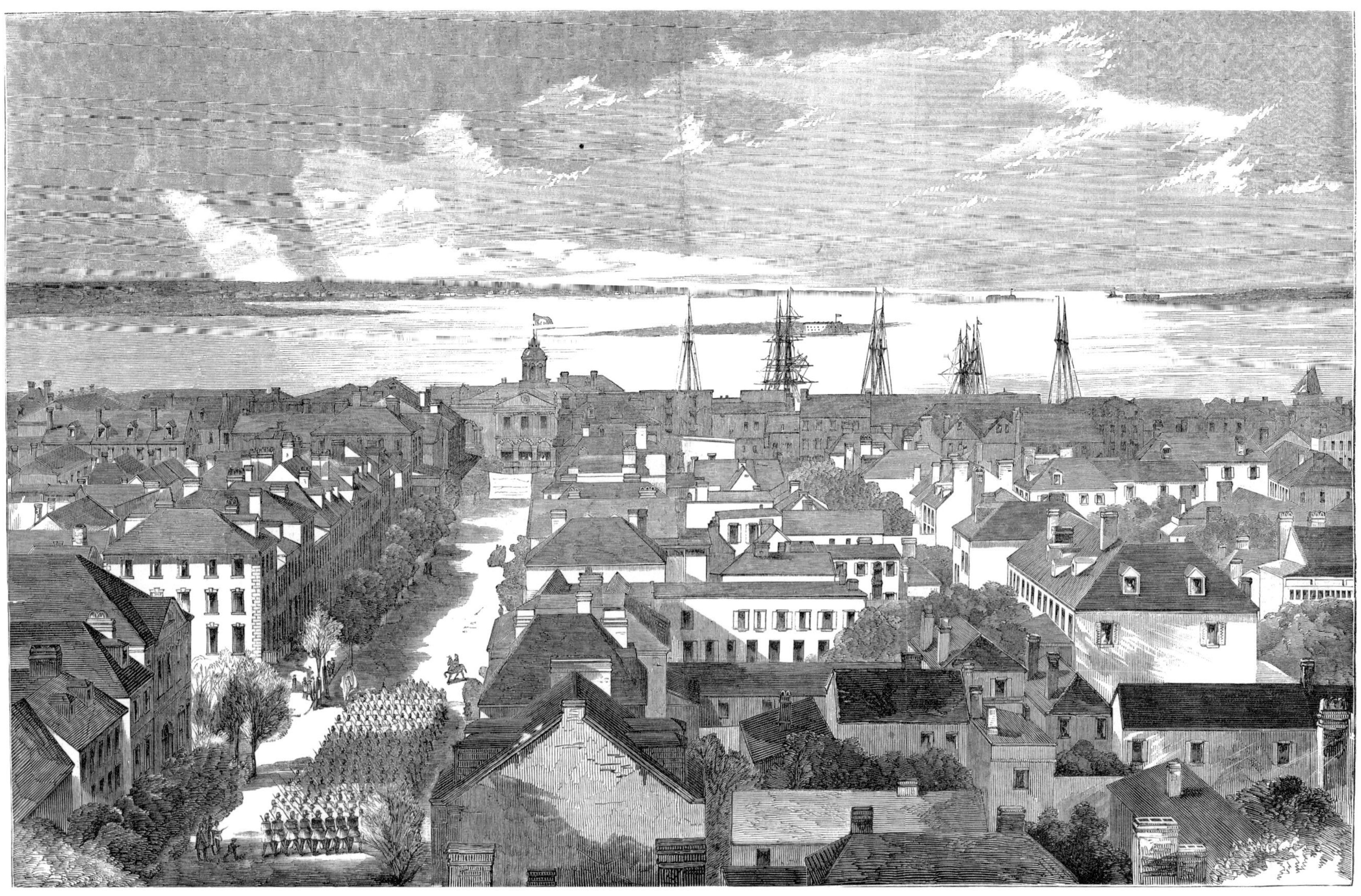

The City of Charleston

Artist: unknown
Harper's Weekly

This engraving provides an excellent bird's-eye view of Charleston from St. Michael's steeple. Note the volunteer troops marching down Broad Street. A short commentary in *Harper's Weekly* notes, "Many merchants have their offices here; it is, in fact, the Broadway of Charleston."

St. Michael's steeple provided a view of the lower peninsula, as well as of the physical relationship of Castle Pinckney, Fort Moultrie and Fort Johnson. Not surprisingly, the only Broad Street office noted is that of the *Charleston Mercury*. The *Mercury* and its owner, fiery secessionist Robert Barnwell Rhett Jr., were frequently condemned by the Northern press.

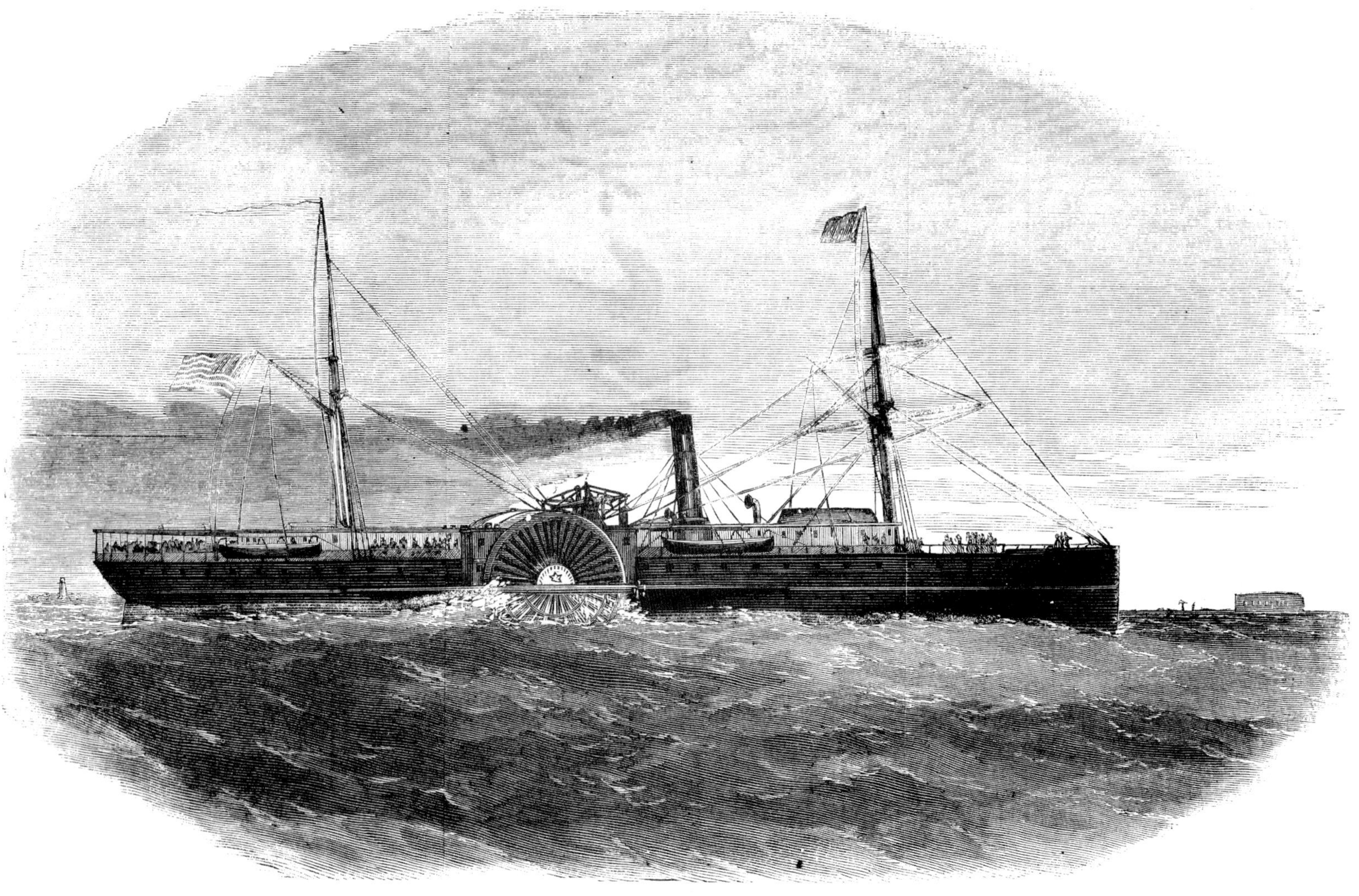

The *Star of the West* Artist: William Waud
Frank Leslie's Illustrated Newspaper

On orders from Pres. James Buchanan, the *Star of the West*, a leased steamer, left New York on Jan. 5, 1861, loaded with supplies and 250 troops to outfit and reinforce Fort Sumter. Charleston was quickly alerted to this "secret mission" by an anonymous telegram.

Anticipating its arrival, Gov. Francis W. Pickens placed several guard boats at the entry of the main shipping channel from the ocean and into Charleston Harbor. Authorities extinguished all the harbor beacons and the Morris Island Lighthouse to prevent their use in navigation by Union boat captains. On the morning of Jan. 8, the *Mercury* headlines read, "United States troops hastening from all points southward. The *Star of the West*, with reinforcements for Anderson, due here today." Suffice it to say, both the military authorities and the general population were in a state of alert.

Just after midnight on Jan. 9, the *Star of the West* arrived near the harbor's entrance. At daybreak, the steamer approached and passed the guard boats. One of the boats, *General Clinch*, fired several rockets to alert the batteries of the unwanted visitor's arrival.

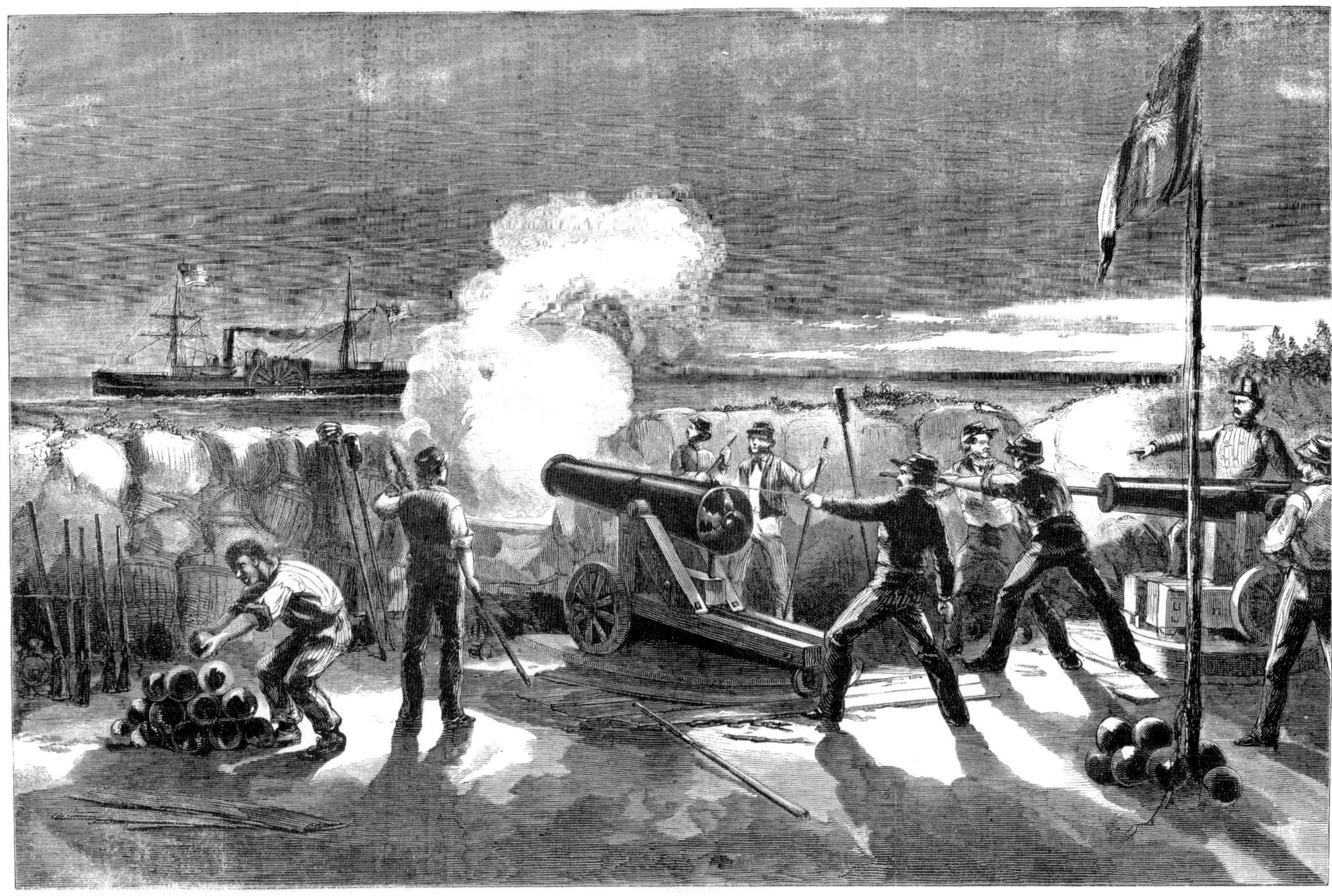

Firing on the *Star of the West*

Artist: unknown
Harper's Weekly

On Dec. 31, 1860, Gov. Francis W. Pickens ordered that a battery be erected on Morris Island, adjacent to the shipping channel coming into Charleston Harbor. This new battery, named Fort Morris, was manned by 40 cadets from the Citadel, the military college of South Carolina. Fort Morris, commanded by Major Peter Stevens, was armed with four 24-lb. field howitzers capable of reaching any vessel moving through the channel.

As the *Star of the West* reached a position opposite the cadet's battery, a warning shot rocketed across the bow. The steamer did not yield and, instead, pushed ahead to fulfill her mission. Stevens ordered the cadets to fire directly on the ship. Shells hit the bow and rudder, and penetrated the ship's rigging. Taking on effective fire and knowing that additional shore batteries would soon be in range, the captain of the *Star of the West* reversed course. He left the harbor without supplying and reinforcing Fort Sumter, and returned to New York, much to the dismay of Major Robert Anderson, his troops and their families who helplessly watched the morning's excitement.

Lieutenant Hall with Flag of Truce

Artist: William Waud
Frank Leslie's Illustrated Newspaper

After the firing on the *Star of the West*, Major Robert Anderson sent a letter under a flag of truce to Gov. Francis W. Pickens. His dispatch read:

> *Sir: Two of your batteries fired this morning upon an unarmed vessel bearing the flag of my Government. As I have not been notified that war has been declared by South Carolina against the government of the United States, I cannot but think this hostile act was committed without your sanction or authority. Under that hope, and that alone, did I refrain from opening fire upon your batteries. I have the honor, therefore, to respectfully ask whether the above mentioned act – one, I believe, without parallel in the history of our country or any other civilized Government – was committed in obedience to your instructions, and to notify you, if it not be disclaimed, that I must regard it as an act of war; and that I shall not, after a reasonable time for the return of my passenger, permit any vessel to pass within range of the guns of my fort. In order to save, as far as in my power, the shedding of blood, I beg that you will give due notification of this, my decision, to all concerned. Hoping, however, that your answer will be such as will justify a further continuance of forbearance on my part, I have the honor to be very respectfully,*

Your obedient servant,
Robert Anderson
Major, First Artillery U.S.A., Commanding Fort Sumter
January 9, 1861

Pickens responded with a lengthy letter, summed up by this response, "The act is perfectly justified by me." F. W. Pickens

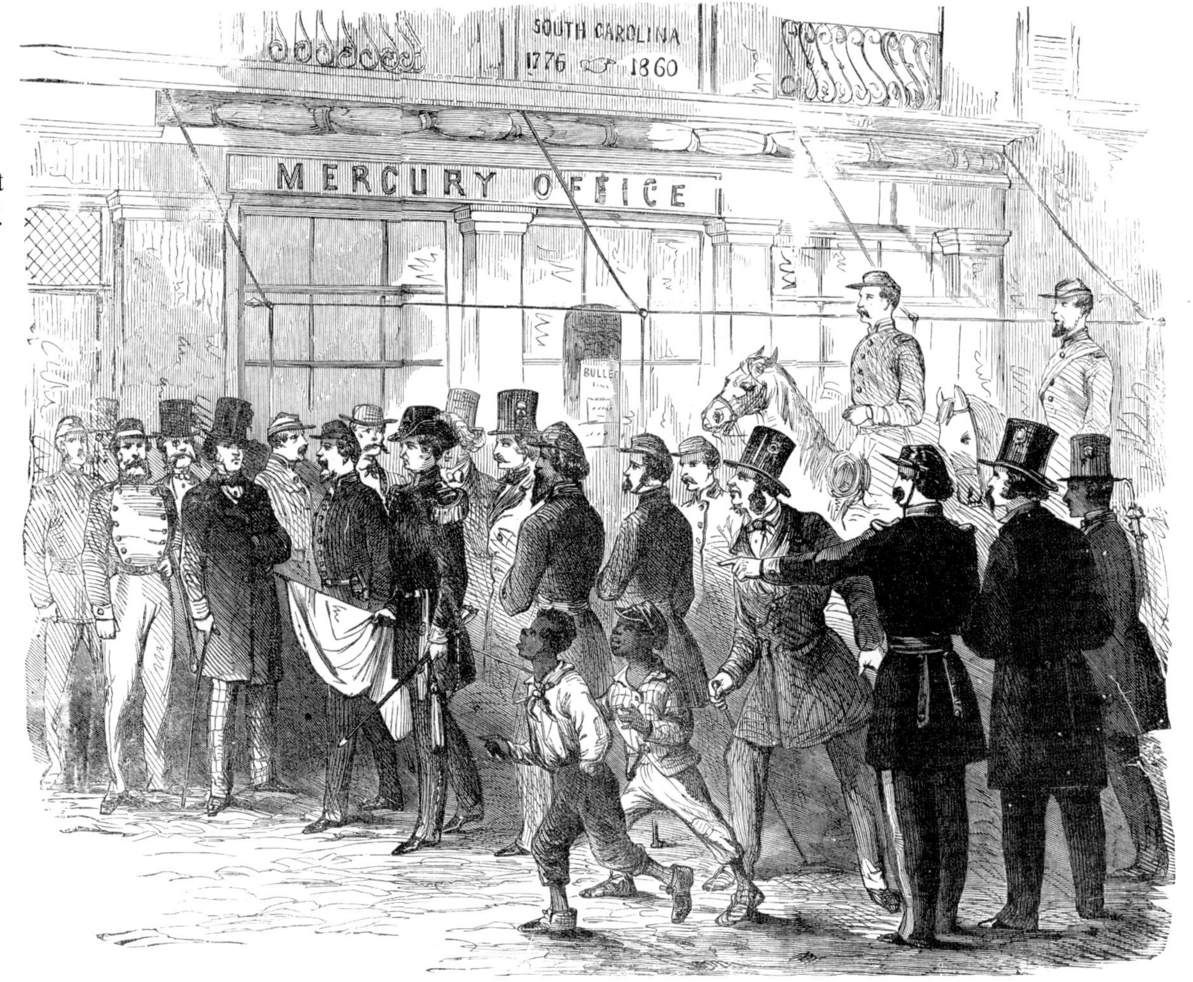

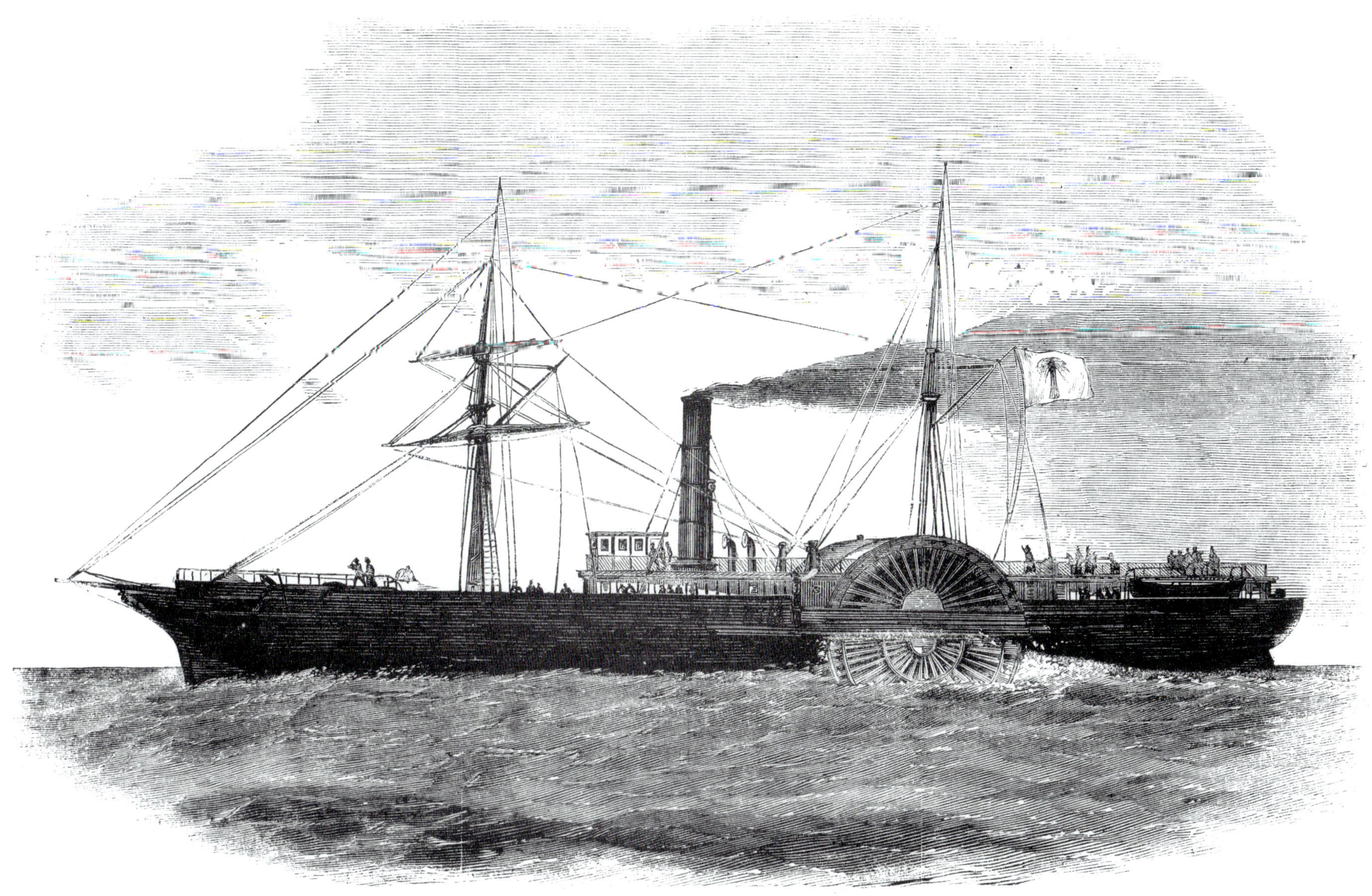

The Steamship *Marion*

Artist: unknown
Harper's Weekly

As Gov. Francis W. Pickens began to realize the federal government might not leave Fort Sumter peacefully, he pushed to gain a better stronghold and further secure the harbor. On Jan. 10, 1861, state authorities seized the steamship *Marion*.

The *Marion*, an 800-ton steamship built in 1851, was commanded by Capt. Sam Whiting and provided cargo and passenger service between Charleston and New York. After its seizure, the steamship was converted to a man-of-war and patrolled the harbor and shipping channel.

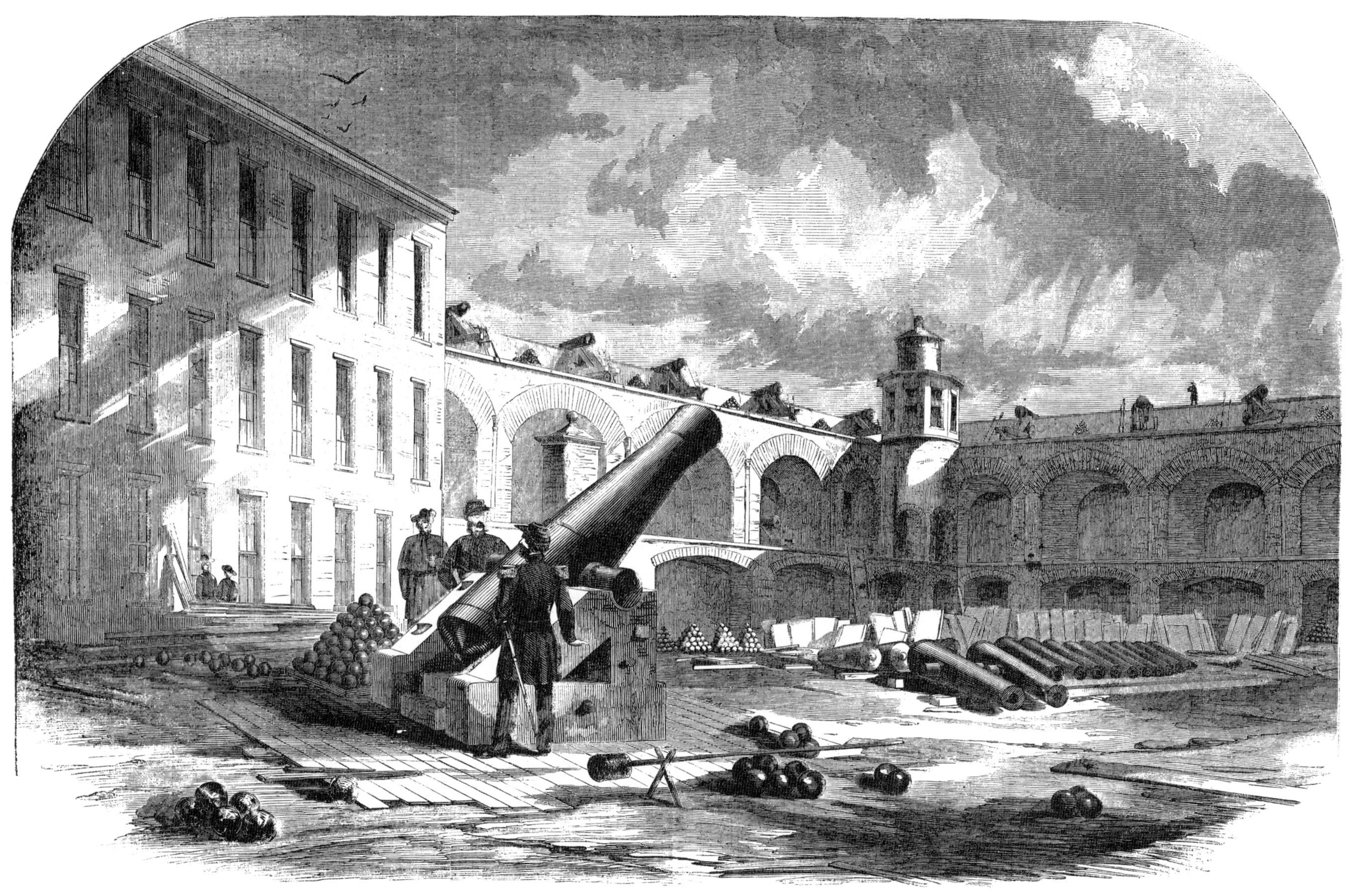

A 10-inch Columbiad at Fort Sumter

Drawn by an officer in Major Anderson's command
Harper's Weekly

Fort Sumter was not yet finished when Major Robert Anderson and his small garrison arrived. A number of the guns intended for the fort had not been delivered. Of those guns on the grounds, many weren't in place.

Fort Sumter was designed to face a naval attack from the harbor, not to defend itself from land batteries on three sides as was then the case. The first task of the garrison was to complete the installation of as many guns as possible.

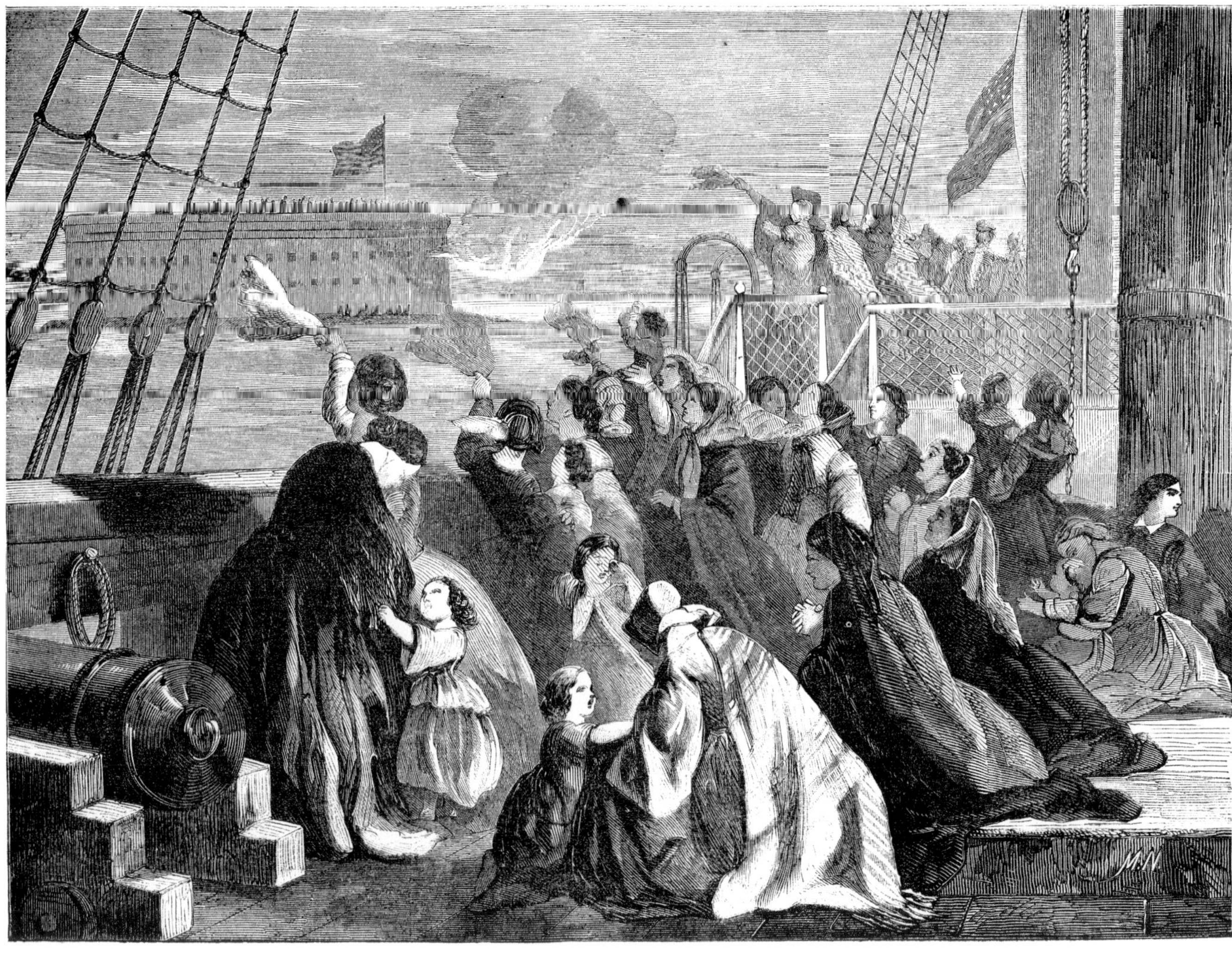

Goodbye to Sumter

Artist: M. N.
Harper's Weekly

As tensions mounted between the small federal garrison at Sumter and the South Carolina authorities, the presence of women and children in Fort Sumter became an increasing concern for both parties. This was particularly so for Major Robert Anderson. He was concerned that these loved ones might find themselves in harm's way, but they were also contributing to the depletion of a sparse food supply.

Anderson requested permission from Gov. Francis W. Pickens to have the women and children evacuated and sent by ship to New York. On Feb. 3, the steamer *Marion* was made available as requested, and the women and children boarded for the long trip. One of the wives aboard the *Marion* recorded as they pulled away:

> *When the ship was passing, [the fort] fired a gun and gave three heart-thrilling cheers as a parting farewell to the dear loved ones on board, whom they may possibly never meet again this side of the grave. The response was weeping and waving adieux to husbands and fathers. A small band put up in an isolated fort, and completely surrounded by instruments of death, as five forts could be seen from the steamer's deck, with their guns pointing toward Sumter.*

Governor Pickens

Drawn from a portrait
Frank Leslie's Illustrated Newspaper

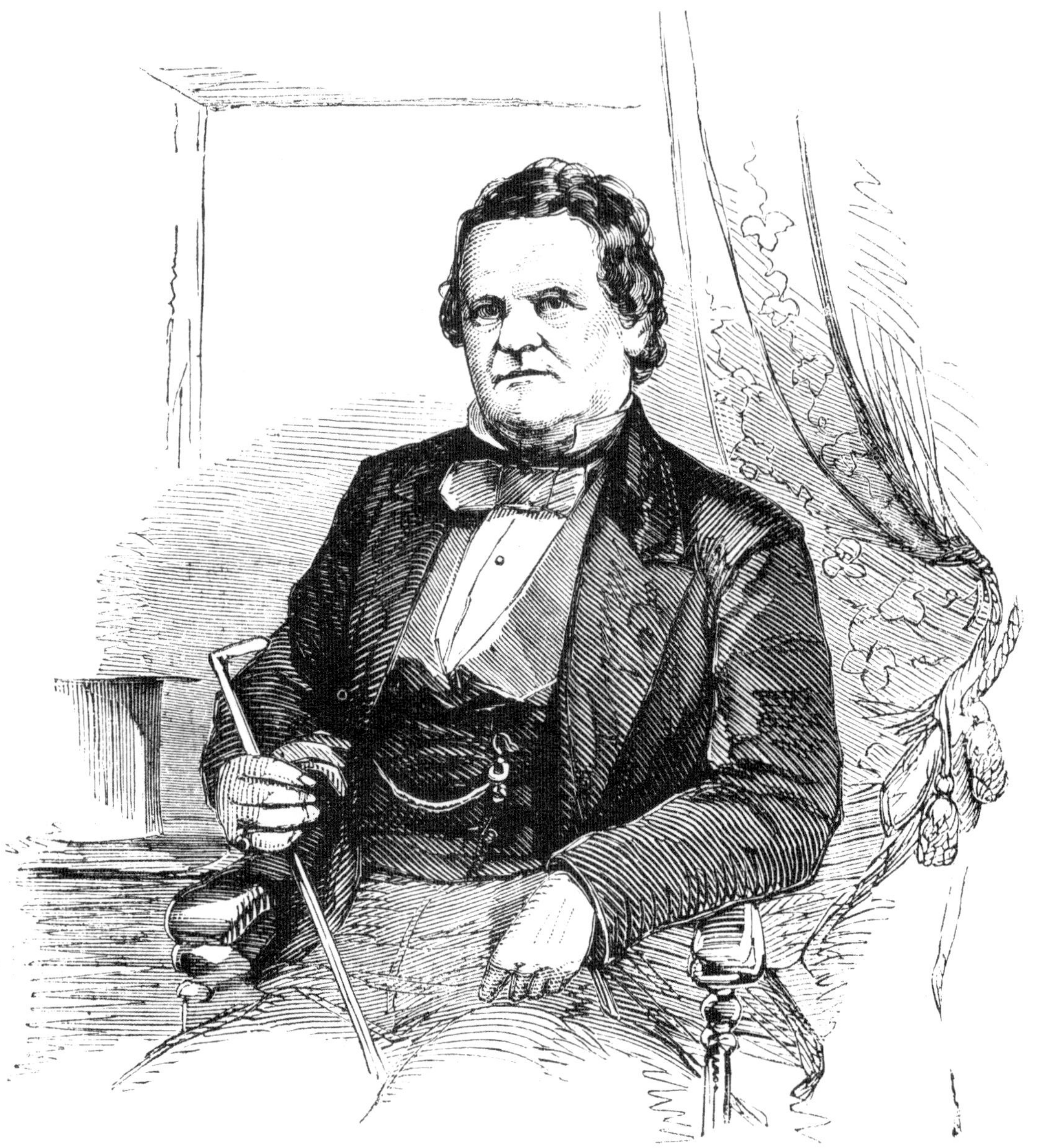

Francis W. Pickens was elected governor of South Carolina on Dec. 14, 1860, just six days before South Carolina voted to secede from the Union. He came with an impressive South Carolina pedigree as the son of former Gov. Andrew Pickens and the grandson of Revolutionary War hero Andrew Pickens. He was also an experienced politician, having served in the South Carolina Legislature for four years, in the U.S. Congress for nine years, and a two-year term as the U.S. minister to Russia before being elected governor. Though he was anxious to take on the job, nothing could have prepared him for the challenges he would face during his two-year term.

Pickens demonstrated capability in his early decisions dealing with Anderson and by installing the early defenses in Charleston. By early February, even as the Confederacy was forming at a convention in Alabama, Pickens prepared to fire on Fort Sumter. Many powerful men – from former Pres. John Tyler to South Carolinians attending the convention – urged Pickens to delay any action. After the formation of the Confederate government and the election of Jefferson Davis, Pickens was informed that any decisions regarding Fort Sumter were the right and responsibility of the Confederate government. He vehemently disagreed and telegrammed the convention at Alabama that he still had the right and authority to attack Sumter and was continuing in his preparations.

After several communications, Confederate Secretary of War Leroy P. Walker telegrammed Pickens a definitive response: "This Government assumes the control of the military operations at Charleston and will make demand of the fort when fully advised. An officer goes tonight to take charge." The un-named officer was Brig. Gen. P. G. T. Beauregard.

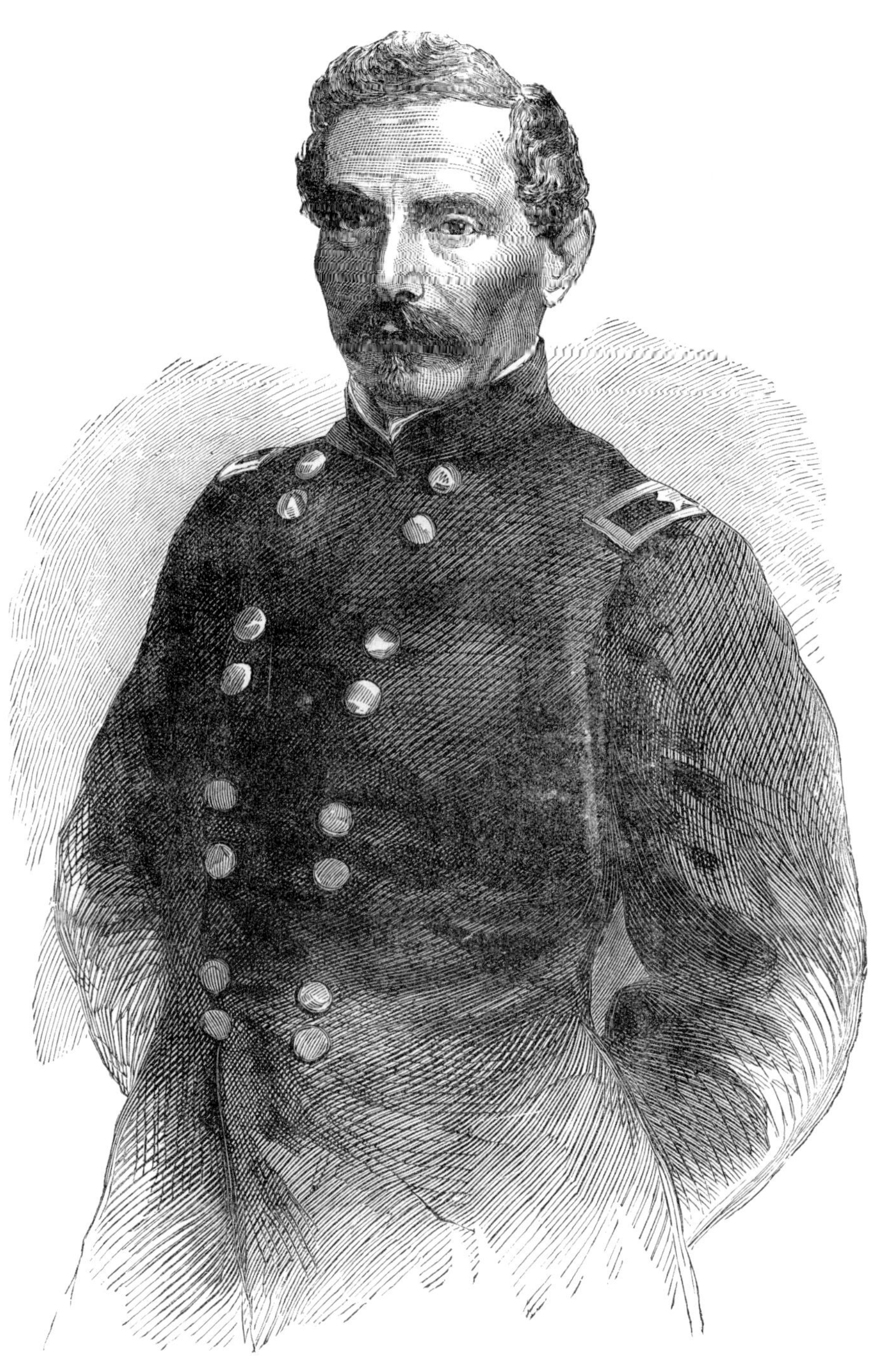

P. G. T. Beauregard

Artist: unknown
Frank Leslie's Illustrated Newspaper

Pierre Gustave Toutant Beauregard was born in New Orleans to Welsh and French parents. Being from a Southern aristocratic family, his appointment to West Point was assured. Beauregard graduated second in his class in 1838. His favorite professor, with whom he became close friends, was professor of artillery Robert Anderson. After graduation, Beauregard stayed on at West Point for a time as Anderson's assistant instructor.

He served with great distinction in the Mexican War as a member of Gen. Winfield Scott's staff. After the war, he commanded the army on the Mississippi and in Louisiana.

In November 1860, Beauregard was appointed superintendent of West Point. He accepted the appointment but notified the President he would resign if Louisiana seceded from the Union. Beauregard assumed command in late December 1860 only to have his appointment revoked five days later.

He traveled to New York to find passage back to New Orleans. In New York, he learned of Louisiana's decision to secede. While at the docks, he witnessed the return of the *Star of the West* from Charleston. He was invited on board and entertained by the commander. Beauregard inspected the damage to the ship inflicted by the Citadel cadets.

In February 1861, Jefferson Davis appointed Beauregard to the rank of brigadier general and instructed him to assume command of the Confederate operations against Fort Sumter.

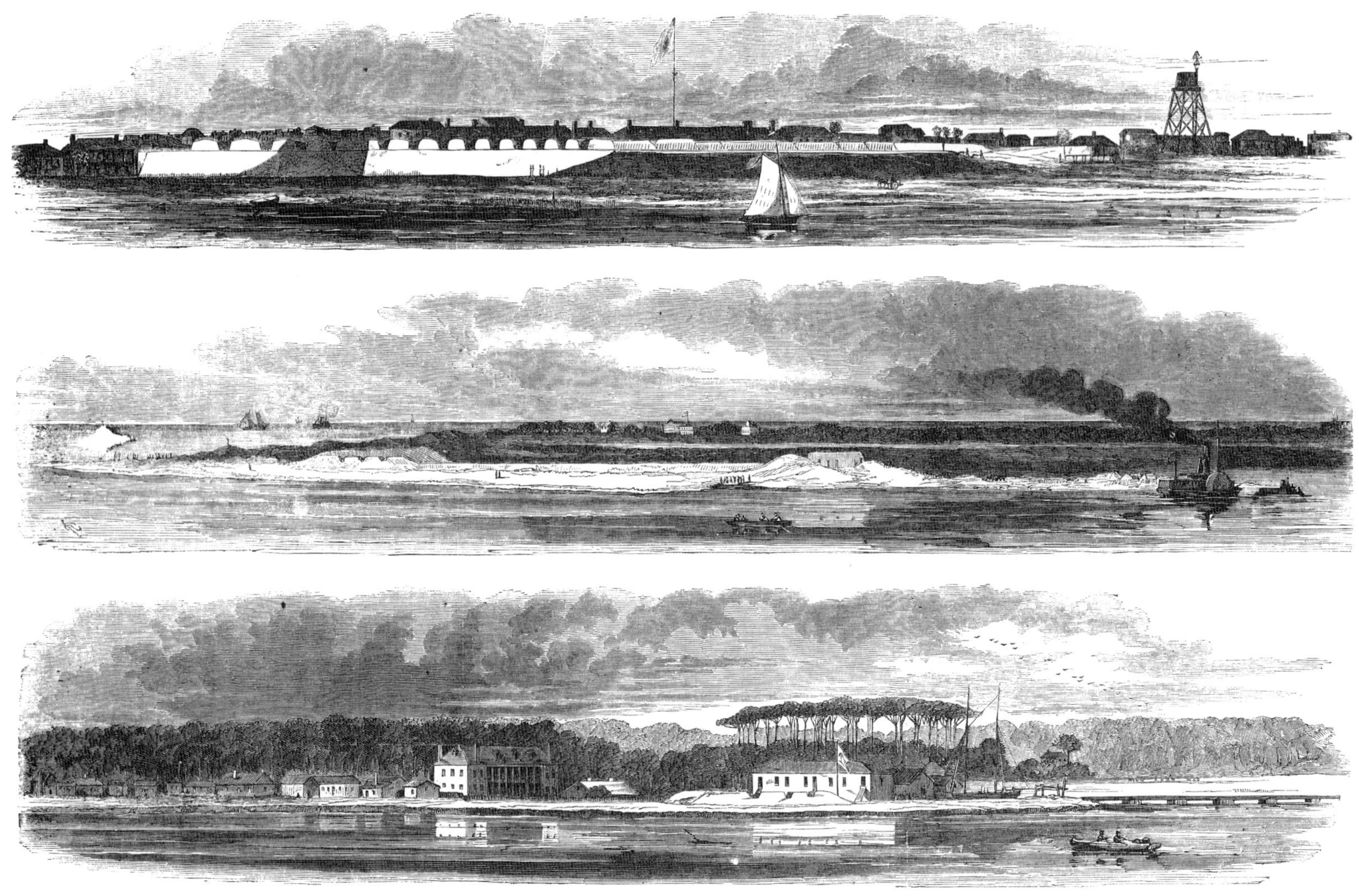

Fort Moultrie, Morris Island and Fort Johnson

Drawn by an officer of Major Anderson's command.
Harper's Weekly

Major Robert Anderson and his officers kept careful watch of the progress made by Confederate authorities in the construction of the harbor batteries. Knowing of P. G. T. Beauregard's arrival, his reputation as an excellent tactician, and the lack of reinforcements for the small garrison, Anderson must have felt like the noose was tightening.

The three engravings provide excellent detail for these positions. Though they were obviously familiar with Fort Moultrie, Anderson's officers carefully monitored the improvements and repairs made by the new occupants. The Morris Island engraving (*middle*) shows the new batteries built on the island, along with the lighthouse keepers' house and complex in the distant background.

In the Fort Johnson engraving (*bottom*), the growing fortifications and barracks are shown. On the left is Johnsonville, the summer village of James Island planters. Local cotton planters moved their families there annually from May to October to benefit from the ocean breeze and avoid the summer fevers.

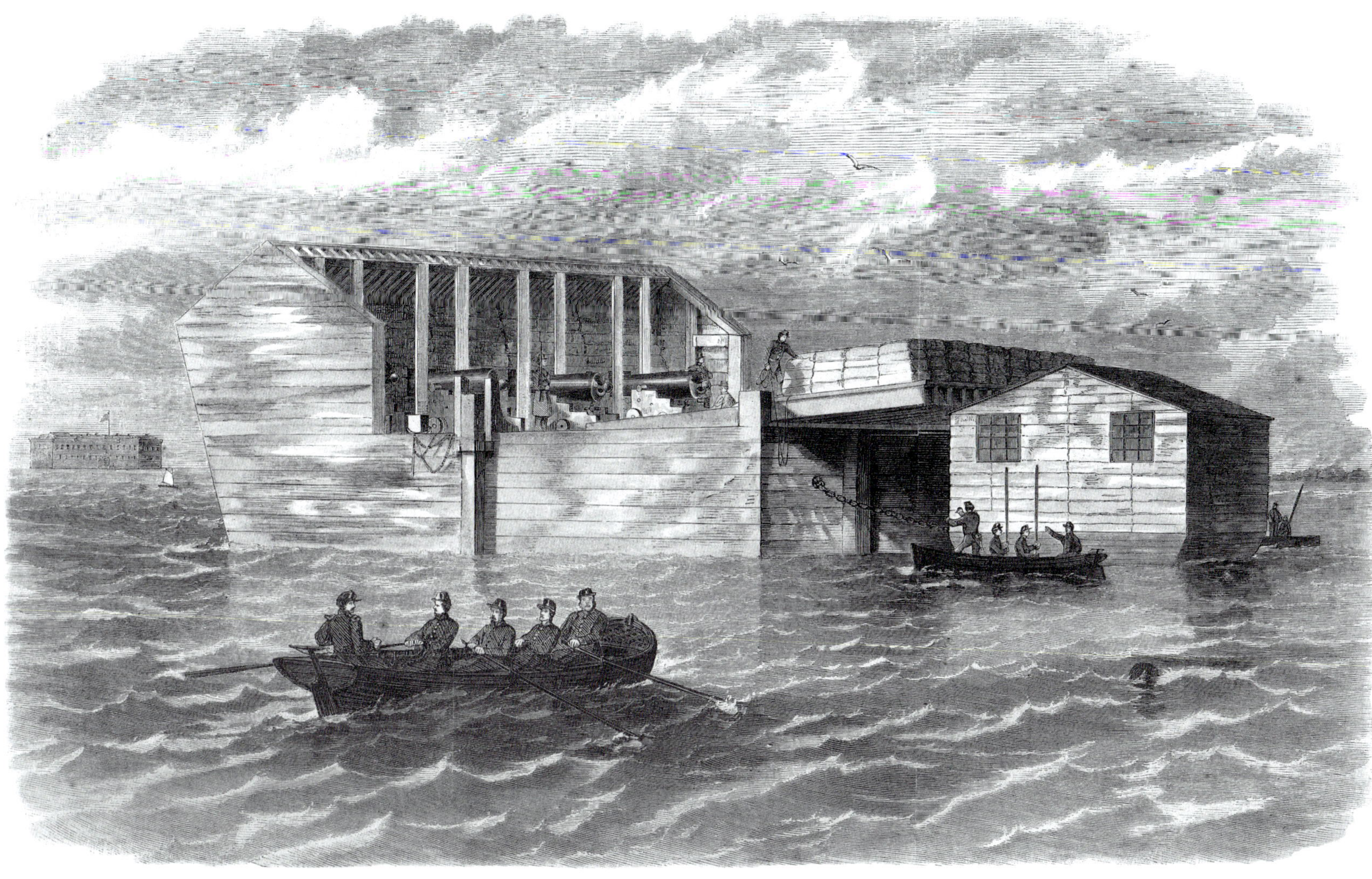

The Floating Battery

Artist: William Waud
Frank Leslie's Illustrated Newspaper

Capt. John Hamilton, CSN, late of the U.S. Navy, developed the idea of a floating barge to act as a movable battery in the eventual assault on Fort Sumter. Supporters called it a marvelous innovation in naval warfare, while critics called it a "slaughter pen." Permission was granted to build the 100-ft. x 25-ft. floating battery. It was constructed of heart pine timbers sawed 12-in. square and reinforced on the face with two layers of railway iron installed vertically and four layers of boiler iron, all bolted to the timbers.

The battery was designed for four heavy caliber guns and was installed with two 42-lb. guns and two 32-lb. guns. The magazine was built in the rear of the hold, surrounded by a six-ft. thick layer of sand bags. The immense weight of the sand bags also served an important function as a counter balance to the large guns.

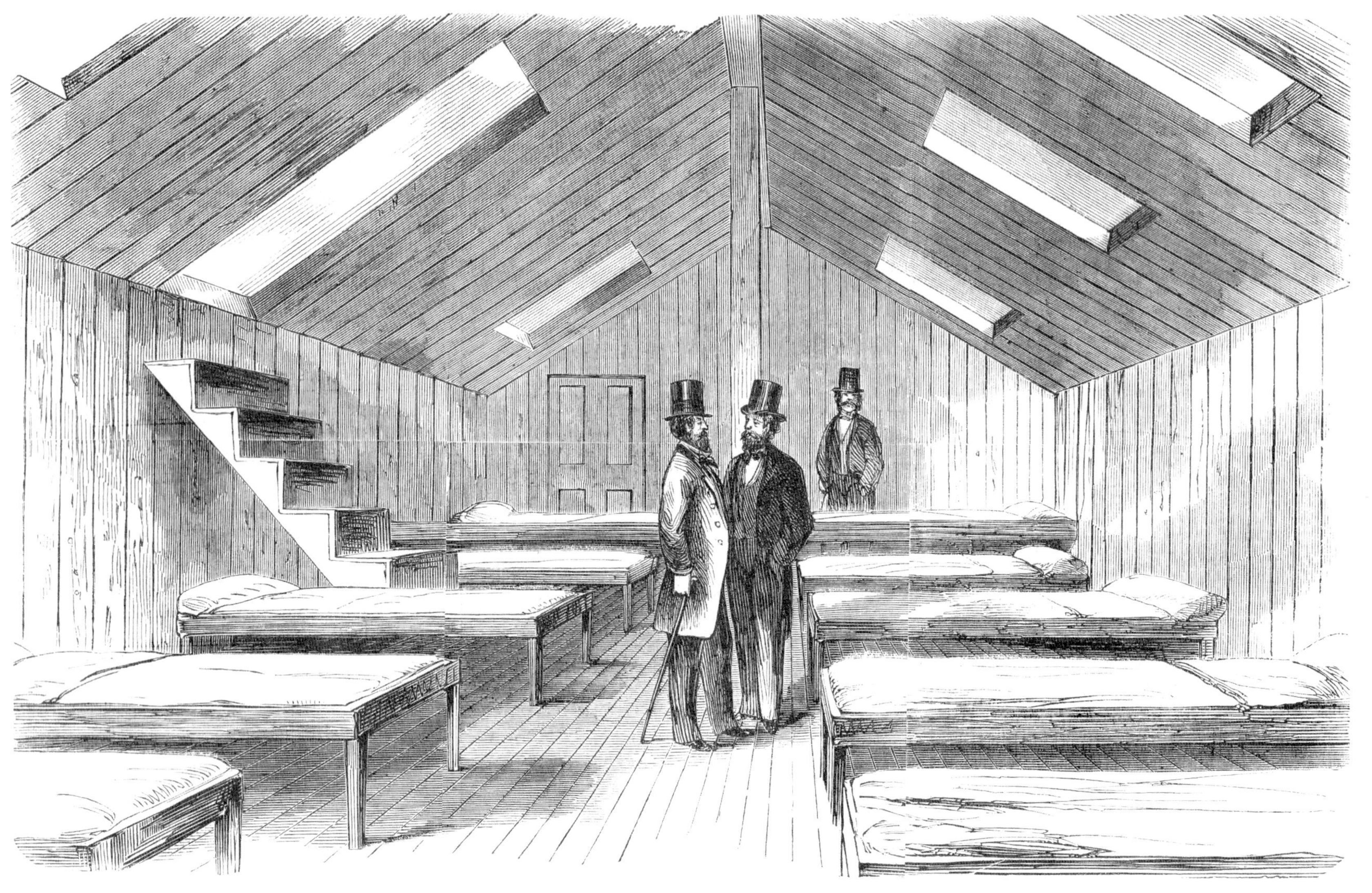

Interior of the Hospital

Artist: William Waud

Frank Leslie's Illustrated Newspaper

A floating hospital was also constructed and attached to the rear of the floating battery. The hospital, run by Dr. DeVega, was protected from horizontal fire by the iron-clad battery in front. There was a concern, though, that the hospital was still vulnerable to mortar fire dropping in on it.

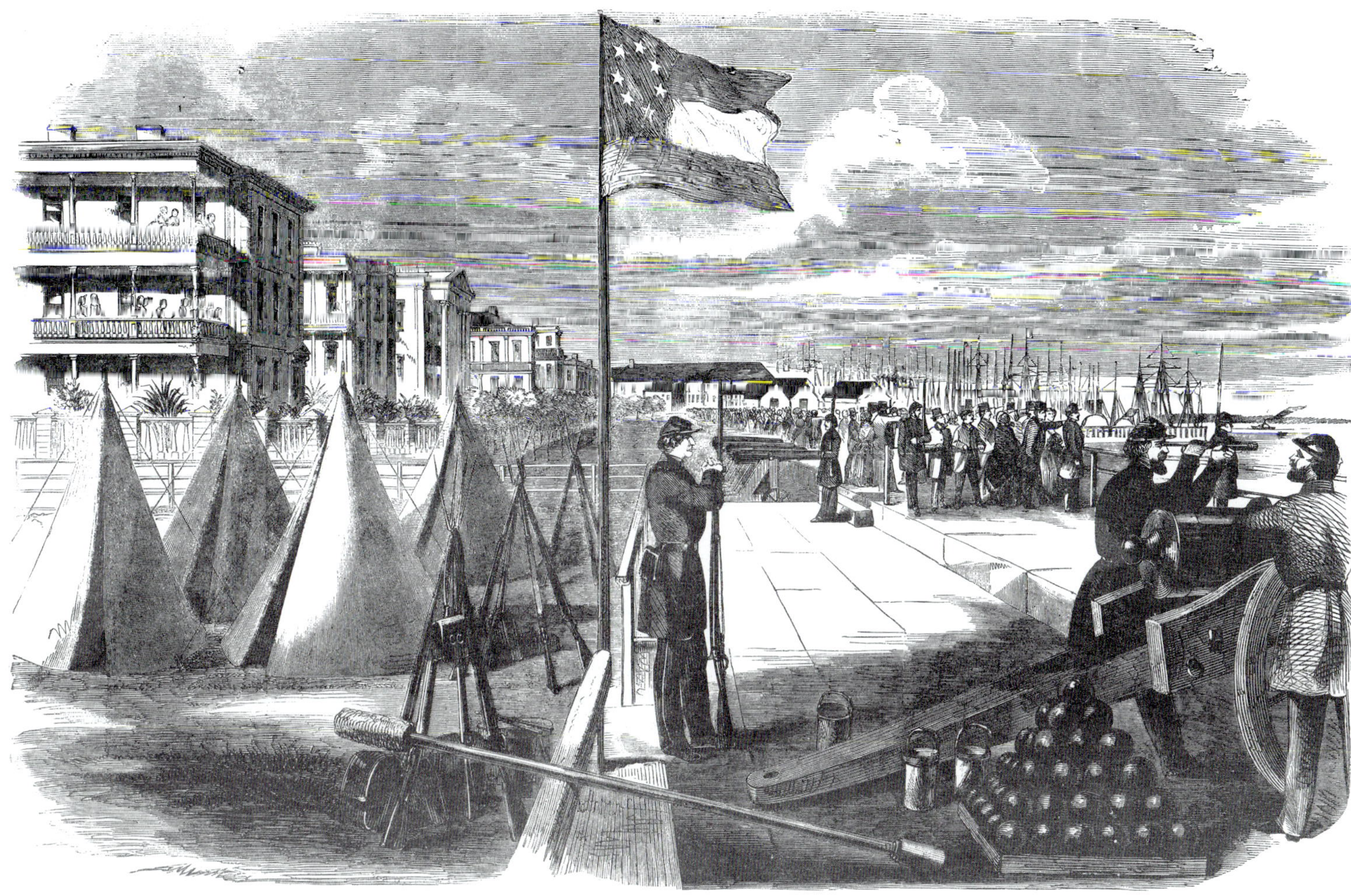

The Battery at Charleston

Artist: unknown
Harper's Weekly

By early April 1861, Gov. Francis W. Pickens and Gen. P. G. T. Beauregard were aware that a naval expedition was en route to Fort Sumter from New York. Word spread quickly throughout Charleston, creating both excitement and anxiety. Was this expedition simply sent as a relief mission? Everyone was aware that the federal garrison at Sumter would soon exhaust its food rations. Beauregard was concerned that a large amphibious assault would be staged on Morris Island as this naval expedition arrived. Citizens gathered at the Battery daily to watch for any developments in the impending confrontation.

On April 11, three of Beauregard's aides delivered a letter to Major Robert Anderson demanding the surrender and evacuation of Fort Sumter. In his proposed terms, Beauregard suggested, "All proper facilities will be afforded for the removal of yourself and your command, together with company arms and property, and all private property, to any post in the United States which you may select."

Anderson met with his officers to read Beauregard's demand. After the unanimous agreement of all the officers, Anderson refused to surrender the fortification saying, "It is a demand with which I regret that my sense of honor, and obligations to my government, prevent my compliance."

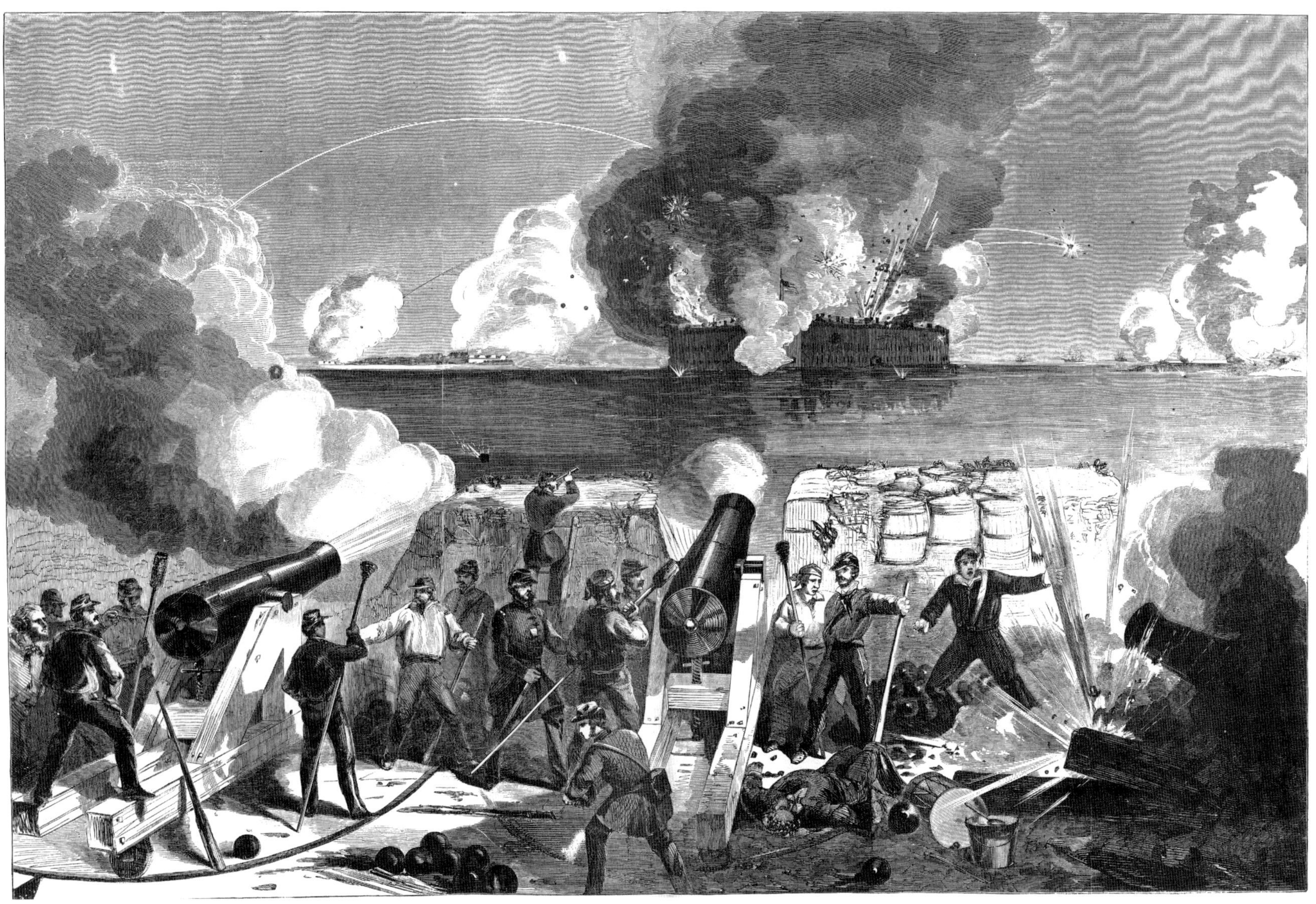

Bombardment of Fort Sumter

Artist: unknown
Harper's Weekly

On April 12, 1861, after last-minute efforts failed to obtain a clear agreement between Gen. P. G. T. Beauregard and Major Robert Anderson, Col. James Chesnut, at Fort Johnson, ordered Capt. George James to fire a 10-in. mortar over Sumter, signaling the beginning of the bombardment. By 5 a.m., Fort Sumter was receiving fire from all the Confederate batteries, which nearly surrounded the fort.

In his official report to Confederate Secretary of War Leroy P. Walker, Beauregard observes, "During the day the fire of my batteries was kept up most spiritedly, the guns and the mortars being worked in the coolest manner, preserving the prescribed intervals of firing. Towards the evening it became evident that our fire was very effective... "

Watching the Bombardment of Fort Sumter

Artist: unknown
Harper's Weekly

On hearing the first shots, citizens of Charleston rushed to their rooftops and along the wall of the Battery downtown to watch the drama unfold. As her husband was at Fort Johnson ordering the first shot of the bombardment, Mary Chesnut was asleep in Charleston. In her diary, she recorded her reaction to the start of the conflict: "At half past four the heavy booming of cannon. I sprung out of bed, and on my knees prostrate, I prayed as I never prayed before."

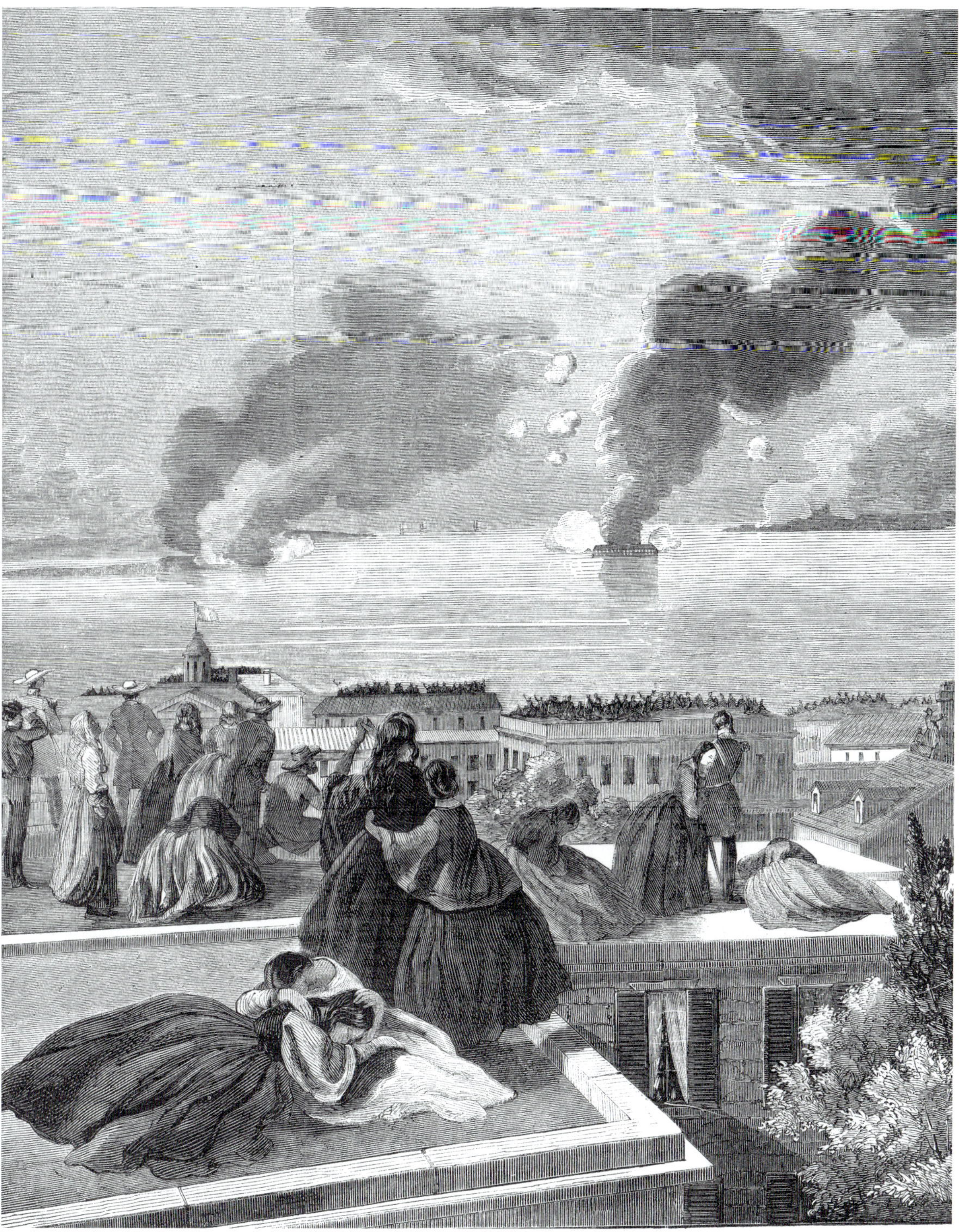

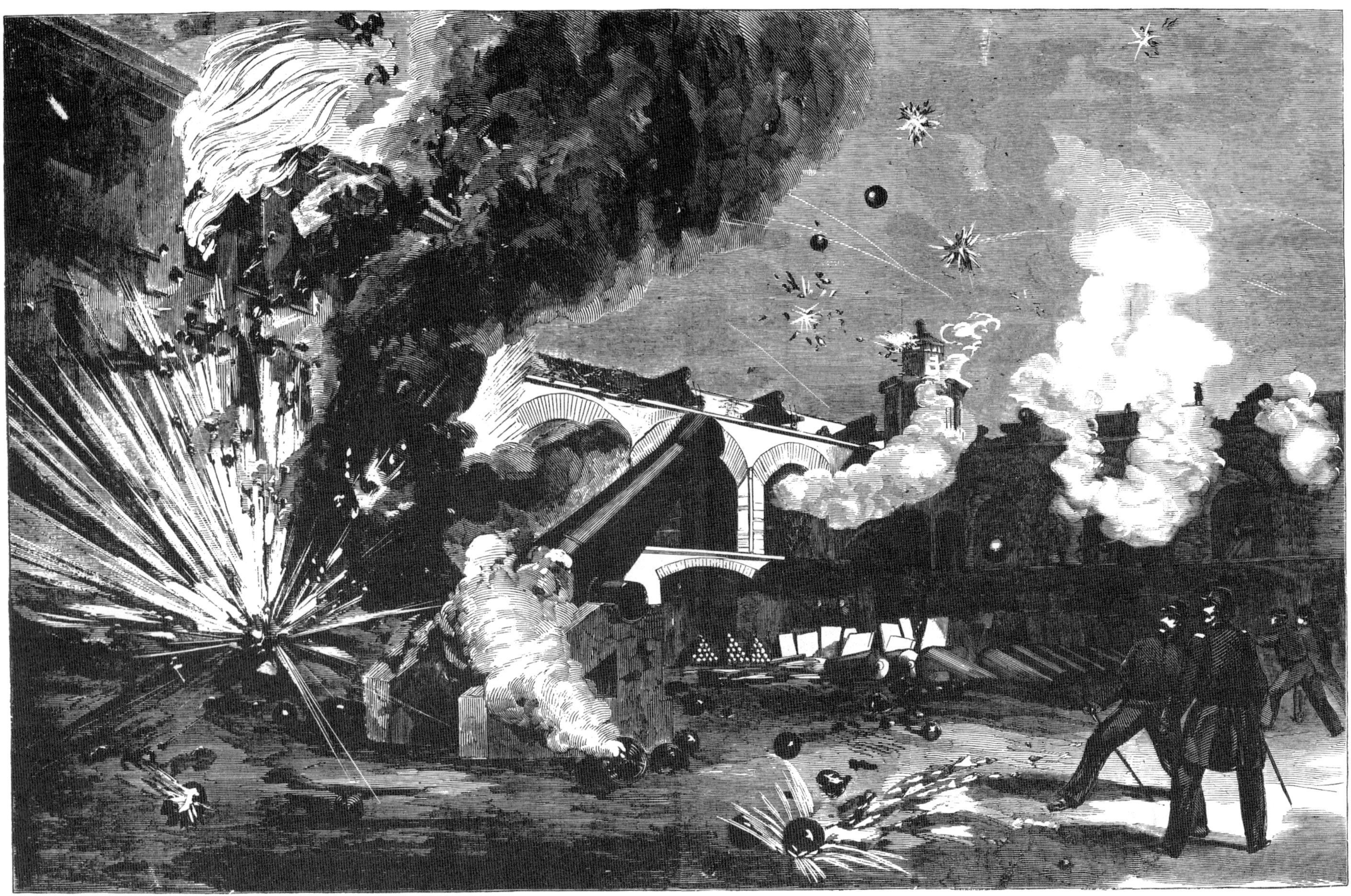

The Interior of Fort Sumter

Artist: unknown
Harper's Weekly

Even in the rain, spectators remained at every vantage throughout Charleston to watch the battle. The firing on Fort Sumter continued through the night. As morning arrived, the firing on Major Robert Anderson's small garrison picked up pace. The decision was made to fire "hot shot" onto Fort Sumter from Fort Moultrie. These pre-heated balls would test the barracks at Sumter, which were reputed to be fireproof. They failed the test. The buildings within the fort ignited, creating suffocating conditions for the over-matched federal garrison.

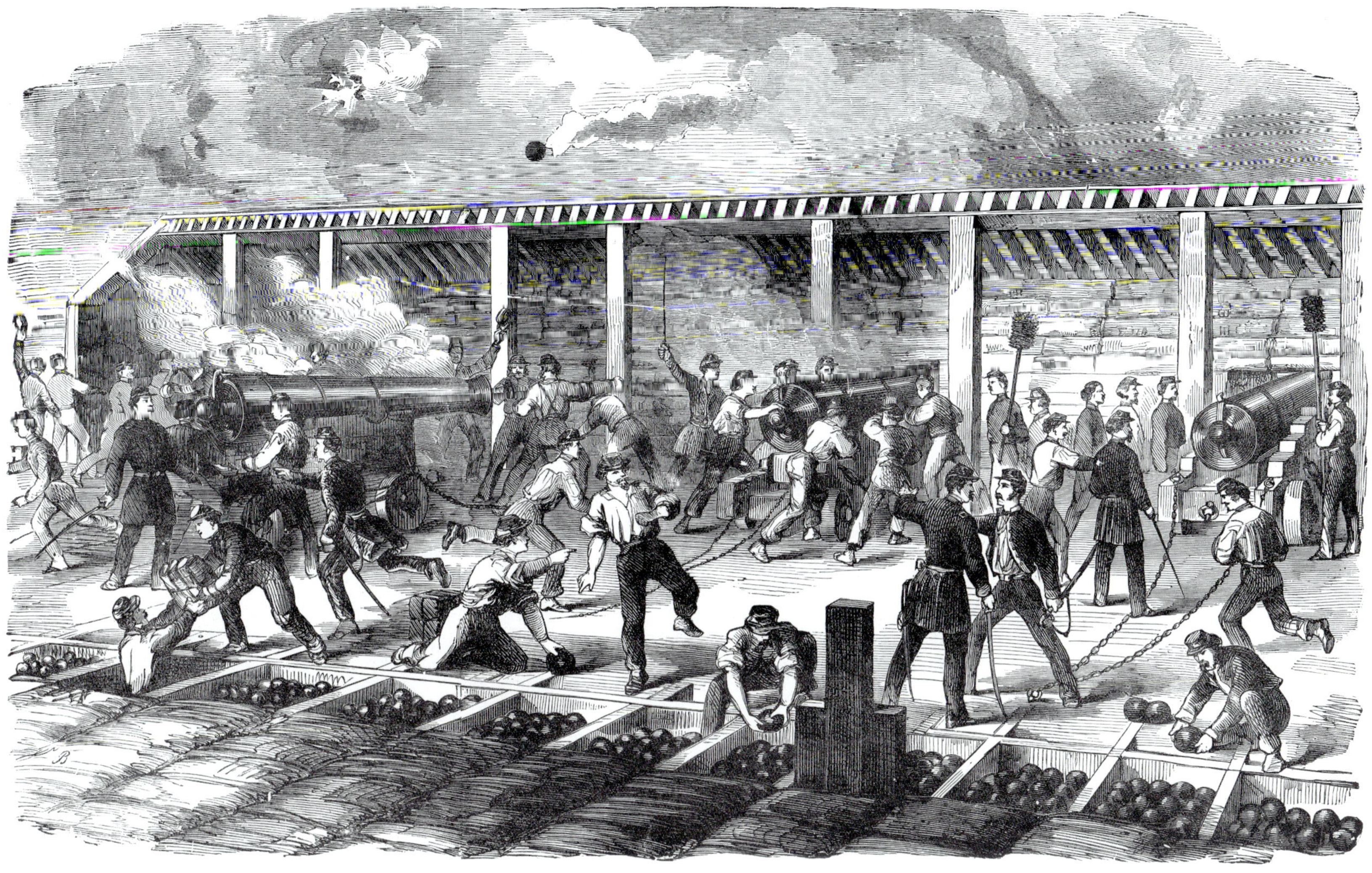

The Floating Battery during the Bombardment

Drawn by Confederate officer on board
Frank Leslie's Illustrated Newspaper

Several officers expressed concern over the seaworthiness of the floating battery as the bombardment neared. The decision was made to beach the barge at Cove Inlet between Sullivan's Island and Mt. Pleasant, making the untested innovation a fixed battery for the upcoming engagement.

The size of the battery and number of guns required a unit of 60 men to operate efficiently. In the bombardment against Fort Sumter, the floating battery proved itself, silencing its many doubters and critics. Not only did the battery fire effectively onto Sumter, the range and positions of the guns made it impossible for Major Robert Anderson to man and fire the barbette guns on the top wall of the fort. Men firing these guns would be easily exposed and vulnerable to fire from the battery. This had a great strategic impact on Anderson because his most powerful guns were on the barbette.

During the engagement against Fort Sumter, the battery received a number of direct hits against the front wall but sustained little damage.

Removing Powder from the Magazine

Artist: unknown
Harper's Weekly

The barracks were the first structures within Fort Sumter to ignite, followed by the hospital. Major Robert Anderson's men could not control the fire, which soon approached the fort's powder magazine. While ample powder was a precious commodity for the fort under fire, the issue of safety was suddenly paramount. With more than 300 barrels of powder, if fire invaded the magazine, the resulting calamity could threaten the fort and its occupants well beyond any threat imposed by the Confederate batteries.

Men were dispatched to remove the powder barrels with great haste. After only one-third of the powder was removed, the heat from the approaching fire became too intense. The magazine was closed, the entrance covered with dirt. A small trench filled with water was quickly installed in front. Soon even the powder that had been removed was in danger of exploding. With no alternative, Anderson ordered that five barrels of powder be retained and the rest thrown over the walls of the fort to the waters of the harbor.

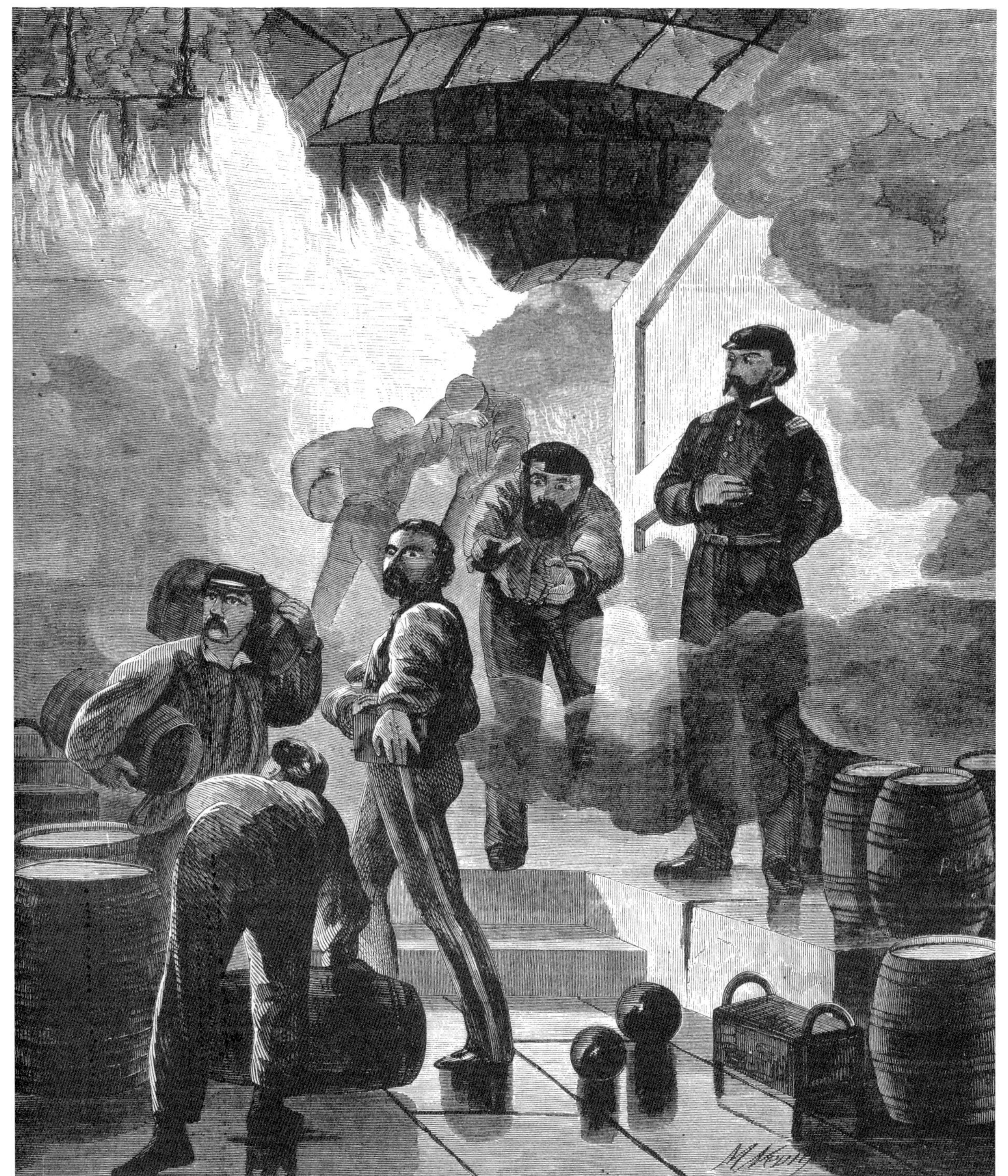

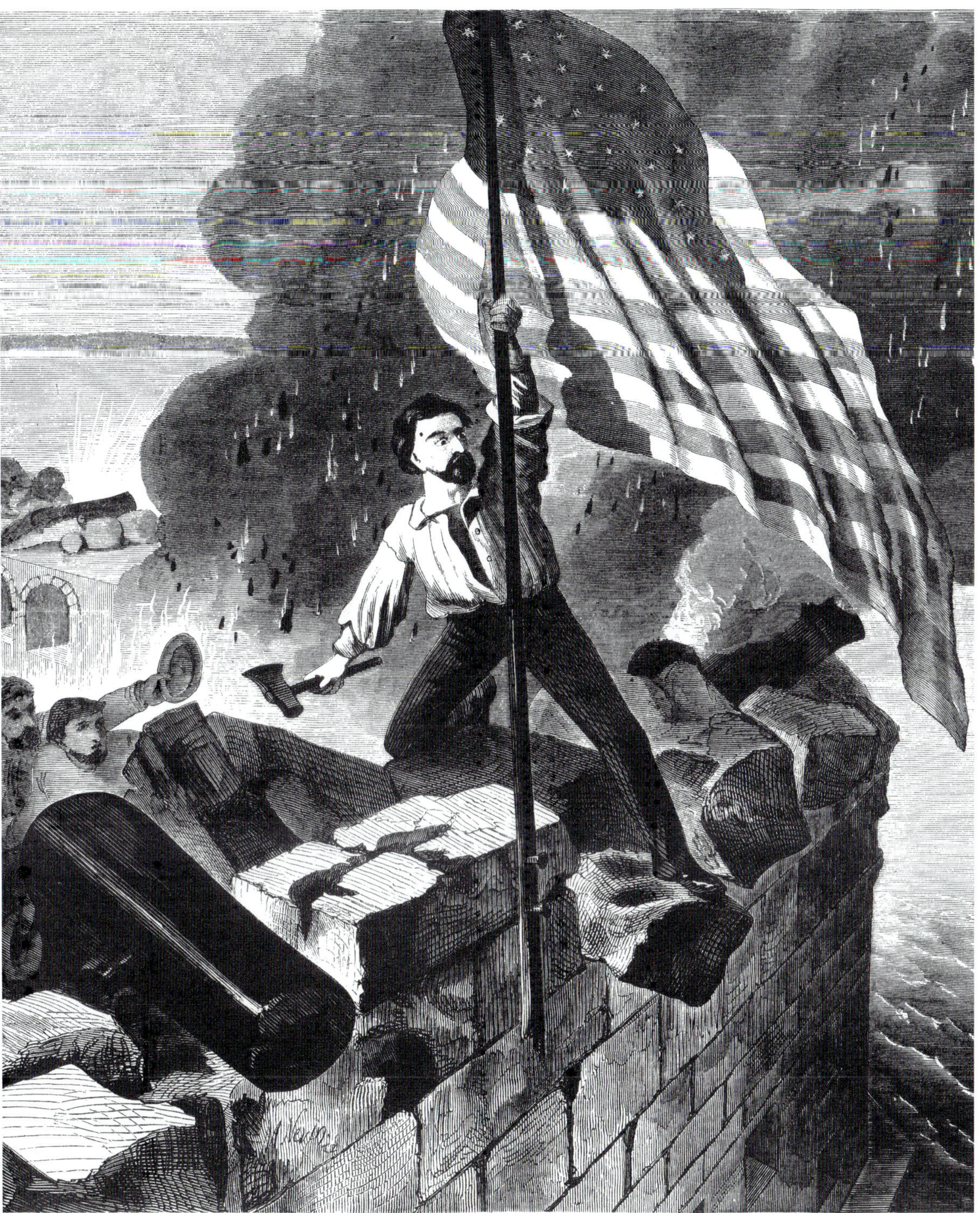

Police-Sergeant Hart Nailing the Flag

Artist: unknown
Harper's Weekly

Police Sgt. Peter Hart's presence at Fort Sumter was quite unintended. In December, when Major Robert Anderson seized Fort Sumter, his wife, an invalid, was in New York. Upon hearing the news of the developing situation in South Carolina, she urgently wanted to see her husband. Despite doctor's orders to the contrary, she made plans to travel from New York to Charleston. Knowing she'd need help to make the journey, she sought out Hart, a New York police-sergeant, and a man who had faithfully served her husband in Mexico.

When Mrs. Anderson and Hart arrived in Charleston, Gov. Francis W. Pickens allowed her passage to Fort Sumter to visit her husband. Pickens permited Hart to accompany Mrs. Anderson on the pledge he would not take up arms. After a several-hour visit, Mrs. Anderson left Fort Sumter to return to her children in New York. Honoring his pledge, Hart never took up arms, but stayed behind to support his former commander.

When the firing on Fort Sumter commenced, Hart assisted the garrison by putting out fires within the fort. At one point in the bombardment, the garrison flag was shot down. The Confederate authorities thought perhaps the flag had been lowered as an act of surrender. Seeing the flag down, amid intense bombardment, Hart nailed the flag to a temporary flagstaff and nailed this staff to the highest point of the remaining fortification.

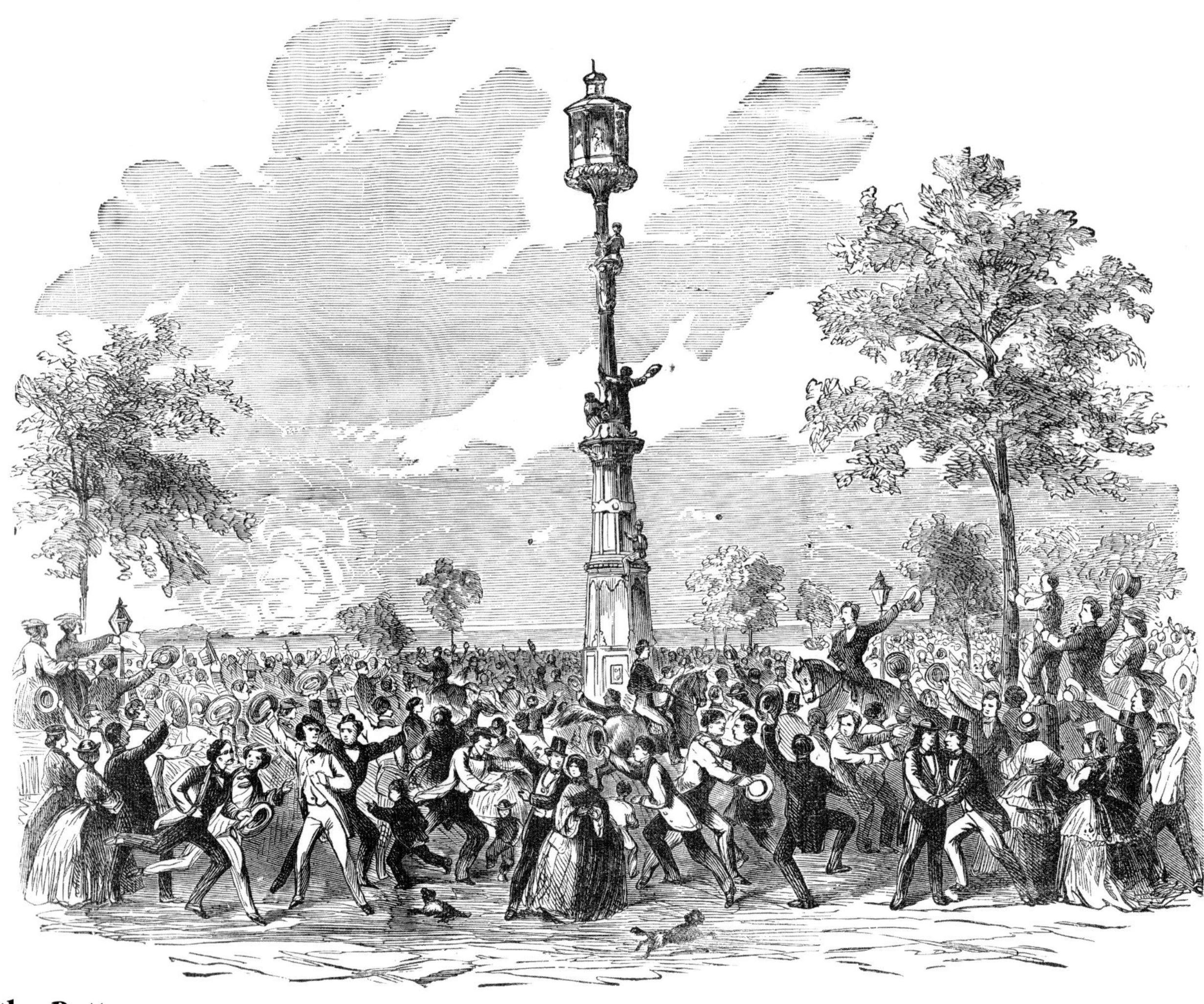

Demonstrations on the Battery

Artist: William Benson
Frank Leslie's Illustrated Newspaper

At 1:30 p.m. on Saturday, April 13, 1861, with the fort in flames, out of powder, having endured the brunt of more than 3,300 shells and hot shot, Major Robert Anderson ordered the garrison flag lowered and a bed sheet raised over the fort. Gen. P. G. T. Beauregard's aides were dispatched to Fort Sumter where Anderson agreed to a truce and evacuated the fort on the original terms offered by Beauregard before the bombardment. Incredibly, not a single man in Fort Sumter was killed during the bombardment.

Celebrations broke out across the harbor and throughout the city. Soon the harbor filled with boats loaded with civilians wanting to get a close view of the embattled fortification.

The formal evacuation of the fort took place on April 14. At 2 p.m., the garrison flag was retired and the federal troops began firing a 50-gun salute, signaling their exit. On the 17th shot, there was a premature explosion of the gun, killing Pvt. Daniel Hough, the only fatality of the siege. The federal troops boarded a ship that took them to a federal ship anchored outside the shipping channel to the harbor.

Anderson and his men arrived in New York by boat on April 18. Given the evacuation, they were concerned how New York might receive them as they assembled on the deck of the *Baltic* in full uniform. As the ship entered New York harbor, the many ships and thousands of people in the harbor rang bells and cheered in tribute to Anderson and his men.

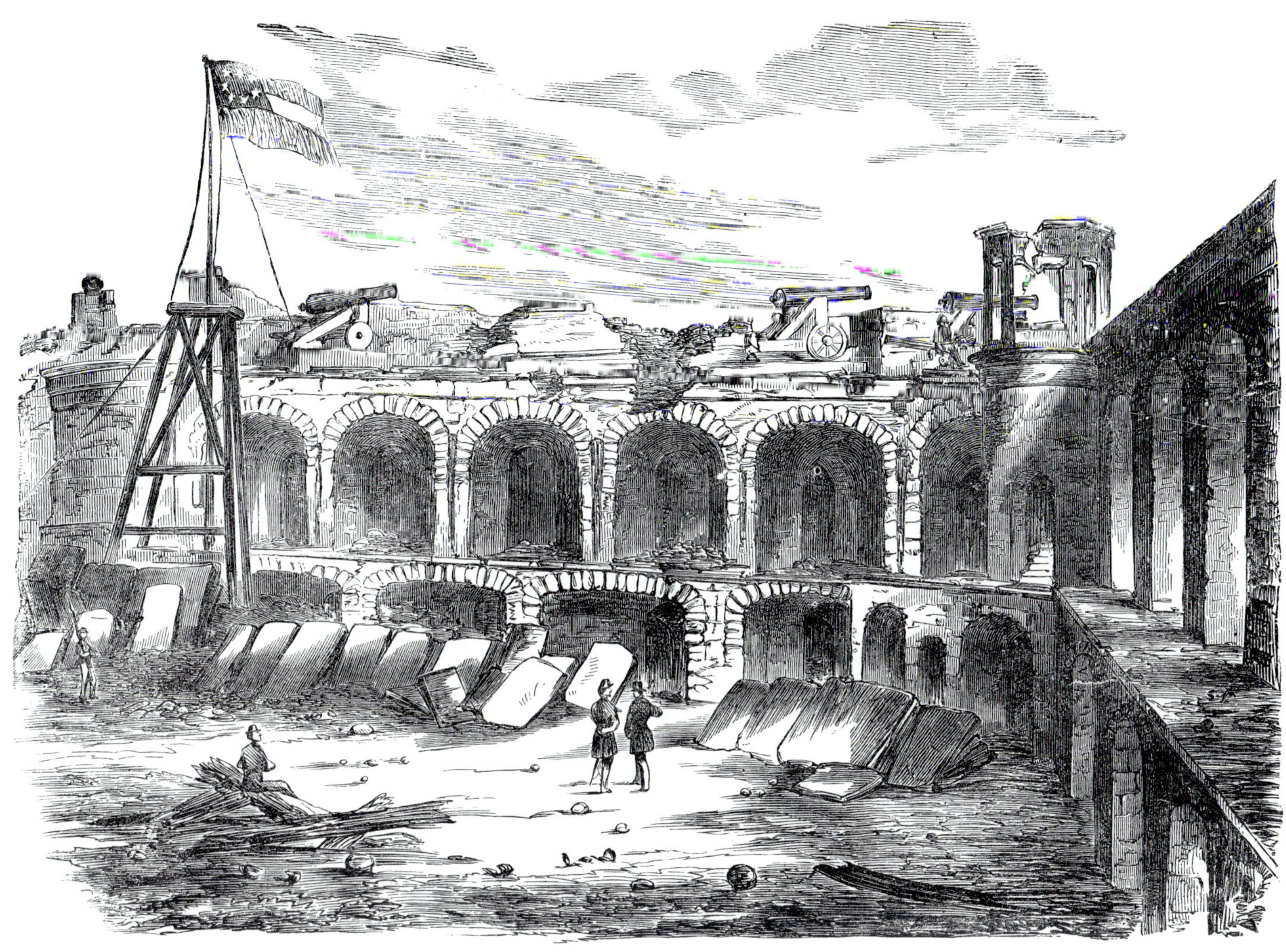

Fort Sumter after the Bombardment

Artist: William Waud
Frank Leslie's Illustrated Newspaper

When Confederates gained entry to Fort Sumter, they saw firsthand the devastation left as a result of the heavy bombardment. On April 15, the *Mercury* offered this view:

> *Every point and every object in the interior of the fort, to which the eye was turned, except the outer walls and easements, which are still strong, bore the impress of ruin... The walls of the internal structure – roofless, bare, bleak and perforated by shot and shell – hung in fragments, and seemed in instant readiness to totter down. Near the centre of the parade ground was the hurried grave of the one who had fallen from the recent casualty... And so it was that the garrison, compelled to yield the fortress, had at least the satisfaction of leaving it in a condition calculated to inspire the least possible pleasure to its captors.*

Both the Confederate and Palmetto Flags were raised over Fort Sumter. The Palmetto Guard, commanded by Lt. Col. Roswell Sabine Ripley was given the honor of occupying the fallen fort, the prize of Charleston. The fall of Fort Sumter also provided Pres. Abraham Lincoln with what he needed and desired – public support in the North to quell the rebellion of the Southern states.

The Enemy Returns

After Fort Sumter, the Confederate command and Charleston recognized that it was only a matter of time before the Union command sent an expedition to the South. For many months in 1861, the lookouts in Charleston harbor were vigilant, watching for any signs of threat.

The threat did come, but not to Charleston. On Nov. 7, 1861, the Union Navy launched an attack against Fort Beauregard and Fort Walker at Port Royal, 50 miles south of Charleston. For the Union, the decision was a good one. The one-day battle of Port Royal was the first Union victory of the new war. More importantly, Port Royal was an excellent strategic location to base operations for the Union Army and Navy in the South. By December, the blockade of both Charleston and Savannah was in place.

On March 15, 1862, federal authorities created the Department of the South based at Port Royal. Major Gen. David Hunter was assigned to command this theater of operations, covering South Carolina, Georgia and Florida.

Command of Confederate forces in Charleston was given to Major Gen. John C. Pemberton, replacing Robert E. Lee, who went to Virginia to accept command of the Army of Northern Virginia. Pemberton's tenure as commander was characterized by constant disagreements with his subordinates and Gov. Francis W. Pickens. Pemberton believed that he should abandon and destroy the harbor fortifications, defending Charleston from the city itself. Ultimately, Lee disagreed and required the defense of the harbor positions.

By mid-May 1862, Union boats were spotted at the mouth of the Stono River. Through the rest of the month, Union gunboats probed the river, testing Confederate defenses. On June 2, Union troops landed on James Island and quickly encountered the Confederates. A skirmish commenced. Over the next several days, more Union troops from transports and from across John's Island, crossed to James Island setting up camp on the southwestern portion of the island. On June 10, a second skirmish occurred, resulting in a Confederate victory, followed by a third skirmish on the 13th.

Lee, in his dispatches from Richmond, made clear to Pemberton the importance of defending and holding Charleston and Savannah. "If the harbors are taken then the cities are to be fought street by street, house by house," writes Lee.

Hunter instructed his subordinate Gen. Henry W. Benham to hold his forces in position on James Island and await further reinforcements. Benham, feeling threatened by a Confederate position at the Tower Battery in the village of Secessionville, defied Hunter's order. On June 16, he launched a pre-dawn attack. The Union forces, which totaled 6,600 men organized in two divisions, attacked a Confederate battery of 500 men.

Lt. Iredell Jones, of the 1st S.C. Infantry, recalls the action:

> *The battery was contested on the ramparts in a hand to hand fight, and a log was rolled from the top to sweep the enemy from the sides of the breastwork. All credit is due to the Charleston battalion and Lamar's two companies of artillery... But while we give all credit to our own troops, let us never again disparage our enemy and call them cowards, for nothing was ever more glorious than their three charges in the face of a raking fire of grape and canister, and then at last, as if to do or die, they broke into two columns and rushed against our right and left flanks, which movement would have gained the day, had not our reinforcements arrived.*

The result was an astonishing defeat for the Union Army with casualties four times higher than those of the Confederates. Hunter was outraged that Benham disobeyed his orders and embarrassed that his army had been defeated. Hunter filed charges against Benham, had him arrested and sent North on a steamship with the full report of the battle. Benham was court-martialed. Later, though, he was given a presidential reprieve and reassigned to the U.S. Corps of Engineers.

By July 8, the Union Army vacated James Island and retired to Port Royal. The threat against Charleston was, at least temporarily, neutralized. In a letter to Pemberton, Lee made clear his views about the strategic importance of Charleston: "The loss of Charleston would cut us off almost entirely from communication with the rest of the world, and close the only channel through which we can expect to get supplies from abroad, now almost our only dependence."

If Charleston had fallen in 1862, the war would not have persisted until 1865.

Sinking the Stone Fleet

Artist: unknown
Harper's Weekly

The federal government needed to find an effective method to blockade key Southern ports without maintaining a large fleet in every location. Much like the Confederacy had done earlier in the year, the Union Army blocked the harbors of Charleston and Savannah using sunken schooners. The presence of the sunken ships would prevent deep-draft ships from safely negotiating their way through the harbor.

Twenty-five schooners left New Bedford, Mass., on Nov. 20, 1861, bound for Charleston and Savannah. Loaded with granite, the schooners arrived in Charleston harbor on Dec. 19. The Union Navy carefully placed 15 of the schooners in position and pulled plugs that had been previously installed in each ship. The schooners quickly made their way to the bottom of the shipping channel, leaving their upper rigging exposed. The remaining 10 schooners set sail for Savannah to repeat the process.

The swift current in Charleston harbor dismantled the sunken schooners and swept the debris out to sea. The Union Navy sank 13 additional schooners in January 1862.

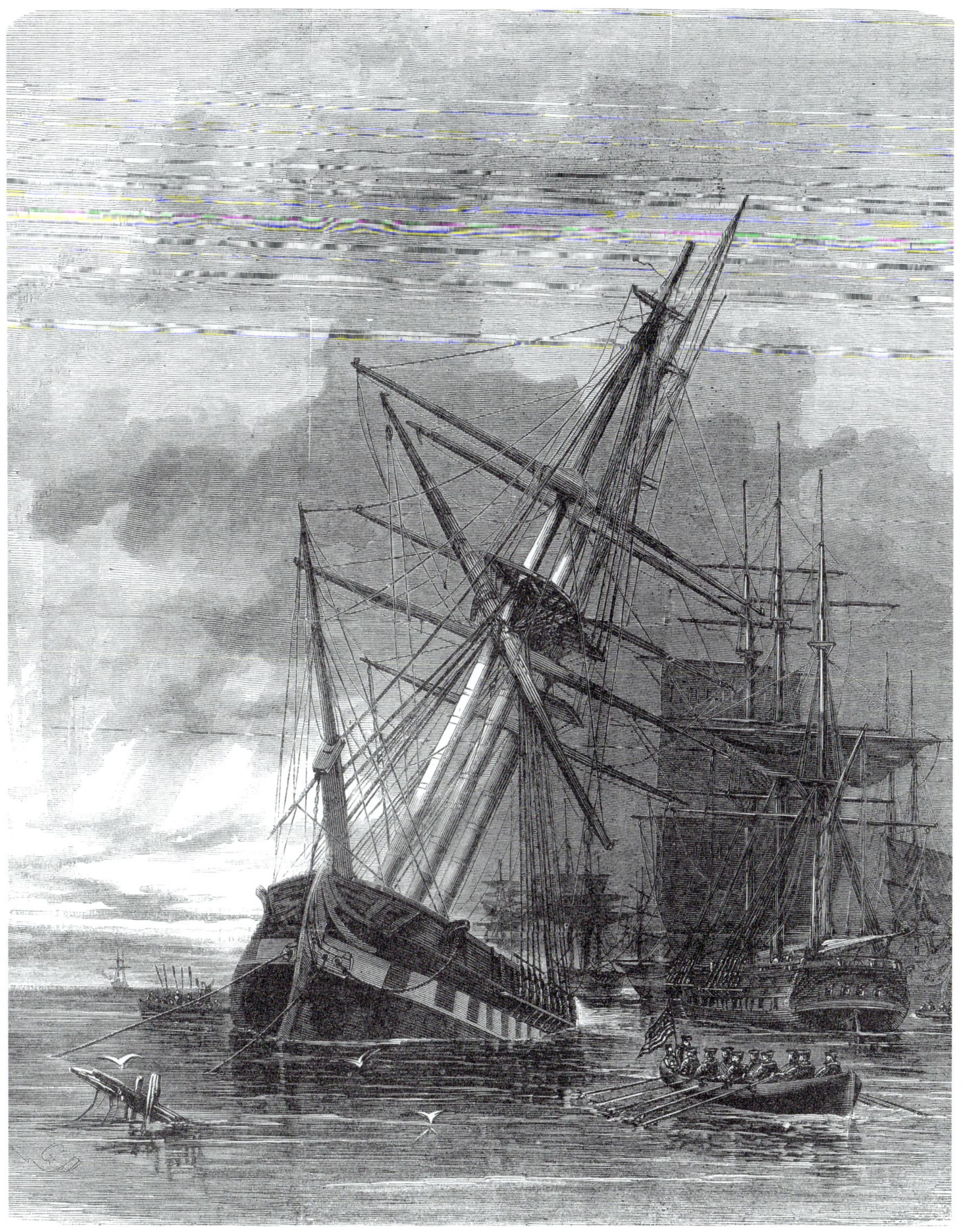

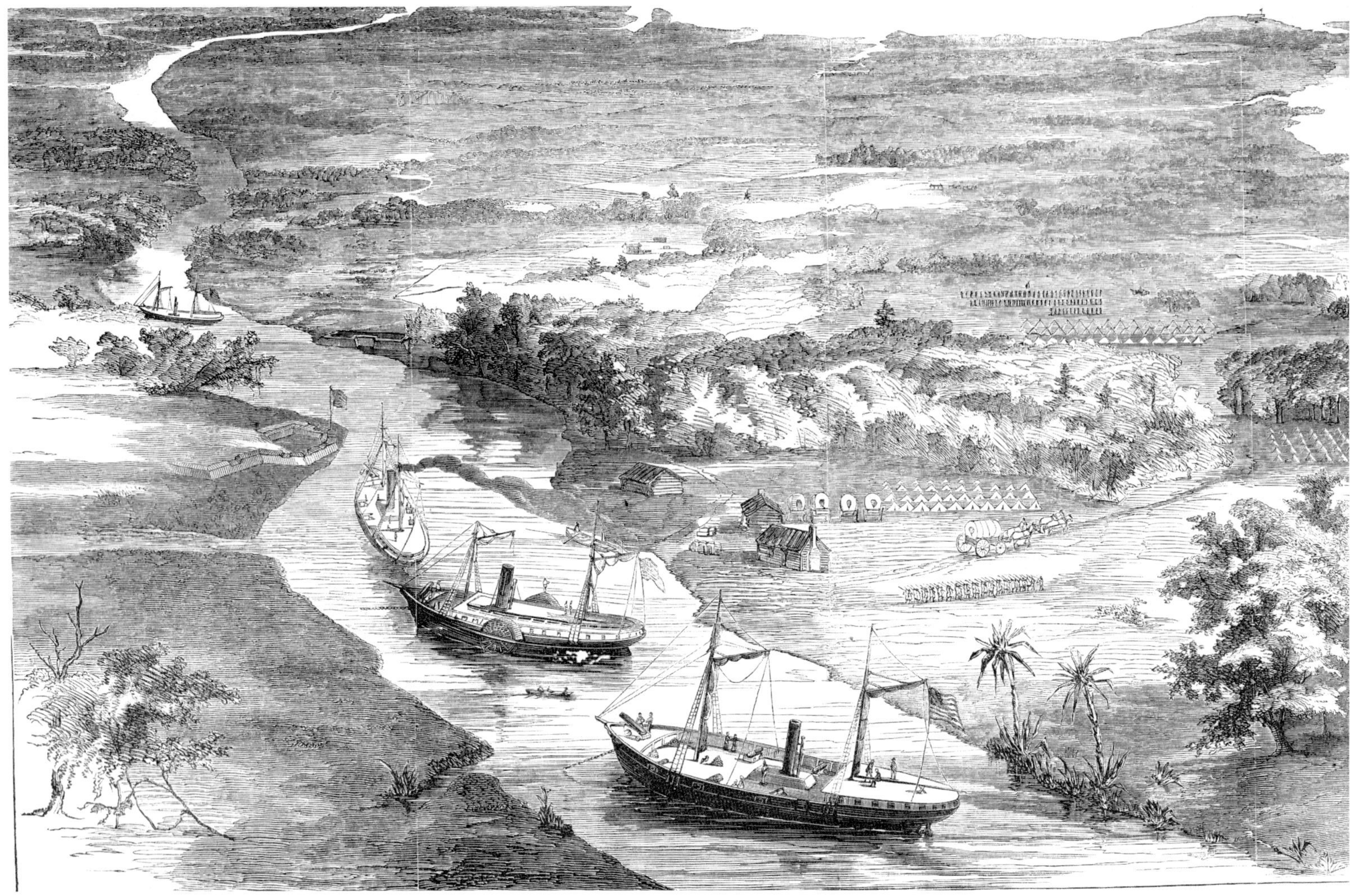

Union Gunboats in the Stono

Drawing by a Union Officer
Harper's Weekly

Major-Gen. David Hunter, planning his attack to take Charleston, followed the lead of the British army in its successful siege of Charleston in 1780. He planned to approach James Island from the west by the Stono River, then quickly move across the island and take Fort Johnson. With control of James Island in hand, multiple batteries could be established on the island, making it easy to direct fire into the city and provoke a quick fall of Charleston.

The Confederates assumed the Union Army would adopt England's Revolutionary War strategy. Pemberton and the Confederate command were busy setting defensive positions on James Island in the spring of 1862. On May 19, Gen. Gist, Confederate commander for James Island, issued orders for the civilian evacuation of the island. James Island was home to 21 cotton plantations and two churches. Gist's orders required the planters, with their families and slaves, to vacate the island immediately, leaving only one male and one female slave to watch over each plantation in their absence.

The same day that Gist issued his evacuation order, a squadron of federal gunboats appeared at the Stono River. On June 2, Union troops landed at Grimball Plantation at the southwest corner of James Island on the Stono River. The Union troops quickly established positions at Grimball Plantation and further south on Sol Legare Island.

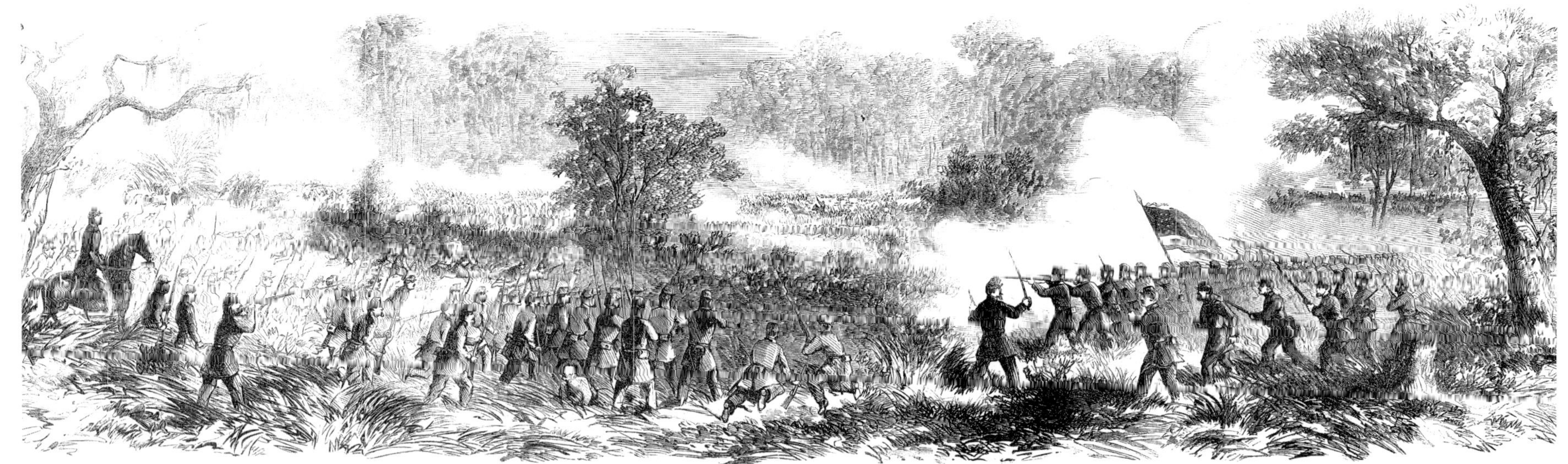

Skirmish on James Island

Drawn by a Union officer
Frank Leslie's Illustrated Newspaper

The first encounter between the armies occurred on June 3, 1862, at Sol Legare Island between the 24th S.C. Infantry and companies of the 28th Massachusetts, 100th Pennsylvania and the 79th New York. The skirmish resulted in the capture of a number of Union troops and an officer.

By June 8, Confederate Gen. J. C. Pemberton estimated Union forces on James Island had grown to 10,000 troops with three light batteries and a similar size force on John's Island. Though Pemberton grossly over-exaggerated the Union force, he was correct in his belief that a Union attempt to take James Island was under way.

On June 10, Pemberton ordered the Confederate lines to establish a battery near Grimball Plantation, putting them in a position to fire on the Union ships in the Stono River and the Union stations at Grimball and Sol Legare Island. This movement led to the second skirmish between Union and Confederate forces. The heavy fire of the Union gunboats and the Union division commanded by Brig.-Gen. Horatio G. Wright prevented the Confederates' advance. By the end of the skirmish, Union forces suffered 16 casualties; Confederates suffered 47.

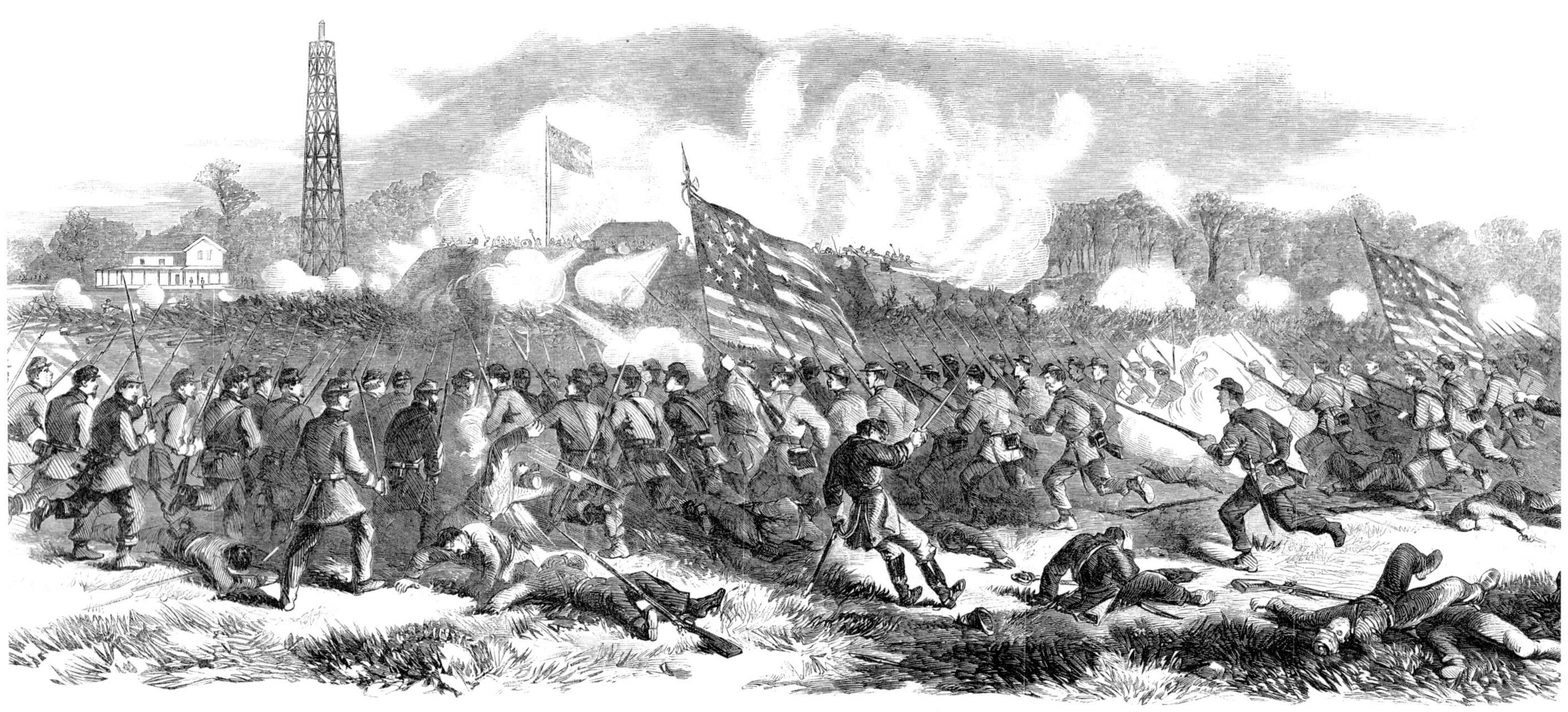

Battle of Secessionville

Drawn by a Union officer
Frank Leslie's Illustrated Newspaper

In mid-June, the Union army busily moved supplies and troops onto James Island while Confederate troops worked frantically to complete the breastworks at Secessionville. Exhausted, Confederate Col. T. G. Lamar allowed his troops to sleep in their positions. At 3 a.m. on June 16, 1862, Lamar awoke to find a large formation of Union troops advancing on his position. With the enemy only 100 yards away, a 24-lb. gun was fired at 4:30 a.m. to awaken the sleeping Confederates. Though in dispute, reports indicate that Lamar himself pulled the lanyard that fired the wake-up shot.

Intense firepower from the Tower Battery hit the advancing federal column, the 8th Michigan Infantry. Joined by the 7th Connecticut and the 28th Massachusetts, Union troops continued their advance. Crack troops from the 79th New York Highlanders were held in reserve.

Confederates were able to reinforce Lamar by way of a bridge connected to Clark Plantation across an expanse of marsh. This proved to be key to the battle. The Union gunboats in Lighthouse Inlet tried to weaken the Confederate position, but as reports would later reveal, the federal fire hit Union troops as often as it did the Confederate position.

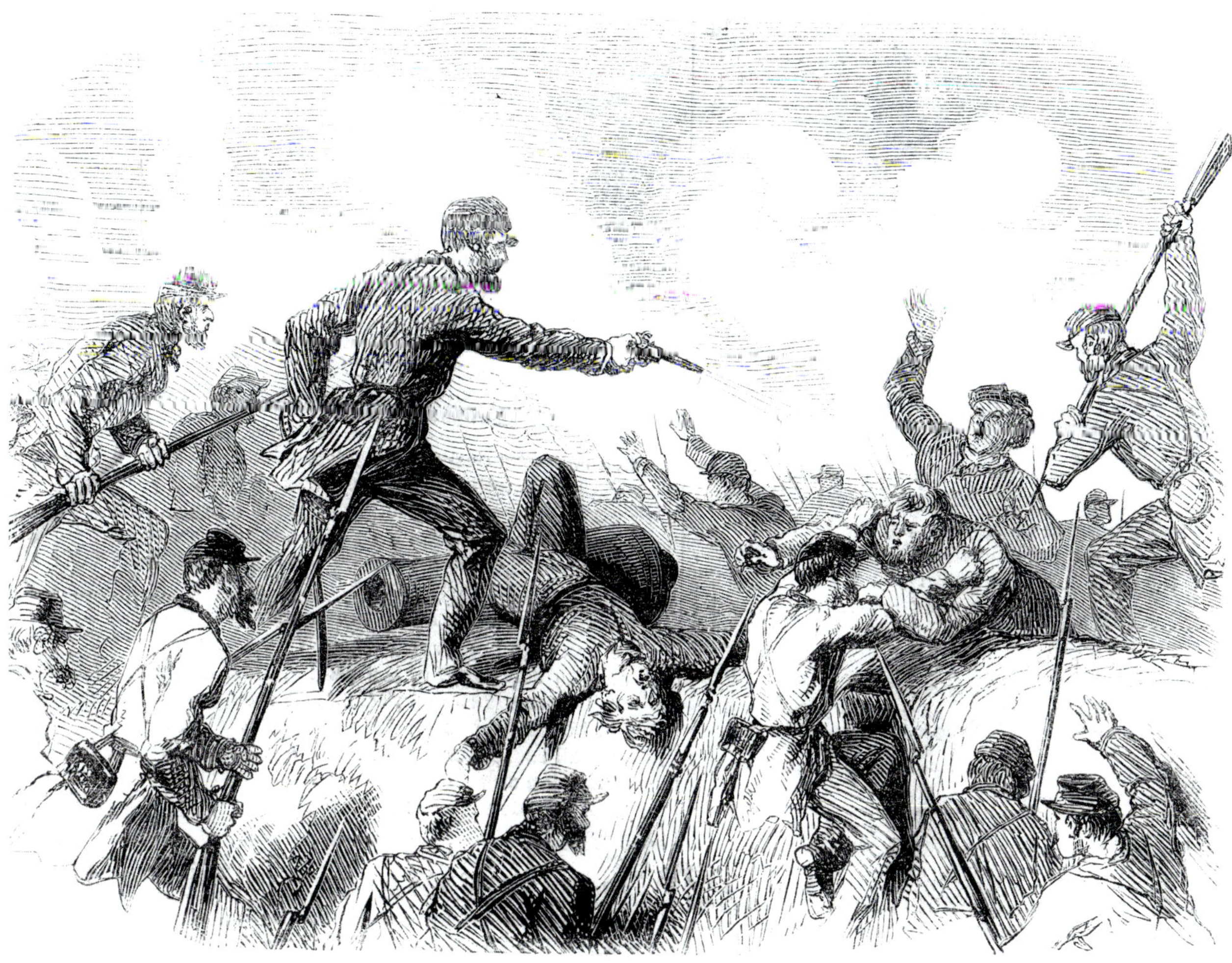

Fighting at the Tower Battery

Drawn by a Union officer
Frank Leslie's Illustrated Newspaper

During the fierce battle, Confederate Col. T. G. Lamar suffered a serious neck wound that forced him to turn over command to Lt. Col. P. C. Gaillard, though he never left the Tower Battery. Most of the fighting took place immediately in front of and even on top of the battery.

The illustration depicts Union Lt.-Col. David Morrison leading the advance of the 79th Highlanders on the parapet of the Tower Battery. Much of the gruelling fight was hand-to-hand. As Morrison reached the top of the battery urging his men to move forward, he was shot in the head by a minie ball. With blood almost blinding him, he still pushed the attack.

Union Col. Daniel Leasure of the 100th Pennsylvania Infantry later recalls:

> *I advanced with the left flank of the Highlanders, cheering them to the charge, till when within about one hundred yards of the works three immense guns bellowed out a perfect cloud of grape, canister, old chains, empty porter bottles, nails and even brickets, and just cut the regiment in two... Panic and disaster were imminent every minute...*

The 8th Michigan had causalities totaling a third of its unit. The 79th Highlanders also suffered great losses.

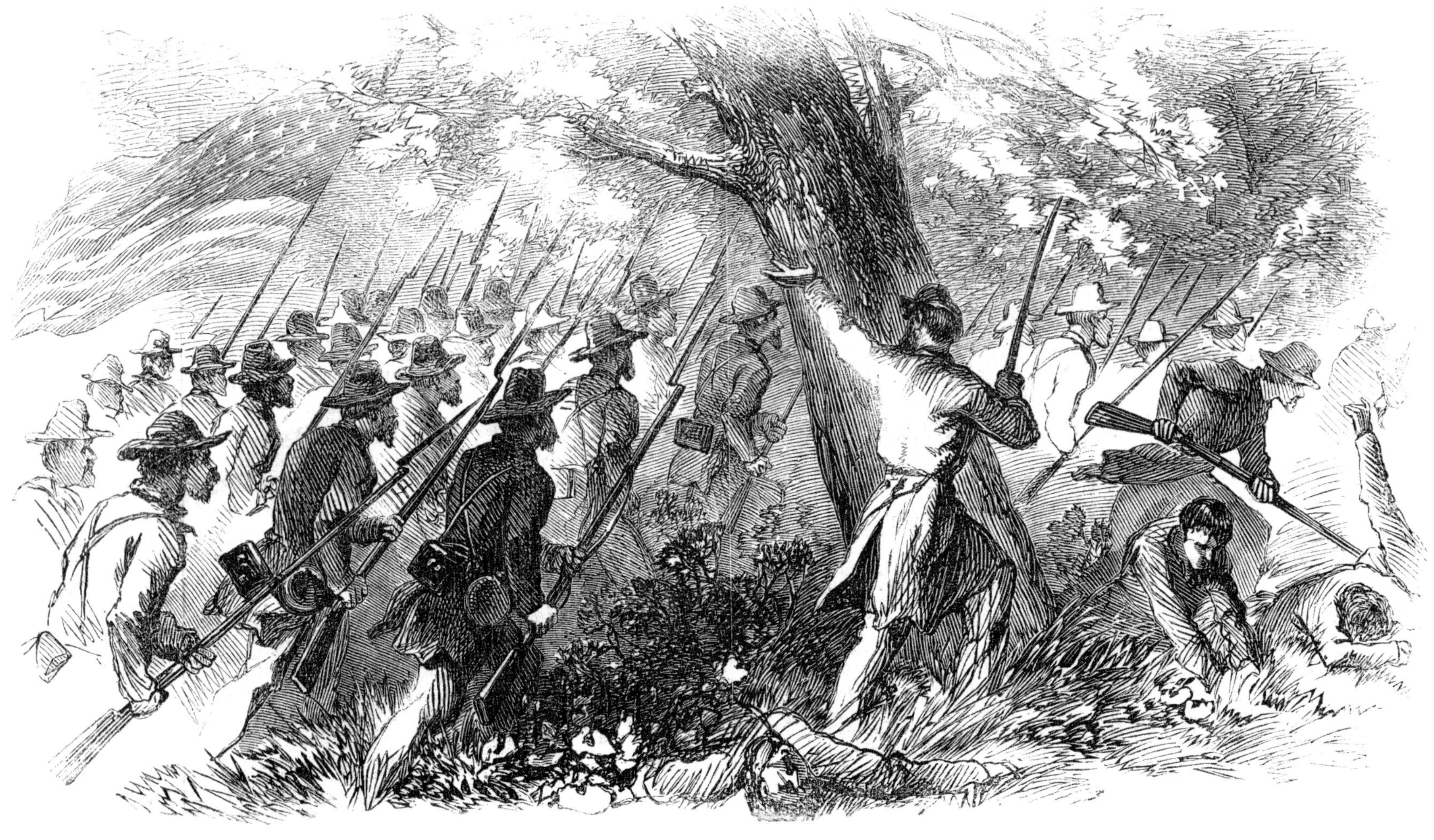

3rd Rhode Island Volunteers

Drawn by a Union officer
Frank Leslie's Illustrated Newspaper

The 3rd Rhode Island and the 3rd New Hampshire, part of Col. Robert Williams brigade, tried to flank the Confederate position at the Tower Battery. As they advanced, they found themselves in a ring of fire from Confederate positions at the battery, the Eutaw Battalion to their left and the advance and reinforcement provided by the 4th Louisiana Battalion.

After three assaults on the Confederate position and two-and-a-half hours of fierce fighting, Union Brig. Gen. Henry Benham ordered a general retreat.

In all, Union forces registered almost 700 casualties. Confederates suffered 150. Col. T. G. Lamar reported that 341 Union soldiers were buried on the field in front of the Tower Battery.

Leslie's summed up the outcome as disastrous. The newspaper further reported that Lamar had 8,000 men at the Confederate position at Secessionville. In truth, the Confederate forces were badly outnumbered by the Union forces commanded by Benham.

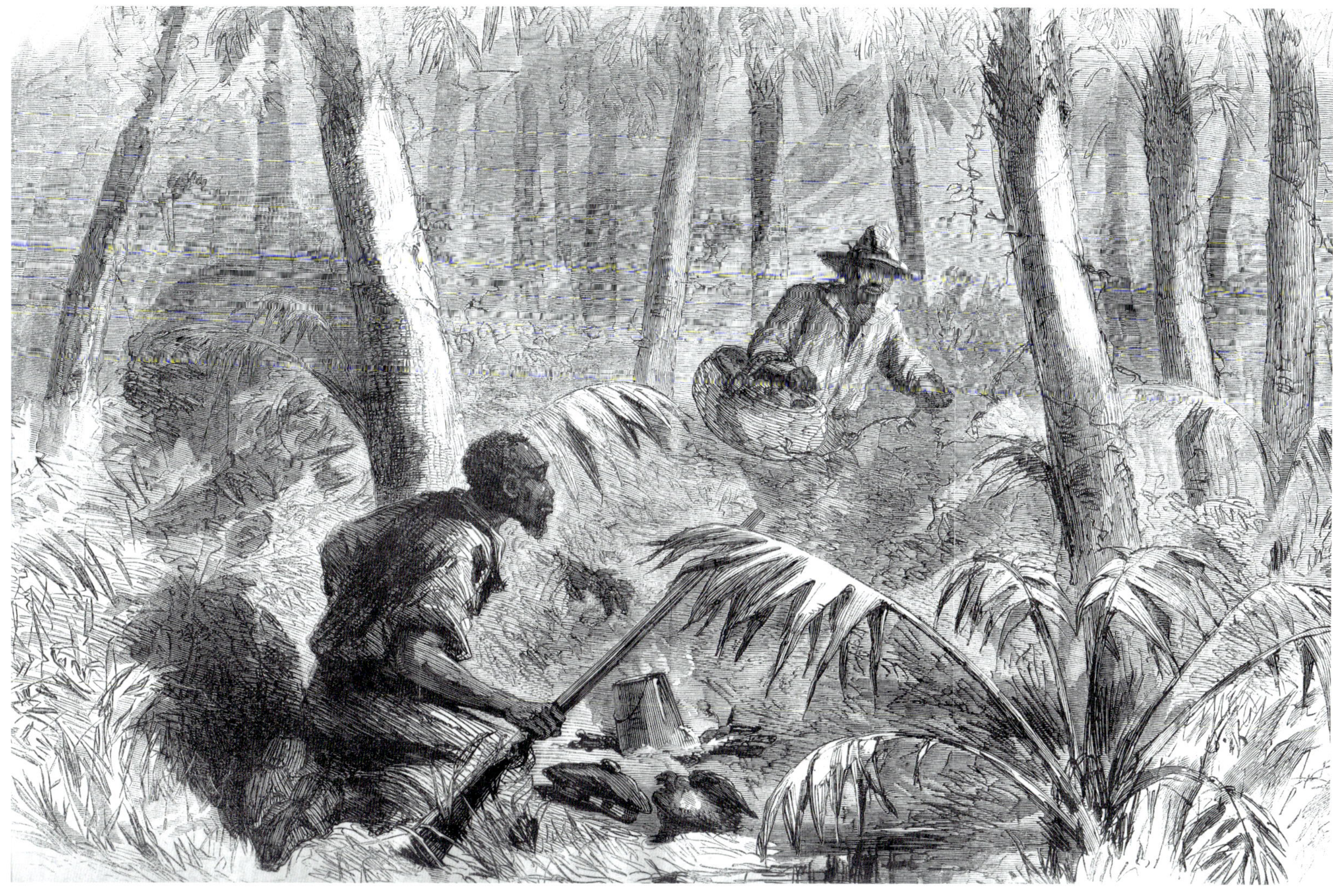

Runaway Slave

Artist: William Waud
New York Illustrated News

The illustrated newspapers in both New York and London focused a great deal of attention on the plight of the slave. This illustration was offered to the reader, depicting a runaway slave hiding in the swamp near Charleston. *The New York Illustrated News* writes:

> *When a slave is ill treated or gets tired of work, he retires to the nearest swamp, where he stays until he is hunted out, or as usually is the case, he gets sick of hiding in the woods, and longs for the comfortable quarters on the plantation, where he will produce himself some morning and go to work in the most assiduous manner... Before the bombardment of Fort Sumter, there were thirty runaways in the Parish of St. Andrews, close to Charleston, who upon hearing the continued firing become* [sic] *so alarmed that all returned quietly to labor.*

The illustration shows a slave hiding in the swamps of St. Andrews Parish and receiving provisions from a friend.

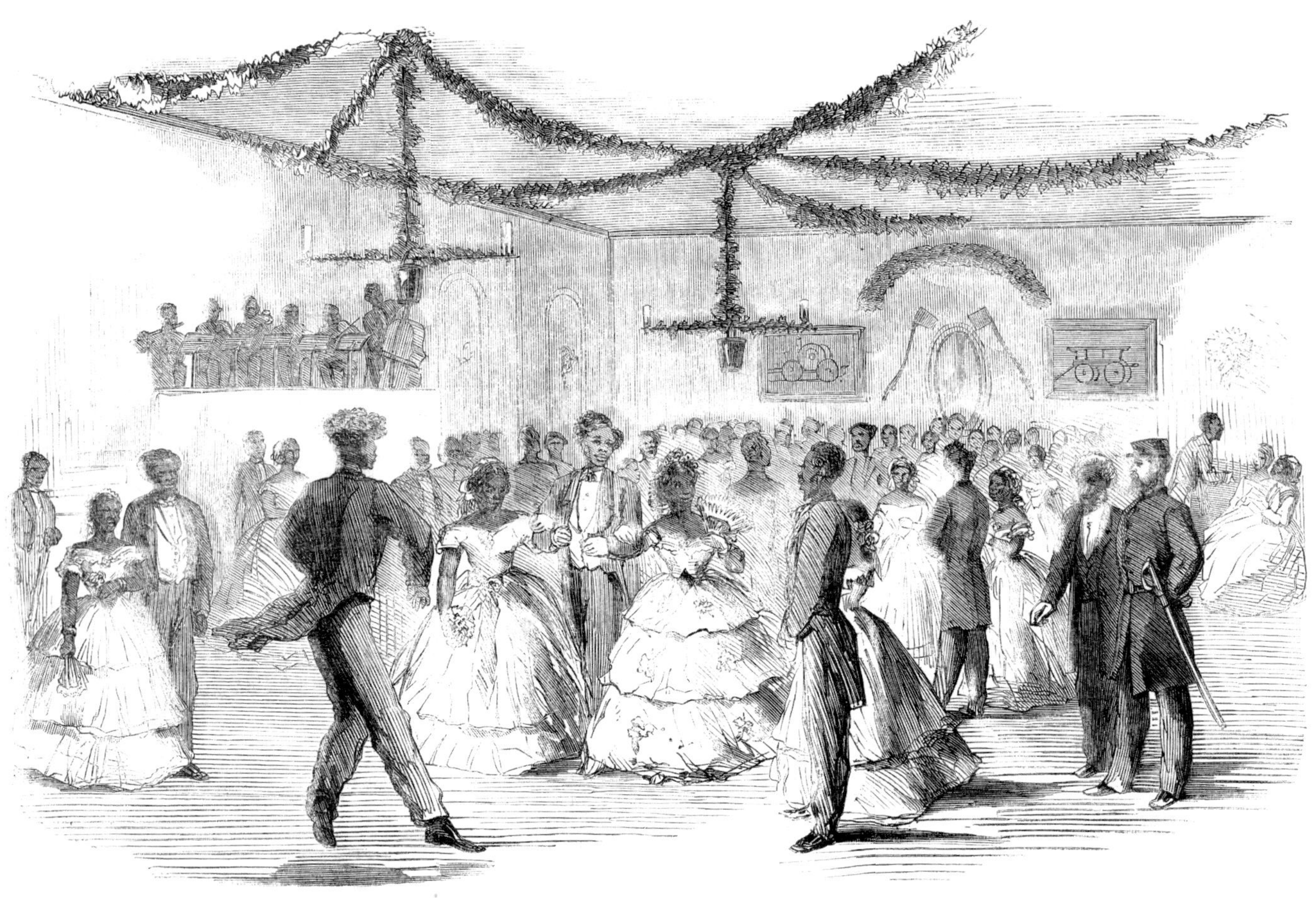

Black Firemen's Ball

Artist: William Waud
New York Illustrated News

Artist William Waud attended the Charleston "Negro Fireman's Ball" in 1862 and forwarded his illustration and observations to the *New York Illustrated News*. Slaves were allowed, with the permission of their masters, to volunteer for service with one of the 10 city ward engine companies that served in addition to the white volunteer fire companies. Each city ward engine company was staffed with slaves under the command of three white managers. As was the tradition with the white volunteer fire companies, the city sponsored a firemen's ball for the members of the 10 ward companies.

William Waud writes:

> *The Hall was fashionably crowded and the ladies and gentlemen (all slaves) well, in some cases, elegantly dressed; the mistresses often attiring their favorite female slaves with great care, providing them with dresses and lending them their own jewels. The excessive gallantry of the men, and the coy little airs of the colored belles were very amusing; everything was conducted in the most orderly manner, the city furnishing them with a couple of policemen (one of whom is represented in the cut) to prevent the intrusion of evil disposed persons. A supper followed the ball, excellently laid out, and very choice in material, the only restriction being placed on wines and liquors, none of which is allowed to be introduced. The overpowering politeness displayed to the ladies during the repast, and afterward in the shawling and escorting home, was beyond all praise.*

Siege of Charleston

The siege of Charleston was the longest and, arguably, most brutal confrontation between Union and Confederate armies during the Civil War. That Charleston withstood the force of an army with far greater numbers and resources for 19 grueling months is testament to the resilience and determination of the Charleston people.

The defense conceived by Brig. Gen. P. G. T. Beauregard contributed in no small measure to that resilience. During the siege, both armies deployed effective and ingenious innovations in 19th-century warfare. The design and use of ironclads; the many varied torpedoes and mines developed by the Confederates; the use of Drummond lights for nighttime illumination by both sides; the Confederate torpedo boats; extending the range of guns to lengths never before achieved; and the first submersible to successfully sink an enemy ship were all elements of the siege of Charleston.

This period of the war began with Adm. Samuel Du Pont's ill-fated ironclad attack on Fort Sumter in April 1863. The one-day battle between what was thought to be the invincible Union ironclad fleet and the Confederate batteries resulted in the damage of several ironclads and the sinking of the *U.S.S. Keokuk*. A seaman aboard the *U.S.S. Catskill* remarked, "Officers and men were astounded to see the injuries done to these supposed invulnerable ironclads."

After withdrawing to Port Royal, the federal government, embarrassed by the defeat, replaced both the top army and naval commanders. Gen. Quincy Gillmore, now commander for the Department of the South, planned the next move against Charleston. In the Union attack on Secessionville and the ironclad attack on Fort Sumter, the Union command believed it could make a quick strike and force an early defeat of Charleston. Despite the earlier losses, Gillmore assumed the same in his decision to assault Battery Wagner on Morris Island.

The Union Army established a foothold at the southern end of Morris Island to position itself to attack Battery Wagner. On July 11, soldiers, led by Gen. George C. Strong, reached the ramparts of the Confederate position only to endure a terrible defeat with more than 400 casualties. Confederates suffered 24 casualties.

Gillmore believed that his only mistake was the lack of artillery support for his attacking column and planned the next assault for seven days later. Amassing three brigades for the attack and providing immense artillery support by land batteries and the Union fleet in the harbor, Gillmore confronted the Confederates with a frontal assault. The defeat of his men was of a magnitude that none of the Union command could conceive as imaginable. Lt. Augustus McKethan, of the 51st N.C. Infantry, writes of the artillery assault: "The sand being our only protection, fortunately one shell would fill up the hole made by the last, or we would have been annihilated."

After 11 hours of bombarding Battery Wagner, Gillmore was ready to send his troops. Col. Haldimand S. Putnam, in one of the lead units, remarked to his officers, "We are all going into Wagner like a flock of sheep." During the assault, Putnam would die with a bullet through his head.

The 54th Massachusetts, the first black regiment raised in the North, led the attack. Col. Robert Shaw said to his men, "Take the fort or die there." At 7:45 p.m., the infantry attack began. The units in the first brigade were shredded by Confederate fire. Lt. Henry G. Webber, of the New Hampshire Infantry, later writes, "All was wild uproar, with the groans and cries of the wounded; men calling for their officers, officers calling for their men, and many in wild excitement yelling for no apparent reason... "

Shaw's statement to his men when he led them into battle had a chilling prescience. "Take the fort or die there" – Shaw, along with half the men of the 54th Massachusetts, died.

In recalling the fateful charge, Lt. Daniel West, 6th Conn. Infantry, writes:

> *I had been in several battles before in Virginia..., but nothing in my experience compared with the slaughter in front and in Fort Wagner that night.... The dead and wounded covered it [the seaward wall] so that it was impossible to get around. All of our commanding officers were either killed or disabled...*

West was captured at Battery Wagner and held as a prisoner until the fall of Charleston.

The second Union brigade entered the fray at 8:30 p.m. Tragically, after dusk, the second brigade could not make out the identity of men near the fortification and fired on their own troops, forcing them to return fire to protect themselves. With their ammunition exhausted and finding it difficult to move through the dead and wounded littering the beach, the federal attack collapsed before the third brigade ever engaged.

By 10:30 p.m., the fight was over. The next morning, even the Confederates at Wagner were horrified at the sight. A Confederate soldier with the 32nd Georgia Infantry described the scene:

> *I never saw such a sight as presented itself on Sunday morning at day brake* [sic] *– as far as the eye could reach could be seen the dead and dying on all sides... I volunteered to go out to collect the wounded Yankees. I had a chance to see what was to be seen – in the ditch to our left there was about 115 killed in a space of about 100 feet – So you can see that there was some brave Yankees engaged – I never saw such a sight, men with heads off many with legs shot off – feet, hands and in fact any part of the body – Such complete destruction of life...*

For the third time, the Union command failed to force a quick and decisive victory. Charleston would not surrender. Gillmore's only choice was to initiate a lengthy and determined siege on Battery Wagner and the rebel-infested city of Charleston. More than seven weeks would pass before Gillmore would take Wagner. One soldier from North Carolina stationed at Battery Wagner and part of the evacuation of the island summed up his feeling about his time there:

> *I have heard preachers talk about Hell, a great big hole, full of fire and brimstone, where a bad fellow was dropped in, and I will allow it used to worry me at times, but Gentlemen, Hell can't be worse than Battery Wagner. I have got out of that, and the other place ain't going to worry me any more!*

Charleston would hold out another 18 months. But, then, faced with the inevitable prospect of capture, the Confederates finally evacuated.

Gen. W. T. Sherman visited Charleston in May 1865, a month after the fall. In a report to his superiors, he notes:

> *Anyone who is not satisfied with war should go and see Charleston, and he will pray louder and deeper than ever that the country may in the long future be spared any more war... Charleston and secession being synonymous terms, the city should be left as a sample, so that centuries may pass away before that false doctrine is again preached in our Union.* ❧

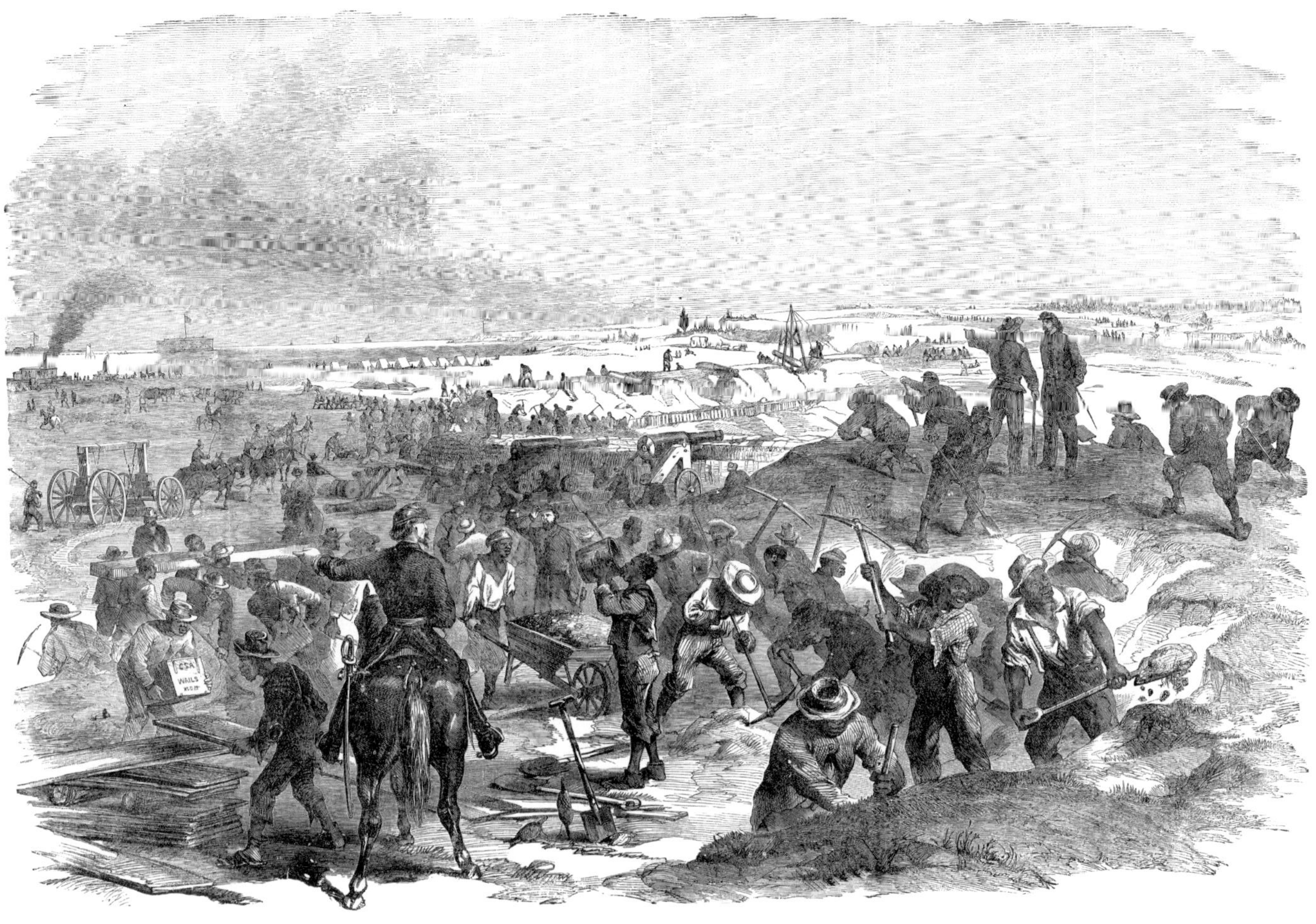

The Confederates Building Fortifications on James Island

Artist: A. P. Palmer, S.C. Volunteers
Frank Leslie's Illustrated Newspaper

As early as October 1862, there were rumors that Union Adm. Samuel Du Pont would attack Charleston. In the month before, Gen. P. G. T. Beauregard returned to Charleston and assumed command of the Department of South Carolina and Georgia. He immediately began work improving the defenses of Charleston, preparing for the anticipated federal attack.

But the Confederates were short of troops, making fortification of the port city challenging. It was clear the only way adequate progress could be made was to use slave labor in the construction of the fortifications. From November 1862 to February 1863, an average count of 755 slaves were actively used in support of the Confederate engineers building the defenses of Charleston.

Beauregard's staff estimated that the federal forces under Gen. David Hunter at Port Royal numbered as many as 40,000 men, in addition to the rapidly expanding fleet commanded by Du Pont. Thomas Jordan, Confederate chief of staff, wrote to the authorities in Richmond that he needed 28,000 men to properly defend Charleston but had only 6,500 troops available. With no prospect of reinforcements, Jordan issued an order in February for "3,000 able-bodied slaves to report for thirty days duty." They were never able to commandeer such numbers. As late as March 27, 1863, Beauregard noted, "The want of a sufficient number of negroes has long been felt, and has materially crippled the artificial defenses of Charleston."

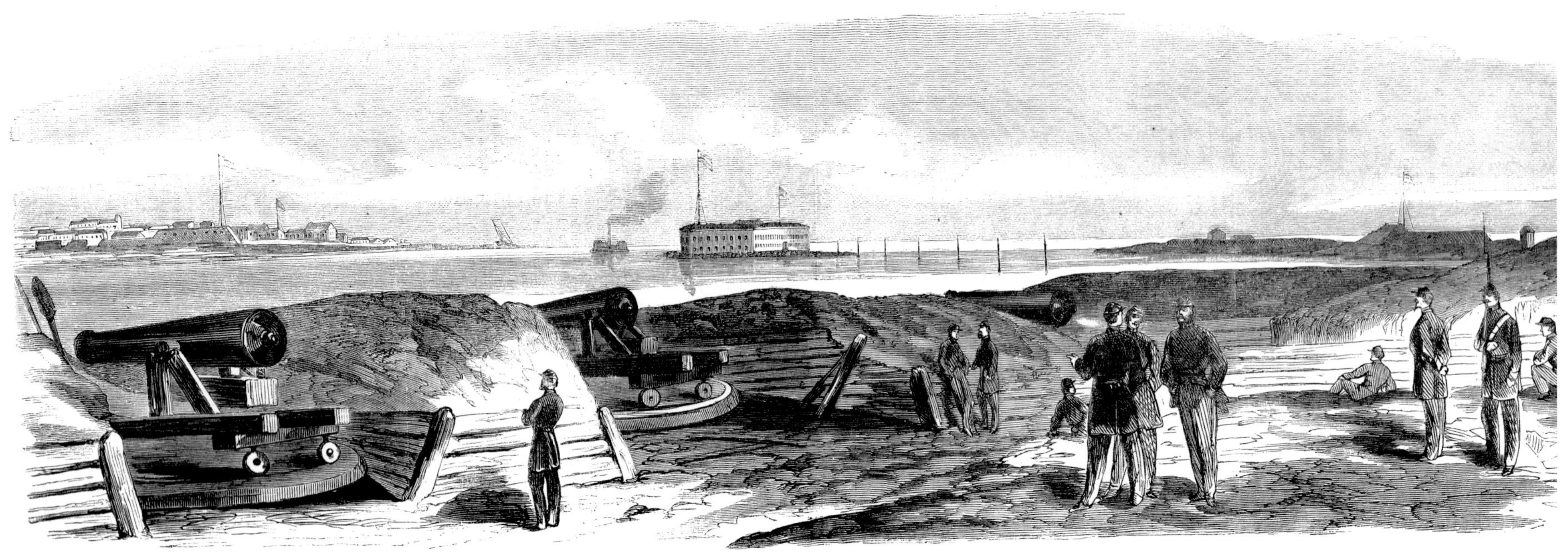

Defenses of Charleston Looking Seaward

Artist: unknown English artist
Harper's Weekly

Gen. P. G. T. Beauregard clearly understood the design for the best defense of Charleston. To repel a ground attack, he knew that his assets needed to focus first on James Island. To defend a naval assault, the main shipping channel needed further fortification. Beauregard made a personal request for the transfer of two officers, Gen. Roswell Sabine Ripley and Col. David Harris, to assist in the design and installation of the Charleston defenses. Both officers were skilled in artillery and defensive fortifications.

As all of Charleston was aware of the impending arrival of the Union fleet, a reporter for the *Illustrated London News* writes: "I have every faith in the results of the coming encounter, for never at any time have the Confederates been more determined to do or die than they express themselves now."

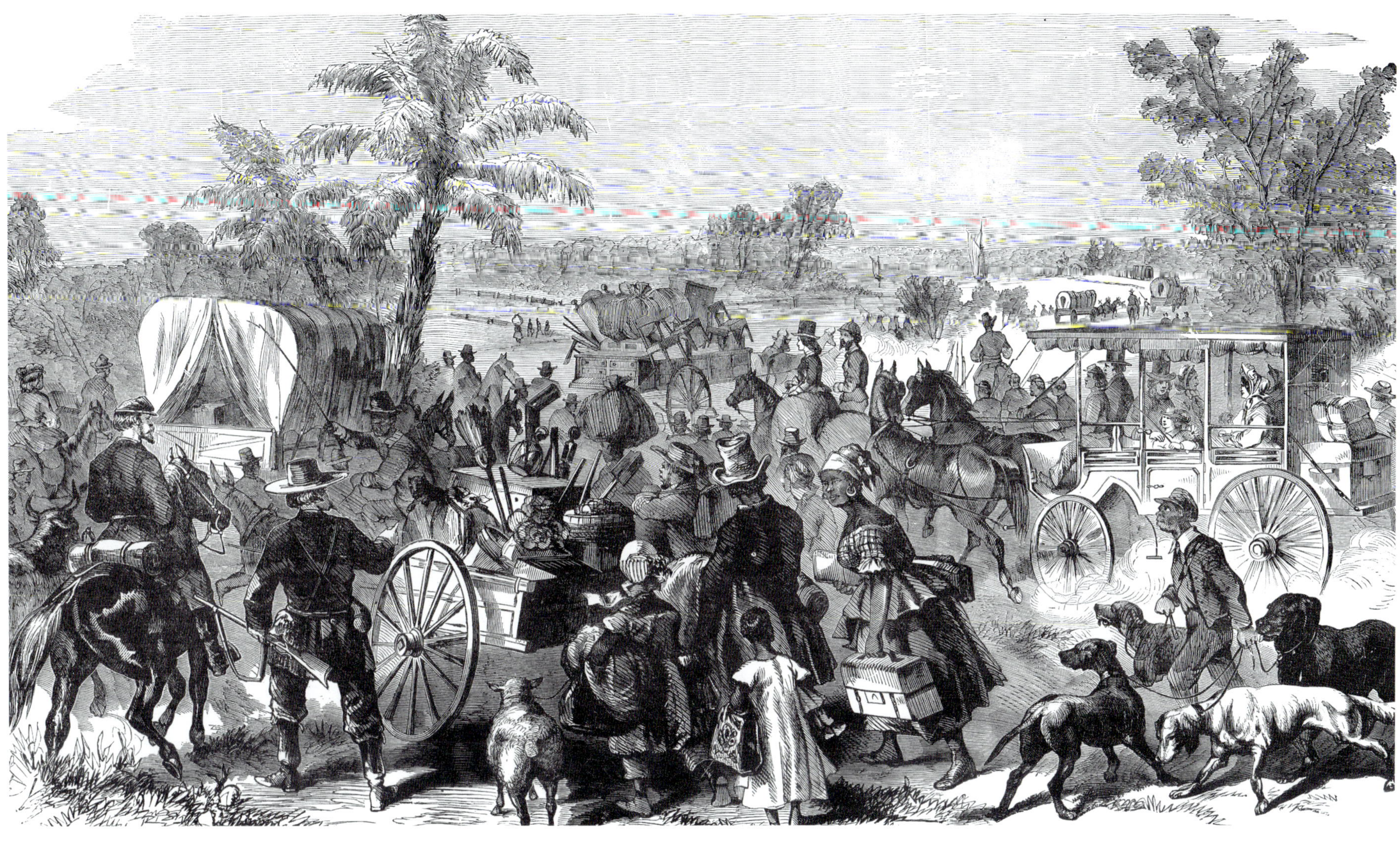

Fleeing Charleston

Artist: unknown
Frank Leslie's Illustrated Newspaper

In early April 1863, several days before the anticipated attack on Charleston by Adm. Samuel DuPont's fleet, Gen. P. G. T. Beauregard issued an order for women and children to leave the city. Despite the scene portrayed here in *Frank Leslie's Illustrated Newspaper*, most people ignored the order. The citizens had absolute confidence in Beauregard and the Charleston defenses.

Reports reaching Beauregard on April 5 told of eight monitors and several steamships leaving Edisto for Charleston. Later that same day, the monitors appeared just outside the shipping channel to Charleston harbor. By the next day, 24 wooden vessels had arrived to join the ironclads. On April 7, Beauregard was advised that more than 20 ships were in the Stono River and many ships with troops were in the North Edisto River.

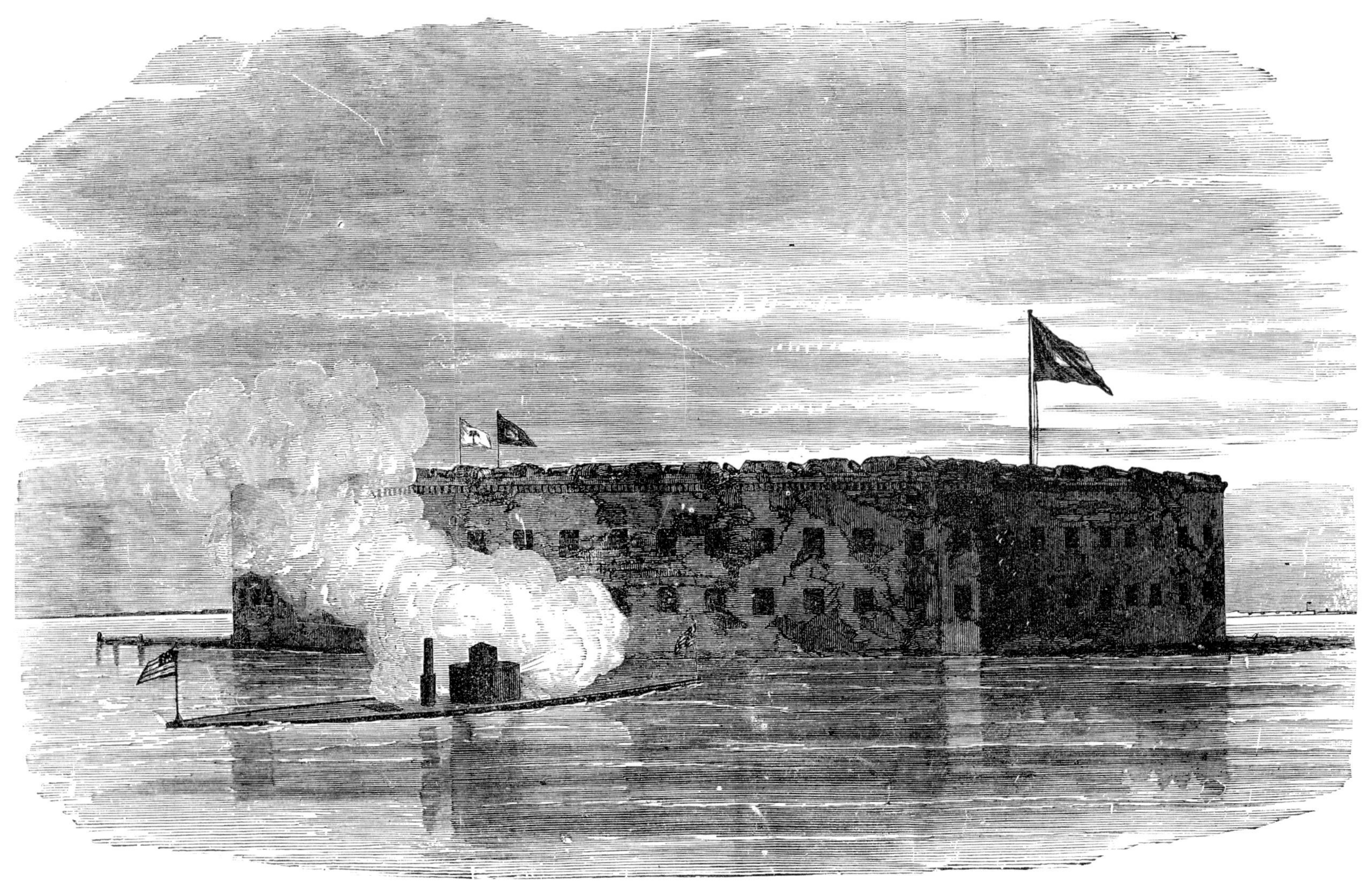

The *Weehawken* Attacks Fort Sumter

Artist: unknown
Frank Leslie's Illustrated Newspaper

For several days, Adm. Samuel Du Pont's fleet lay anchored off the entrance to Charleston harbor. On the morning of April 7, reports arrived at the city that the fleet was moving into the harbor. As the fleet of nine Union ironclads moved through the shipping channel off Morris Island, the Confederate land batteries knew when they were within range when they passed specific buoys. The lead Union monitor, the *Weehawken*, commanded by Capt. John Rogers, moved through the channel to challenge Fort Sumter.

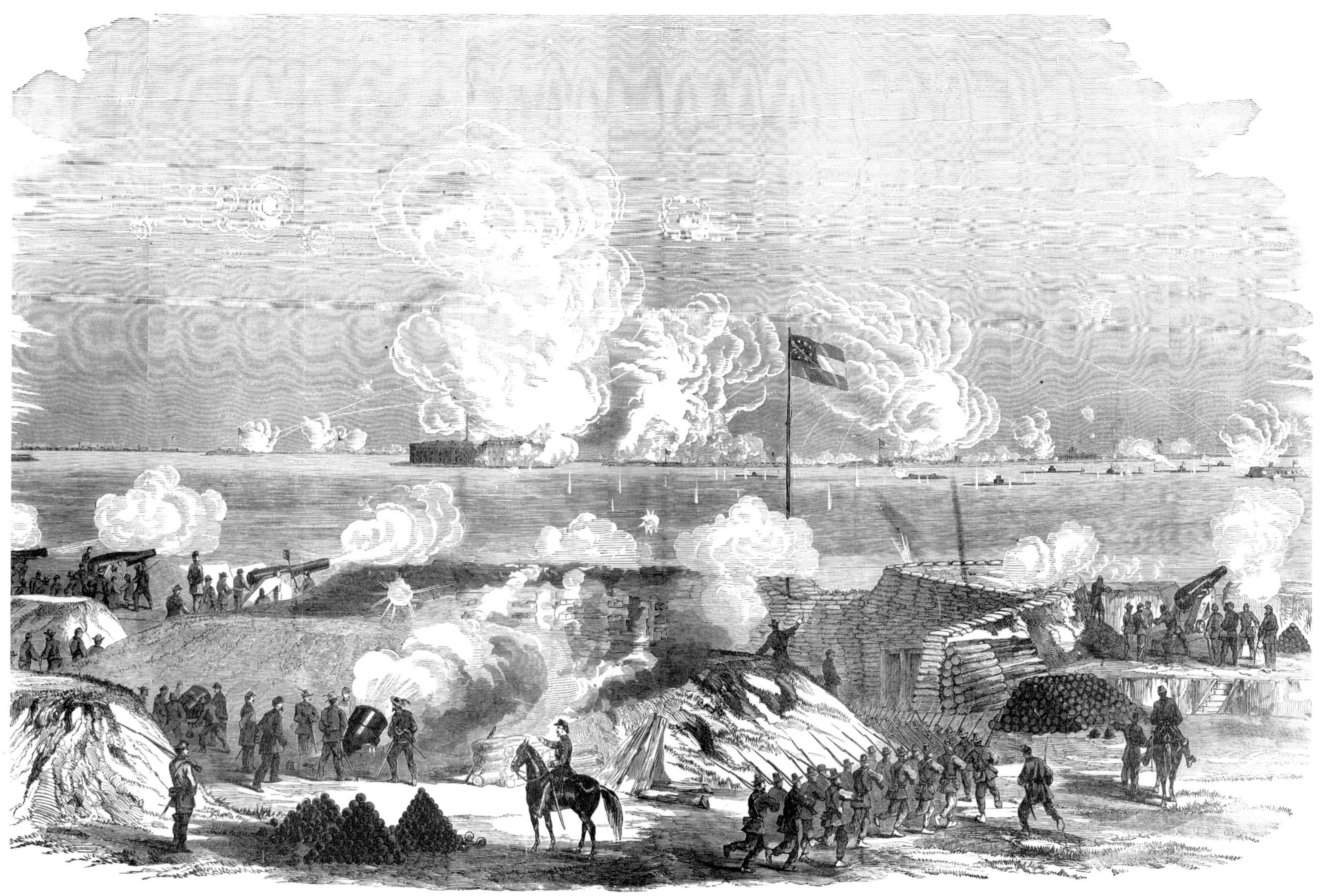

Federal Fleet Opens Fire

Artist: unknown
Frank Leslie's Illustrated Newspaper

With the Union fleet in range, the Confederates at Fort Moultrie, batteries Bee, Beauregard, Gregg and Wagner, and Fort Sumter unleashed their 76 guns. Only the heavy armor on the monitors saved them from the relentless pounding of the guns of Beauregard's defense.

With damage to the turret and the pilot house, the *Passaic* withdrew and anchored. The *Nahant* also sustained substantial damage and retreated. Several other Union monitors had difficulty maneuvering around each other.

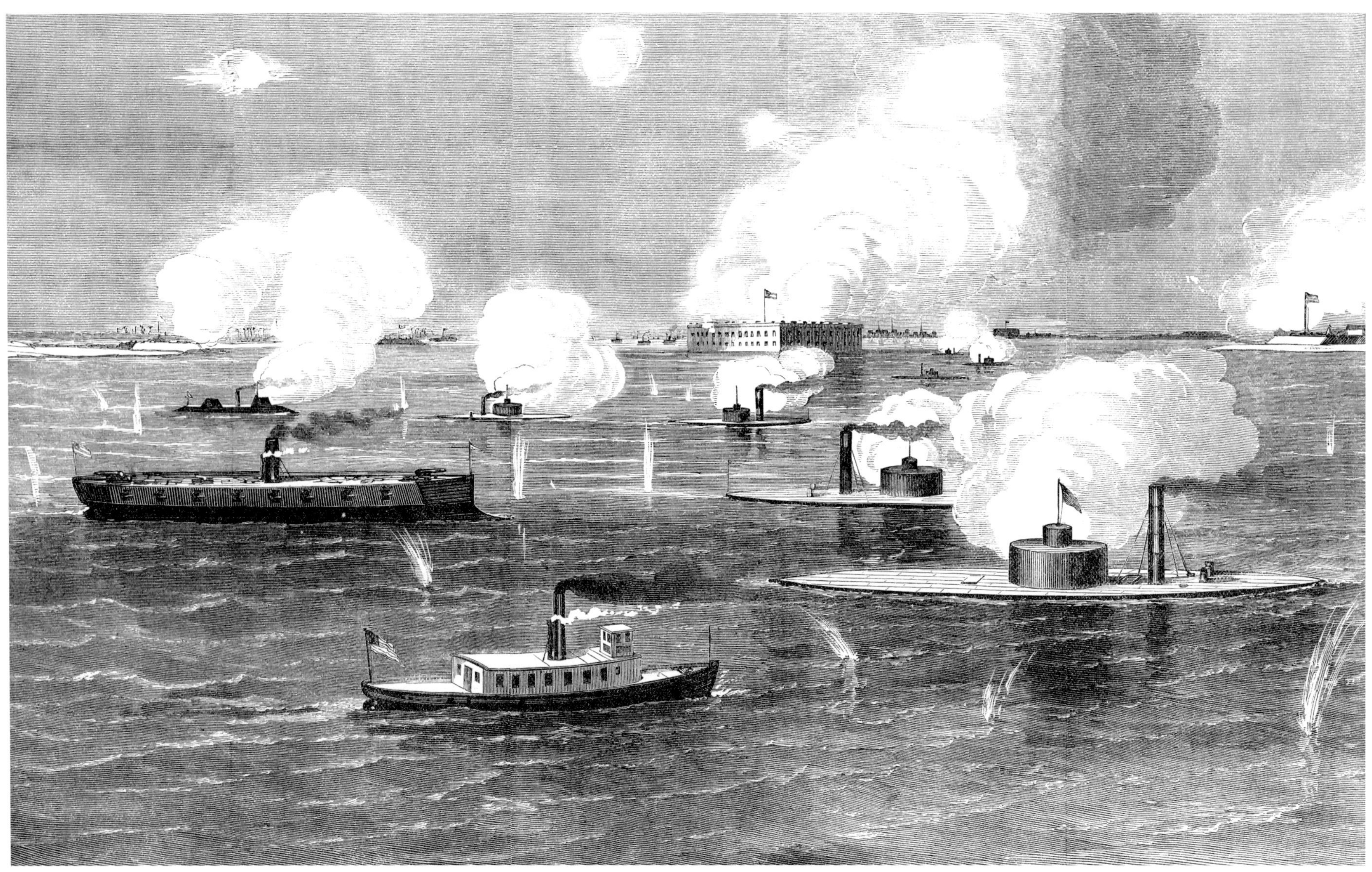

Bombardment of Fort Sumter

Artist: unknown
Harper's Weekly

Fort Sumter, the focus of the attack, received the heaviest fire from the Union ironclads, though little damage was done. Fort Moultrie also received fire, but suffered only one casualty. The fallen man died after being hit by the flagstaff.

With clear skies and good weather the day of the attack, spectators lined the sea walls and filled the rooftops of the waterfront homes to watch the action. Not unlike two years earlier in the Confederate attack on Fort Sumter, the drama of the great military confrontation played out before the citizens of Charleston.

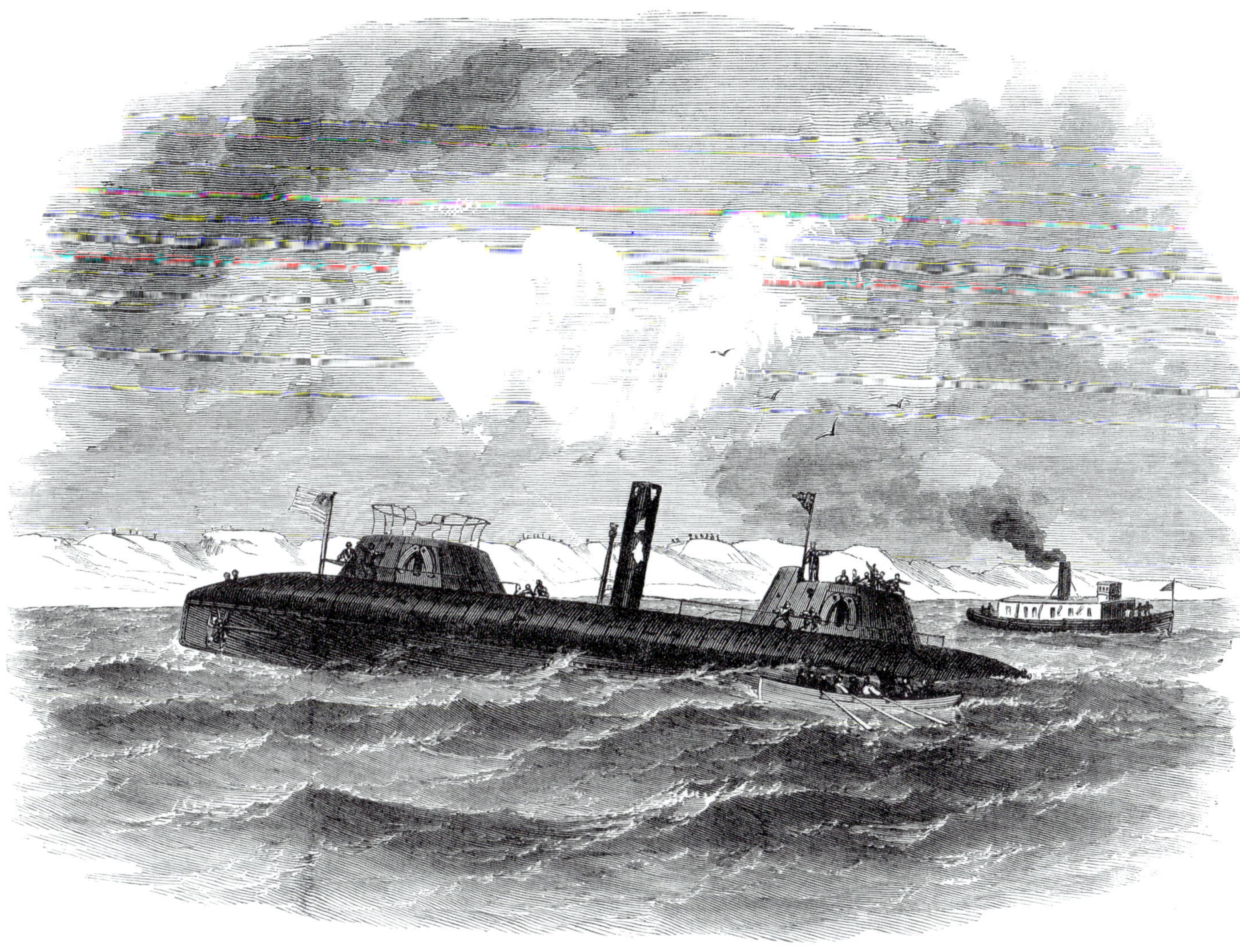

Sinking of the *Keokuk*

Artist: unknown
Harper's Weekly

The iron-clad *Keokuk* was the last in the line of Union ships entering the harbor. With two gun turrets and a bold captain at the helm, she steamed ahead of the other ships to come within 1,000 yds. of the prized Confederate outpost at Fort Sumter. This brought the attention of the guns at Sumter and Morris Island to the monitor. Many shots pierced the turrets and the water line of the iron-clad ship. After receiving 90 shots, the *Keokuk* withdrew.

By the next morning, the once proud ship was sinking in the waters just off Morris Island. Thirteen of her crew had been wounded; two of them were expected to die. Though the *Keokuk's* designer, C. W. Whitney of New York, had boasted of the "shot-proof" design, the ship sustained 19 holes as a result of Confederate gunfire.

Later, Gen. P. G. T. Beauregard had the two guns from the *Keokuk* salvaged for use at Forts Sumter and Moultrie.

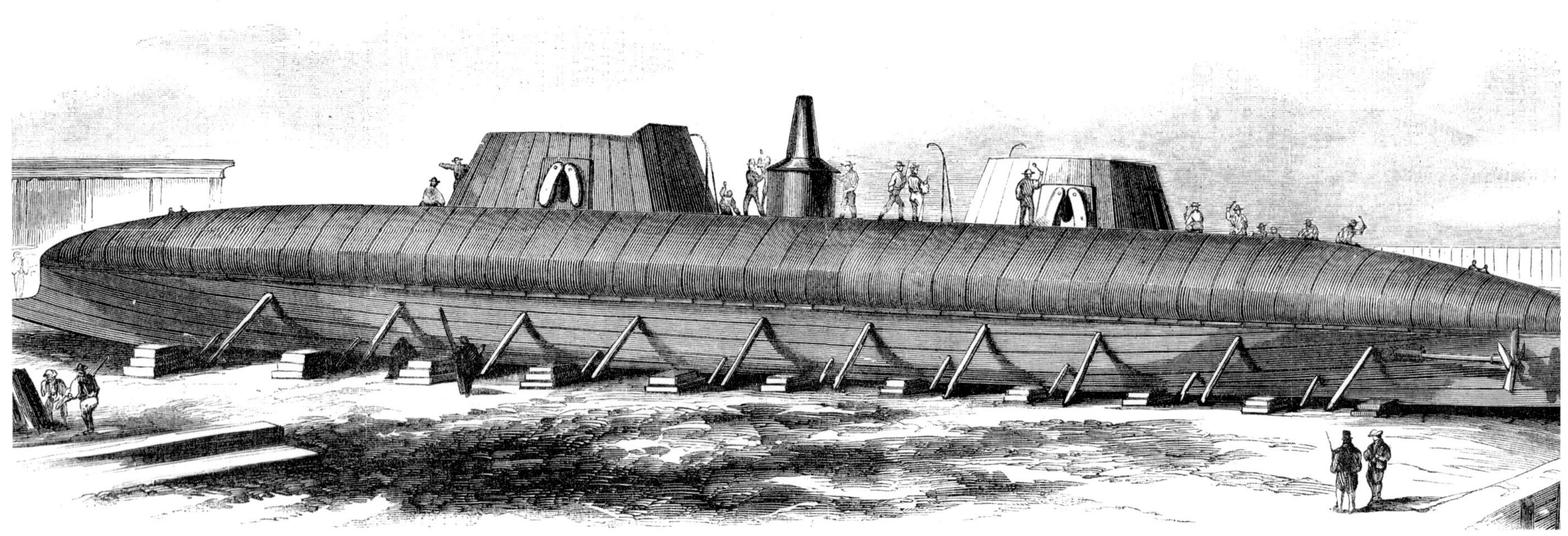

The *Keokuk* before Launching

Artist: unknown
Harper's Weekly

The *Keokuk* left New York for Port Royal in March 1862. Built in late 1861, she was the newest member of the U.S. Navy's "shot-proof fleet," sporting two turrets, each with an 11-in. gun, firing a 180-lb. shot. The ironclad was 159.5 ft. long, 36 ft. wide, 13.5 ft. tall and drew 9 ft. of water. Capable of moving the ship at 10 knots, she had two propellers powered by two 500-lb. engines.

The *Keokuk* was designed with a ram on the bow and outfitted with a "torpedo-catcher" that extended from the bow to protect the ship. Though smaller than the old class of monitors, the *Keokuk* could carry 100 men. She had storage space to handle the necessary provisions and two magazines to carry 200 11-in. shot and 150 11-in. shells.

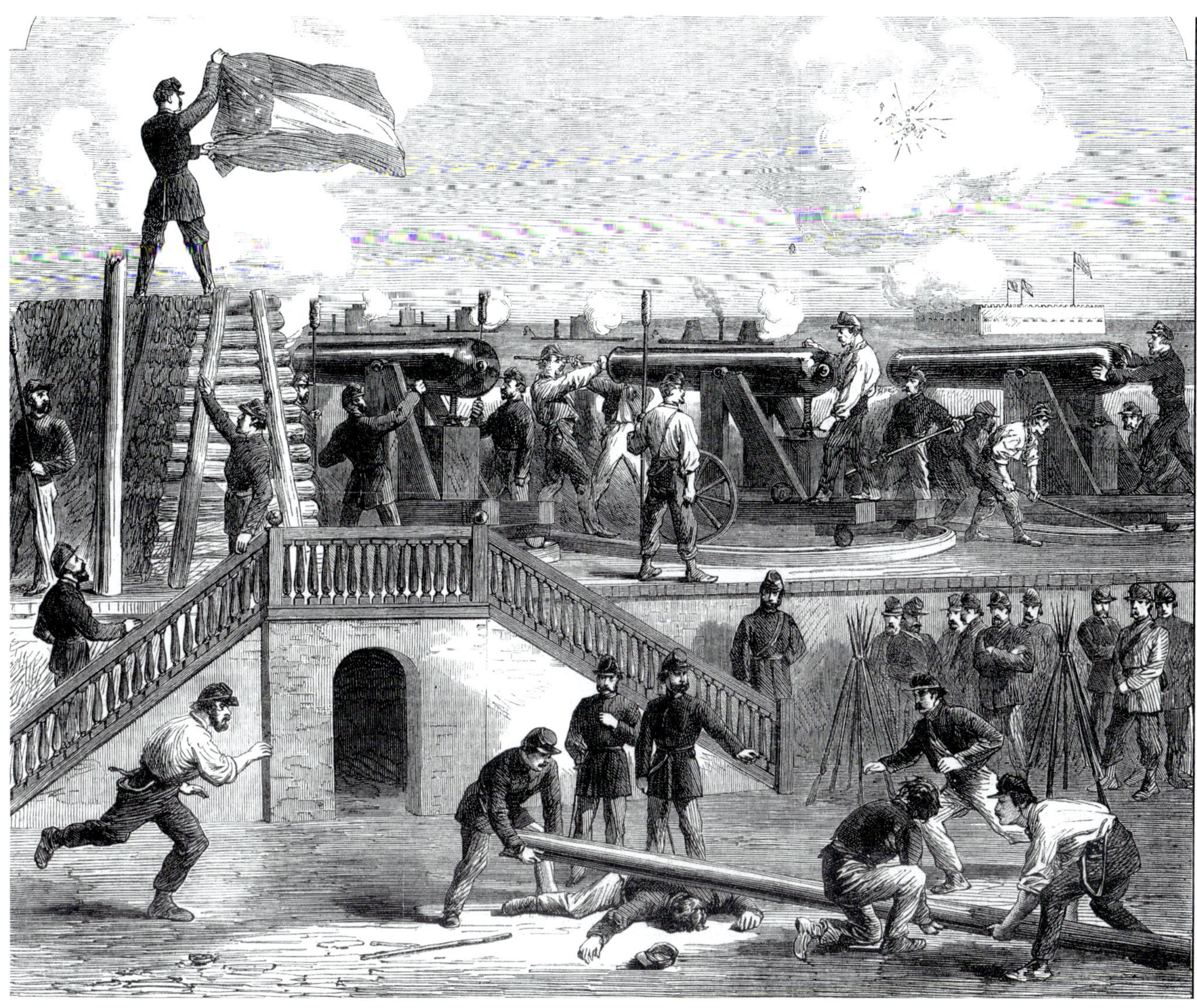

Fort Moultrie during the Bombardment

Artist: Frank Vizetelly
Illustrated London News

The artist describes the illustration in his report to his London editor:

> *The sketch I send you illustrates one of the most gallant feats in the bombardment of Fort Moultrie. I had just left my position in Battery Bee and reached Fort Moultrie just in time to witness it. The action was at its height when a ball cut the flagstaff in two just above the traverse, and as it fell it struck a poor fellow on the back of the head, killing him on the spot. The quartermaster of the battalion in the fort immediately sprang forward, seizing the fallen flag tore it from its hold and leapt on to the traverse, where he stood under the heavy fire immovable, until a jurymast was rigged and raised in the place of the shattered staff. The soldiers in the foreground of my sketch are removing the broken staff from the body of the poor fellow, who lies beneath it, and was the only man killed by the Federal fire.*

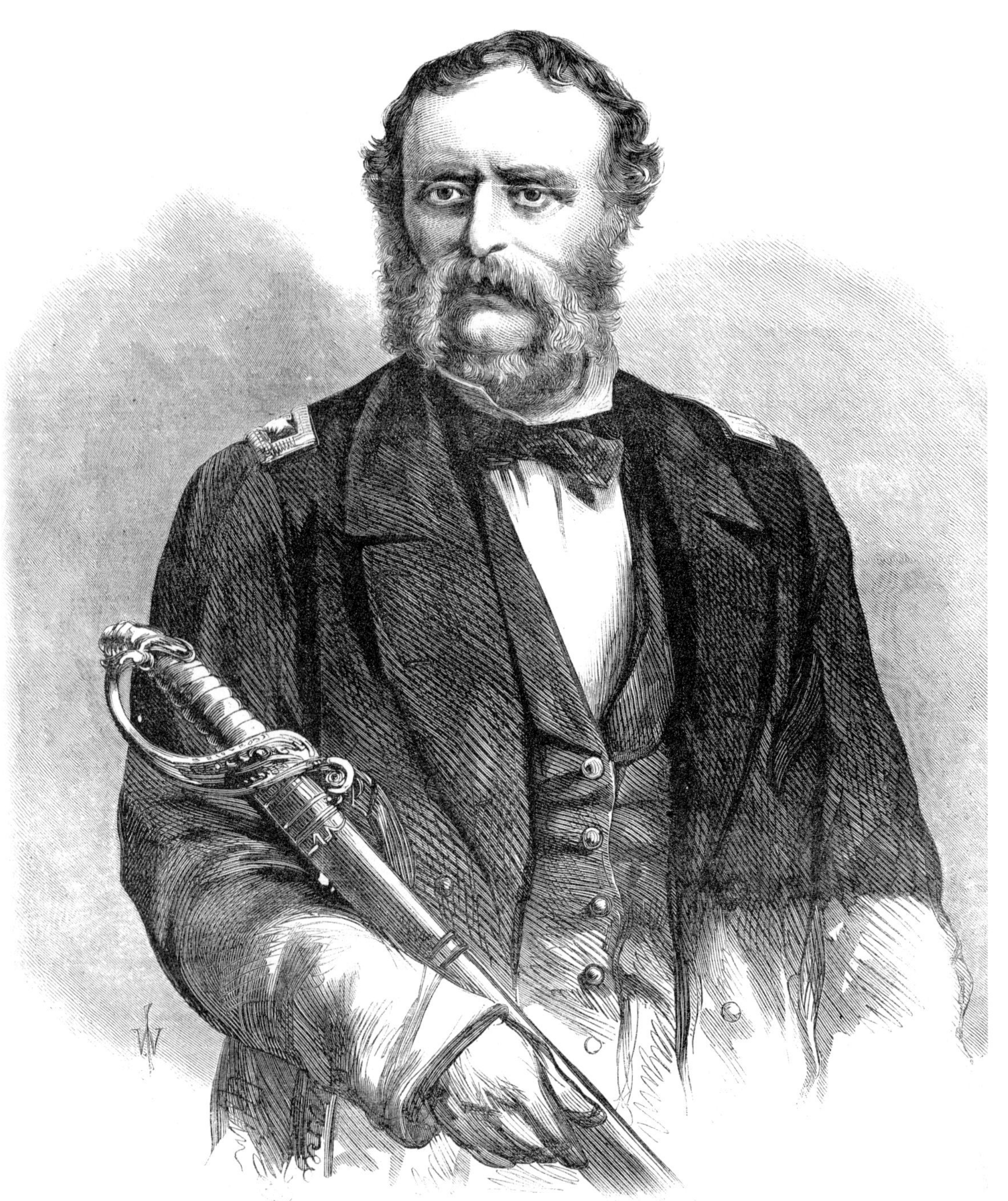

Admiral Samuel F. Du Pont

From a photograph by Guterunst
Harper's Weekly

Adm. Samuel Du Pont, a native of New Jersey and grandson of Pierre Samuel du Pont de Nemours, had served in the U.S. Navy since 1815. As the Civil War broke out, he was appointed to the rank of commodore and given command of the federal naval expedition against Port Royal, S.C. In recognition of that successful attack, Du Pont was promoted to rear admiral.

Against Du Pont's advice, U.S. Secretary of the Navy Gideon Wells ordered him to attack Charleston with the ironclad monitors. The Union fleet, unable to take Fort Sumter, limped out of the harbor and beyond range of Confederate guns. After anchoring overnight, Du Pont's fleet withdrew to Port Royal the next morning. The resounding defeat of the great Union fleet caused great embarrassment in Washington. In a communication to Major Gen. David Hunter, Du Pont writes, "I attempted to take the bull by the horns, but he was too much for us. These monitors are miserable failures where forts are concerned." By early June, Du Pont was relieved of his command of the South Atlantic fleet by Wells.

Harper's Weekly notes, "Had we destroyed Fort Sumter and occupied Charleston, there would have been good ground for expecting the early collapse of the rebellion."

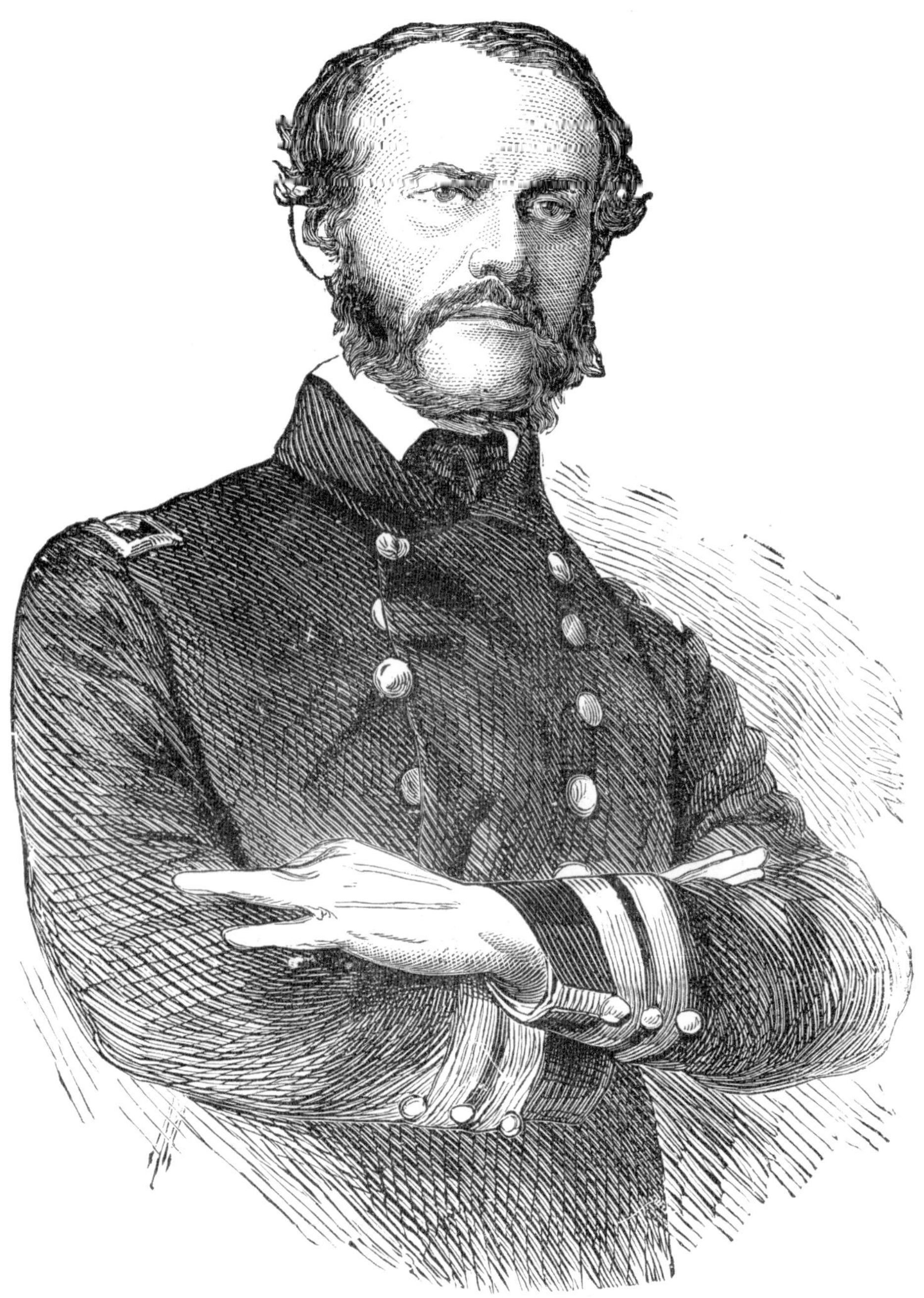

Admiral John A. Dahlgren

Artist: unknown

Harper's Weekly

John A. Dahlgren, a native of Philadelphia, joined the navy as a midshipman in 1826. Diligently working his way up the chain of command, he was given the position of commandant of the U.S. Navy Yard at Washington, in April 1861, after the previous commandant resigned to join the Confederacy. By 1862 Dahlgren was promoted to captain.

After Rear-Adm. Samuel Du Pont's embarrassing defeat at Charleston harbor in June 1863, Dahlgren was tapped to replace him as head of the South Atlantic Blockading Squadron. As he assumed his new command, Dahlgren was quickly promoted to rear admiral.

In the 1850s, Dahlgren published four books on naval ordinance and armament, and through his career, he was credited with many improvements in naval ordinance. His design for the 9-in. and 11-in. smoothbore guns became the favorite of U.S. seamen. The "Dahlgren Smoothbores" were noted for their lightness, range and accuracy.

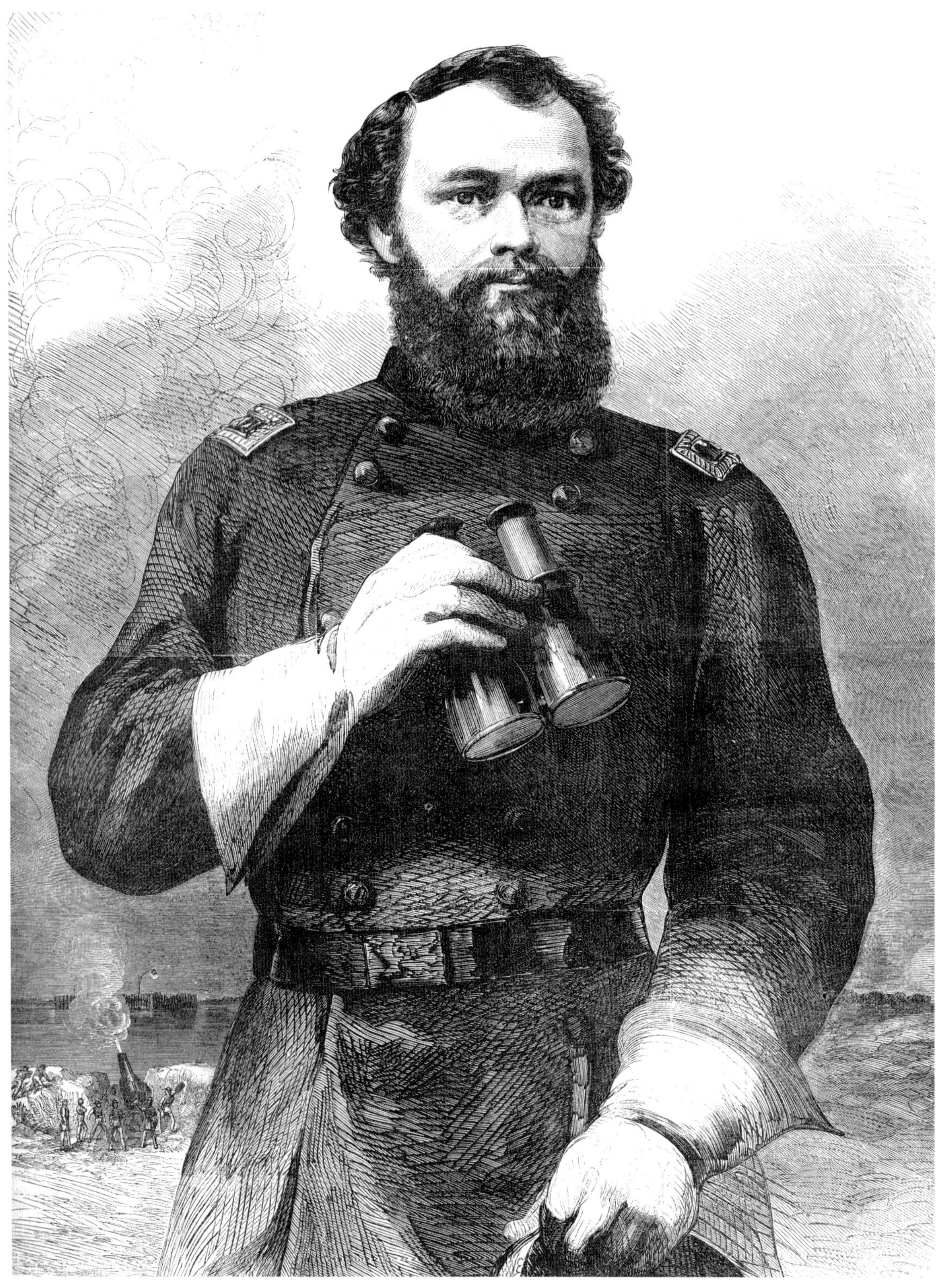

General Quincy A. Gillmore

Drawn from a portrait
Harper's Weekly

Quincy A. Gillmore, a native of Ohio, was graduated from West Point in 1849, first in his class. Lt. Gillmore proved himself a capable officer, quickly rising through the engineers to the rank of captain. From 1852-1856, he served as instructor of "practical military engineering" at West Point. In 1861, he accompanied Gen. William T. Sherman to Port Royal to began the war. While in South Carolina, Sherman promoted Gillmore to the rank of brigadier-general and placed him in charge of the siege of Fort Pulaski in Georgia.

Gillmore was given command of the Department of the South on June 12, 1863, replacing Gen. David Hunter. His appointment occurred at the same time as Adm. John A. Dahlgren, who replaced Adm. Samuel Du Pont after his failed first naval attack on Charleston.

Gillmore's first assignment was the siege of Charleston, covering the city that Northerners regarded as the "head of the snake." Interestingly enough, after the war's end, Gen. Gillmore accepted an appointment with the U.S. Army Corps of Engineers, living in Charleston. He directed the effort to design and build the Charleston Jetties in the harbor's shipping channel off Morris Island.

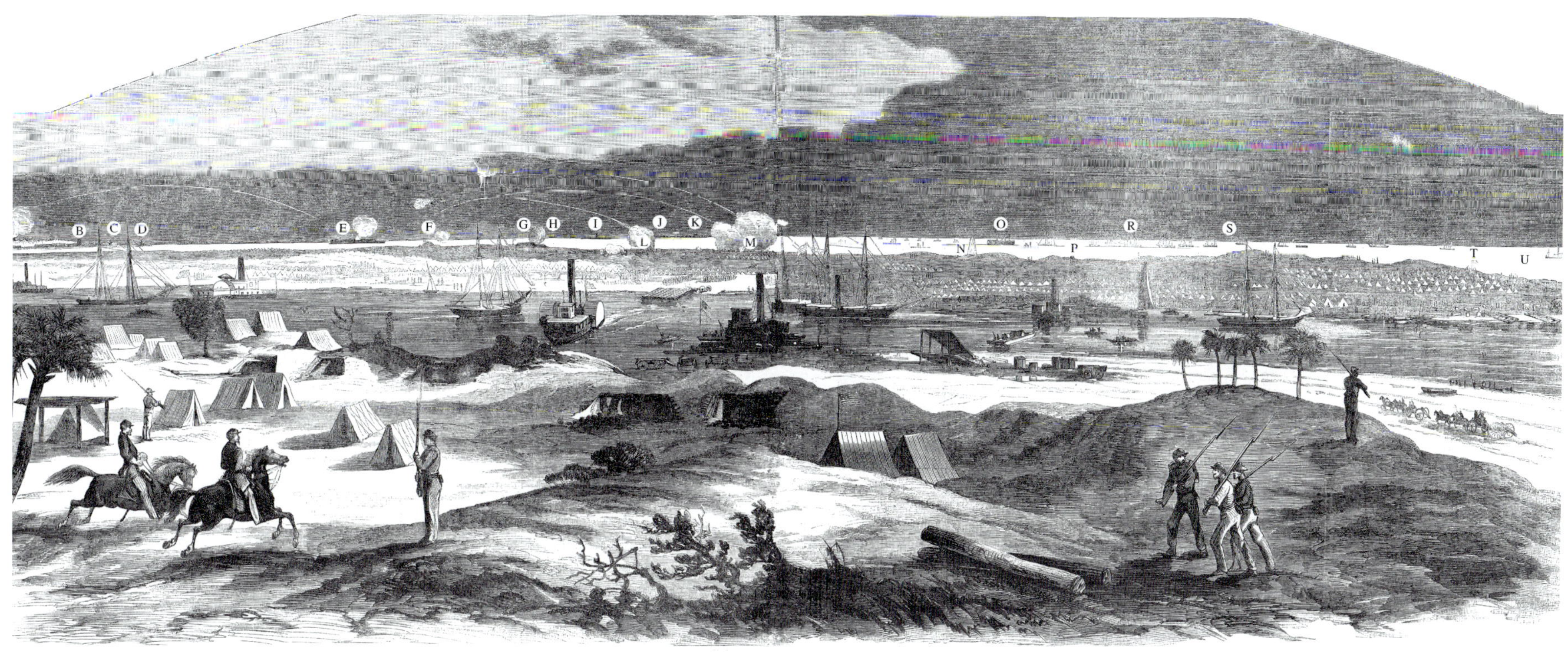

View of Morris Island from Folly

Artist: "Occasional Correspondent"
Harper's Weekly

Gen. Quincy Gillmore moved his troops from Port Royal to the sea islands near Charleston. Initially finding a foothold on Folly Island, the troops soon crossed to the southern end of Morris Island and established a sizable encampment and field batteries. This illustration provides an effective view of the federal encampment on Morris Island from Folly Island. The artist notes the following landmarks:

A– New rebel works on James Island
B– Rebel lookout
C– Fort Johnson
D– Rebel iron-clad
E– Fort Sumter
F– Battery Gregg
G– Fort Wagner
H– Battery Bee
I– Fort Moultrie
J– Battery Beauregard
K– Moultrie House [hotel]
L, M– Union batteries
N– Union lookout
O– New Ironsides
P– Ruined lighthouse
R– Flagship
S– Union fleet
T– Gillmore's headquarters
U– The ocean

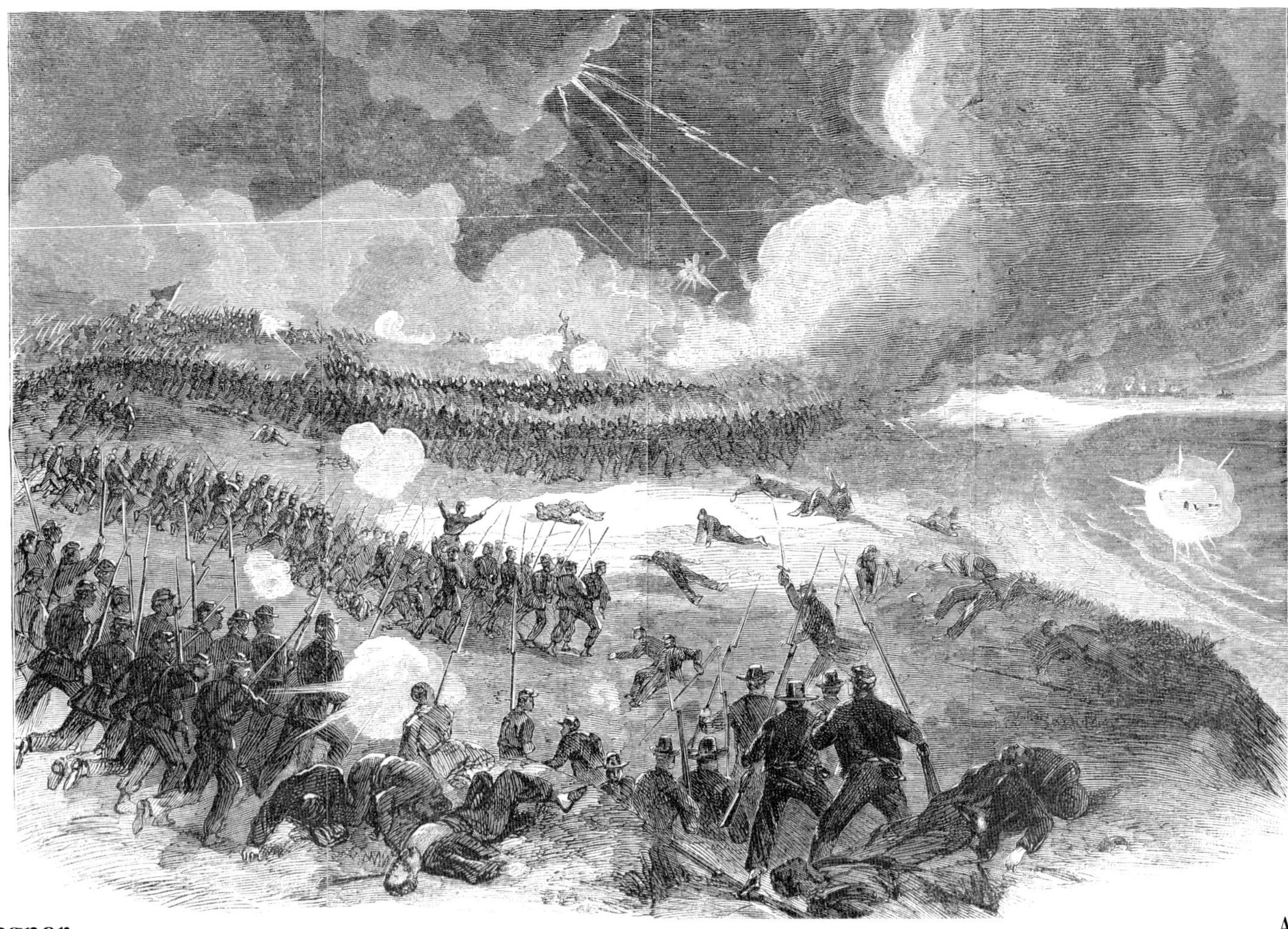

Attack on Fort Wagner

Artist: unknown
Harper's Weekly

Gen. Quincy Gillmore and Rear Adm. John A. Dahlgren decided to attempt a frontal assault on Battery Wagner with naval support as the first stage to take control of the harbor and, ultimately, Charleston. At midday on July 18, 1863, Union ironclads and land batteries began an intense bombardment of the Confederates in Battery Wagner.

Gen. George C. Strong was given the dubious honor of leading the assault with a brigade, including the notable black regiment (54th Massachusetts), the 6th Connecticut, the 48th New York, the 3rd New Hampshire, the 76th Pennsylvania and the 9th Maine.

The 1st Brigade made its way to the parapet, but was slaughtered. The 2nd Brigade, led by Col. Haldiman S. Putnam, had difficulty manuvering through the dead and wounded even to reach Wagner. The planned charge of the 3rd Brigade never occurred, and it withdrew without engaging the enemy.

Union officers Gen. George C. Strong, Col. Robert G. Shaw, Col. John L. Chatfield, Col. William B. Barton, Col. Green, and Col. J. H. Jackson all fell. As the Union troops withdrew, they were further demoralized by hearing the rebel shouts and cheers of victory that could be heard even above the guns of Fort Sumter and Battery Gregg.

All told, the Union Army suffered 1,527 casualties, compared to only 222 for the Confederate defenders.

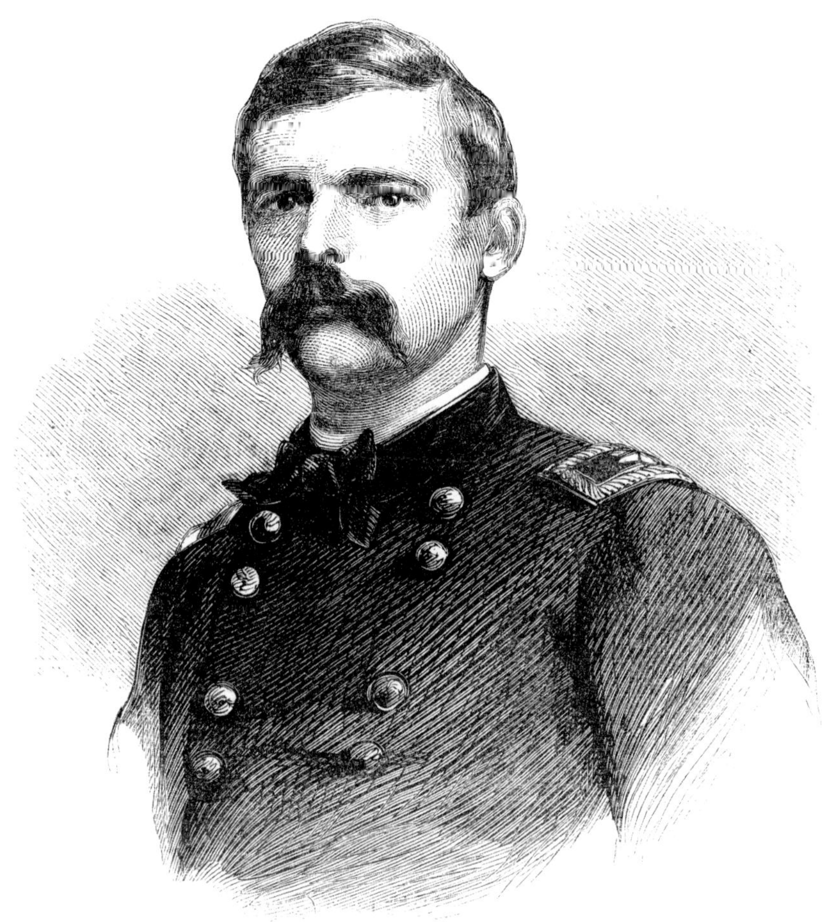

Brigadier General George C. Strong

Drawn from a photograph by Brady
Harper's Weekly

Brig. Gen. George C. Strong died of tetanus on July 30 from wounds he received while leading the bold attack on Battery Wagner.

He was a native of Massachusetts and an 1857 graduate of West Point. Strong served at Bull Run and was Gen. Benjamin F. Butler's chief of staff in New Orleans. At the personal request of Gen. Quincy Gillmore, he was placed in command of a brigade for the Department of the South.

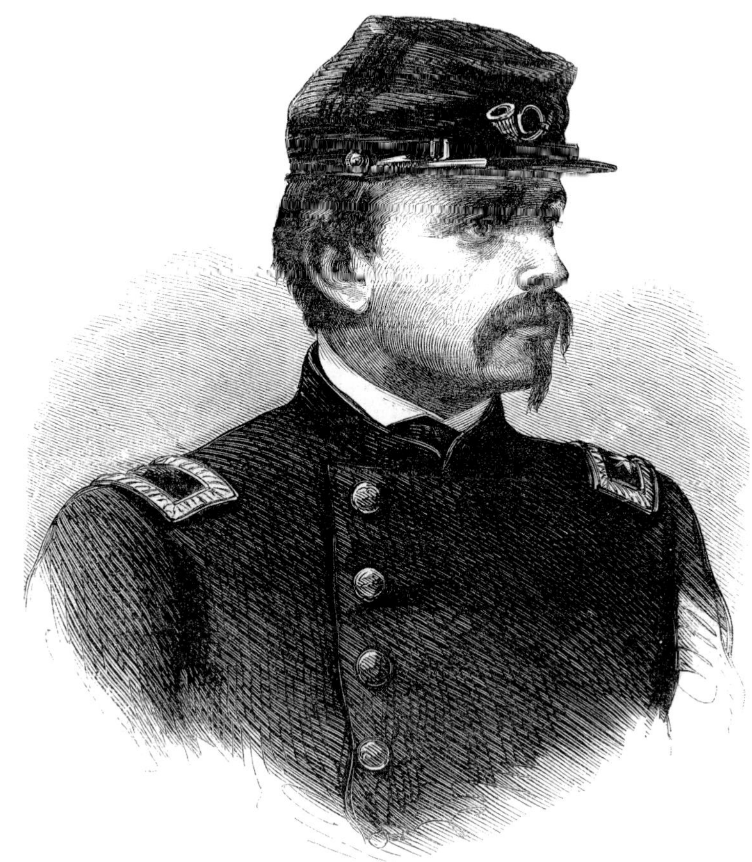

Colonel Robert G. Shaw

Drawn from a family portrait
Harper's Weekly

Brig.-Gen. George C. Strong, at Col. Robert G. Shaw's insistence, finally allowed the black regiment to meet the Confederates in a significant engagement. Just as the 54th Massachusetts reached the parapet at Battery Wagner, Shaw was killed at the head of his regiment. The Confederates buried Shaw in a mass grave along with many of his men.

While in the field hospital, Strong was quoted:

> *The* 54th *did well and nobly. Only the fall of Col. Shaw prevented them from entering the fort. They moved up as gallantly as any troops could, and with their enthusiasm, they deserved a better fate.*

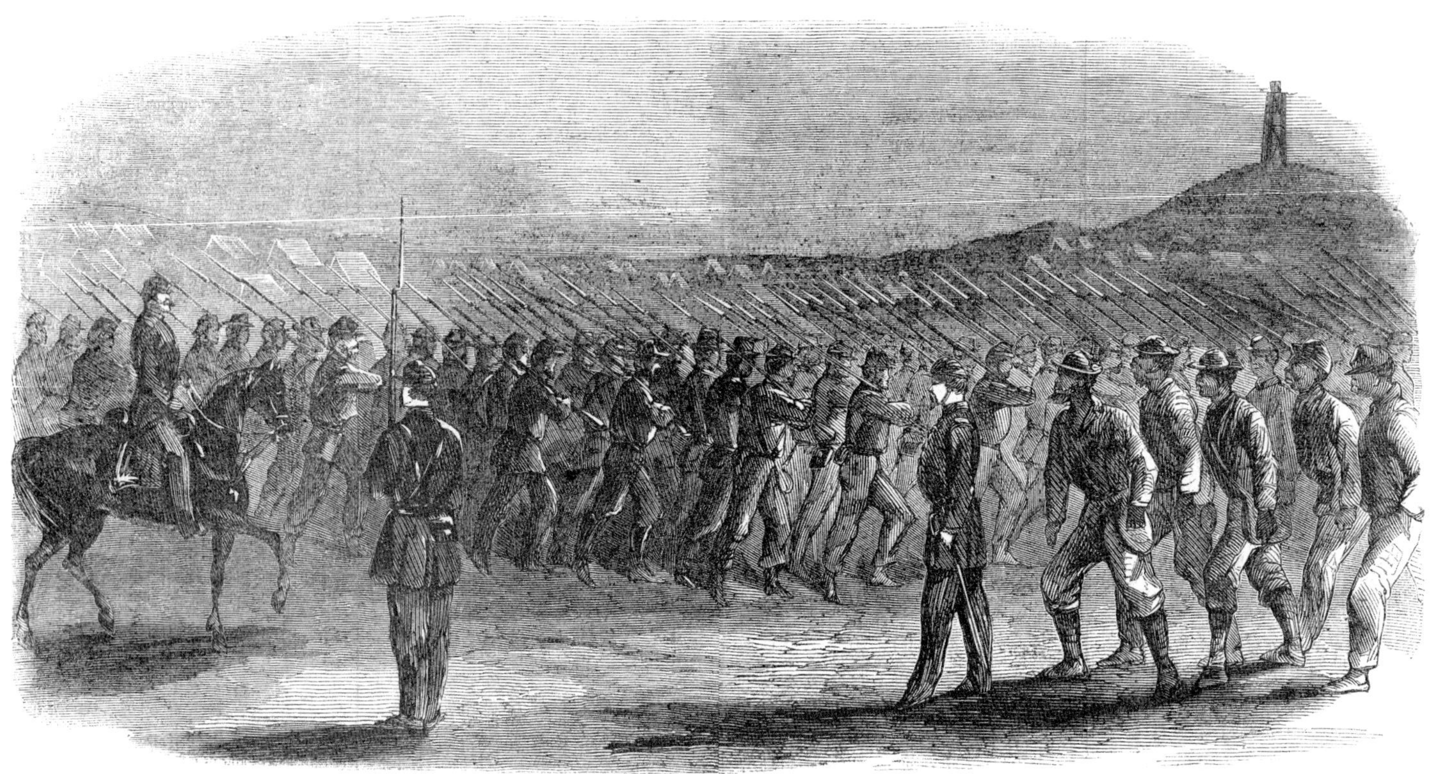

In The Trenches before Wagner

Artist: unknown
Harper's Weekly

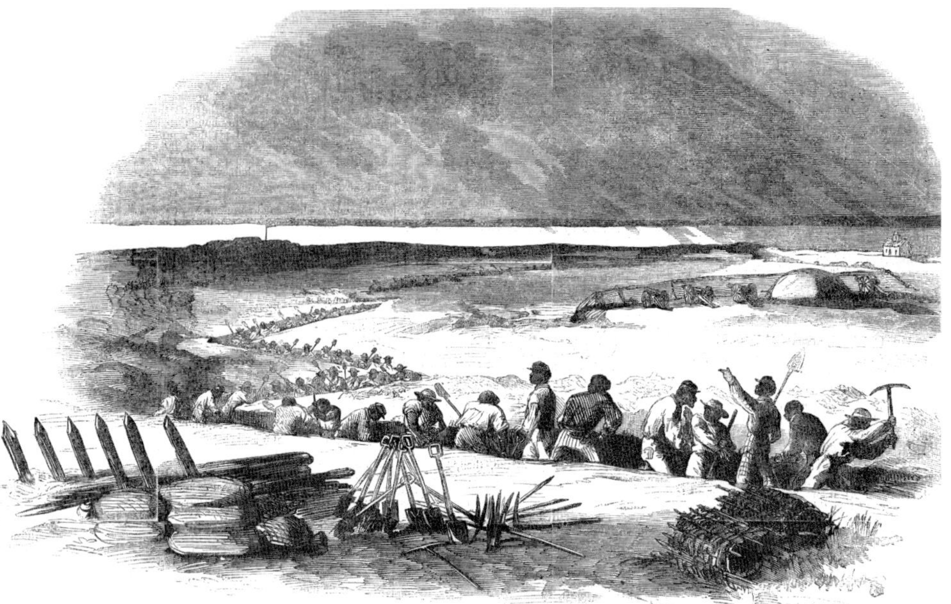

After the failure of the first assault on Battery Wagner, Gen. Quincy Gillmore determined his best course of action was to initiate a siege on the formidable Confederate position. He and his engineers designed a series of zig-zag trenches to be installed as a means of advancing his batteries against Wagner. The first batteries were set up 1,600 yds. from Battery Wagner, and the long, grueling process of advancing foot by foot began.

The conditions were anything but favorable for this work. The workers digging the trenches, called fatigue parties, were under constant gunfire from batteries at Wagner and James Island. Being on a sandy island virtually at sea level, it was difficult to dig far without striking water. The heavy guns had to be moved by as many as 100 men with horses and mules as the batteries advanced through the sand. Once the advance got within 1,000 yds. of Battery Wagner, the Union troops also had to contend with the Confederate sharpshooters.

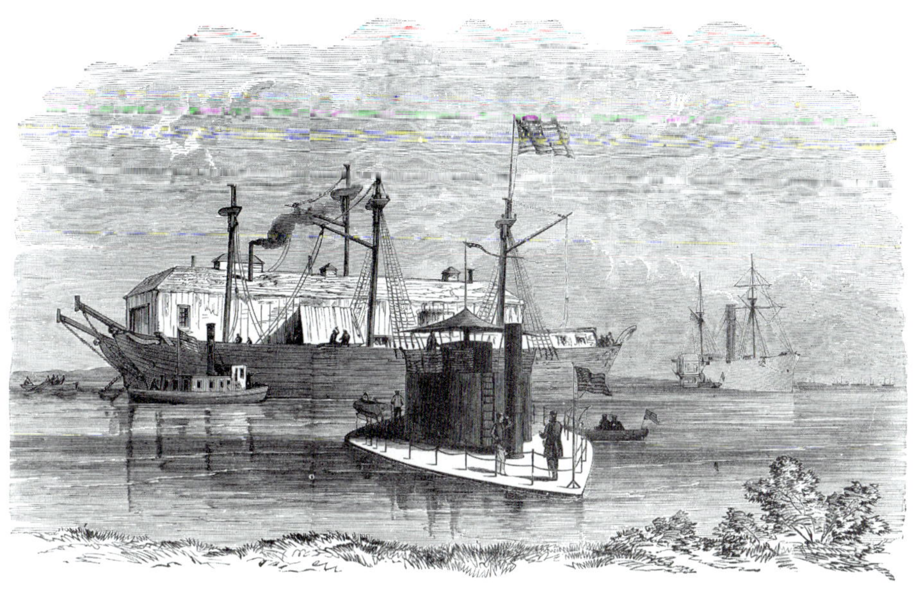

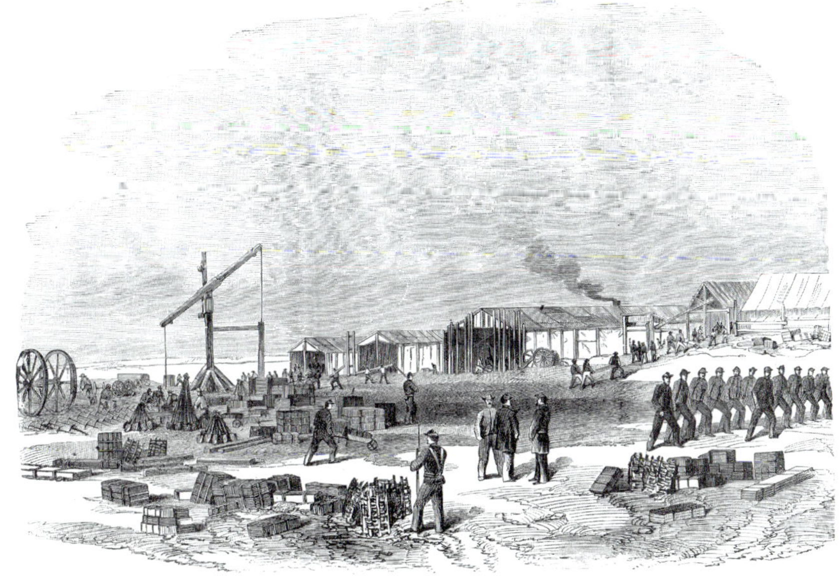

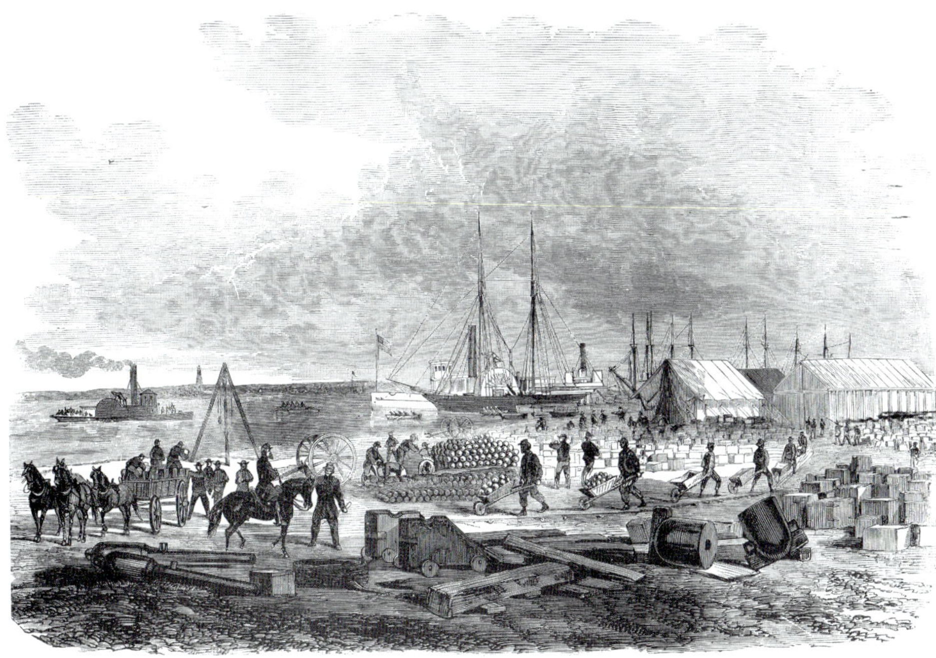

Machine Shop
Engineers and Supply Depot
Ordinance Depot

Artist: unknown

Frank Leslie's Illustrated Newspaper

A siege that combined the coordination of more than 11,000 men, close to 100 pieces of heavy artillery and a large fleet of ironclads and gunboats, required extensive support. On Folly Island and on the southern end of Morris Island, engineers and supply depots were established along with a massive ordinance depot. Additionally, the Union Navy required the use of a floating machine shop to support the ironclads in the fleet.

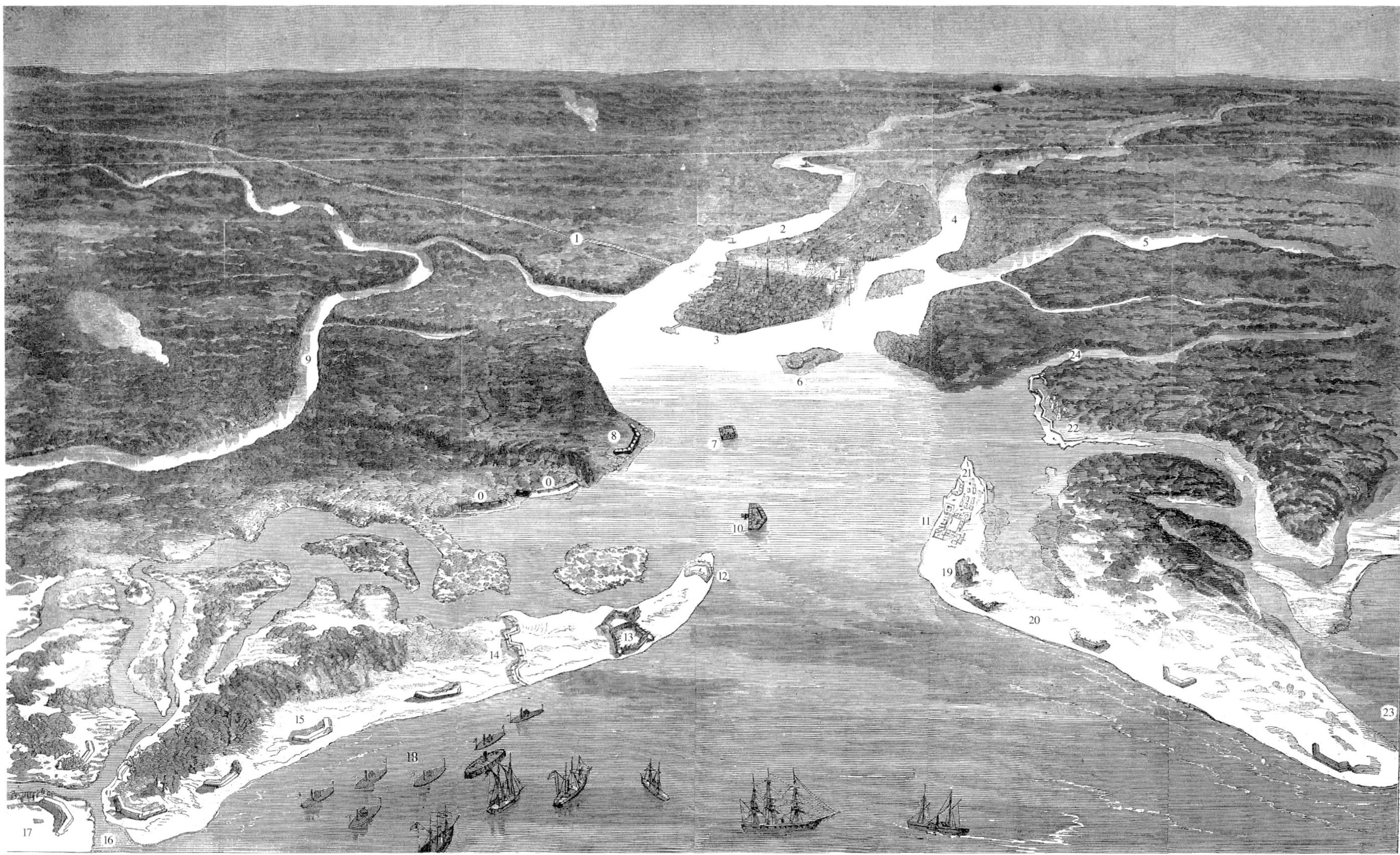

Bird's-Eye View of Charleston

Artist: unknown

Harper's Weekly

This *Harper's Weekly* illustration provides an excellent bird's-eye view of the harbor defenses, the Union Army and fleet, and the significance of them all to the harbor of Charleston during the long siege and blockade.

1– Charleston & Savannah Railroad
2– Ashley River
3– Charleston
4– Cooper River
5– Wando River
6– Castle Pinckney
7– Fort Ripley
8- Fort Johnson (James Island)
9– Stono River
10– Fort Sumter
11– Fort Moultrie
12– Battery Gregg (Cummings Point)
13– Fort Wagner
14– General Gillmore's advanced batteries
15– Captured works–Morris Island
16– Lighthouse Inlet
17– Union Battery–Folly Island
18– Ironclads and wooden ships
19– Hotel
20– Sullivan's Island and rebel batteries
21– Moultrieville
22– Mount Pleasant
23– Breach Inlet
24– Shem Creek
0,0– Rebel batteries on James Island

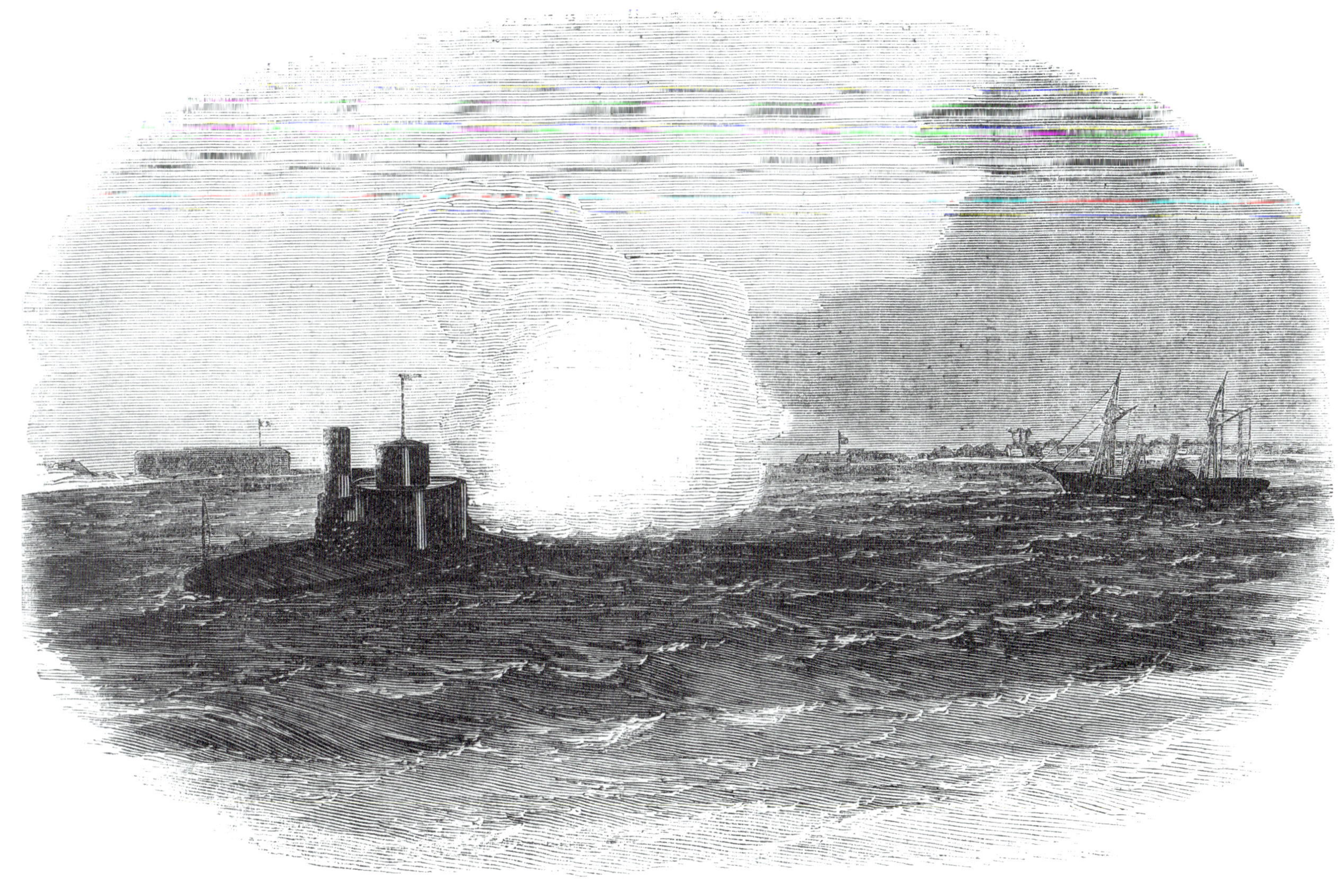

Sinking a Blockade Runner

Artist: unknown
Harper's Weekly

A large iron sidewheel steamer had made its way through the Union fleet on July 19, 1863. Capt. John Rogers, commanding the *Catskill*, moved into position to intercept the daring blockade runner. Firing his 11-in. and 15-in. guns, Rogers forced the steamer to alter course, eventually causing it to run ashore at Sullivan's Island. As the *Catskill* approached, her guns found their mark and set the steamer ablaze. In publishing the illustration, *Harper's Weekly* asserted: "[Let this be] a warning to all Anglo-Rebels to keep away from Charleston during the present siege."

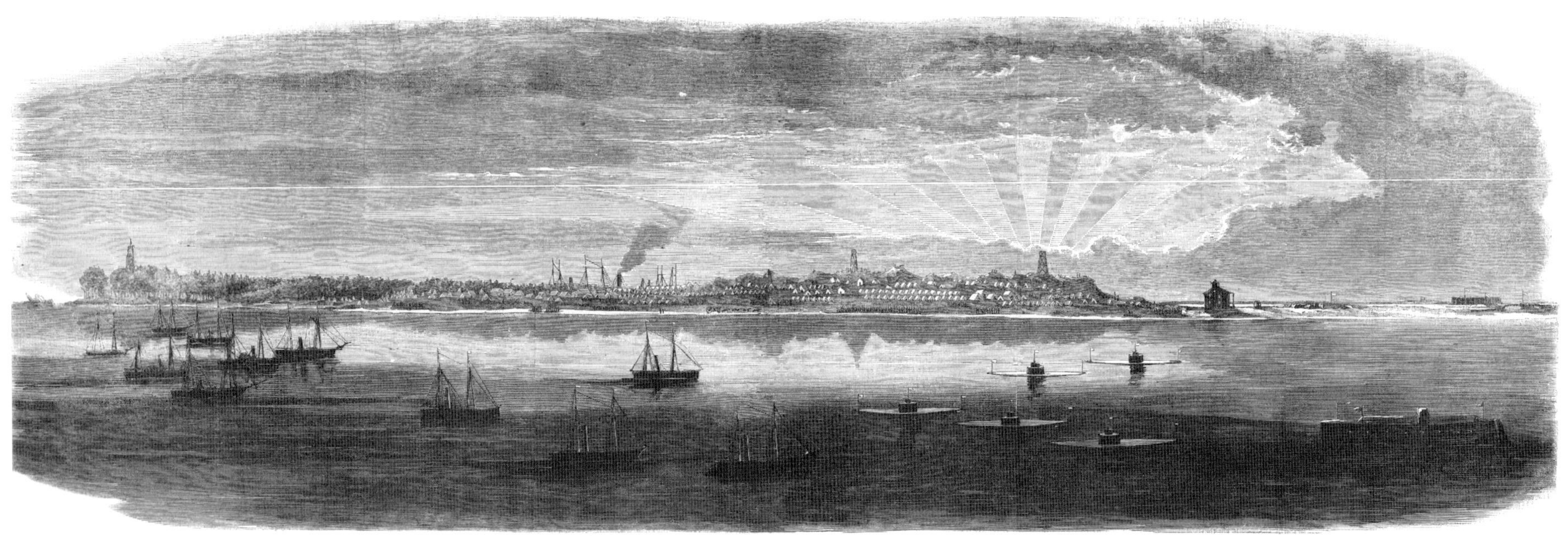

Union Troops on Morris Island

Artist: unknown
Harper's Weekly

Harper's Weekly published an interesting sketch done by an officer of the U.S. Navy. It provided a perspective of Morris Island from the shipping channel and harbor entrance. The Union Army took initial positions on Folly Island and the southern end of Morris Island, while the Union fleet anchored off the shipping channel and out of range of the Confederate guns. The ships' masts and smokestack in the left background belong to Union ships in the Folly River past Lighthouse Inlet. The building on the right side of the island is the lighthouse keeper's for the now destroyed Morris Island Lighthouse. Fort Sumter can be seen on the far right.

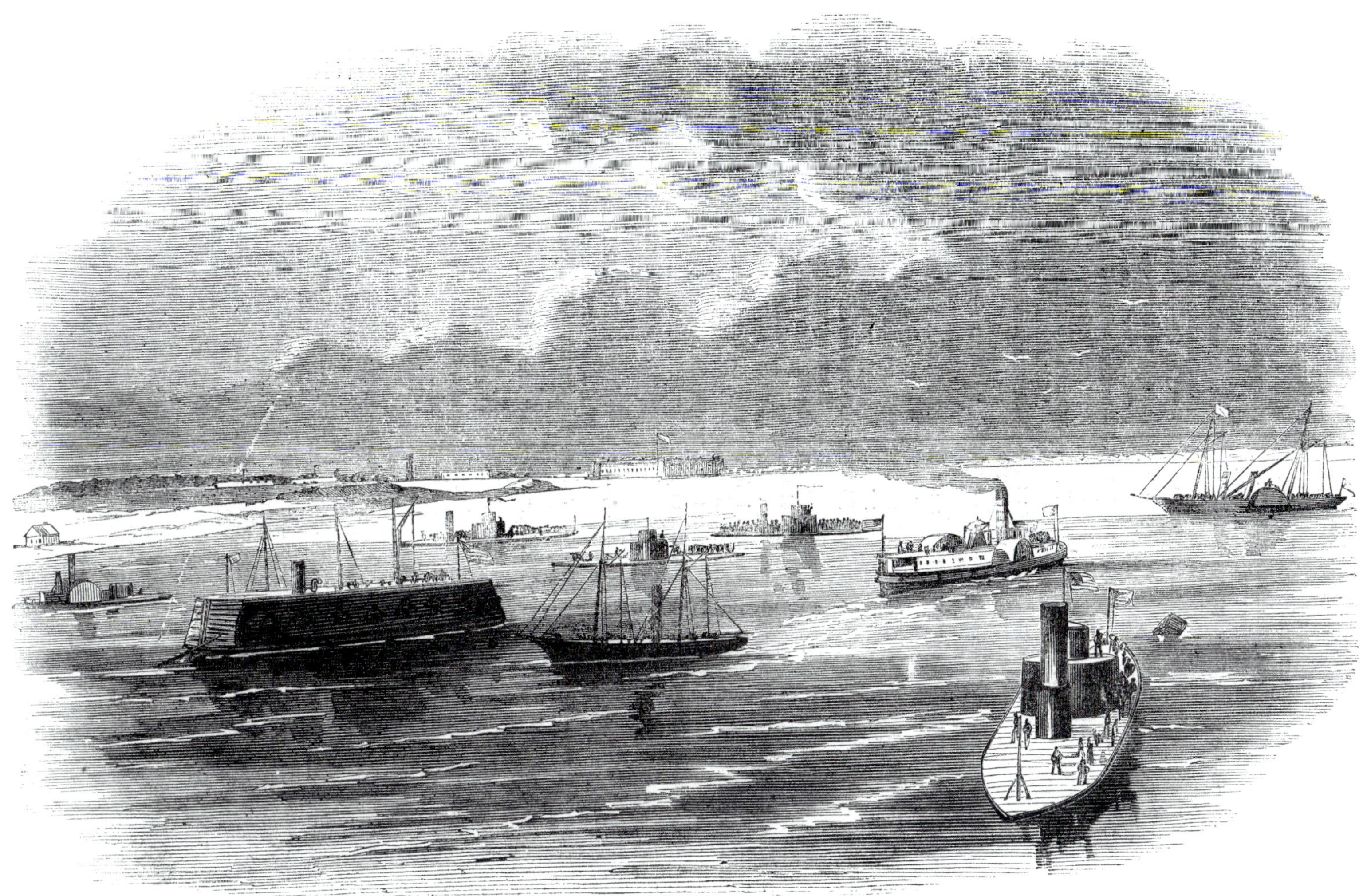

Exchange of Prisoners

Artist: unknown
Harper's Weekly

Gen. Quincy Gillmore sent two officers under a flag of truce to Battery Wagner to arrange a prisoner exchange on July 21, 1863. Brig.-Gen. P. G. T. Beauregard had instructed Brig.-Gen. Johnson Hagood at Wagner to negotiate the exchange, provided the disposition of the black Union prisoners was not be discussed. At the negotiations, the Union officers brought the body of Confederate Lt. John S. Bee, which was exchanged for the body of Col. Haldiman S. Putnam. It was agreed that the remaining prisoners, mostly wounded, would be exchanged on July 24 at 10 a.m. between ships off Morris Island. It was further agreed that a number of the Union prisoners would be returned home and released from further duty to account for the difference in the number of prisoners on both sides.

At the appointed time, the Confederate blockade runner *Alice*, loaded with 105 wounded Union prisoners, moved to the harbor. The Union Navy sent the *Cosmopolitan*, a hospital ship with 40 captured Confederates and five surgeons and assistant surgeons. The prisoners were exchanged; however, one Union prisoner died while aboard ship. The Union officers inquired about the noticeable absence of any black troops. The Confederate officers offered no comment and returned to Charleston with their men.

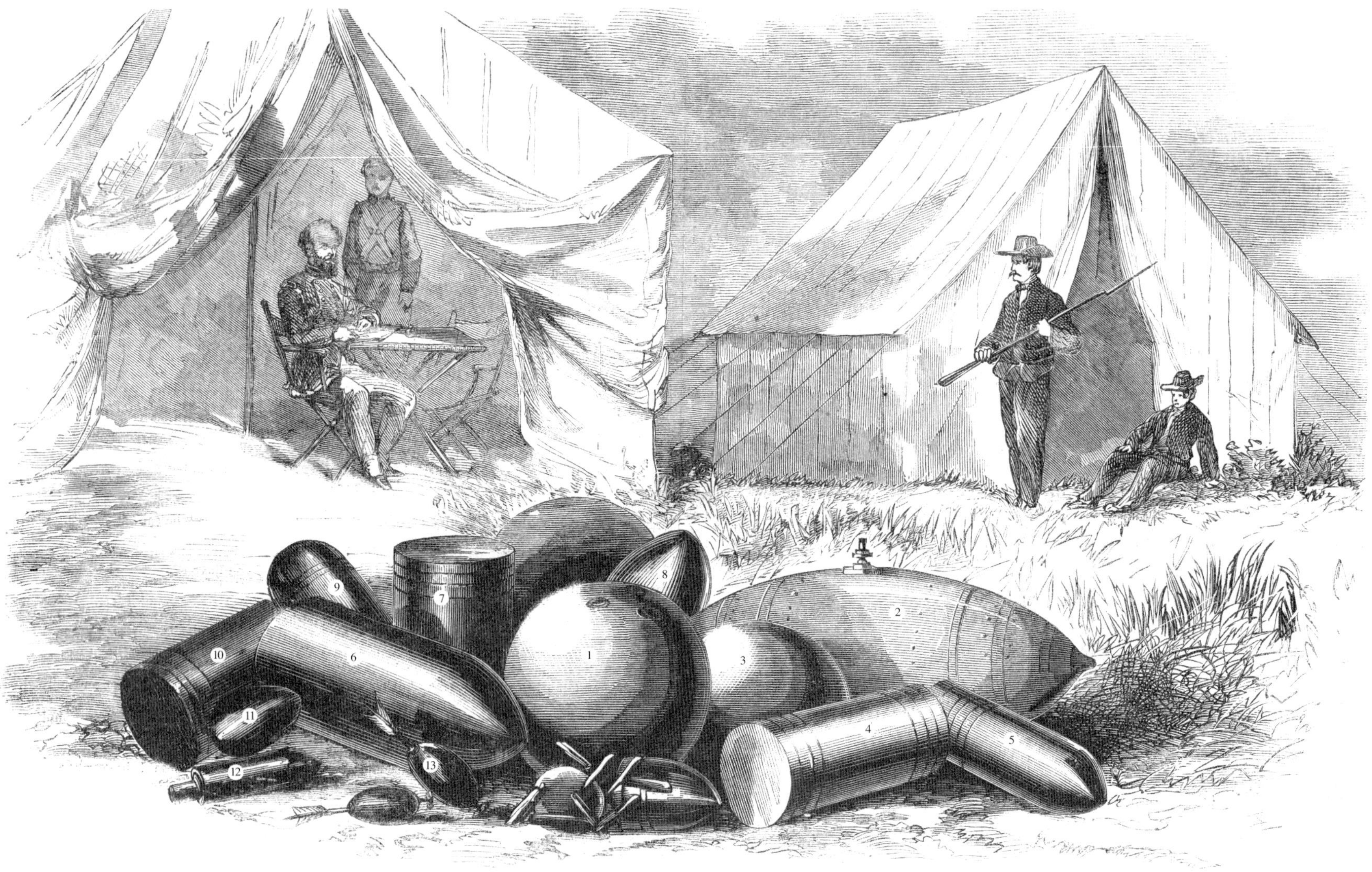

Shot and Shell

Artist: Theodore R. Davis
Harper's Weekly

During the siege of Charleston, there were as many types of shot and shell used as there were guns to fire them. Each type of ordinance had a specific purpose or held an advantage over other choices. *Harper's Weekly* artist Theo Davis sketched the many different types of Union and Confederate shells at Gen. Quincy Gillmore's headquarters.

1 – 15-in. shell
2 – Torpedo
3 – Mortar shell
4 – Brooks (rebel)
5 – 100-pounder Parrot
6 – Brooks (rebel)
7 – Brooks (rebel)
8 – 200-pounder (rebel)
9 – Whitworth Belt (rebel)
10 – Brooks (rebel)
11 – James
12 – Anglo-rebel
13 – Hand-grenade
14 – Greek fire

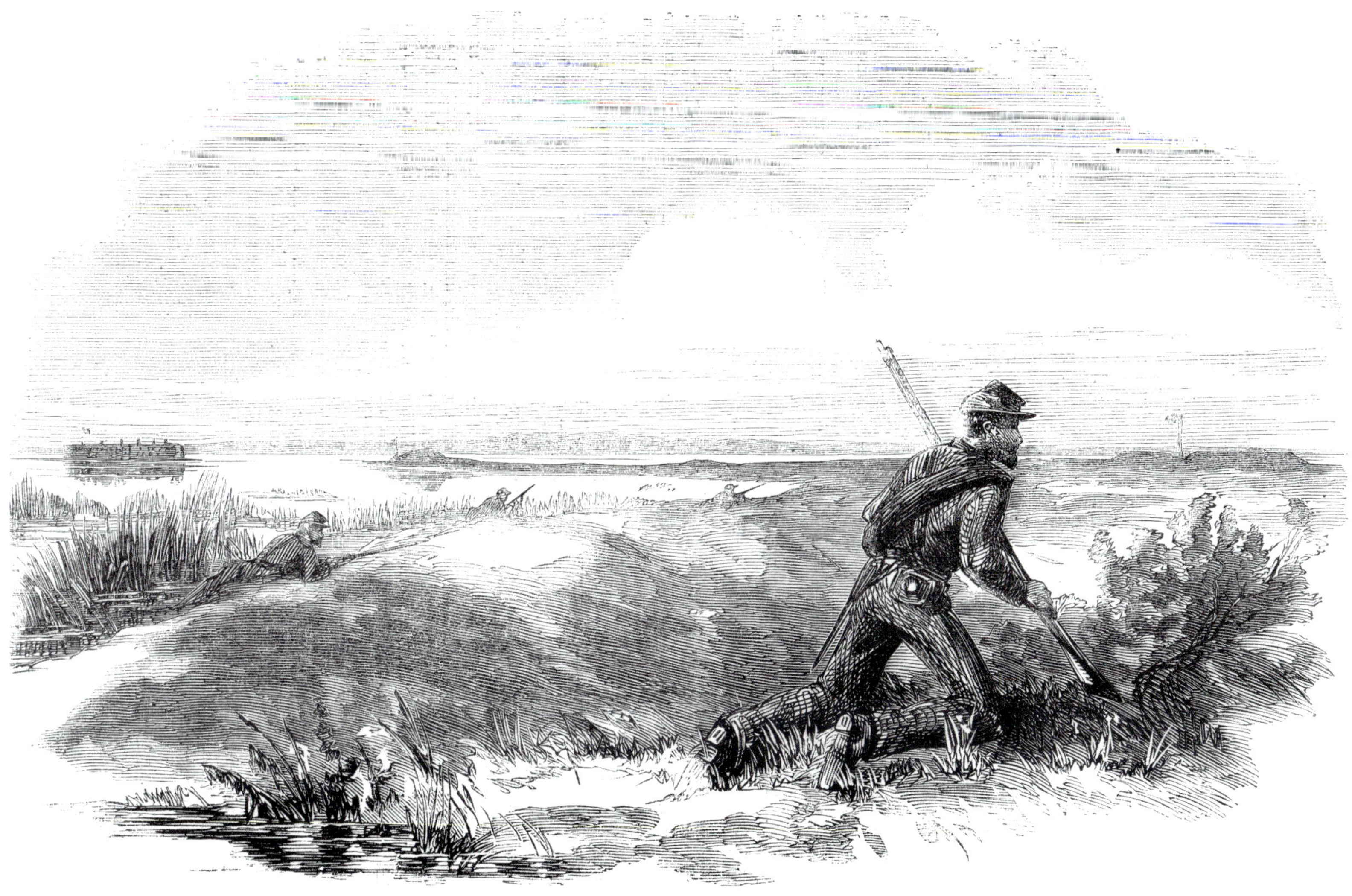

Union Sharpshooters

Artist: unknown
Harper's Weekly

Capt. Thomas B. Brooks wrote to Gen. Quincy Gillmore, complaining about the Union sharpshooters. The letter is dated Aug. 2, 1863: "The present so-called sharpshooters are inefficient. First, they are not good shots; second, their arms are not in good condition; third, they are not sufficient in numbers, even if they were efficient; and fourth, they are not properly officered."

Gillmore ordered that all the Union troops participate in target-shooting contests to determine the best shots at their disposal. He further ordered, "These men [are] to be organized into a company, encamped by themselves, and provided with the best arms that can be procured." Approximately 60 men were selected and placed under the command of two officers who themselves were excellent marksmen.

This company of sharpshooters was placed on duty on Morris Island to shoot the defenders at Battery Wagner – when the opportunity presented itself.

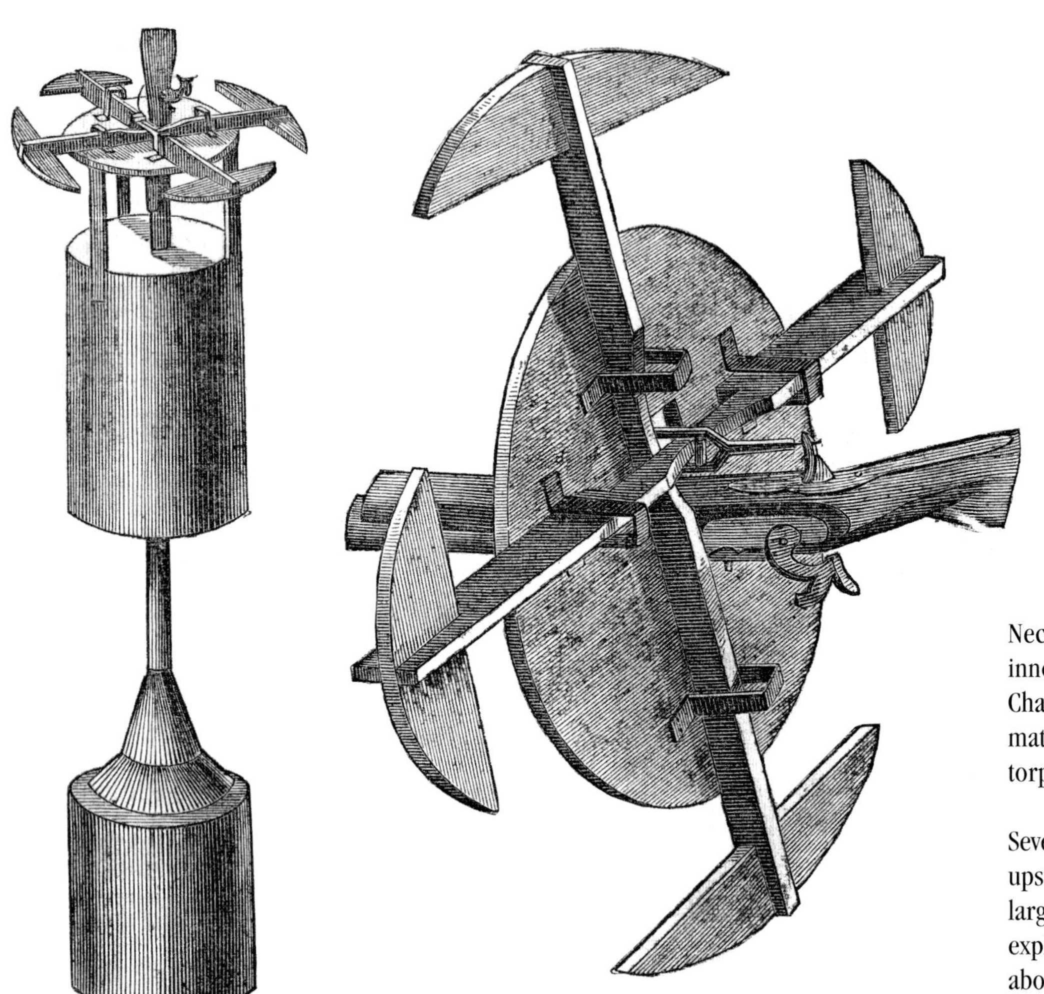

Rebel Torpedo

Artist: unknown
Harper's Weekly

Necessity being the mother of invention, engineering and military innovations cropped up in abundance during the course of the siege of Charleston. Where the Confederates might lack machine shops or raw materials, they simply improvised. Such was the case with a Confederate torpedo recovered from the Stono River on the night of Aug. 16, 1863.

Several Union gunships were in the Stono River and the Confederate soldiers upstream sent a surprise the way of the Union ships on the outgoing tide. A large explosion under the stern of the *Pawnee* shook the entire ship and exploded her launch. Two more explosions erupted nearby. Once the men aboard gathered themselves, they detected floating "torpedoes" in the water moving with the tide.

It appeared that the Confederates sent 10 torpedoes downriver in pairs, all connected by a rope several hundred feet in length. Two of the torpedoes floated to the bar and exploded there. Two others moved up the Folly River. One torpedo was carefully recovered for study.

The torpedo was made of two cylinders of tin with 60 lbs. of powder in the bottom and the empty cylinder on top, which acted as a buoy. The two cylinders were connected by an iron tube placed in the stock of a musket at the top. As the ropes connecting the torpedoes became entangled with the intended target and pulled tight, it would fire the trigger on the stock and ignite the powder in the cylinder.

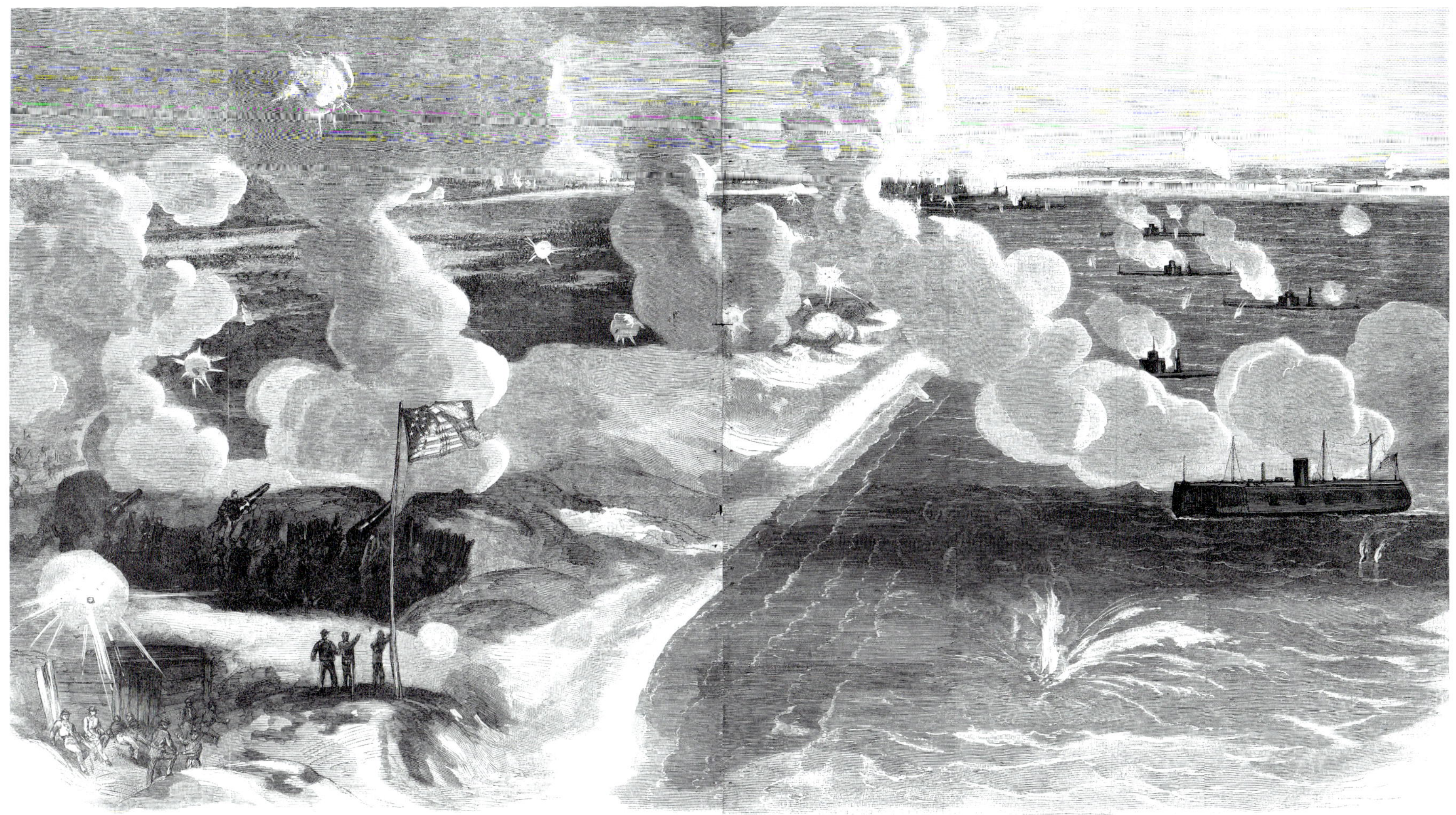

Bombardment of Forts Wagner and Sumter

Artist: unknown
Harper's Weekly

Gen. Quincy Gillmore and Adm. John A. Dahlgren planned the second major offensive for mid-August. At 5 a.m. on Aug. 17, the Union Army fired a shot toward Fort Sumter signaling the beginning of the attack. The Union land batteries followed with an intense bombardment directed at both Fort Sumter and Battery Wagner. By 7 a.m., Dahlgren sent the ironclads up the channel to fire on Wagner.

With the continued intensity of the fire, the small garrison at Wagner was forced to retreat to the safety of its bombproofs. This allowed the Union wooden gunboats to join the attack as well, further intensifying the firepower focused on the two Confederate positions.

The heavy pounding of solid shells at Fort Sumter crumbled the brickwork walls. The percussion shots, exploding on impact, pulverized the masonry. While at first devasting, the bombardment created a rubble barrier that, ironically, protected the fort. The rubble effectively served to absorb the impact of the shells. Battery Wagner's walls were mostly sand. By day's end, almost 700 shells had been fired by the Union Army and Navy at Fort Sumter, yet the small Confederate garrison endured.

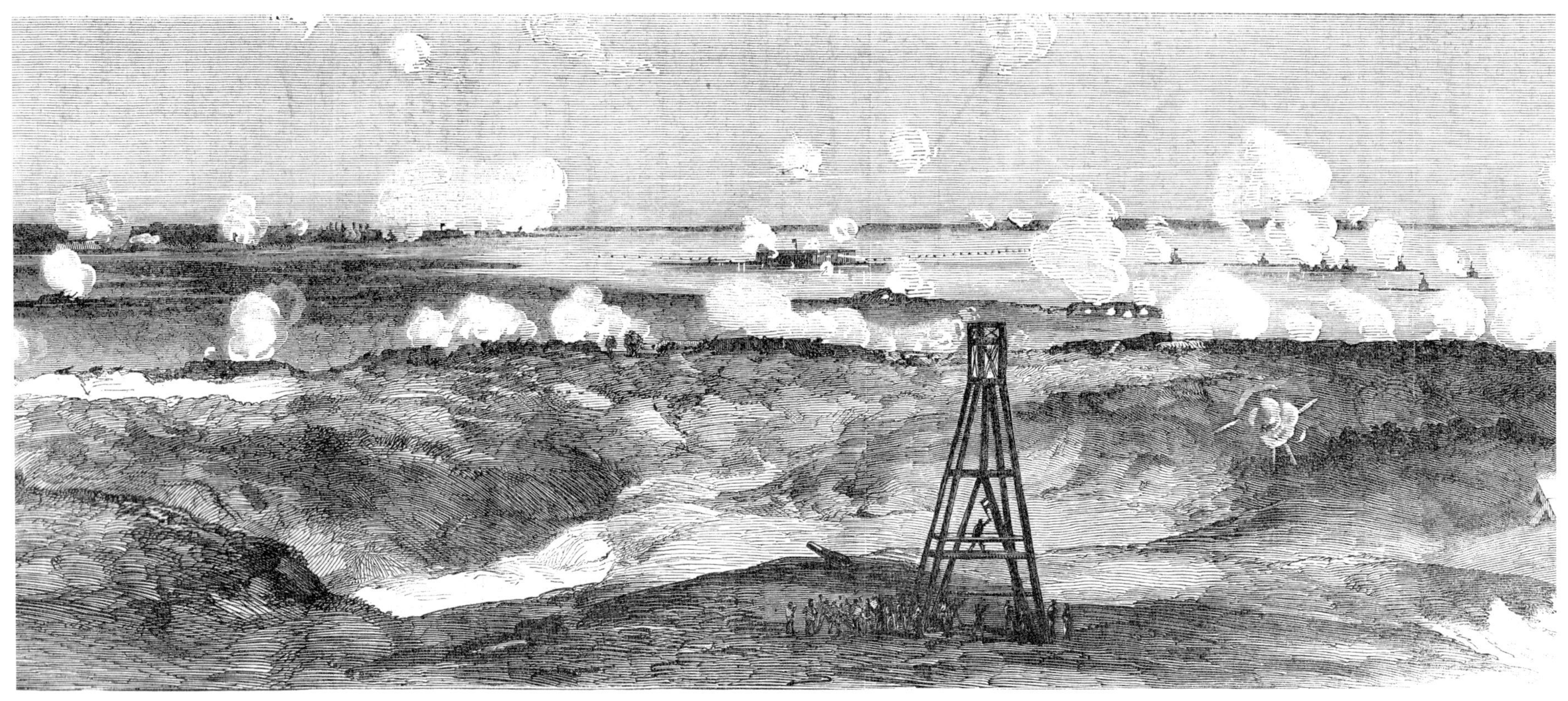

The Fleet Engaging Wagner and Gregg

Artist: Mr. J. P. Hoffman
Harper's Weekly

The illustration shows the Union fleet in action early Aug. 17, 1863. The ironclad monitors fired on batteries Wagner and Gregg, as well as Fort Sumter. The ironclad frigate *New Ironsides* focused her large and powerful guns, firing broadsides on Battery Wagner.

The intense action also allowed the Union troops on Morris Island to advance their work on the trenches moving ever closer to Wagner.

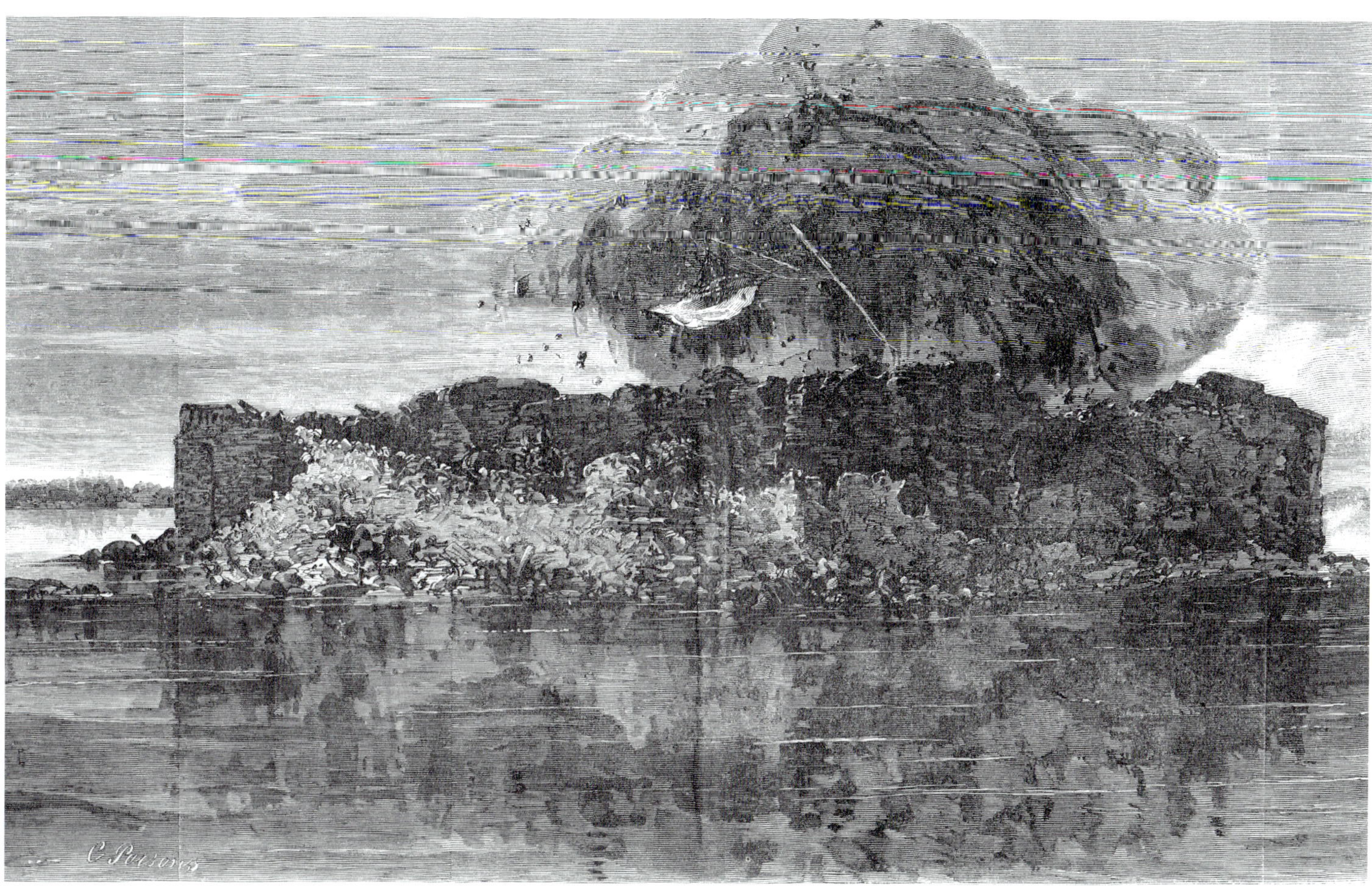

Fort Sumter after Six Days Bombardment

Artist: An "Occasional Contributor"
Harper's Weekly

The Union bombardment of Fort Sumter continued for six long days. During the campaign, more than 5,000 shells were fired at the island rubble held by the determined Confederates. Despite the relentless pounding, only three men were killed and 35 wounded at the fort.

In his report to federal authorities, Gen. Quincy Gillmore writes: "Fort Sumter is today a shapeless and harmless mass of ruins. My chief of artillery, Col. J. N. Turner, reports, 'By a longer fire it could be more completely a ruin and a mass of broken masonry, but could scarcely be more powerless in defense of the harbor.'" Time would show that both Gillmore and Turner underestimated the fortitude of the Confederate garrison to hold Fort Sumter and, with the land batteries, deter the progress of the Union fleet in forcing Charleston to surrender.

Confederate Brig. Gen. Roswell S. Ripley made his report to the chief-of-staff, Brig. Gen. Thomas Jordan:

> *The garrison of Fort Sumter, under Colonel Alfred Rhett and Major Ormsby Blanding, have stood to the defense of their castle with untiring fortitude and bravery. From the nature of the structure and the enemy's projectiles, the exposure during the period when subjected to fire has been great and extremely annoying, and yet every duty of repair and details have been carried on without interruption or undue delay.*

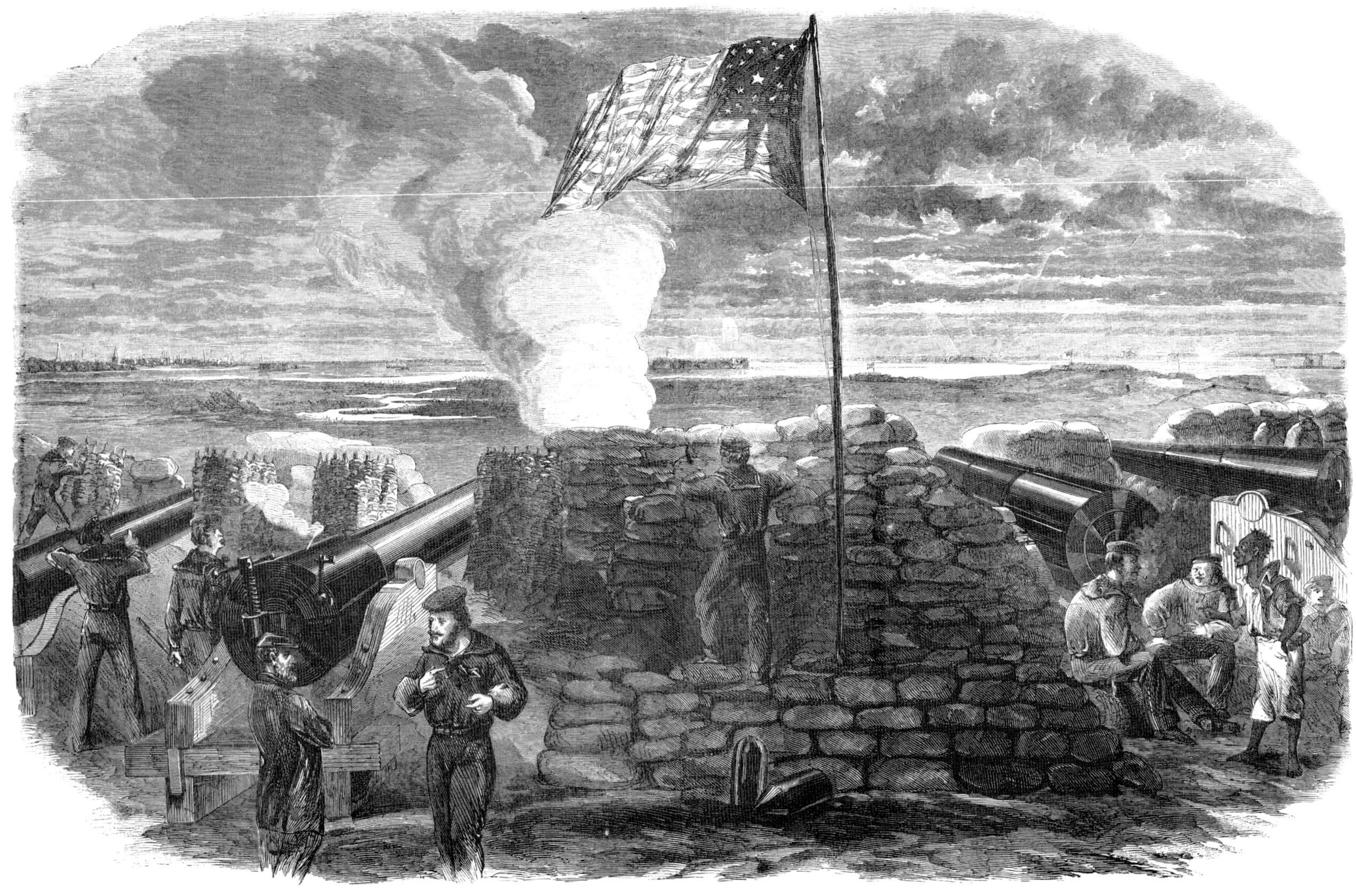

The Morning Call to the Rebels

Artist: Theodore R. Davis
Harper's Weekly

Theo Davis, the artist and correspondent for *Harper's Weekly*, was allowed to move freely through the Union lines and fortifications. At times, the newspaper would publish not only his compelling illustrations, but his written report as well. Such was the case in the Sept. 19 issue.

> *Many readers of the* Journal of Civilization [Harper's Weekly] *will say, as they read the caption to this letter, "sunrise gun; so the night is passed in quiet repose!" Not so, as the reader would certainly know, could he but see each morning the lifeless clay borne from the trenches, all its record being 'Killed in the saps.'*
>
> *The firing at night is not, however, quite so heavy as during the day—maybe the men are fatigued, maybe the gunners are not so sure of their aim. The break of the day is often the time for a salvo that seems to make the whole island shake.*

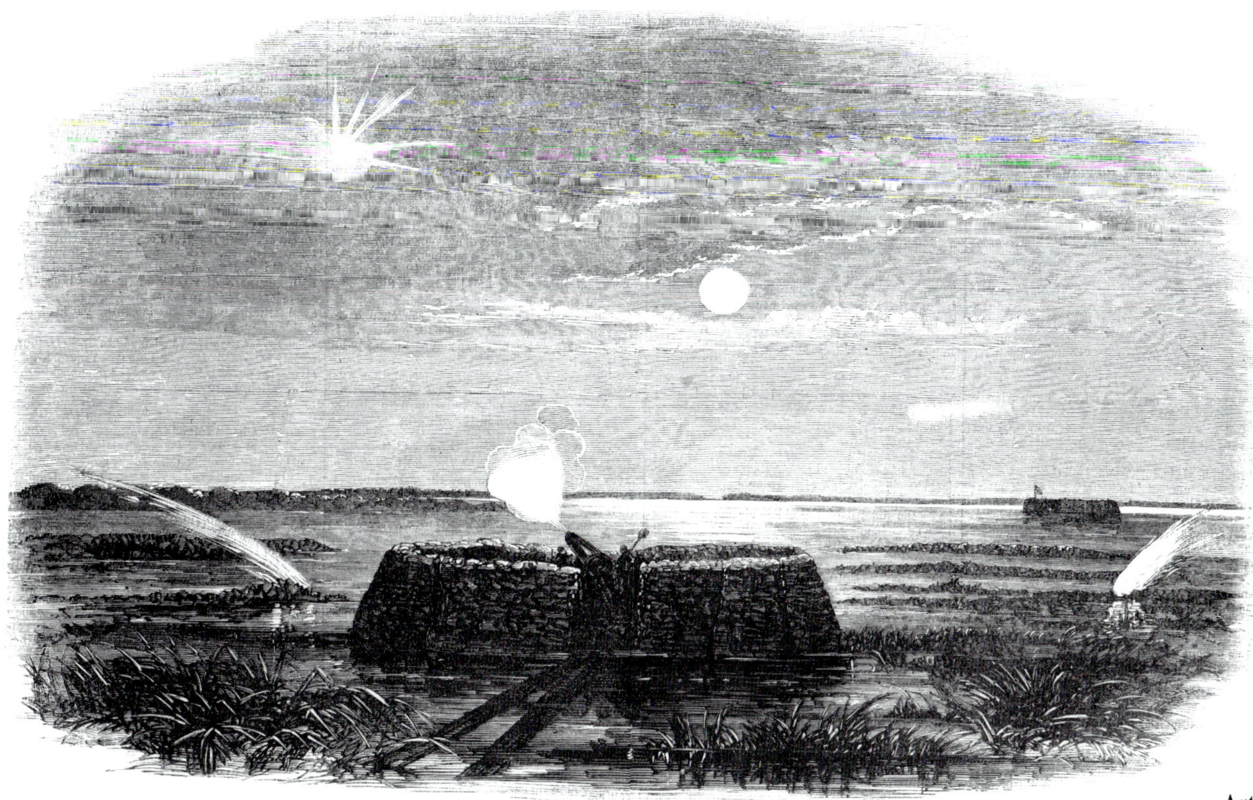

The Swamp Angel

Artist: Theodore R. Davis
Harper's Weekly

Unable to take Battery Wagner, the Union guns were too far from Charleston to fire on the city. Gen. Quincy Gillmore, knowing he could weaken the resolve of the Confederates if he could shell the city, ordered Col. Edward Serrell of the 1st New York Engineers to find a spot between Morris Island and James Island where they could reach Charleston. With only marsh between the islands and the mud in places 12-ft.-deep, building such a battery posed a serious challenge.

An exasperated lieutenant under Serrell actually requisitioned 20 men 18-ft. tall to do the job. He then requested that the regimental surgeon splice three 6-ft. men together to give him his 18-ft.-tall men.

After 17 days of testing and planning, Serrell designed a parapet of logs and sandbags to surround the gun platform that would essentially "float." To build the parapet, soldiers had to carry more than 13,000 sandbags, weighing some 800 tons, across a 2-ft.-wide 1,700-ft.-long wooden plank causeway in the oppressive Charleston summer heat. One Union soldier remarked, "We're building a pulpit on which a Swamp Angel will preach." The name "Swamp Angel" stuck, but this was meant to be an angel of death for those in Charleston.

To reach Charleston, the gun was elevated to an angle never before used for the large 150-lb. shells fired by the Parrott gun. At 1:30 a.m. on Aug. 22, 1863, the Swamp Angel sent its first shot shrieking into the city. That night, a total of 16 shells were fired into Charleston. Ten of the shells were laced with "Greek fire," an incendiary chemical that was an early form of napalm.

The shelling of Charleston resumed on the evening of Aug. 23. A hairline crack developed in the Swamp Angel, a trait that was characteristic of the larger Parrott guns. In an effort to continue the shelling, two lanyards were tied together on the gun. As each shot was readied, the men moved outside the battery before firing in case the gun exploded. Finally, on the 13th shot of that evening, the 36th shot to be fired on Charleston from the Swamp Angel, the angel of death met her own demise. The gun's barrel could no longer contain the force of the 150-lb. shell, and it burst.

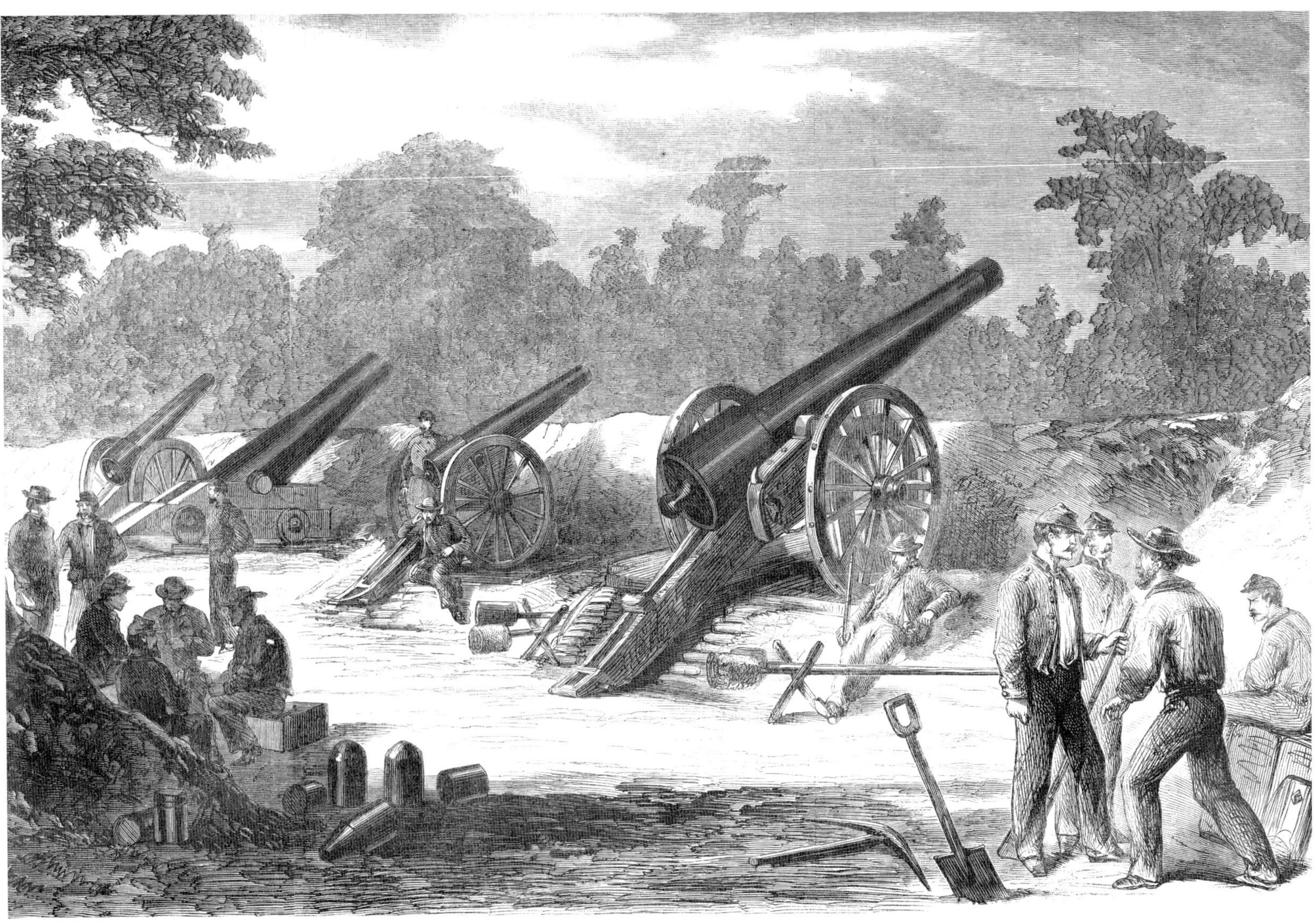

The New Black Island Batteries

Artist: Theodore R. Davis
Harper's Weekly

After the experience with the "Swamp Angel," Gen. Quincy Gillmore ordered a four-gun battery be established on nearby Black Island. Like the site of the Swamp Angel, Black Island was located between Morris Island and James Island, 4.5 miles from Charleston. The guns at Black Island could reach Charleston, but once the Union Army controlled all of Morris Island, the battery was used most often in exchanging fire with the many Confederate batteries on James Island.

Black Island still exists today, though it is privately owned and more commonly known as Block Island.

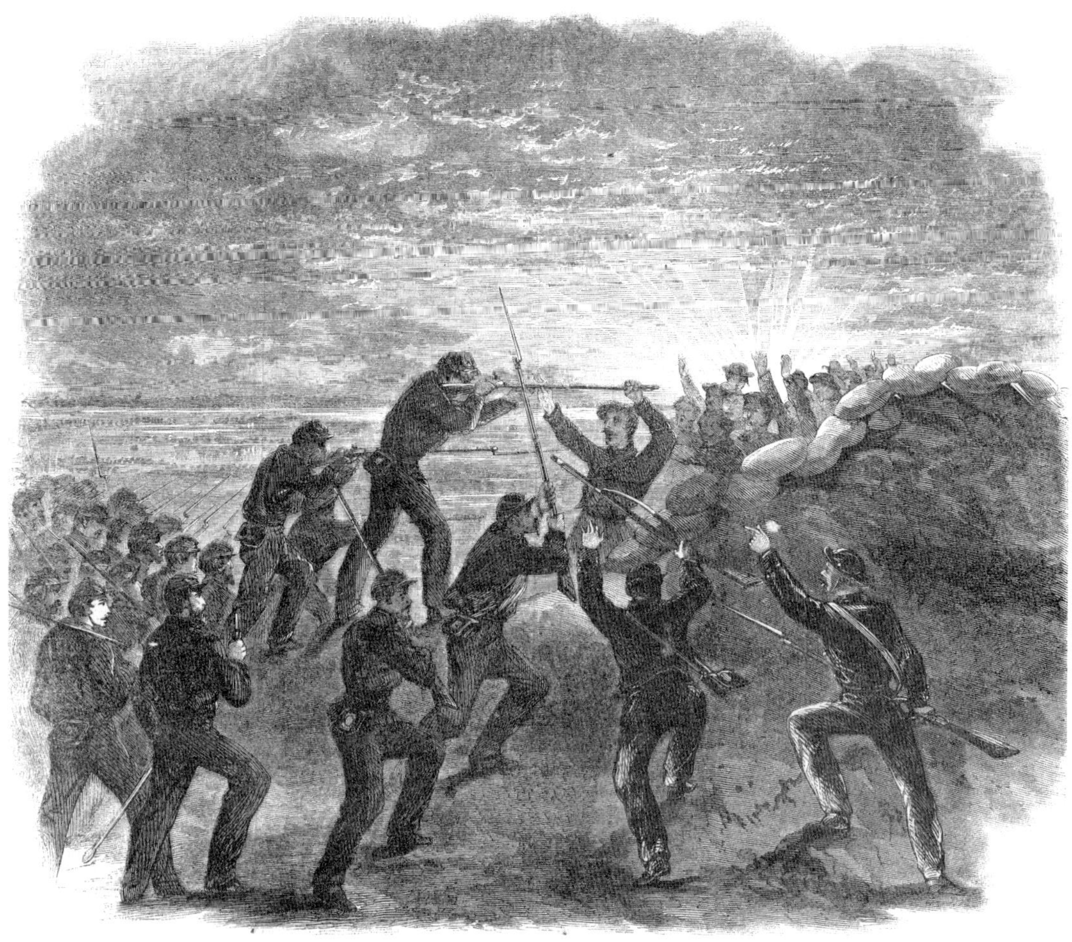

Charge upon the Confederate Rifle-Pits

Artist: Theodore R. Davis
Harper's Weekly

The Confederate command at Battery Wagner had designed an ingenious system of defense after the frontal assault by the Union Army in July. Both Battery Wagner on the north end of Morris Island and the advancing Union positions on the south end were located on the beach front. Extending from Battery Wagner to the south was a significant section of sand peppered with various types of torpedoes. Still further south was a first defense of rifle-pits dug into the sand running the entire width of the highland from the beach to the marsh and manned by Confederate infantry units. The strategic placement of these rifle-pits and the sharpshooters in them significantly slowed the federal advance on Battery Wagner.

The federal advance through the trench system had progressed enough that an assault of the rifle-pits seemed plausible to the Union command. On Aug. 26, 1863, the 24th Massachusetts prepared to advance. Each man had his weapon, extra ammunition and two shovels strapped to his back. If the assault were successful, the regiment would need to quickly dig in to protect itself from the fire that would surely come from Battery Wagner.

At 6:30 p.m., the 24th Massachusetts Volunteers, led by Col. Francis Osbourne and supported by the 3rd New Hampshire Volunteers, charged and quickly overran the 86 men of the 61st North Carolina who were manning the rifle-pits. Nineteen of the Confederates escaped, but the other 67 were taken prisoner, not wanting to attempt an escape through the torpedo infested sand to the safety of Wagner. Immediately, the Union soldiers began digging in the sand to improve their cover from Wagner. The work was so urgent that the Confederate prisoners were forced to dig as well.

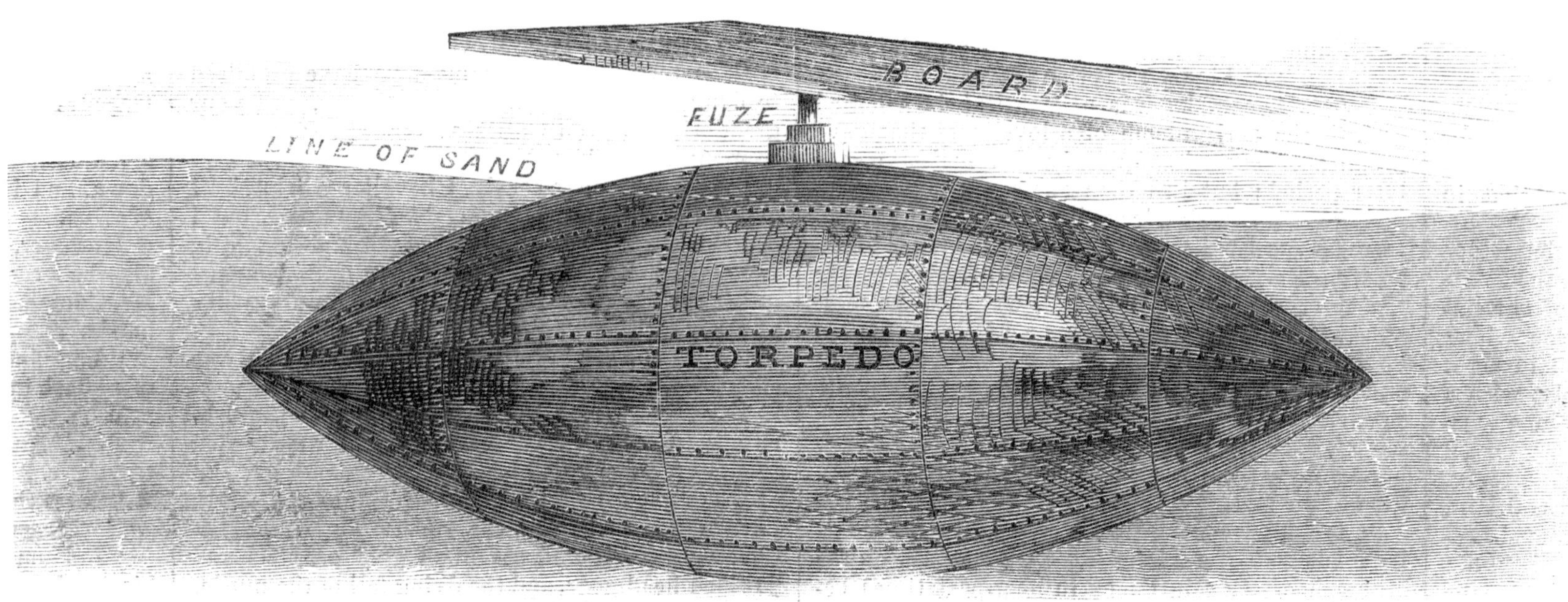

Torpedo in the Sand

Artist: Theodore R. Davis
Harper's Weekly

Once the Union Army controlled the Confederate rifle-pits in front of Battery Wagner, the next major obstacle had to be confronted. Between the Union position and the moat in front of Wagner's walls was a 200-yd. stretch of sand protected by torpedoes. Before the Union trench workers could continue their advance, the torpedoes would have to be removed or disabled — no small task under the watchful eyes of the Confederate sharpshooters on the walls at Wagner. At considerable time and expense, the Union strategy was to keep enough shells firing onto Wagner to force the majority of the Confederates into the bombproof and off the walls, thereby decreasing the threat to their men working in the torpedo field.

Artist Theo Davis illustrates here the predominant type of torpedo the Union Army encountered. Originally designed for marine use, the explosive was a 10-gal. keg with cones on the end, filled with powder. A board or other cover was placed over the plunger on top. Any pressure on the board would set off the charge. The other two types of torpedoes made use of 15-in. navy shells or 24-lb. cannon shells placed in a cylinder and set off by pressure on a plunger or percussion cap.

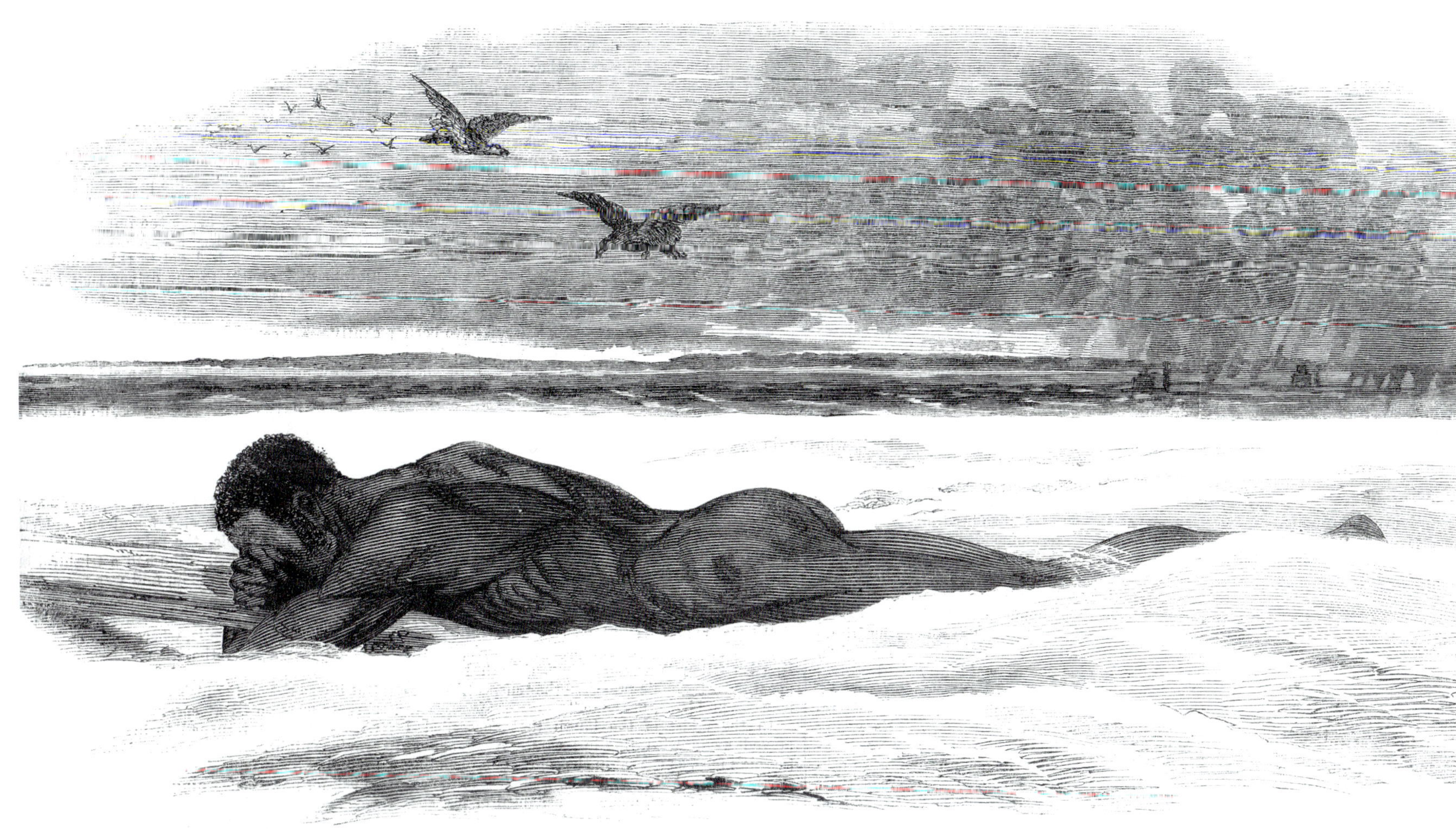

The Rebel's Last Device

Artist: Theodore R. Davis
Harper's Weekly

This illustration, published in *Harper's Weekly* and reported in many northern newspapers, inflamed the public and readers in the Union states. Whether by mistake or by intention, the erroneous story caused quite a stir. On Aug. 26, *Harper's* artist and reporter Theo Davis was in the trenches with the Union soldiers at a forward position. Davis and several soldiers witnessed a black soldier laying on one of the boards over a Confederate torpedo. Quickly realizing he was dead, they were led to the conclusion that the Confederates were baiting the Union soldiers, trying to clear the field by treating the man as a decoy.

The issue was later cleared up by a Union officer, Capt. Frederick Graef, who had been supervising a unit defusing torpedoes the previous day. Apparently, a corporal with the 3rd U.S. Colored Troops was near a torpedo and set it off. The intense explosion ripped away most of his clothing and he landed 25 yards away with his arms resting on the board at yet another torpedo. The man was dead, but the detail could not yet reach the body to remove it.

By the time the story reached many papers in the North, the real story was so corrupted and embellished that the published reports indicated that the Confederates were tying live prisoners to torpedoes as decoys.

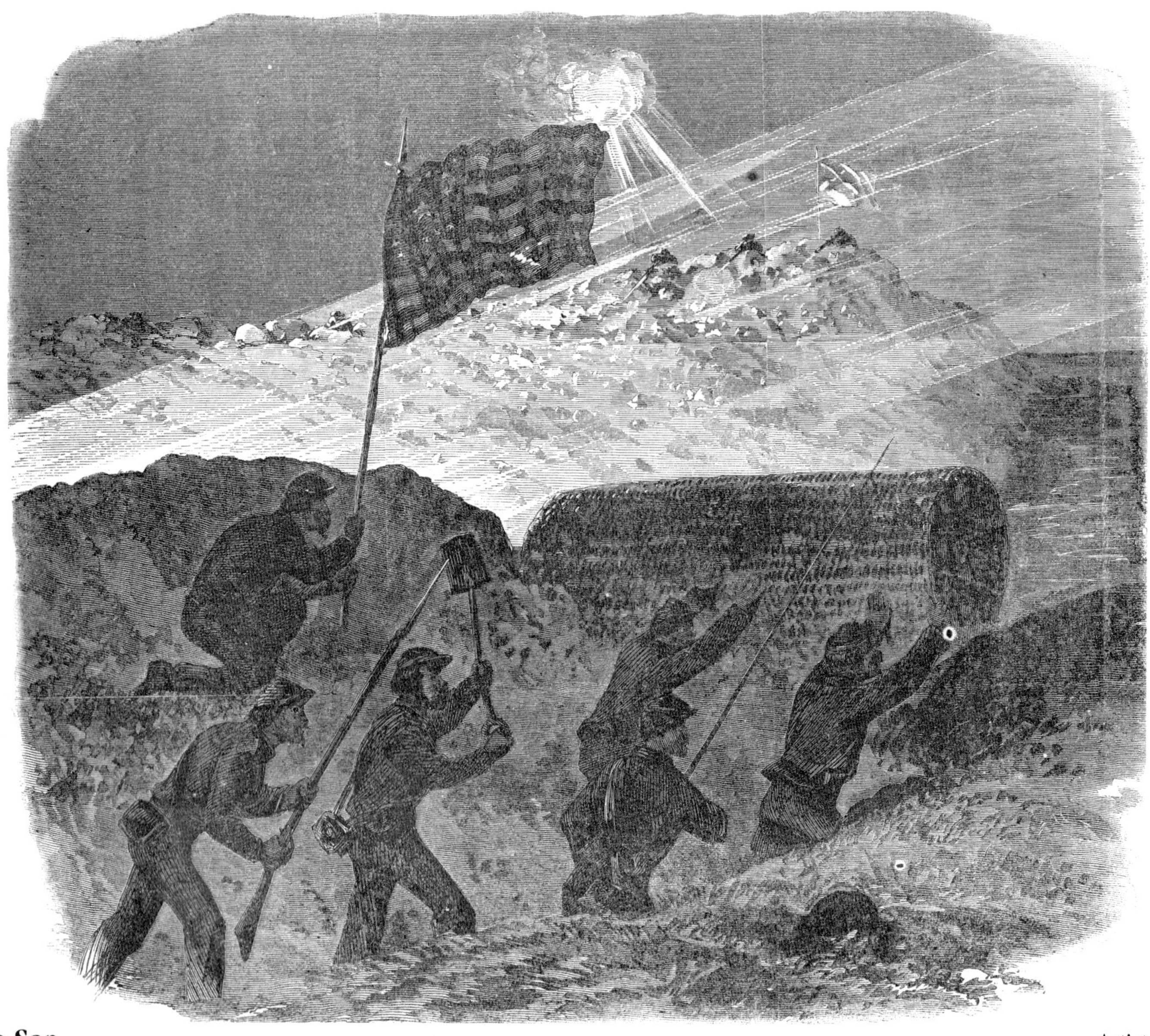

The Head of the Sap

Artist: Theodore R. Davis
Harper's Weekly

The sap roller was a particularly effective innovation by the Union engineers that allowed some degree of protection from the Confederate sharpshooters for the soldiers digging the trenches. The sap roller was a large wooden cylinder filled with sand. Nine-ft. long and 4-ft. in diameter, it was moved just ahead of the trench work to provide cover for those men behind. The roller was placed and moved by a sapping brigade, which consisted of eight men, called artificers, and two non-commissioned officers divided into two squads, alternating duty. The trench dug behind the sap roller was generally 4-ft.-wide and 2-ft.-deep.

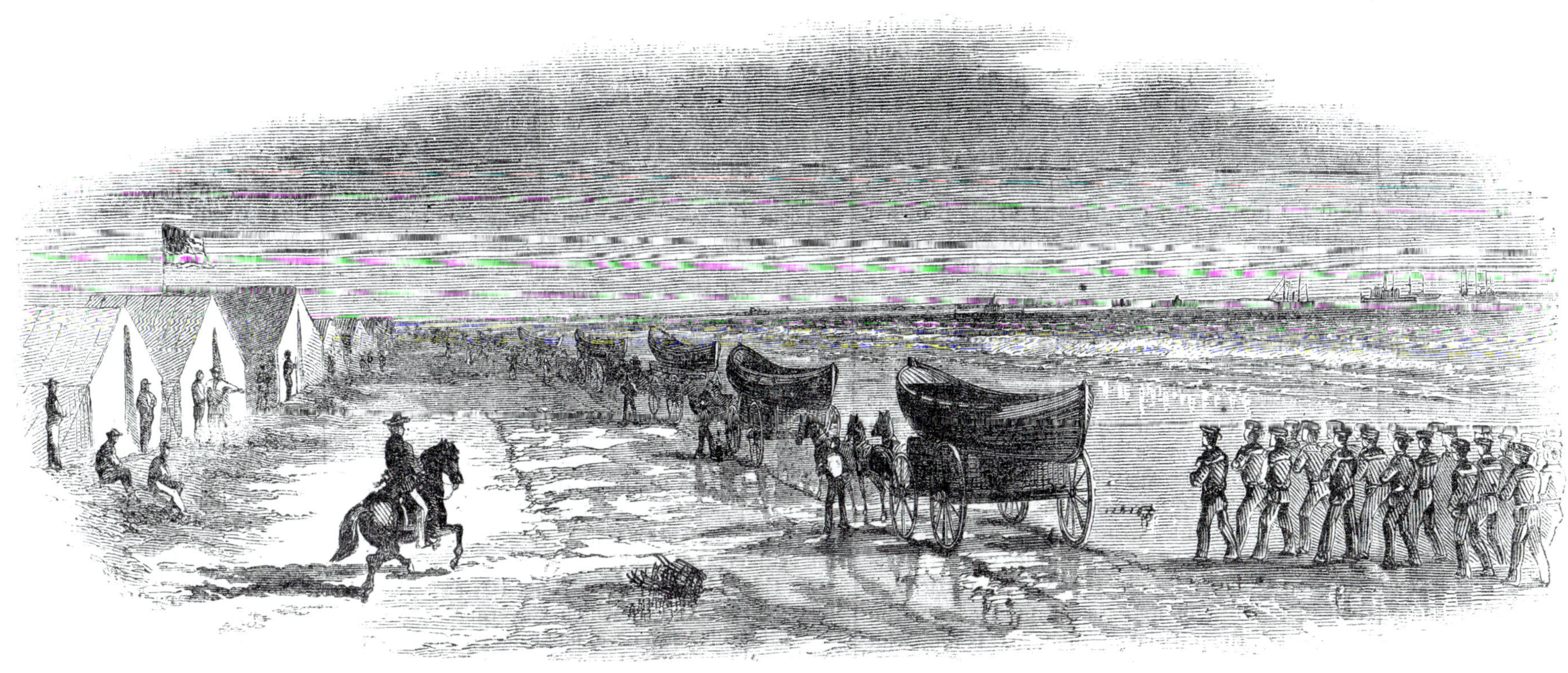

The Boats for the Attack under way

Artist: Theodore R. Davis
Harper's Weekly

In an effort to end the Confederate presence on Morris Island, Gen. Quincy Gillmore planned a night attack on Battery Gregg. His plan was to land troops at Battery Gregg by boat, surprising the Confederate garrison, then seizing control of the fortification. After spiking the guns and destroying the magazine, the troops would withdraw before the Confederates elsewhere could respond. This would serve to further isolate the garrison at Battery Wagner, increasing the chance for Union victory in the eventual assault there.

On the evening of Sept. 5, 1863, the Union force of five units commanded by Major Oliver Sanford of the 7th Connecticut assembled at the Union camp on the south end of Morris Island. Adm. John A. Dahlgren assisted by supplying several hundred sailors to act as oarsmen for the boats.

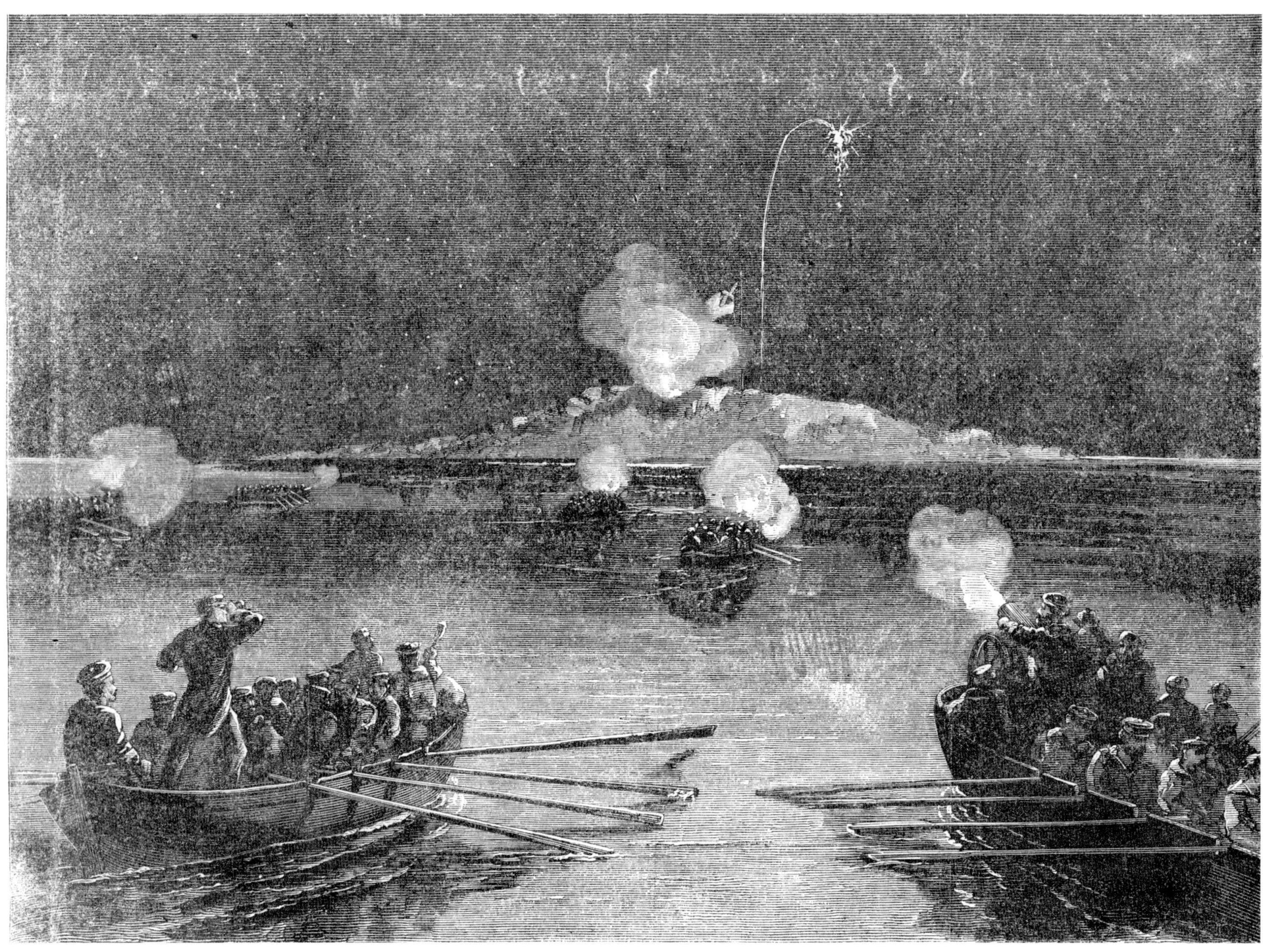

Attack on Battery Gregg

Artist: Theodore R. Davis
Harper's Weekly

The Confederate command had considered the possibility of an infantry attack on Battery Gregg initiated by a boat landing at Cummings Point. As a precaution, Confederate commanders strengthened the garrison at Battery Gregg and positioned infantry in the sand-hills between Gregg and Battery Wagner.

To divert the attention of the Confederates, the Union Army launched a mortar assault against Battery Wagner. Shortly after 1 a.m., Capt. H. R. Lesesne at Battery Gregg spotted 15 to 20 boats carrying Union troops. The boats were approaching his position near the junction of Vincent and Schooner creeks. Major James Gardner of the 27th Georgia ordered his infantry to open fire on the invaders. Intense fire ushered forth from Battery Gregg with supporting fire from Fort Moultrie and Battery Bee, forcing the Union boats to withdraw without ever landing and mounting an attack on Battery Gregg.

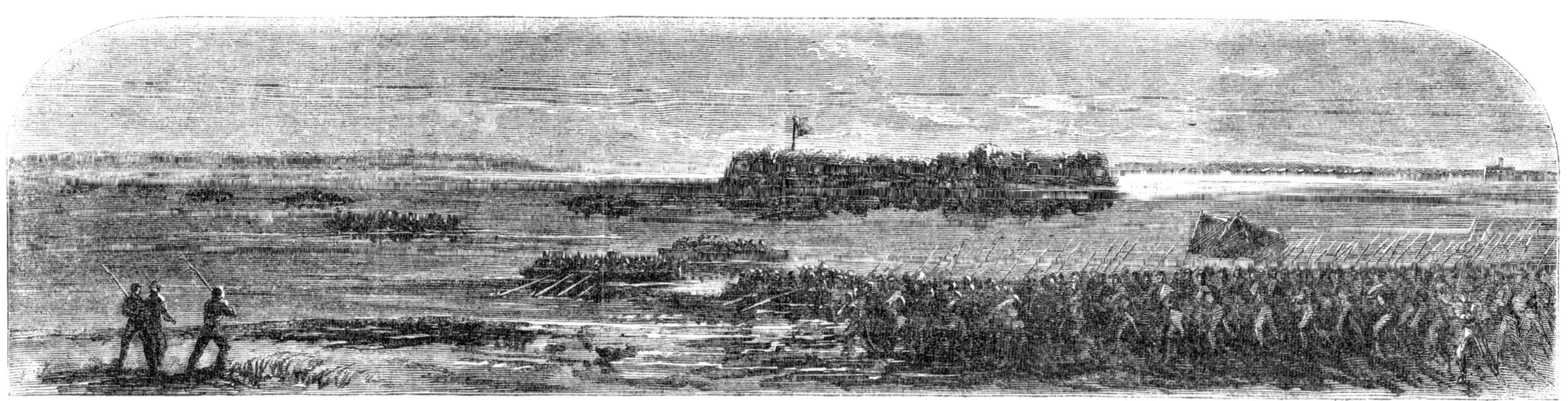

Evacuation of Morris Island

Artist: Theodore R. Davis
Harper's Weekly

With the fall of the rifle-pits and the approaching Union trenches, Gen. P. G. T. Beauregard and his staff undertook plans to evacuate Morris Island. Confederate commanders feared that if a federal assault on Wagner or Gregg were successful, many needed troops would be lost or captured. The thwarted Union attack on Battery Gregg on Sept. 5 confirmed such fears. The sappers continued their advance and the ironclads were unrelenting in their bombardment of Battery Wagner. It was clear, Wagner could no longer be defended.

The next day, the sappers made their way to the large moat outside the Battery Wagner wall. Gen. Quincy Gillmore and his staff planned a major assault on Battery Wagner for 9 a.m. the next morning.

The night of Sept. 6, the Confederates in the garrison at Battery Wagner evacuated their positions and left Morris Island by boat. The Union forces were unaware of the evacuation of the battery by more than 1,000 men. The Confederates disabled Wagner's guns and set a fuse to blow the powder magazine as the last of the men departed. Union gunboats happened upon the last three boats leaving Morris Island, capturing the 50 men aboard including Lt. Charles H. Hasker and the crew of the Confederate boat *Chicora*. The fuse to the magazine failed and it did not explode.

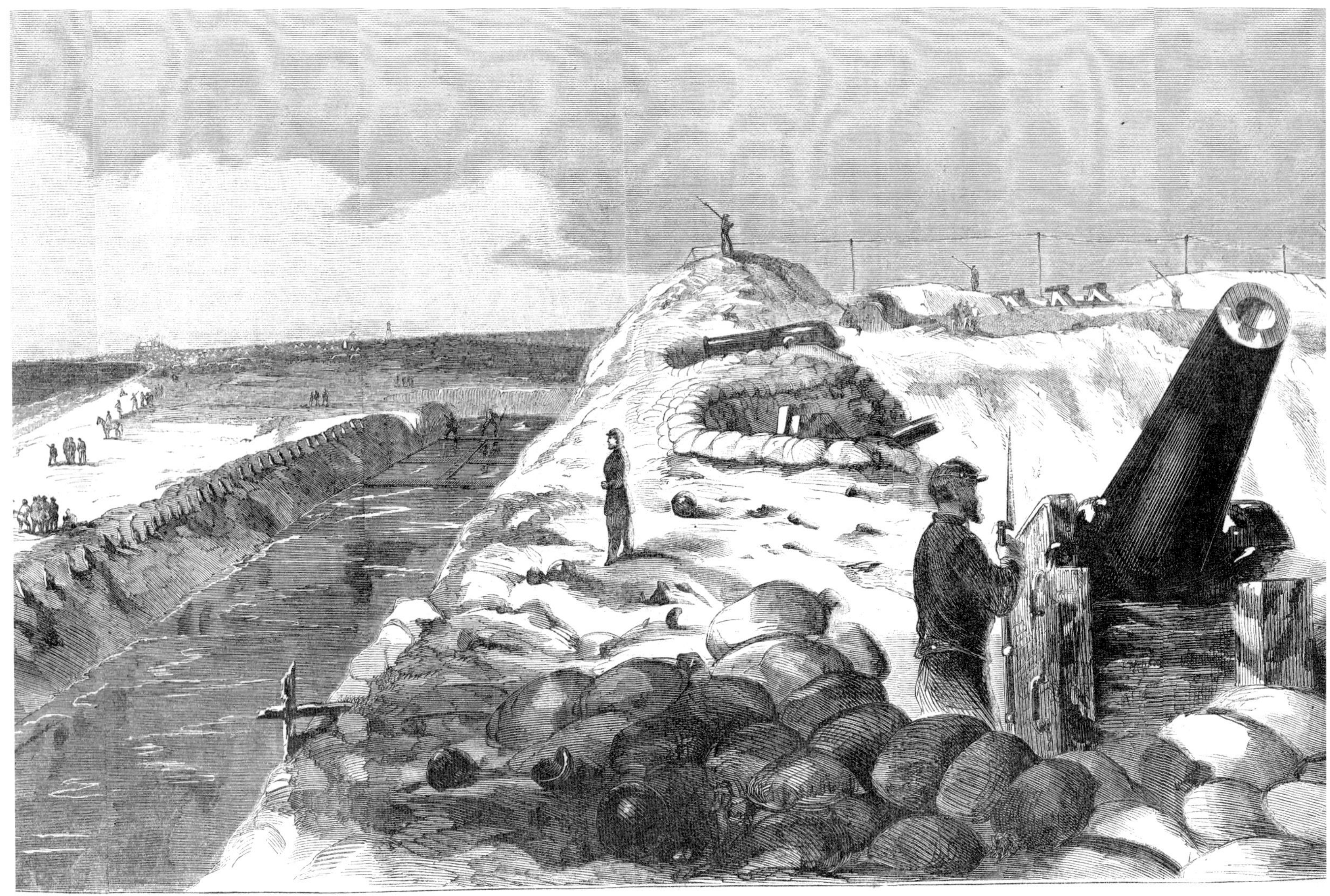

The Sea-Face of Fort Wagner

Artist: Theodore R. Davis
Harper's Weekly

The Union Army learned of the Confederate evacuation of Battery Wagner from deserters crossing Union lines on the morning of Sept. 7, 1863. At 5:10 a.m., Gen. Quincy Gillmore signaled to Adm. John A. Dahlgren, "The whole island is ours, but the enemy has escaped us."

Later that same day, Gillmore filed a report to Gen. Henry W. Halleck, commander-in-chief in Washington:

Fort Wagner is a work of the most formidable kind. Its bombproof shelter, capable of containing 1,800 men, remains intact, after the most terrific bombardment to which any work was ever subjected. We have captured 19 pieces of artillery and a large supply of excellent ammunition. The city and harbor of Charleston are now completely covered by my guns.

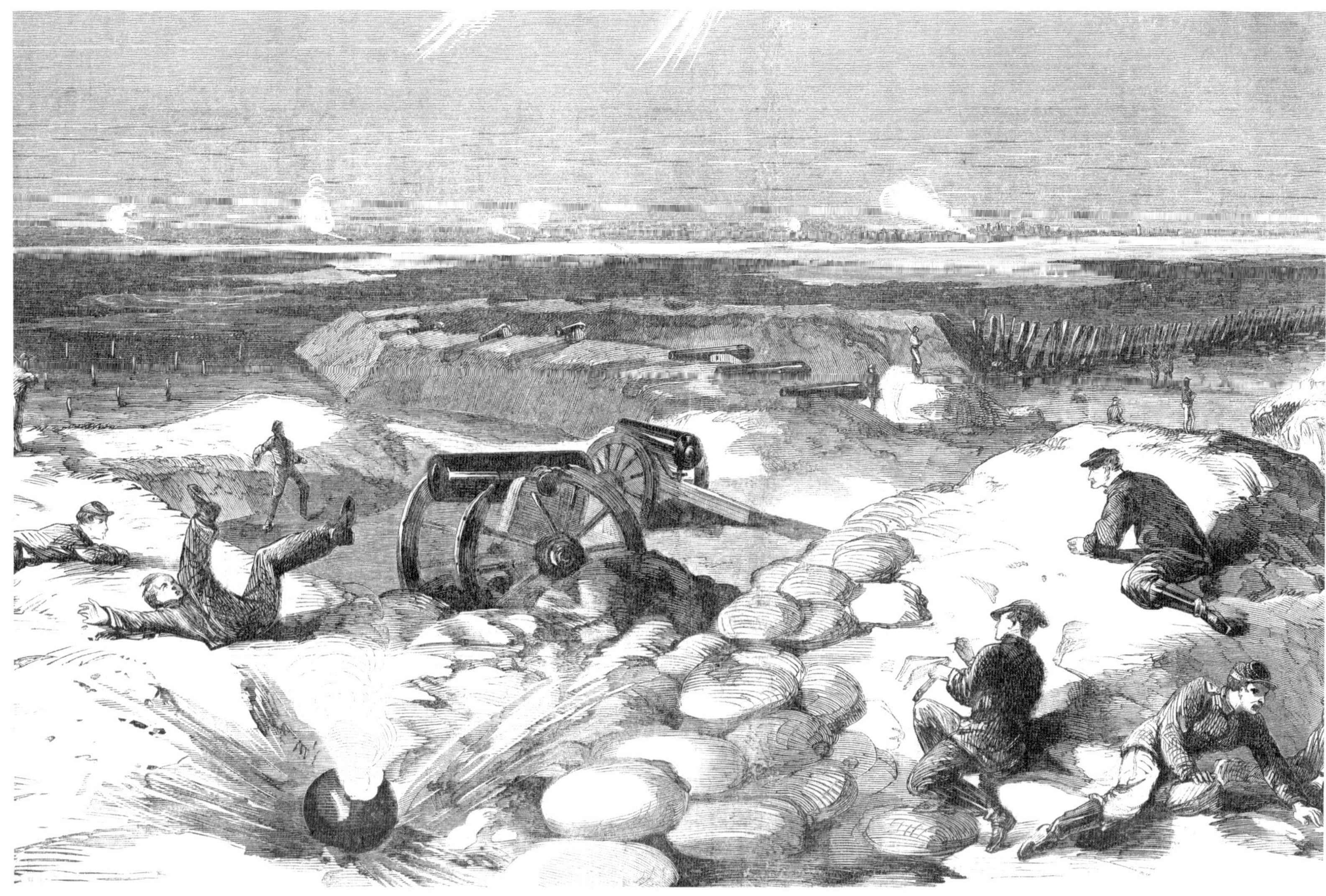

A Shell from Fort Johnson

Artist: Theodore R. Davis
Harper's Weekly

At daylight, Confederates at batteries Simkins, Cheves and Fort Moultrie opened fire on Battery Wagner.

Harper's Weekly artist Theo Davis entered Battery Wagner with the first of the Union troops. A shell fired from a Confederate battery on James Island landed nearby, covering him in sand and saltwater. Fearing that he might have been hit, soldiers rushed to help Davis. He was sandy and soaked, but appeared fine. Davis overheard soldiers in conversation about his presence in such a dangerous place when he didn't have to be there. One soldier remarked, "the artist man [is] loony."

Shortly after, Davis left, but he sketched an illustration capturing his own experience at Battery Wagner. Note Theo Davis with his sketch pad in the foreground.

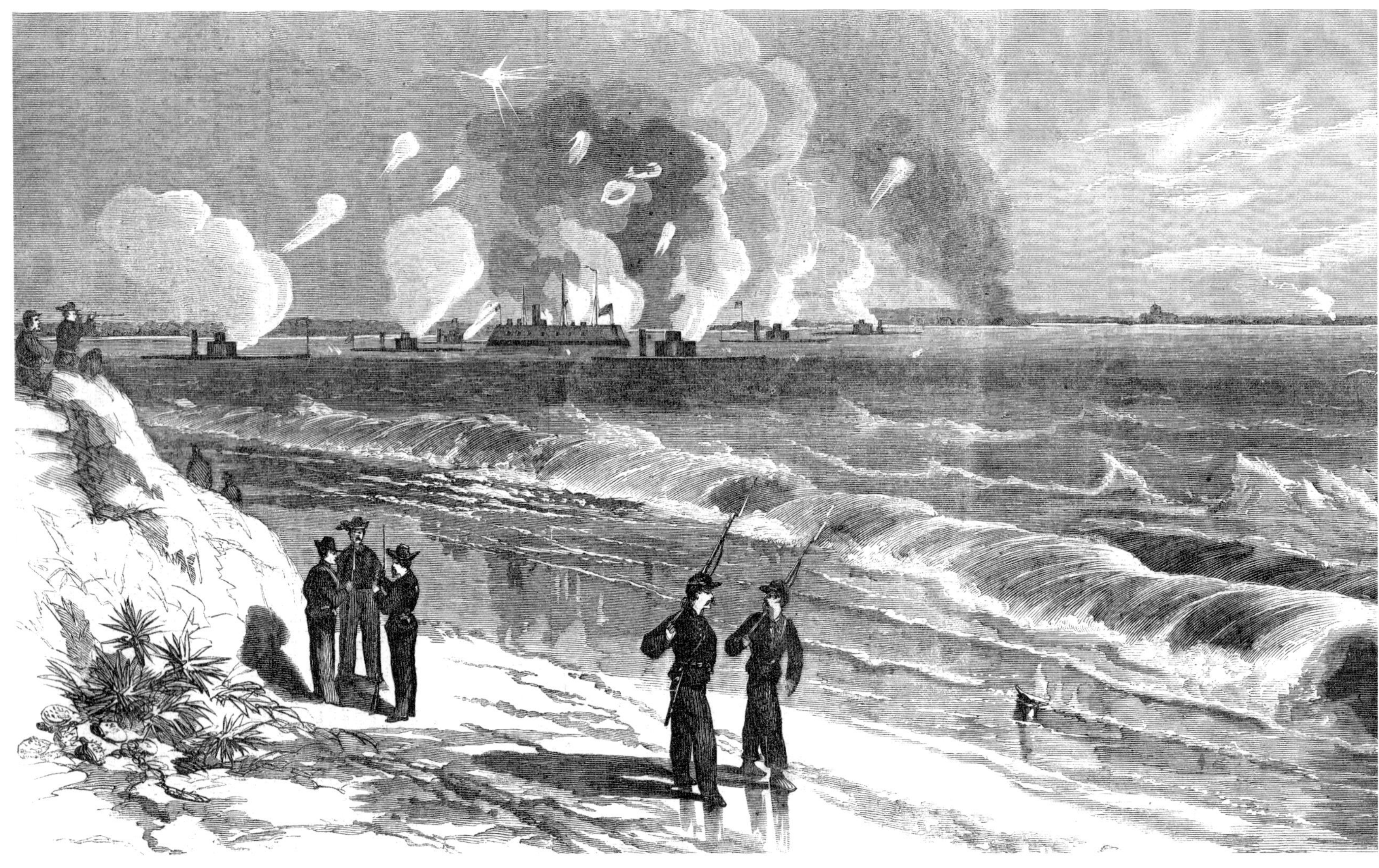

Bombardment of Fort Moultrie

Artist: Theodore R. Davis
Harper's Weekly

Adm. John Dahlgren, bolstered by the Confederates' evacuation at Morris Island, demanded the surrender of the garrison at Fort Sumter, but was refused. The next day, he ordered his fleet into action. The ironclad *Weehawken* tried to maneuver between Fort Sumter and James Island, but quickly ran aground. Several other monitors and the *New Ironsides* moved into position to fire on Fort Moultrie and the Sullivan's Island batteries and to draw fire from the disabled *Weehawken*. They sustained a constant bombardment for five hours before withdrawing for lack of ammunition.

The *Weehawken* was hit 24 times, but only suffered minor damage and three causalities. Finally, as the tide rose, she was able to float and move out of range.

The spectacular firefight was on display for all the Union troops on Morris Island to watch. Artist Theo Davis observed: "How reckless men become after a period of constant exposure to shell fire can be seen by the entire indifference exhibited by the soldiers upon the beach."

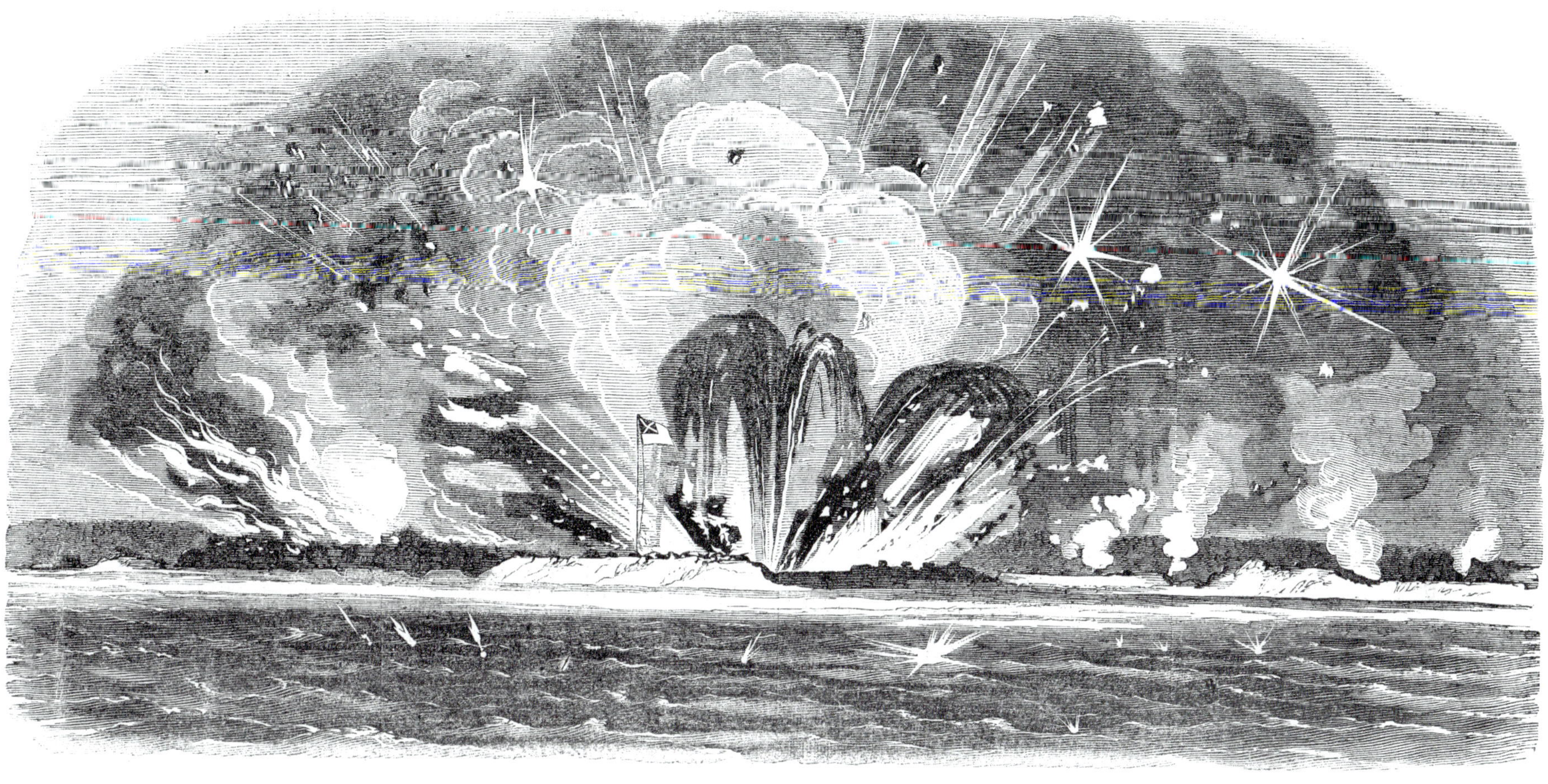

Explosion at Fort Moultrie

Artist: Theodore R. Davis
Harper's Weekly

After breakfast on the morning of Sept. 8, and while the *Weehawken* was still aground, Capt. Edmund Colhoun ordered the crew to open fire on Fort Moultrie. A shot from the *Weehawken* ricocheted off an 8-in. Columbiad in the fort into a number of nearby shell-boxes and ammunition chests. The explosion killed 16 men and wounded 12 others, all from Capt. R. Press Smith's company. Smith narrowly escaped death by jumping from the parapet into the ditch in front of the fort. Lt. D. G. Calhoun, who was officer of the day, worked with a small detachment to extinguish the flames in the fort while constantly under heavy fire from the Union ironclads.

The article filed by Theo Davis with *Harper's Weekly* indicated the entire powder magazine at Fort Moultrie had exploded, but such was not the case.

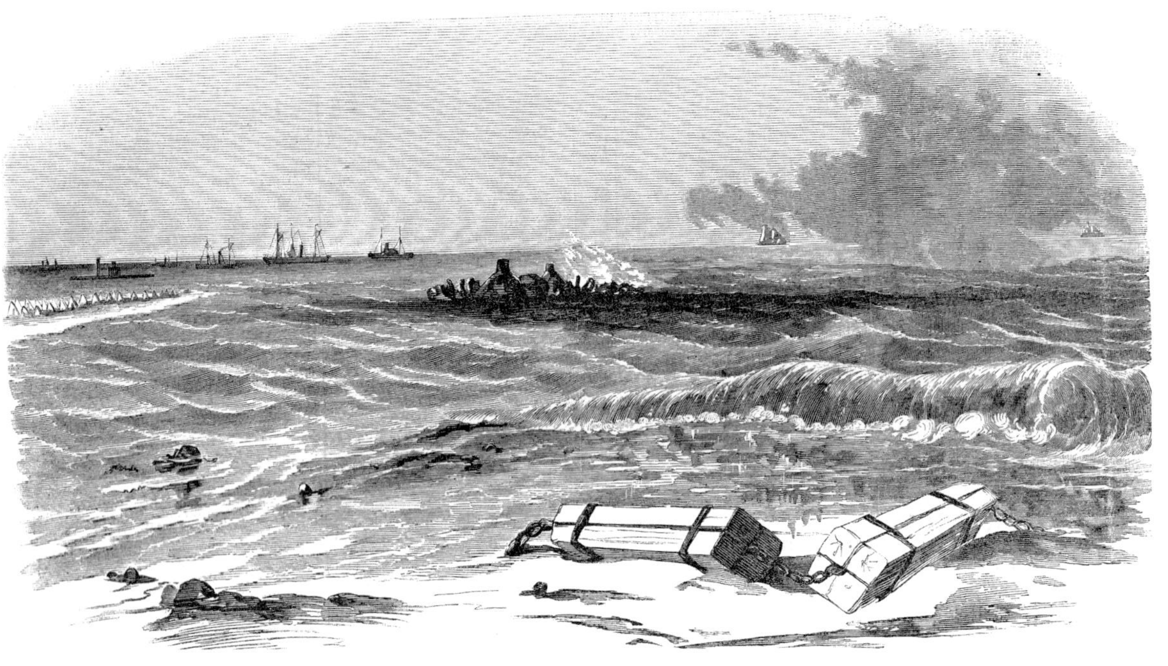

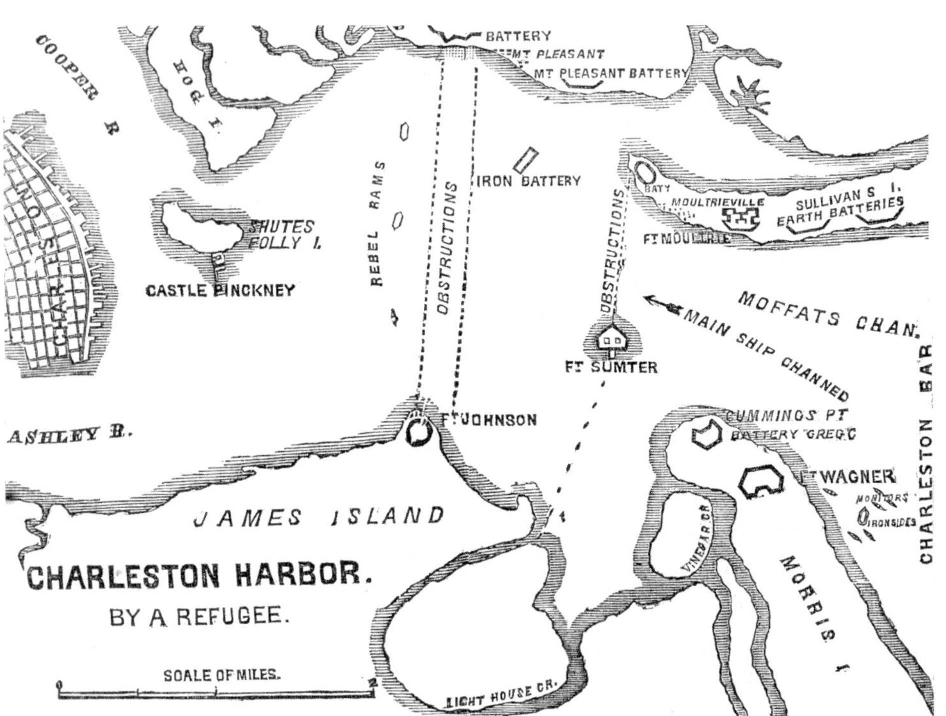

Obstructions in the Harbor

Artist: Surgeon Robinson, 104th Pennsylvania
Harper's Weekly

The defense of Charleston harbor was studied in depth early in the war. Naturally, the harbor fortifications and their guns played a major role. In October 1862, the Confederate government in Richmond established a Torpedo Bureau to advise the Southern ports on the use of such defensive weapons. Both mines and torpedoes were planned for Charleston harbor.

A system of booms, constructed of pine logs bound and tied with iron straps, were placed across the inner harbor as obstructions. The booms often had long ropes attached to catch and entangle the propellers of intruding ships. Dr. John R. Cheves was placed in charge of maintaining these boom and chain obstructions in the harbor.

As noted by surgeon Robinson in September 1863 and published in *Harper's Weekly*, part of the harbor obstruction had broken away and washed ashore on Morris Island.

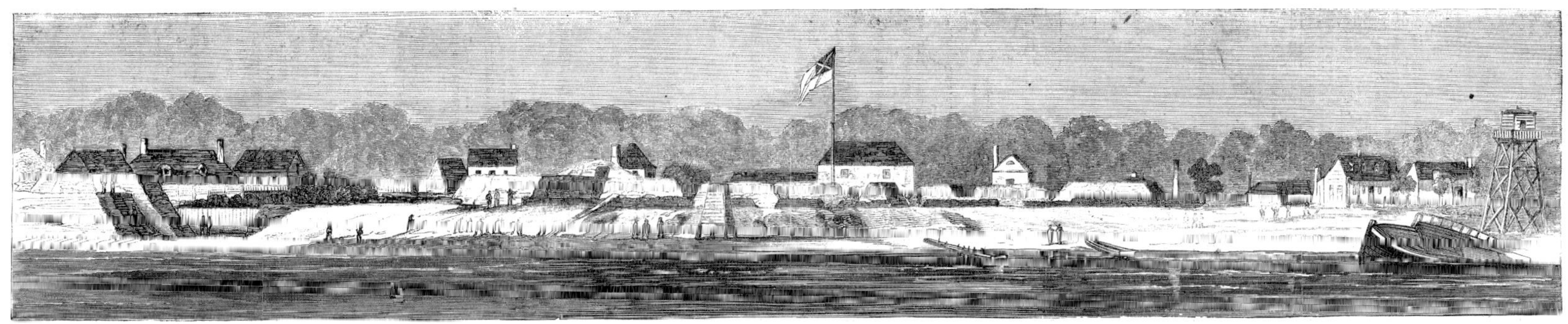

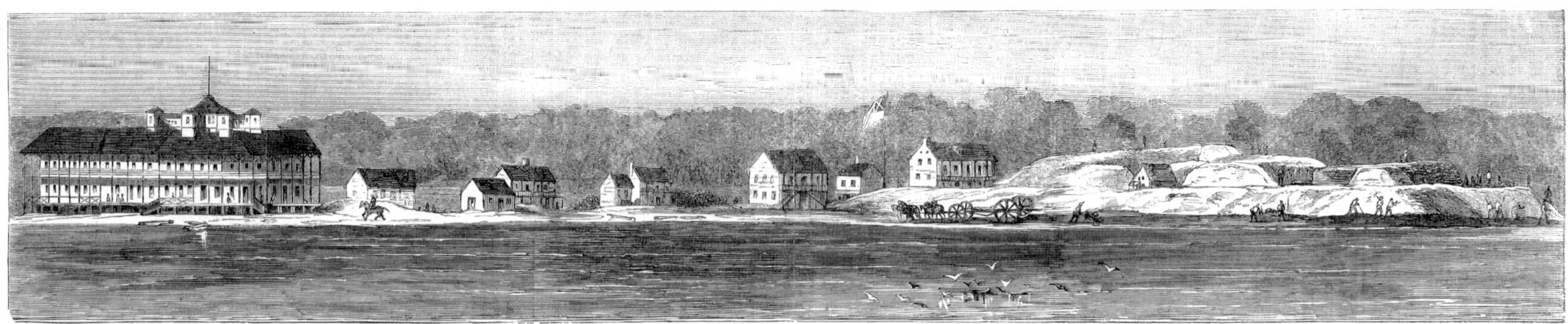

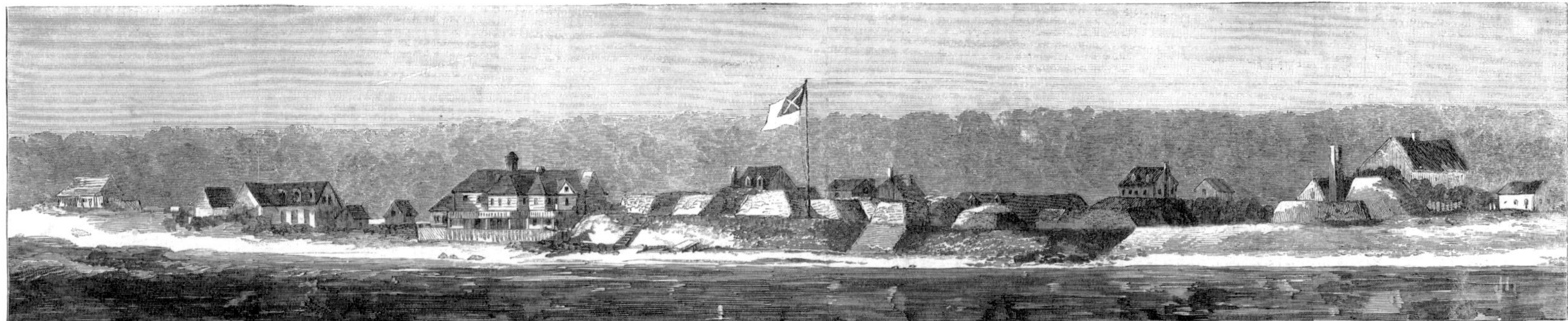

Rebel Batteries

Artist: Mr. O. Enez
Harper's Weekly

Artist O. Enez was on board one of the monitors in the Union fleet making his observations and sketches. Along with drawings he sent to *Harper's Weekly*, he offered the following narrative:

> *The representation of Fort Moultrie shows the effects of the last bombardment by the Ironsides and the Monitors. The effect of the shots is visible on the house standing in the centre of the fort; also on the outside where you see men at work to mend the damages. Those square white patches resting on the embankment are piles of sandbags to protect the gunners, and have been erected since the last fight, giving to the fort a different appearance from what it had three weeks ago. The other batteries, Bee and Beauregard, are all on Sullivan's Island, and will, in the next few days be the scene of a desperate fight.*

Attempt to Blow Up the *New Ironsides*

Artist: An Occasional Contributor
Harper's Weekly

The ironclad *New Ironsides* had been particularly bothersome to the Charleston defenders. The bands of iron had protected the frigate through many firefights, proving much more resilient than the ironclad monitors. Not only did shot and shell have little impact on the ship, her guns were much more powerful than the turret guns on the monitors.

The frigate was 250-ft. long with iron plates more than 4-in. wide protecting her sides. The 14 11-in. guns were certainly feared by the Confederates. John Frasier and Company, the Confederacy's largest blockade running firm, offered a bounty of $100,000 to anyone who could sink the *New Ironsides*, twice the sum paid for sinking an ironclad monitor.

David, a Confederate torpedo boat, slipped out of Charleston harbor on the evening of Oct. 5. Ahead, the crew spotted the coveted target, the *New Ironsides*. Sailors at watch on deck spotted the approaching torpedo boat and began firing. *David's* commander, Lt. W. T. Glassell, managed to get the torpedo in place. An explosion ripped the *New Ironsides* and damaged her but did not sink the frigate.

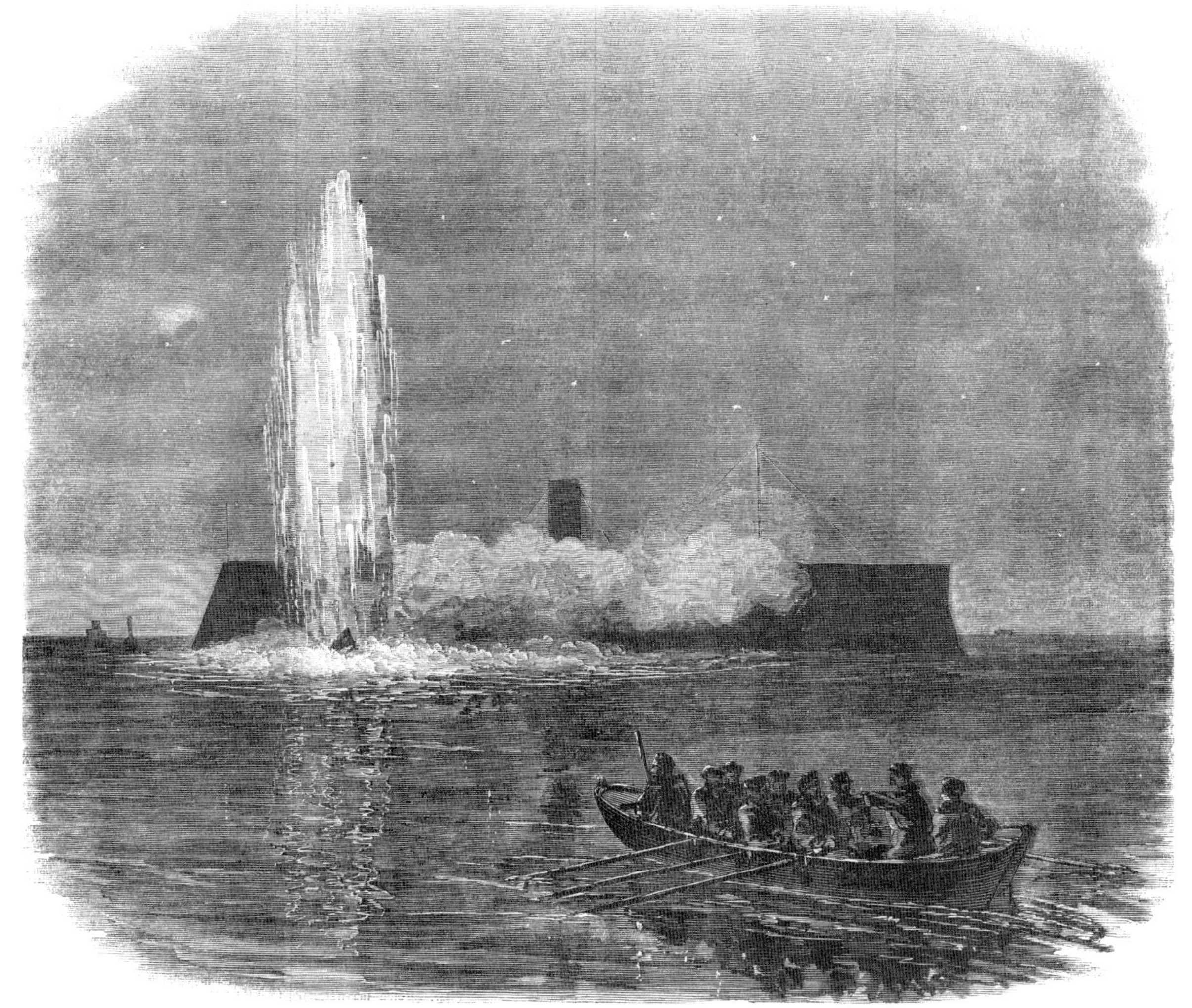

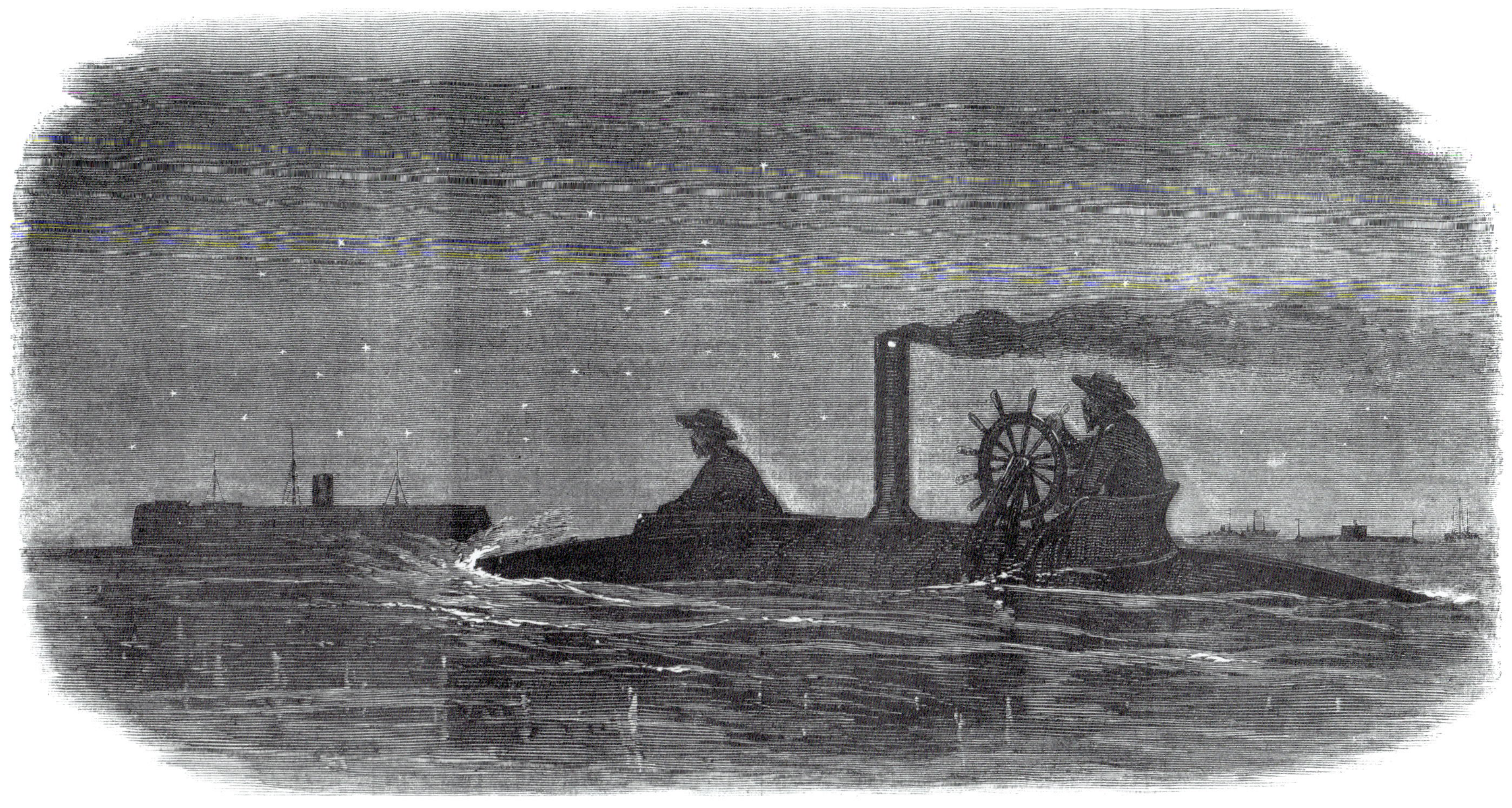

The Rebel Torpedo Boat

Drawn by an occasional contributor
Harper's Weekly

As the torpedo exploded, a wall of water swelled over *David*, extinguishing the boiler and setting her adrift. Lt. W. T. Glassell ordered his three-man crew to abandon ship. One of the crew, J. W. Cannon, however, could not swim. He jumped but held onto the small torpedo boat. Engineer J. H. Tombs returned to *David*, checking on his shipmate. Together, they were able to get the ship's boiler back in operation. With the Union fleet still frantically searching for its attacker, *David* made her way back to Charleston.

Glassell and crewman James Stuart were captured by the Union Navy in the harbor. The illustration was drawn by a naval officer, based on the descriptions of the two Union prisoners. They described the four- to five-man boat as a small steamer with a torpedo attached to the bow, which was designed to contact the bottom of an intended floating target. The *Harper's Weekly* article erroneously stated that the torpedo boat attacking the *New Ironsides* on Oct. 5, 1863, was destroyed and sank in the attack, taking two of the four man crew down with her. The published illustration was a remarkably accurate depiction of the actual boats designed and built by the Confederates.

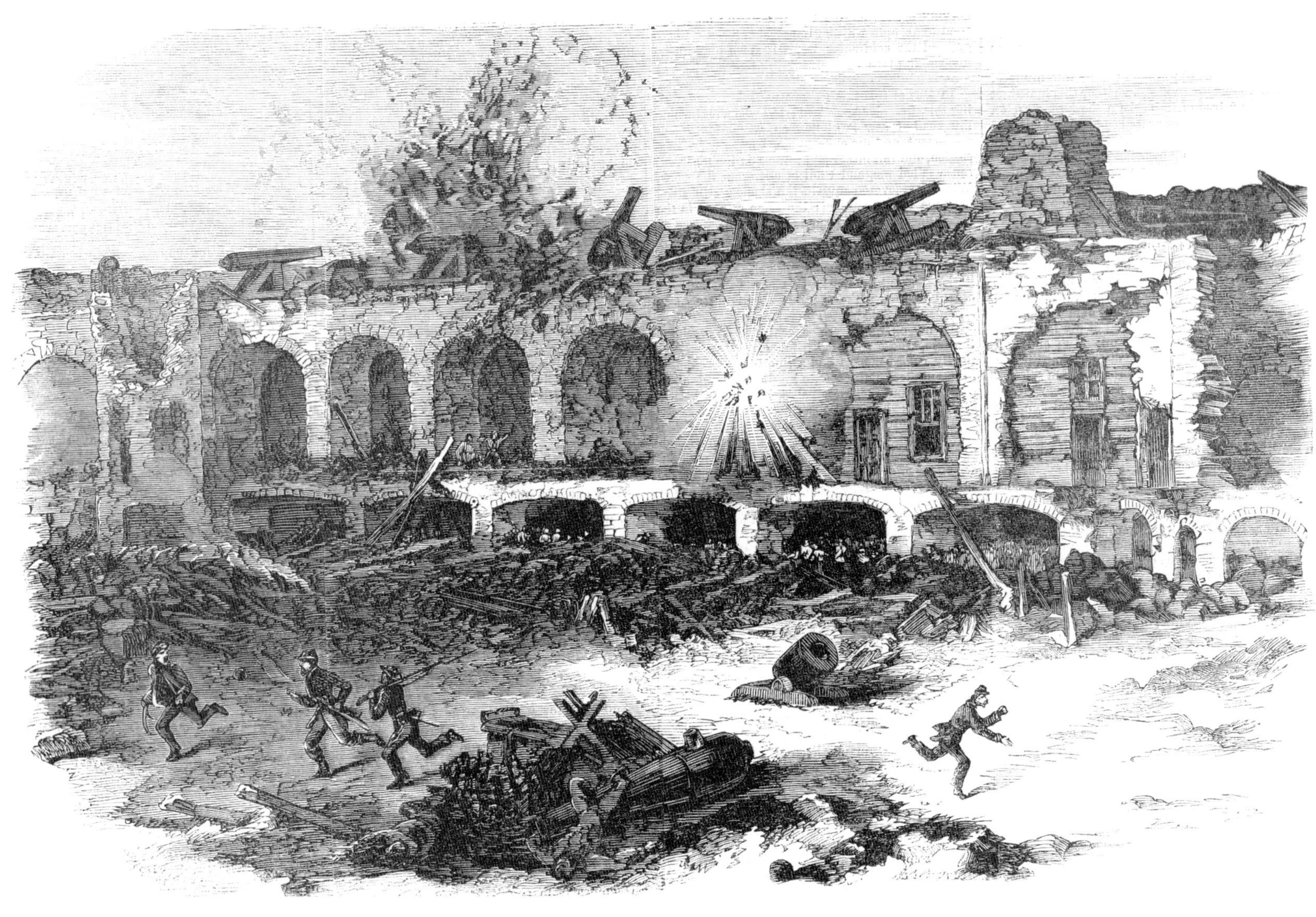

Interior of Fort Sumter

Drawn by an English Artist
Harper's Weekly

On Oct. 26, 1864, the combined federal forces began a second major campaign to force the surrender of the Confederate garrison at Fort Sumter. Adm. John Dahlgren's fleet was now joined by two new Union batteries - Fort Strong (formerly Battery Wagner) and Fort Putnam (formerly Battery Gregg).

The constant bombardment lasted 41 days. The Union Army and Navy fired more than 18,000 shells at Fort Sumter. Remarkably, the Confederate garrison held the fort and, with Sullivan's Island's fortifications, prevented the Union fleet from moving into the inner harbor and forcing the surrender of Charleston.

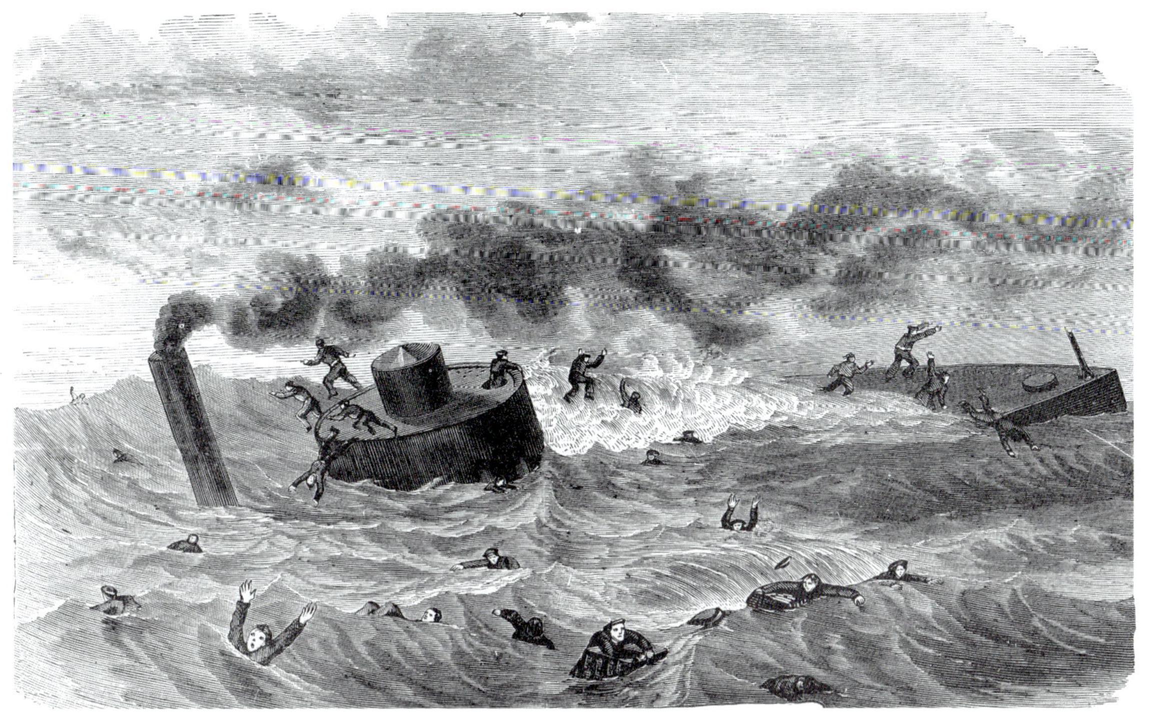

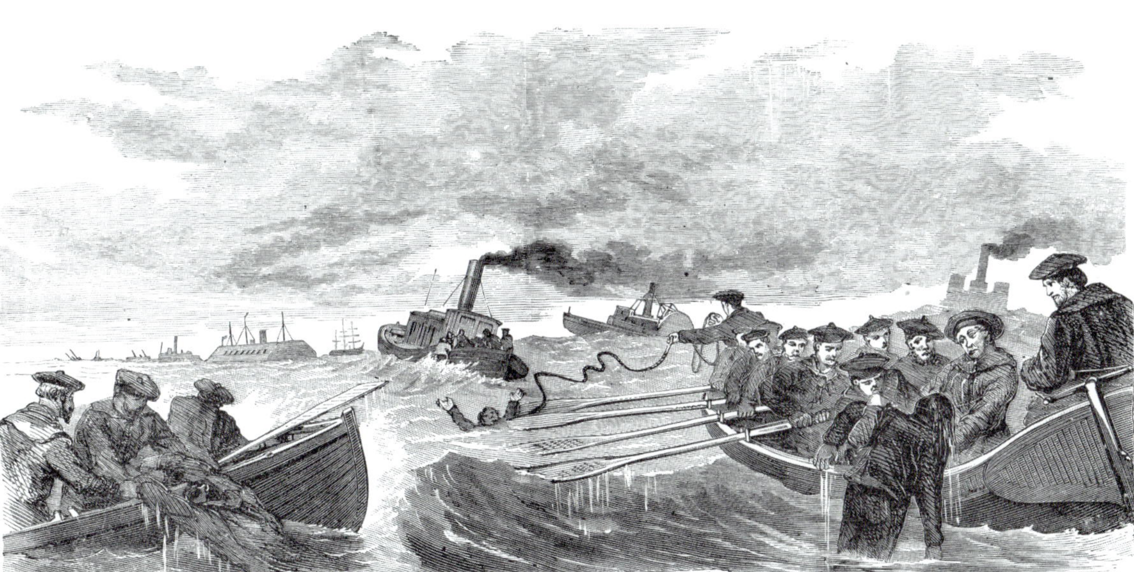

Sinking of the *Weehawken*

Artist: W. T. Crane
Frank Leslie's Illustrated Newspaper

The *Weehawken*, under the command of Capt. John Rogers, had seen considerable action in the siege of Morris Island and the multiple attacks on Fort Sumter. Earlier, the *Weehawken* led a force of nine ironclads in its initial and ill-conceived attack on Fort Sumter. The *Weehawken* sustained more than 60 direct hits from the guns at Sumter and the land batteries. Then, while trying to remove harbor obstructions on Sept. 7, 1863, the *Weehawken* was grounded and took on intense fire from James Island and Sullivan's Island. Still, the ironclad persevered.

On Dec. 6, the *Weehawken* was re-supplied with a large order of ship's supplies and munitions for the continued campaign against Fort Sumter. The weight of these supplies was excessive, causing the ironclad, tied to a mooring buoy off Morris Island, to sit low in the water. As the sea turned rough, she began to take on water through the ports and under the turret. She sank with her four officers and 20-man crew aboard. Help arrived and the crew was rescued. Finally, the rough seas off Morris Island accomplished what the Confederate guns could not—the sinking of the *Weehawken*.

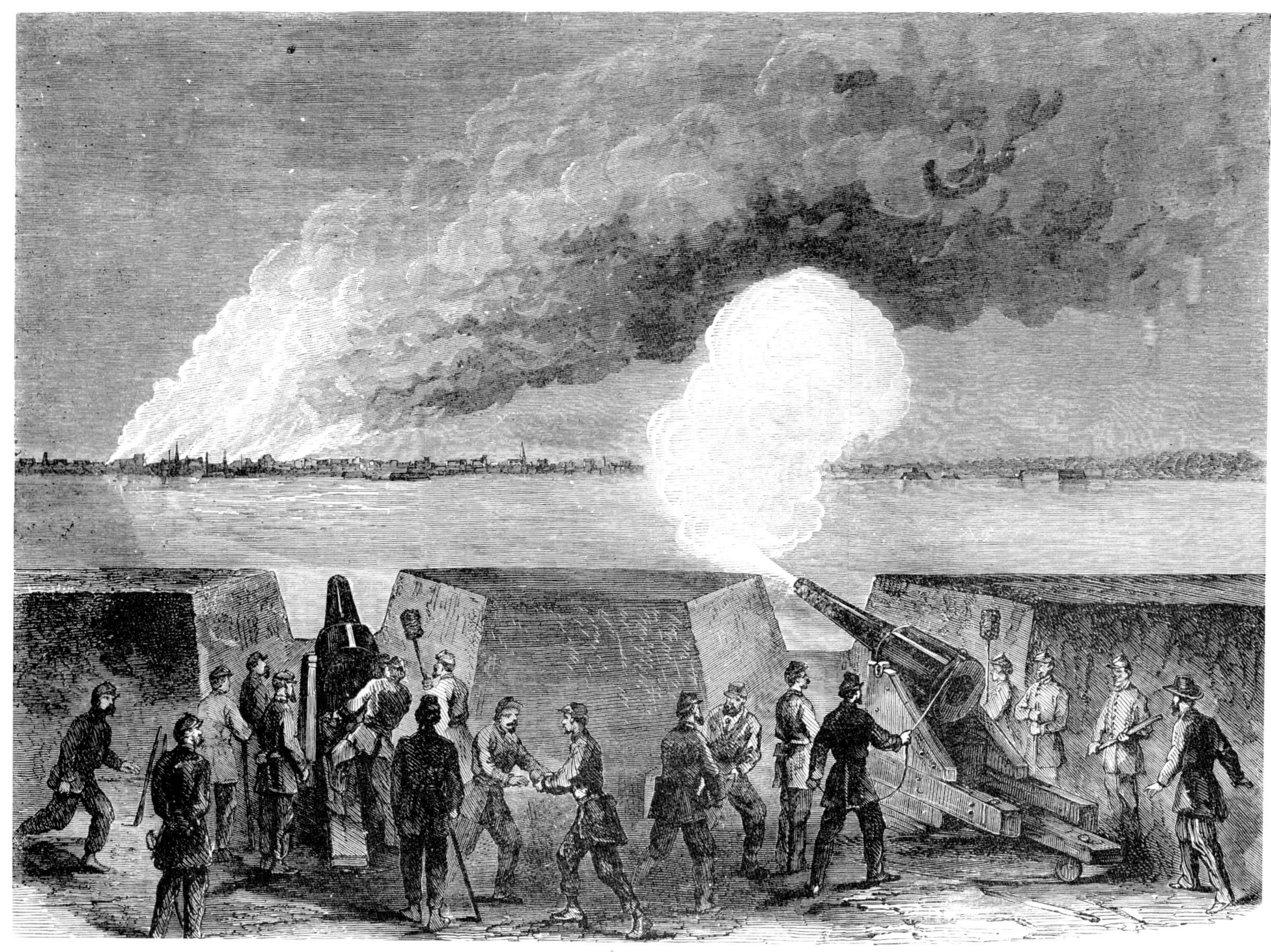

The Doomed City

Artist: unknown
Frank Leslie's Illustrated Newspaper

This illustration drawn by the artist on Jan. 3, 1864, shows the guns at Fort Putnam firing on the city of Charleston. Fort Putnam, the site of what was Confederate Battery Gregg, was named in honor of Col. Haldiman Putnam, killed in the doomed assault on Battery Wagner in July 1863.

With all of Morris Island under Union control, the guns at Fort Putnam and Fort Strong could fire into the peninsula city of Charleston. Over a period of nine days, Union forces fired 1,500 shells into the city, forcing most of the homes, churches, and businesses in the lower peninsula to be deserted.

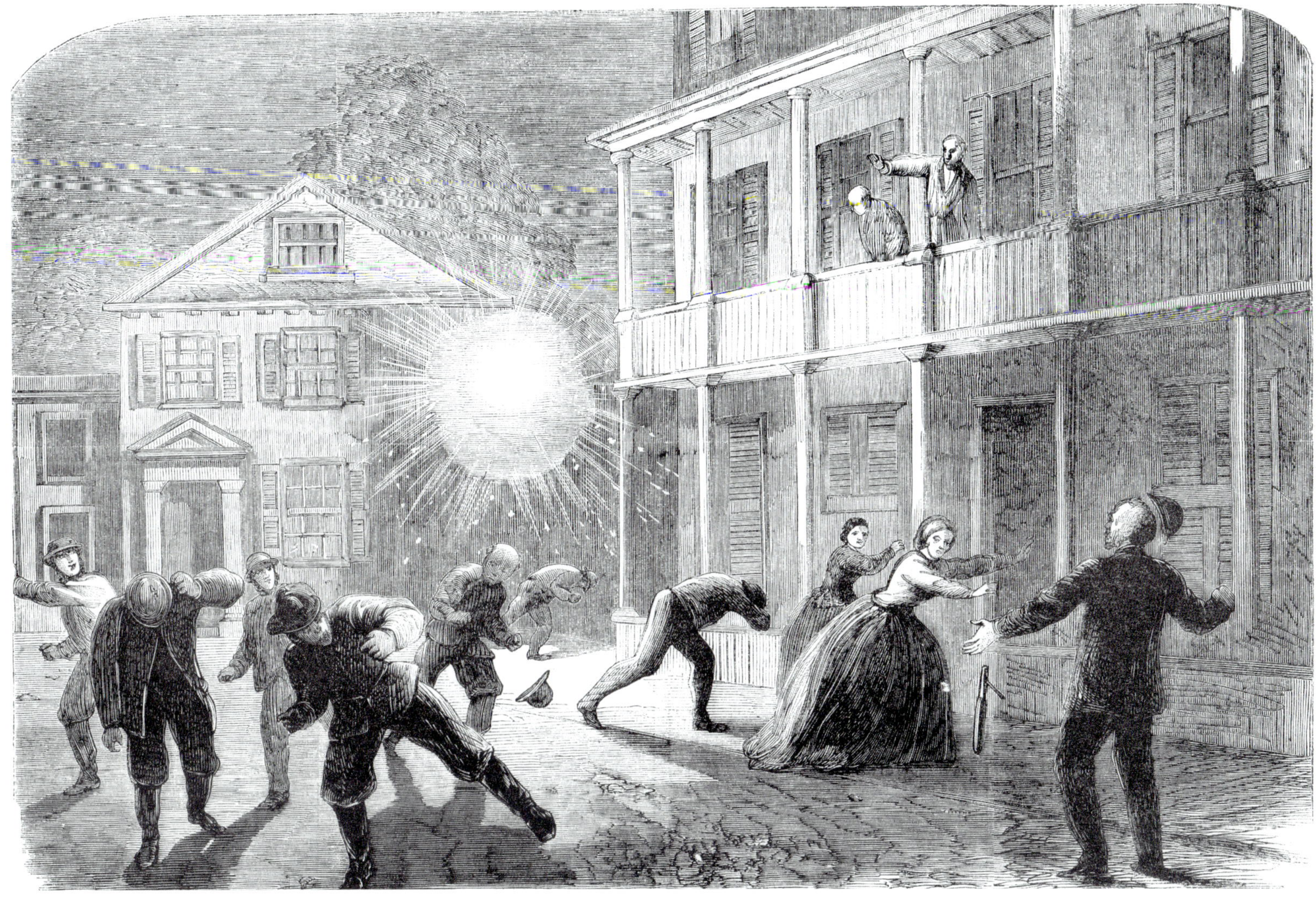

Bursting of a Shell in Charleston

Drawn by an English Artist
Harper's Weekly

The Union Army fired on Charleston on a regular basis through the middle of January 1864. Many shots hit and destroyed homes and businesses, however some landed in Charleston unexploded. On Jan. 9, the Union batteries began shelling Charleston at 11 p.m., firing one shot every 30 minutes. Of the 18 shots fired into Charleston by 6 a.m., one fell short and did not reach the city and nine landed unexploded. The remaining members of the volunteer fire companies stayed busy fighting fires at Broad and Church streets, the hospital, the state bank and on Meeting Street.

After mid-January, firing into Charleston occurred more erratically. Large numbers of Union and Confederate troops were transferred from Charleston and sent south to fight in the Florida Expedition. Confident that the situation in Charleston was under control, the Union Army and Navy were content to leave a small force in place while fronts in Florida and Virginia were given higher priority.

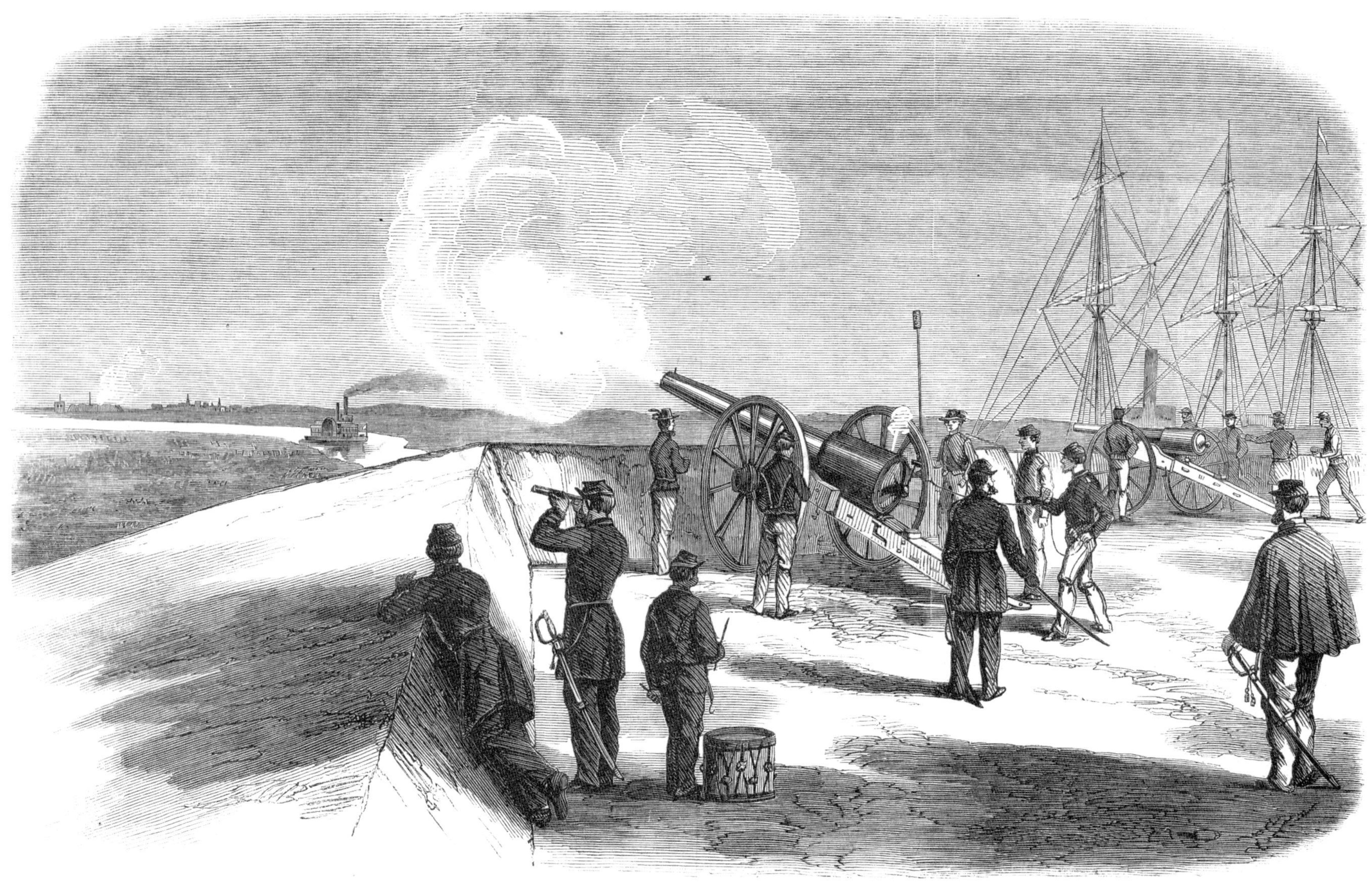

Shelling Secessionville

Artist: W. T. Crane
Frank Leslie's Illustrated Newspaper

Throughout 1864, fire was exchanged between the many Confederate batteries on James Island with Union batteries on Morris and Black islands. *Frank Leslie's* artist W. T. Crane, with the Union artillery at Fort Strong, witnessed the frequent exchange of fire with the Confederate battery at Secessionville. The illustration depicts Gen. John G. Foster ordering fire. Crane reports, "These bombardments are not wanton. They are provoked by the enemy, who fire at our steamers, and especially at the Planter, the boat carried off by Small and other negroes, and the mere appearance of which singularly to ruffle the equanimity of our Southern fellow citizens."

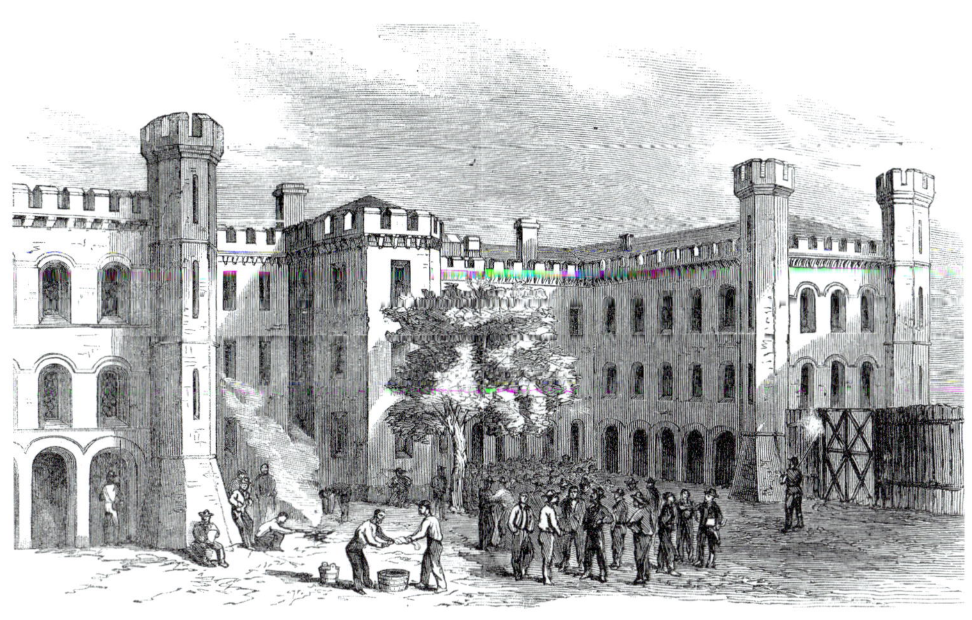

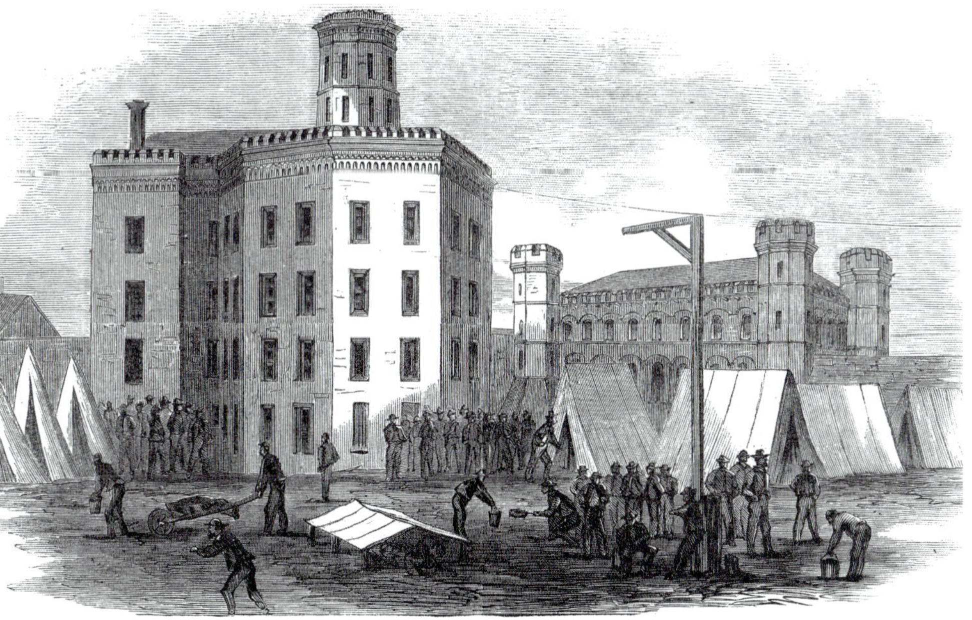

Military Prisons at Charleston

Artist: Lt. F. Millward
Harper's Weekly

While the illustrations in *Harper's Weekly* were titled "military prisons," they actually depict the Workhouse (top) and the Charleston Jail (bottom), both located on Magazine Street in Charleston. The facilities were used as prisons for captured Union soldiers during the war.

The jail, built in 1802, had been expanded and remodeled several times prior to its use during the Civil War. W. S. Glazier, a Union officer who was confined in the jail, provides an insight into its use: "The ground floor of the jail was occupied by civil convicts; the second story by rebel officers under punishment for military offenses; the third story by negro prisoners; and the fourth by federal and rebel deserters... "

Capt. H. A. Coats, of the 85th New York, was held prisoner at the Charleston Jail. In 1867, he testified before Congress, which was investigating the treatment of prisoners of war by the Confederates. He noted that he was one of 400 or more men held in the jailyard, none of whom had blankets or shelter. "There was but one privy, never cleaned out... Later, many enlisted men were brought and filled the jail to overflowing. In the hall was a sutler, who tantalized the prisoners by a display of food held at prohibitory prices, except for a few fortunate ones."

After captured federal officers were moved from Macon, Ga., to Charleston late in the war, the workhouse and Roper Hospital were converted to prisons.

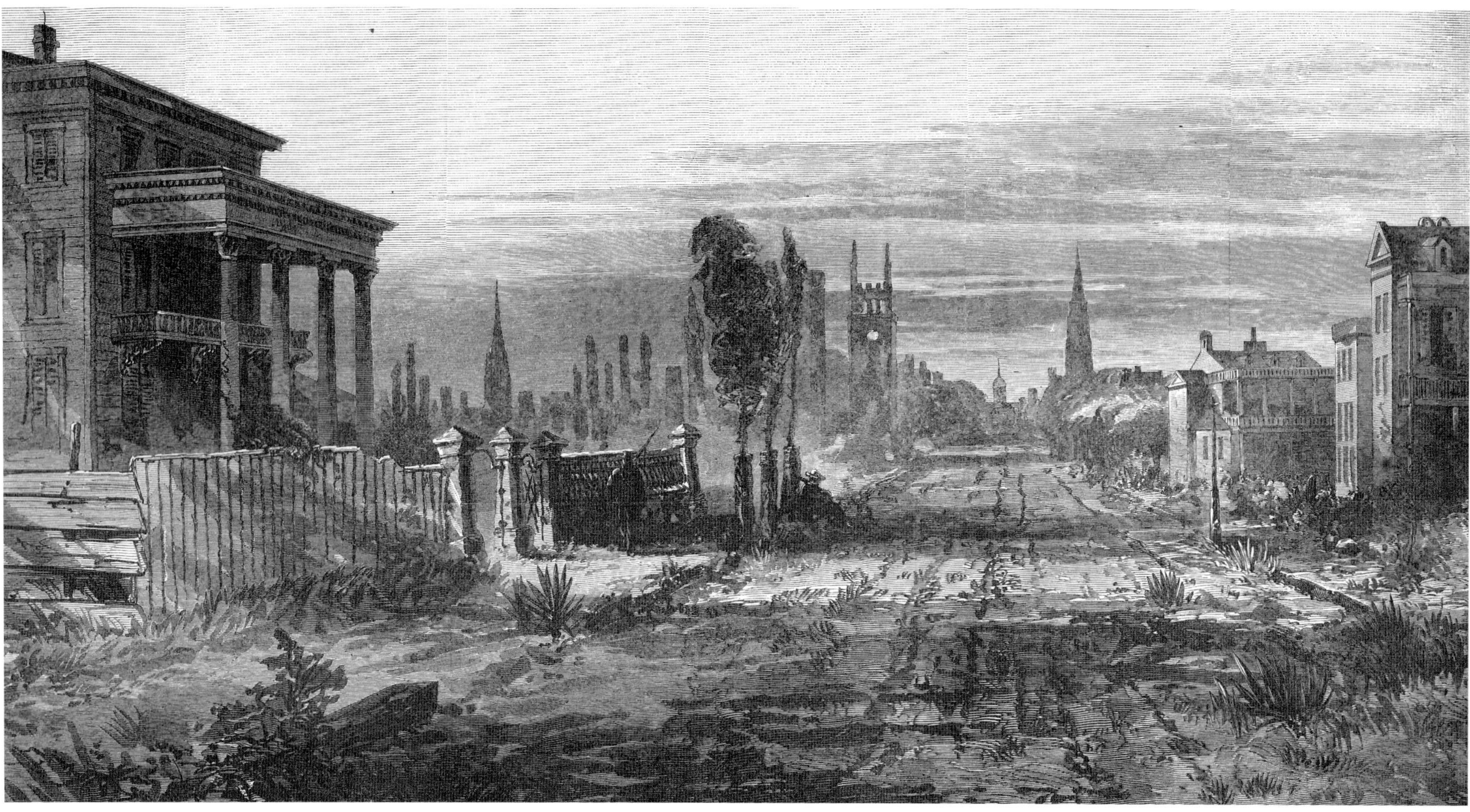

Broad Street under Fire

Drawn by a Union officer
Harper's Weekly

Union prisoners were held at the Charleston Jail and at Castle Pinckney, yet these facilities, crowded as they were, still could hold the many captives taken by the Confederates on James Island and Morris Island. It became routine to hold Union officers prisoner in private homes in Charleston. A number of officers, including Gen. Truman Seymour, were held in a home at the corner of Broad Street and Rutledge Avenue. Seymour was with Major Robert Anderson at Fort Sumter in 1861 and was captured during the assault on Battery Wagner.

This sketch was done by one of the officers housed with Seymour. He writes that federal prisoners were "treated with great indignity; the food was poor and barely able to sustain life." He, perhaps, ignored the fact that the conditions and diet for most people still in Charleston was not much different than his own.

This view, looking toward the Cooper River, shows Broad Street in a desperate state. The Union shelling of Charleston contributed to these conditions, but the great fire of 1861 devastated this part of Charleston as well, the evidence of which could still be seen.

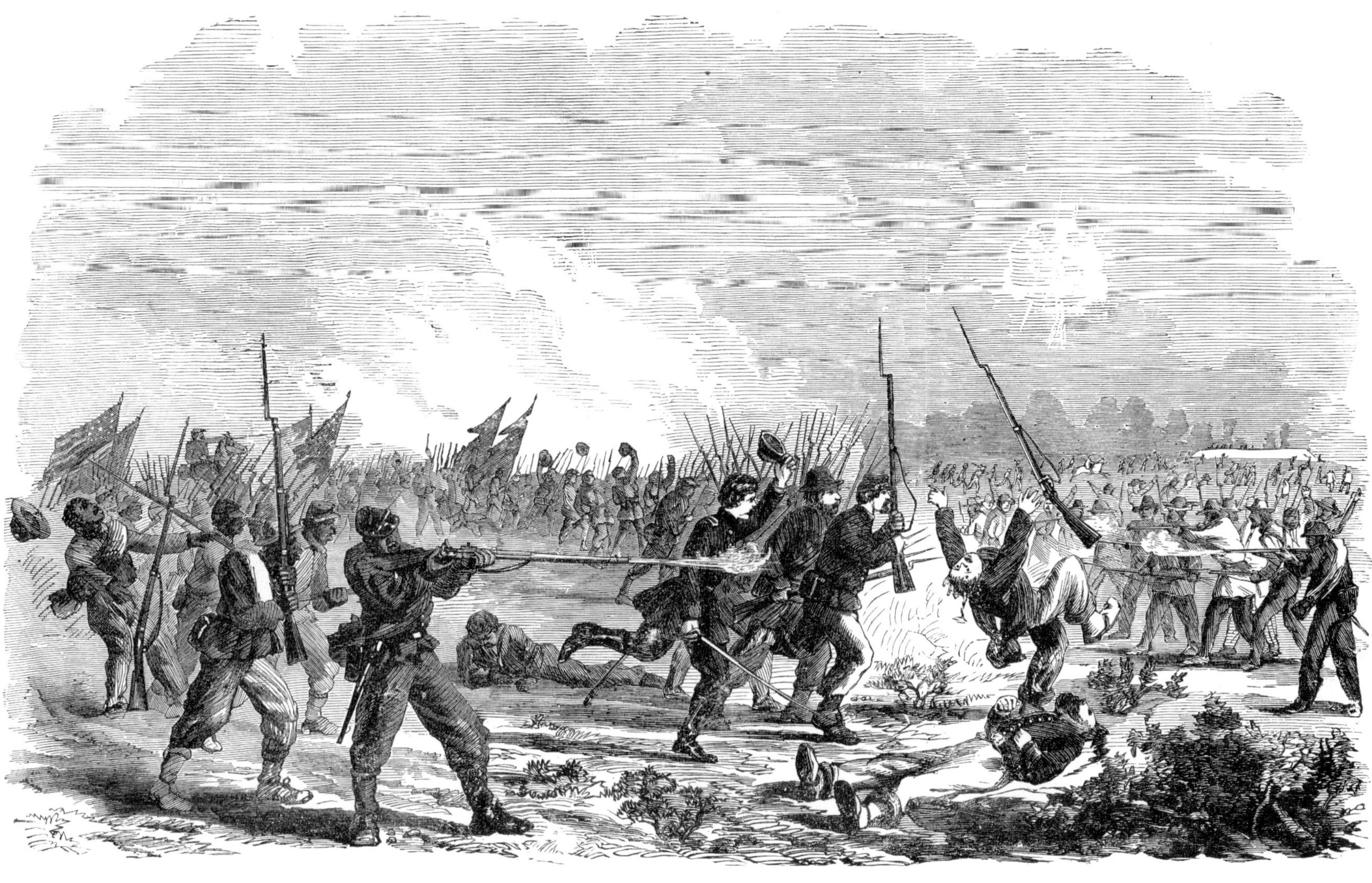

Attack on the Confederate Rifle-Pits

Artist: W. T. Crane
Frank Leslie's Illustrated Newspaper

One of the last battles in the Carolina lowcountry prior to the fall of Charleston occurred in early February 1865. The Union Army planned an amphibious assault on Battery Simkins, located near Fort Johnson on James Island. The barges, loaded with Union troops, neared James Island, drawing intense fire from the batteries on Sullivan's Island and the guns at Battery Simkins. The unrelenting fire forced the barges to withdraw without making a landing.

On Feb. 9, Union troops fashioned an attack on a Confederate position on James Island. With cover fire from two monitors and a mortar schooner, two Union regiments carrying field guns made their way ashore. Their target was a position of rifle-pits held by the Palmetto Battalion, commanded by Major Edward Manigault. The Confederates made a heroic stand, but finally succumbed to superior numbers. In the attack, Manigault was wounded and taken prisoner.

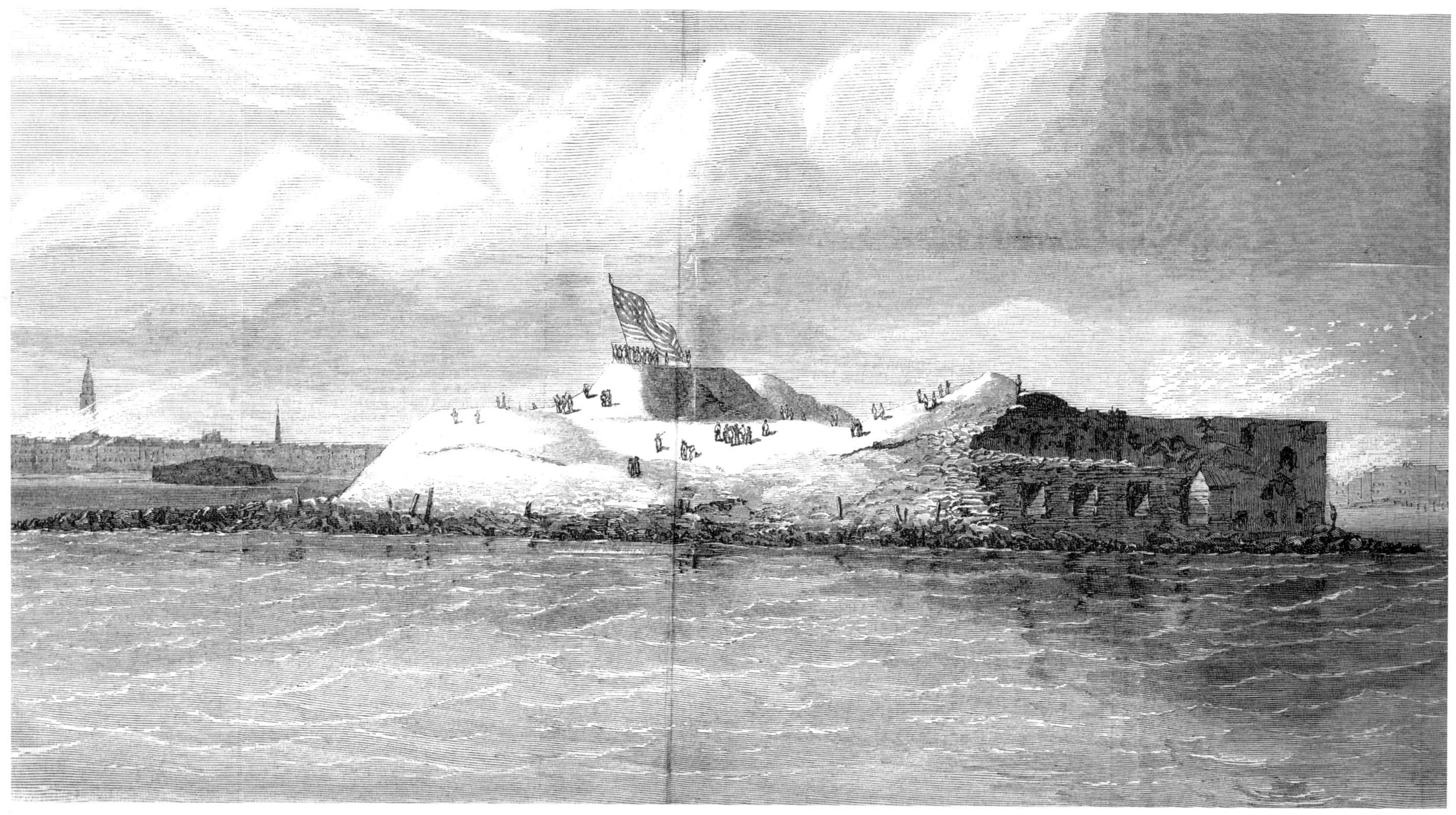

Fort Sumter in Charleston Harbor

Artist: William Waud
Harper's Weekly

By late January 1865, the garrison at Fort Sumter contained approximately 300 men from the 3rd Georgia Volunteers and the 1st S.C. Artillery. On Feb. 16, Gen. P. G. T. Beauregard sent instructions for the prompt evacuation of Charleston, wanting to withdraw the remaining troops to North Carolina.

The Union signalmen on Morris Island, reading messages between Charleston and the harbor forts, knew the evacuation was imminent. On the morning of Feb. 17, the garrison at Fort Sumter raised a new Confederate flag and made preparations to leave the fort. Near 10 p.m., two small steamers arrived at Fort Sumter to pick up the troops.

Interestingly, the last Confederate officer to leave Battery Wagner had also been the last to leave Fort Sumter. Major Thomas A. Huguenin of the 1st S.C. Infantry, recalls:

> *After visiting every portion of the fort, with a heavy heart I reached the wharf, no one was left behind but many a heart clung to those sacred and battle scarred ramparts, I cannot describe my emotions. I felt as if every tie held dear to me was about to be severed; the pride and glory of Sumter was there, and now in the gloom of darkness we were to abandon her, for whom every one of us would have shed the last drop of his blood.*

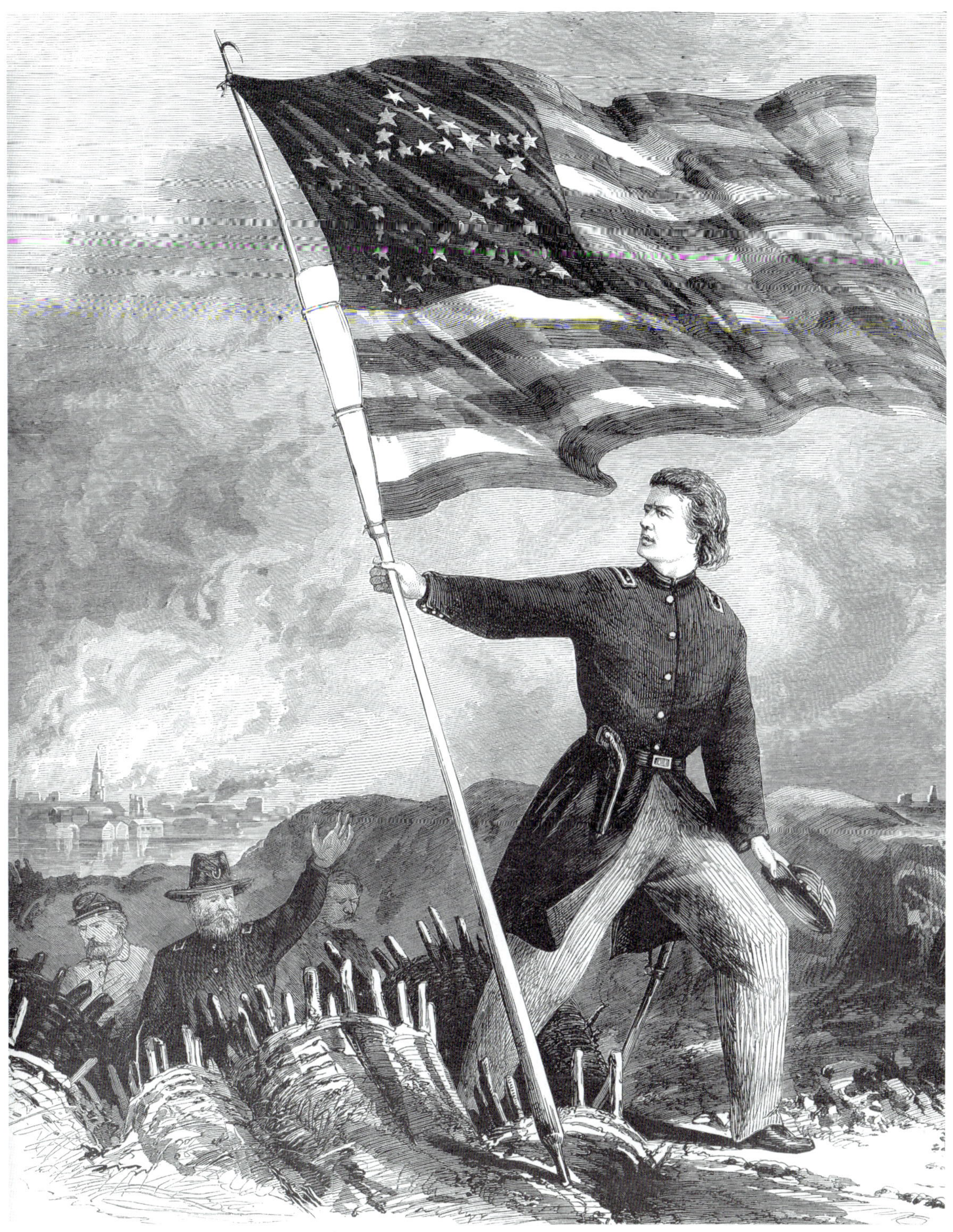

The Old Flag Again on Sumter

Artist: unknown
Frank Leslie's Illustrated Newspaper

Mrs. Lee Harby, a young girl in Charleston at the time of the war, recalls the events of the 17th:

> *It was a terrible, heart-breaking, awful night. The men who were garrisoning Sumter had come over in their small boats, bringing their flags. In the early morning of the 18th, they were gathered in the city on the wharf, and there they cast themselves down on the earth and wept aloud. Some prayed; some cursed; all said they would rather have died in the fort they had so long defended than have her ramparts desecrated by the invader's tread ...*

The next day, when the Union troops realized the Confederates had evacuated the harbor fortifications, several units raced to raise the United States flag at each location. This illustration depicts Capt. H. M. Bragg of Gen. Quincy Gillmore's staff raising the United States flag over Fort Sumter, the site where four years earlier the war began. Note the city of Charleston burning in the background.

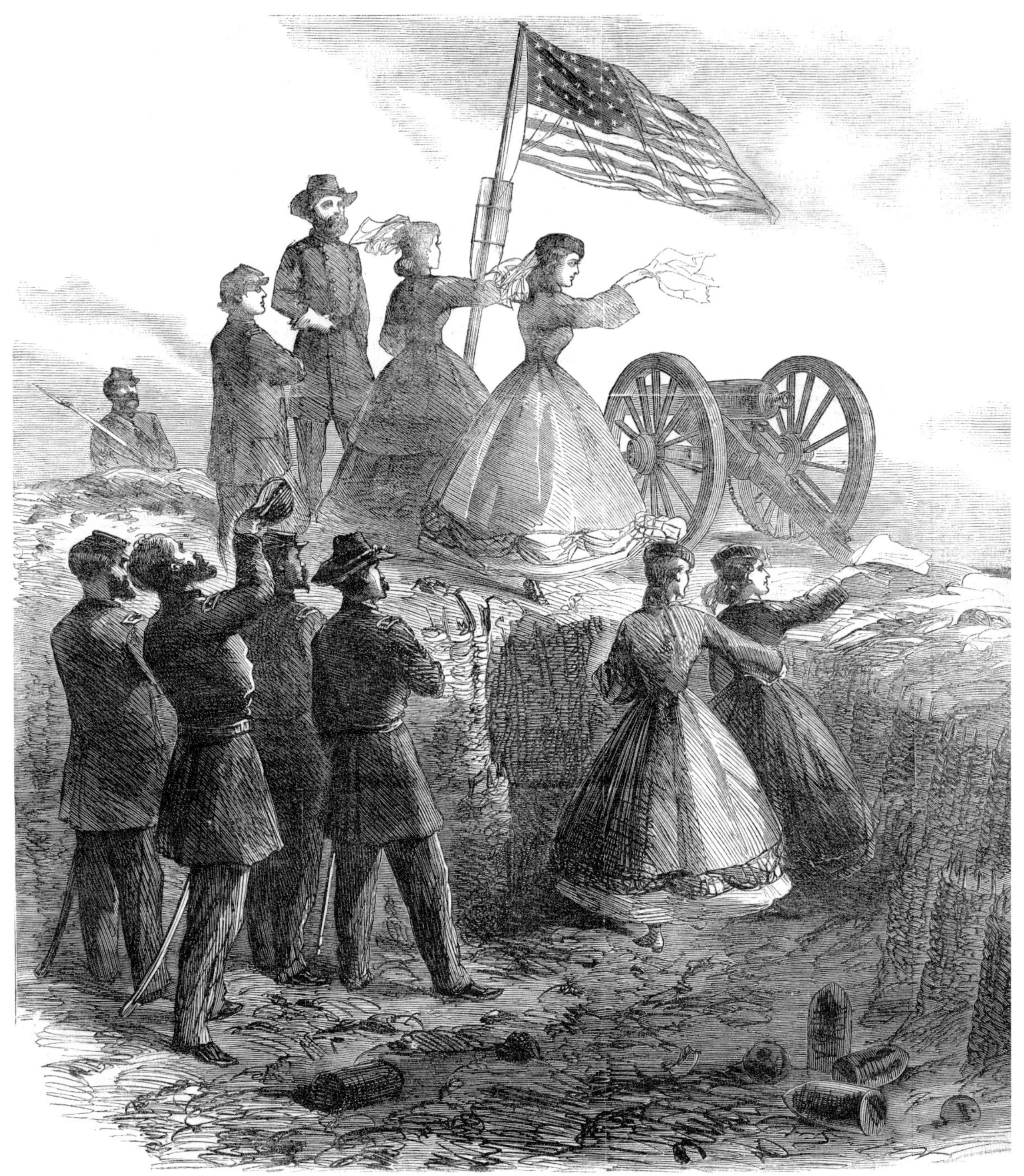

Gillmore Returns to Sumter

Artist: Stanley Fox
Harper's Weekly

On Feb. 21, Major Gen. Quincy Gillmore and his staff toured the ruins of Fort Sumter. In noting the significance of Fort Sumter to the country, *Harper's Weekly* published this:

> *Here the rebellion had its birth, and after four years of a strife, the most terrible as well as the most needless on record, after four years which have done very much toward exhausting the Confederate states, the city which was the first theatre of war, which first heard the rebel shout of victory, has fallen before the prowess of our national arms.*

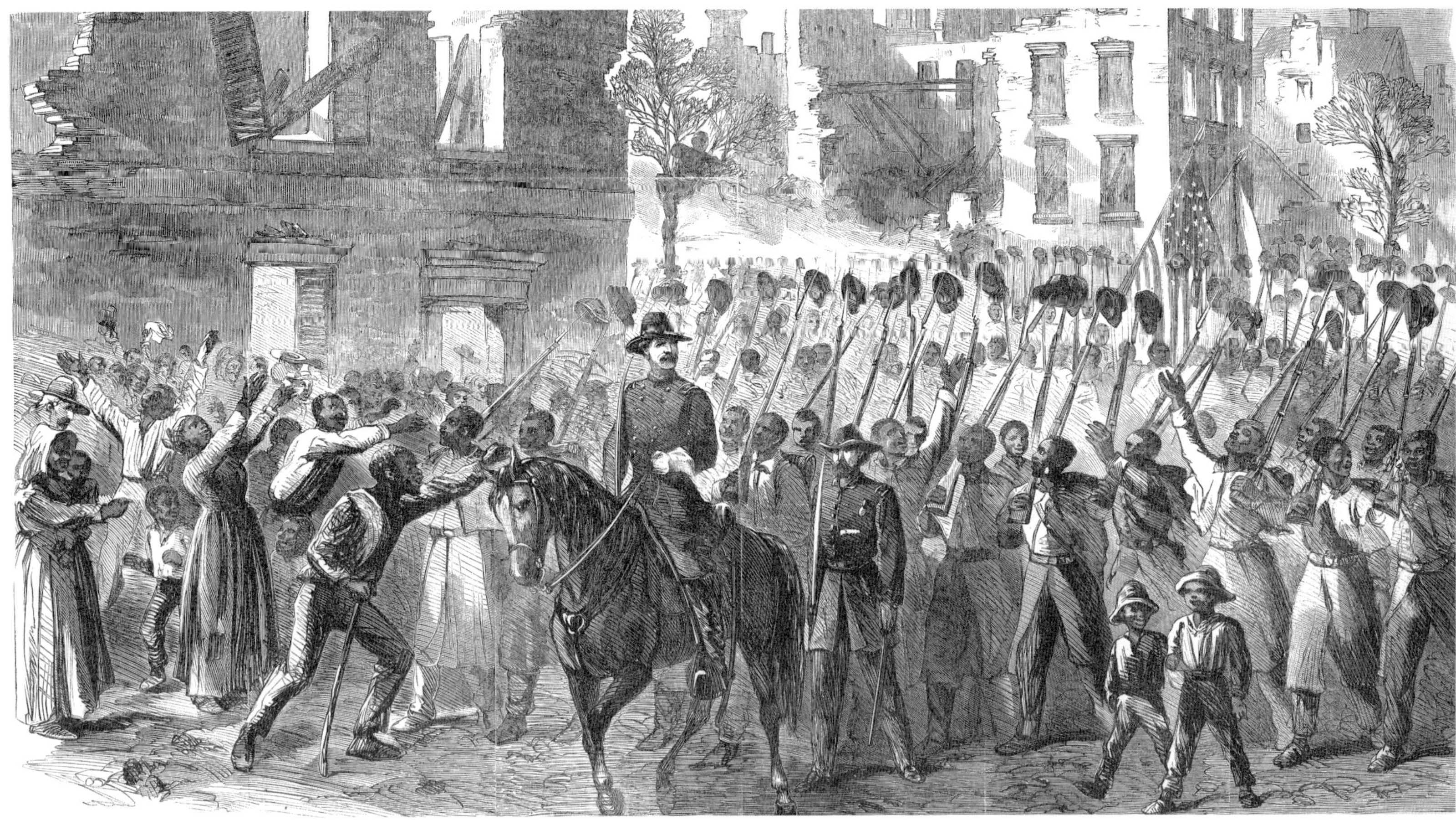

Marching through Charleston

Artist: Stanley Fox
Harper's Weekly

As the Confederate Army evacuated Charleston, it burned the remaining stores of cotton and supplies to prevent them from falling into enemy hands. The few ships in the harbor were destroyed and one fire raged out of control, exploding the railroad depot, killing and injuring many people.

Lt. Col. Augustus G. Bennett of the Union Army was the first to enter Charleston with a small detachment. After receiving the surrender of the city from the mayor, Bennett made his way to the Citadel at Marion Square, establishing the federal headquarters. Later in the day, the 21st U.S. Colored Troops arrived in the city.

This illustration depicts the march through the city on Feb. 21 by the 55th Massachusetts Colored Regiment led by Bennett. As the 55th marched in celebration, it sang *The March of John Brown's Soul*. In recognition of the event, *Harper's Weekly* writes: "If the war itself was a revolution of citizens against their government, it has introduced also a revolution quite as profound in the relation hereto existing between the negro and his master."

Many of the citizens still remaining in Charleston barricaded themselves in their homes to protect their property and possessions. Major-Gen. Quincy Gillmore, in a letter to Brig.-Gen. John P. Hatch in Charleston, writes: "I hear on all sides very discouraging accounts of the state of affairs in Charleston; that no restraint is put upon the soldiers; that they pilfer and rob houses at pleasure; that large quantities of valuable furniture, pictures, statuary, mirrors, etc., have mysteriously disappeared."

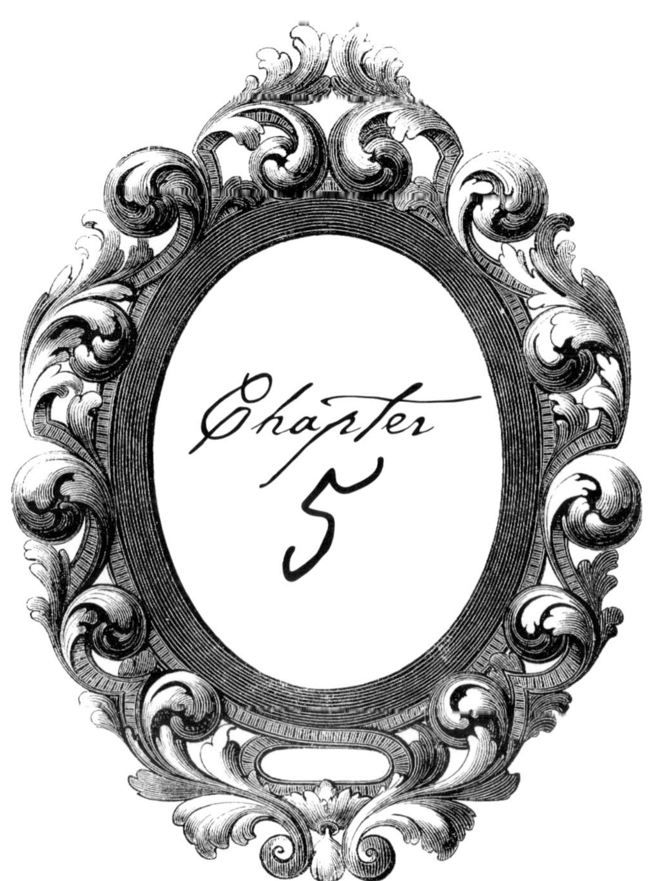

City In Ruins

In March 1865, Secretary of War Edwin M. Stanton issued an order announcing the return of Robert Anderson to the very fort where the war began.

> *That at the hour of noon, on the 14th day of April, 1865, Brevet Major-General Anderson will raise and plant upon the ruins of Fort Sumter, in Charleston harbor, the same United States flag which floated over the battlements of that fort during the rebel assault, and which was lowered and saluted by him, and the small force of his command, when the works were evacuated on the 14th of April, 1861.*

Between the date the order was issued and the April 14th celebration, both Richmond and Petersburg fell and Gen. Robert E. Lee surrendered at Appomattox.

On April 14, a crowd estimated at 5,000 men, women and children gathered at Fort Sumter. The observances were opened by the Rev. Matthias Harris. Harris served as chaplain for Anderson's small garrison at the start of the war. It was Harris who offered the prayer on Dec. 27, 1861, as Anderson raised his garrison's flag for the first time over Fort Sumter. Now, a little more than four years later, Harris again offered the prayer. Others presented prayers and speeches to commemorate the event. But the crowd anxiously awaited the main event.

Anderson stepped up to the flag pole. He was accompanied by his good and faithful friend, police Sgt. Peter Hart, the man who had nailed the flag in place while under intense fire in 1861. Hart reached into his bag, removing Anderson's old flag. The crowd cheered as three sailors attached Old Glory to the halyards and handed them to Anderson.

Filled with emotion, Anderson addressed the crowd:

> *I am here, my friends, my fellow-citizens and fellow-soldiers, to perform an act of duty to my country dear to my heart, and which all of you will appreciate and feel. Had I observed the wishes of my heart it should be done in silence; but in accordance with the request of the Honorable Secretary of War, I make a few remarks, as by his order,*

after four long, long years of war, I restore to its proper place this dear flag, which floated here during peace before the first act of this cruel rebellion. I thank God that I lived to see this day, and to be here, to perform this, perhaps the last act of my life, of duty to my country. My heart is filled with gratitude to that God who has so signally blessed us, who has given us blessings beyond measure. May all the nations bless and praise the name of the Lord, and all the world proclaim, Glory to God in the highest, and on earth peace, good-will toward men.

Anderson raised the tattered old flag as the crowd cheered and the band played. The guns remaining at Sumter fired a salute, followed by the guns at Morris Island and Fort Moultrie. Then a salute was fired from every Confederate fort and battery used against Fort Sumter. Finally, the guns of the Union fleet were fired. The ceremony concluded with a stirring speech by the Rev. Henry Ward Beecher and a benediction by the Rev. Dr. R. S. Storrs Jr.

It was 6 p.m. before the large crowd arrived back in Charleston. The Union fleet again fired a salute at sunset, then hosted a grand military ball that evening at the Charleston Hotel. At the end of the impressive meal were many toasts and speeches, including one given by Maj.-Gen. Abner Doubleday, who served with Anderson at Fort Sumter in 1861. The closing toast was reserved for Anderson. After some introductory remarks and an elegant tribute to Pres. Abraham Lincoln, Anderson raised his glass, and said:

I beg you now, that you will join me in drinking to the health of another man whom we all love to honor, the man who, when elected President of the United States, was compelled to reach the seat of government with an escort, but who now could travel all over the country with millions of hands and hearts to sustain him. I give you the good, the great, the honest man, Abraham Lincoln.

At the moment the audience in the large hall drank to Lincoln, no one assembled knew that at that same moment, the President of the United States lay dying in Washington from an assassin's bullet.

The next several years were a time of great struggle in Charleston. While the city was no longer under military assault, the port city remained a dangerous place. Looting was widespread, the city was under martial law and – as noted by the *Charleston Courier* – gangs infested the city. With a devastated economy, a ruined city and a reversal of the social order, life in Charleston was in upheaval.

Eventually, businesses found the method and means to re-open. The enormous piles of rubble were removed, the railroad repaired, the port re-opened. This was also the time phosphate mining got its start in the lowcountry. Between 1865 and 1872, more than $4.5 million dollars was spent on improvements and projects in the city.

Robert E. Lee visited Charleston in 1870, only six months before his death. During his tour, he remarked to a journalist, "I am astonished to see Charleston so wondrously recuperated after all her disasters."☙

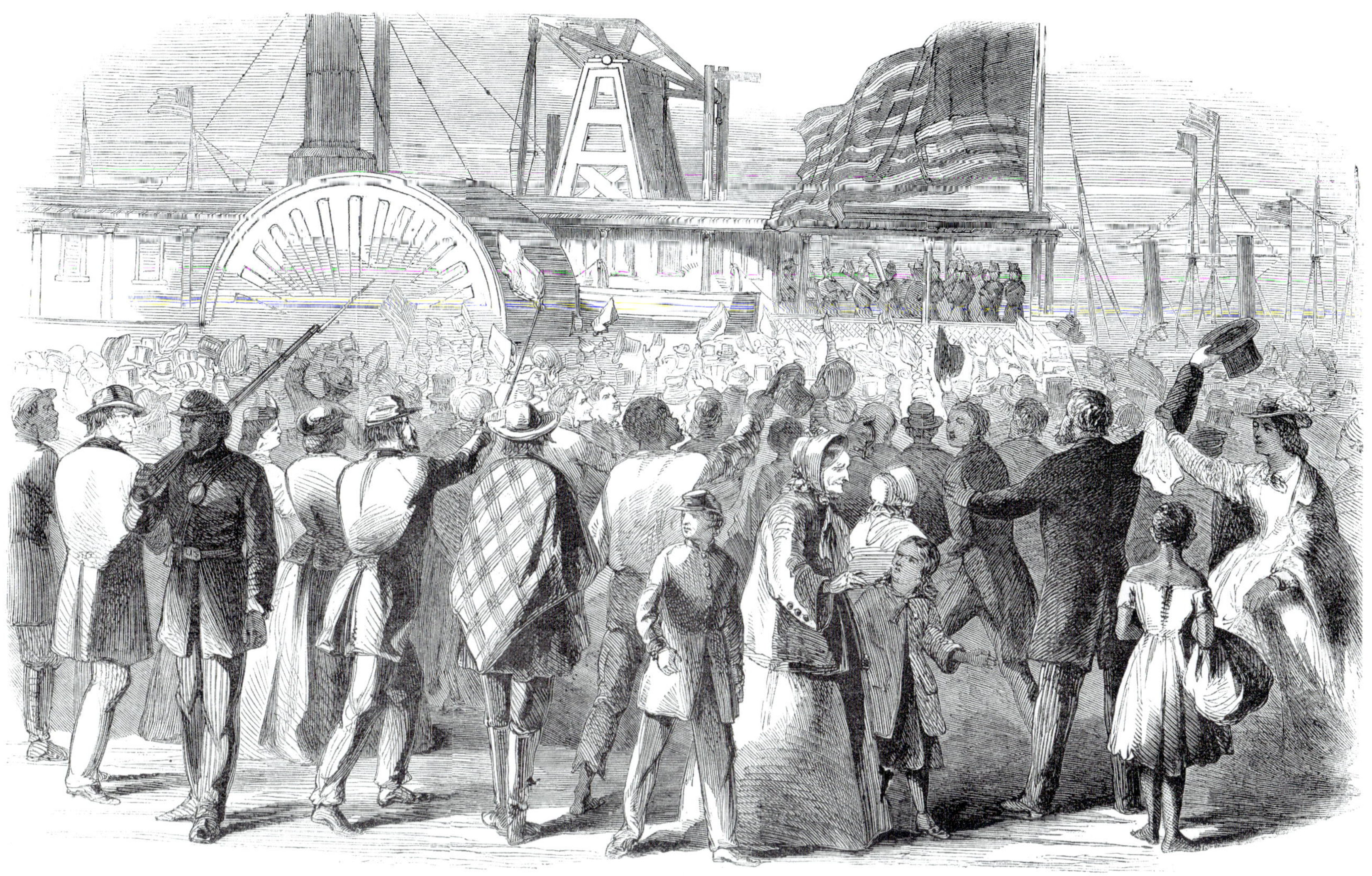

Gillmore Lands in Charleston

Artist: W. T. Crane
Frank Leslie's Illustrated Newspaper

This illustration depicts Gillmore's return to Charleston, landing at Vanderhorst's Wharf on Feb. 20, 1865. In his drawing, W. T. Crane, a *Leslie's* correspondent, shows the landing with a large and enthusiastic crowd gathered to receive Gillmore. Appropriately, Crane writes:

> *Our readers must not too hastily conclude from the sketch that the Charlestonians are repentant – for the mass there assembled was composed principally of colored persons, citizens of Northern birth and what the 'gallant and pure-blooded Chivalry' call 'white trash.'*

With the inclusion of the gentleman on the left and the women with the children at the back of the crowd, Crane effectively demonstrates that not everyone relished the opportunity to welcome Gilmore to the city he reduced to ashes.

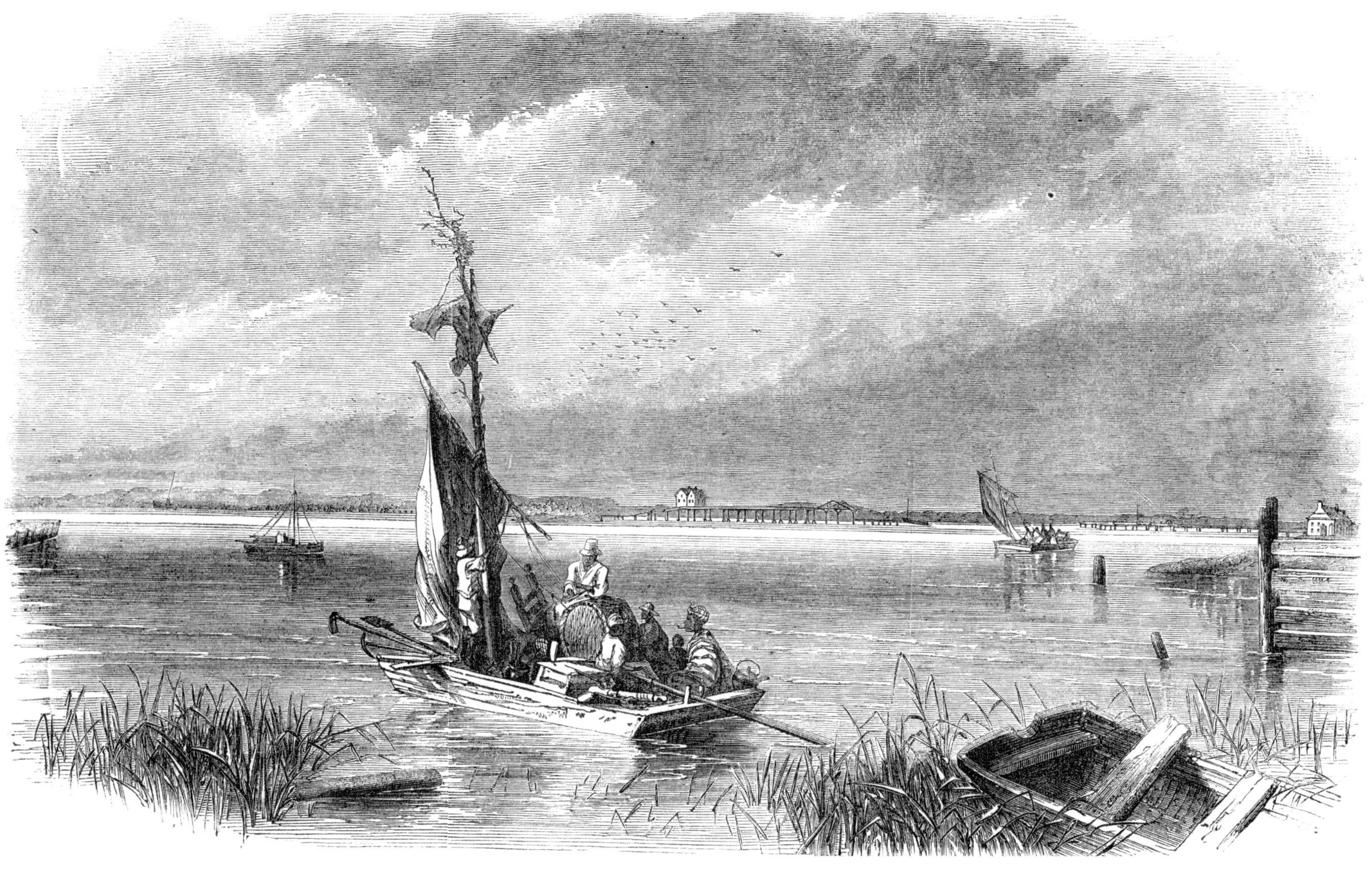

The Ashley River

Artist: W. T. Crane
Frank Leslie's Illustrated Newspaper

By 1865, Charleston was a city in ruins. In one day, the fire of 1861 ravaged the Charleston peninsula. Rebuilding after the fire was impossible since all resources were directed toward the war effort. Nevertheless, it was the siege that cost the city most dearly. As the longest siege of the war, Charleston bled in every way. Not only physically devastating, the seige inflicted a severe economic and emotional toll. As the Confederate Army evacuated Charleston, much of the remaining infrastructure was destroyed to prevent its use by Union forces waiting to enter the city. On every count, by war's end, Charleston was gutted.

In the background of this illustration is the Ashley River bridge, partially destroyed by retreating Confederates in February 1865. In the wake of the war, Charleston families, white and black, were poverty-stricken.

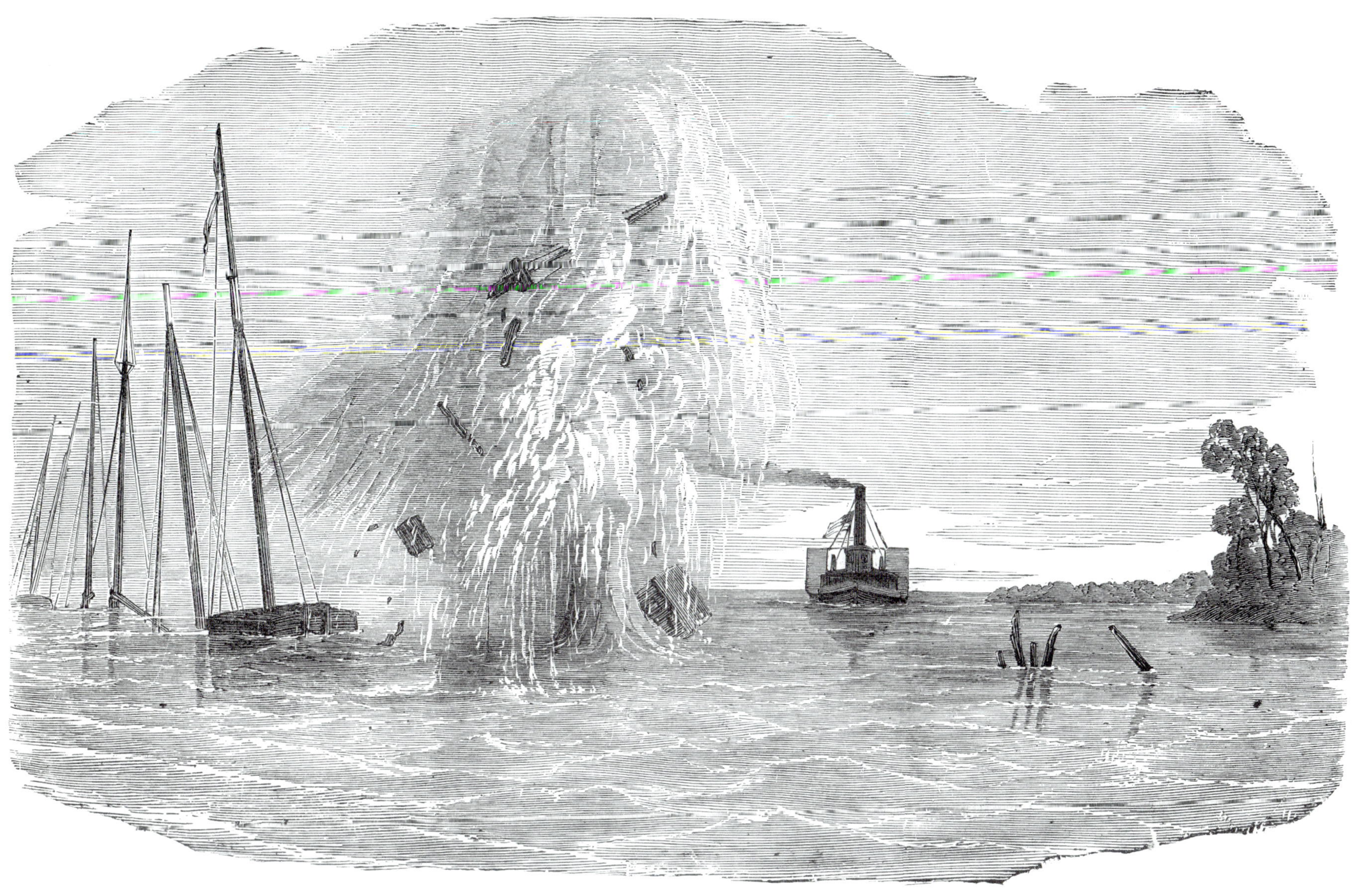

Clearing the Harbor

Artist: unknown
Frank Leslie's Illustrated Newspaper

The U.S. Navy sought to clear the harbor quickly once Charleston was again under control of the federal government. What the swift current didn't remove, the navy did by exploding the remanents of the schooners put in place during the 1862 blockade. Likewise, the iron and pine booms obstructing the harbor at two entrance points were not difficult to locate and remove.

More challenging was the arduous process of searching for and removing mines and torpedoes left in Charleston waterways. Throughout the war, Confederate engineers demonstrated exceptional skill in finding innovative ways to deliver munitions to Union ships moving through the harbor. When the Confederates evacuated Charleston, many explosive devices still lurked in the waterways.

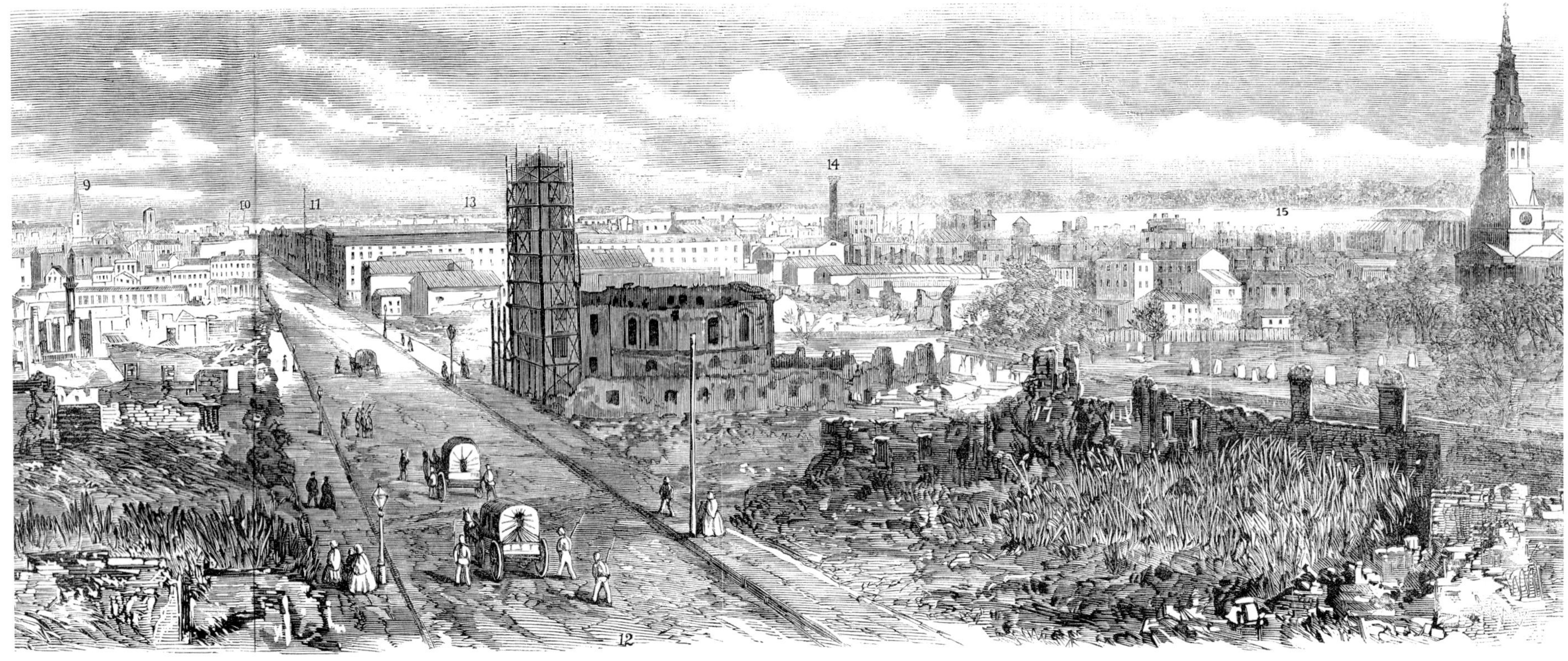

Meeting Street

Artist: W. T. Crane
Frank Leslie's Illustrated News

As Union troops occupied Charleston, *Leslie's* correspondent W. T. Crane sketched this view of Meeting Street, looking north from the Mills House. The illustration shows the devastation that befell Charleston.

The large ruin on the right is the site of South Carolina Institute Hall. In a better day, Institute Hall was host to the 1860 Democratic Convention and was where the Ordinance of Secession was signed, establishing the Republic of South Carolina. The hall burned in the great fire of 1861.

Just to the north of Institute Hall, are the ruins of the Circular Congregational Church, also destroyed in the 1861 fire. In the background to the right, stands the haggard remains of St. Philip's Episcopal Church. During the siege of Charleston, the church was struck 10 times by Union shells, which caused serious damage to the interior. In 1864, while firing from Fort Putnam, federal gunners used the 200-ft. spire to sight their fire. The congregation at St. Michael's Episcopal Church on Broad Street painted the spire of its church black during the siege to prevent federal gunners from targeting that site as well.

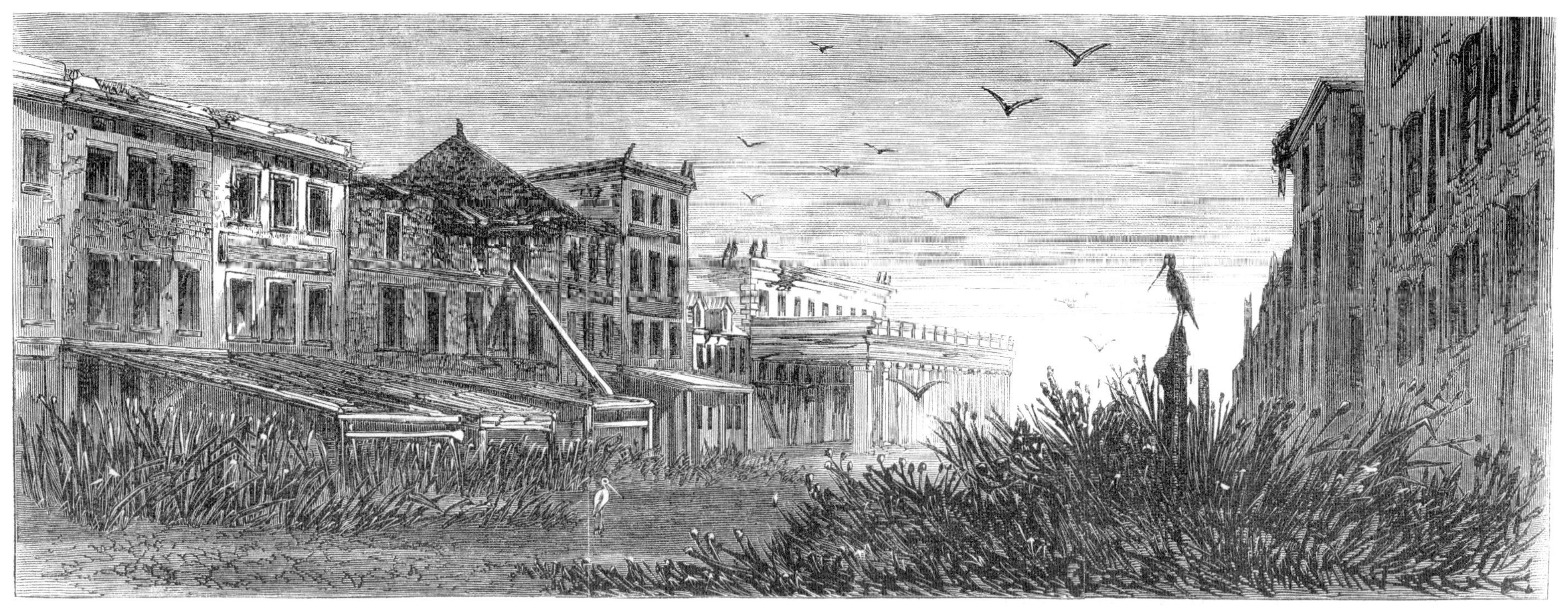

Ruins on Vendue Range

Artist: W. T. Crane
Frank Leslie's Illustrated Newspaper

In this illustration, W. T. Crane offers a view of Vendue Range in Charleston in March 1865. Vendue Range was part of the city that residents called the "Shell District," referring to the fact that it was within range of Union batteries after the Confederate evacuation of Morris Island. Before the war, the area was home to many shops.

Crane offers to the reader:

> *The appearance baffles all description; scarcely a house remains intact; in some instances a dozen shell have entered the same building; glass is invariably shattered in almost every window; roofs are crushed and walls lean, crack, and gape at you as you silently and thoughtfully gaze upon them; grass is growing in the streets;... Crows scream around the ruins; broken bricks, timbers and debris of all kind are heaped around.... Look at it now, and we see the blight of the touch of secession's fingers.*

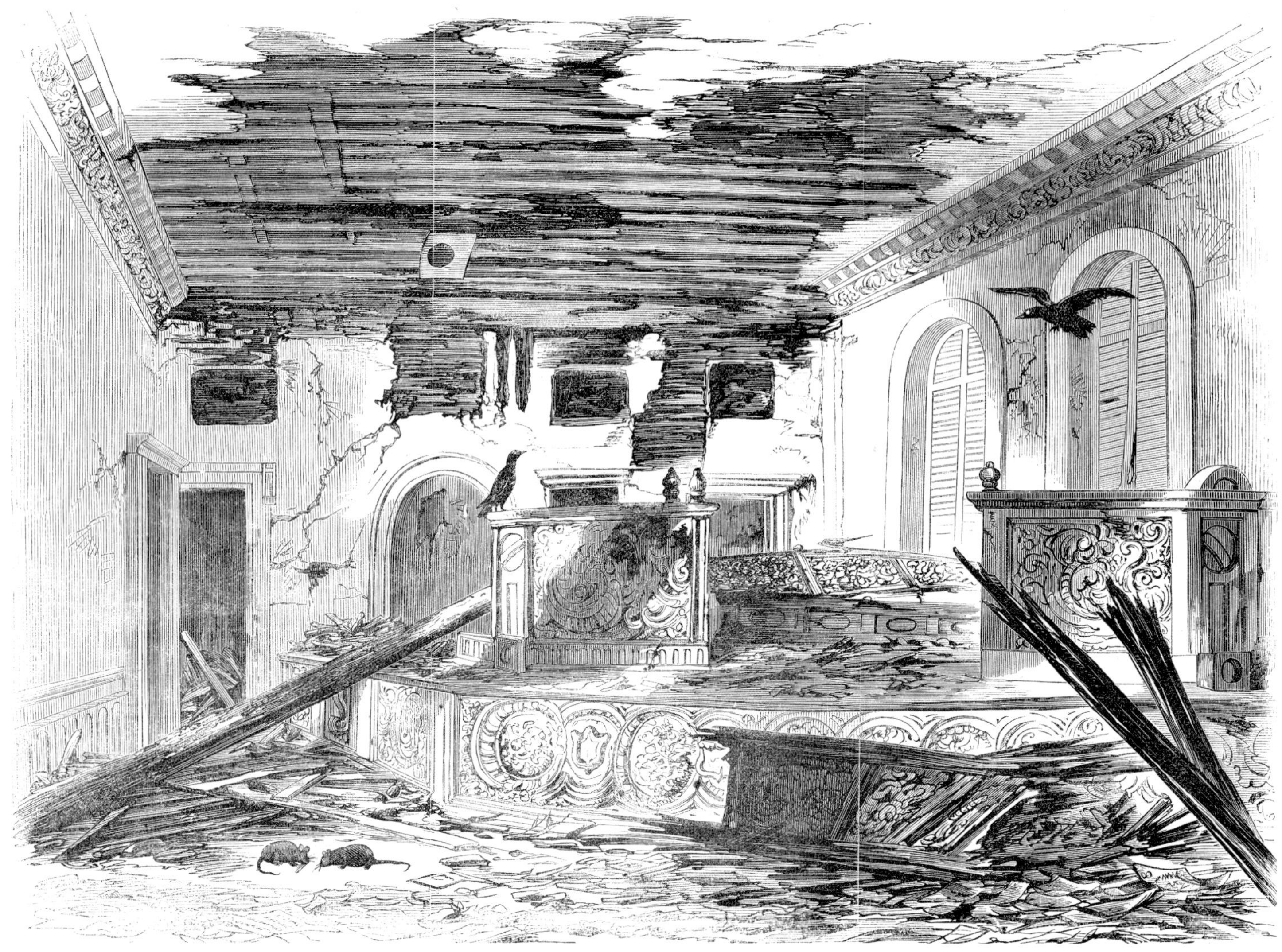

State Bank of South Carolina

Artist: W. T. Crane
Frank Leslie's Illustrated Newspaper

An opportunity perceived as too poetic to pass up, *Leslie's* artist W. T. Crane sketched the State Bank of South Carolina, now part of the ruins of Charleston. *Leslie's* writes:

> *Our Artist found this once wealthy bank in ruins, the furniture destroyed, the walls disfigured by our shells, and the literary matter of the establishment, as cheques and blanks of various kinds, given over to the cunning artificers of rats' nests and crows' nests. The Confederate credit is very fairly indicated by our picture of the bank at Charleston.*

After touring Charleston, Crane writes:

> *I have seldom looked upon a more dismal sight than Charleston is now. We must at least give its citizens credit for the fortitude with which they have endured their siege, for most certainly our officers were not aware of one-half the damage our fire had inflicted.*

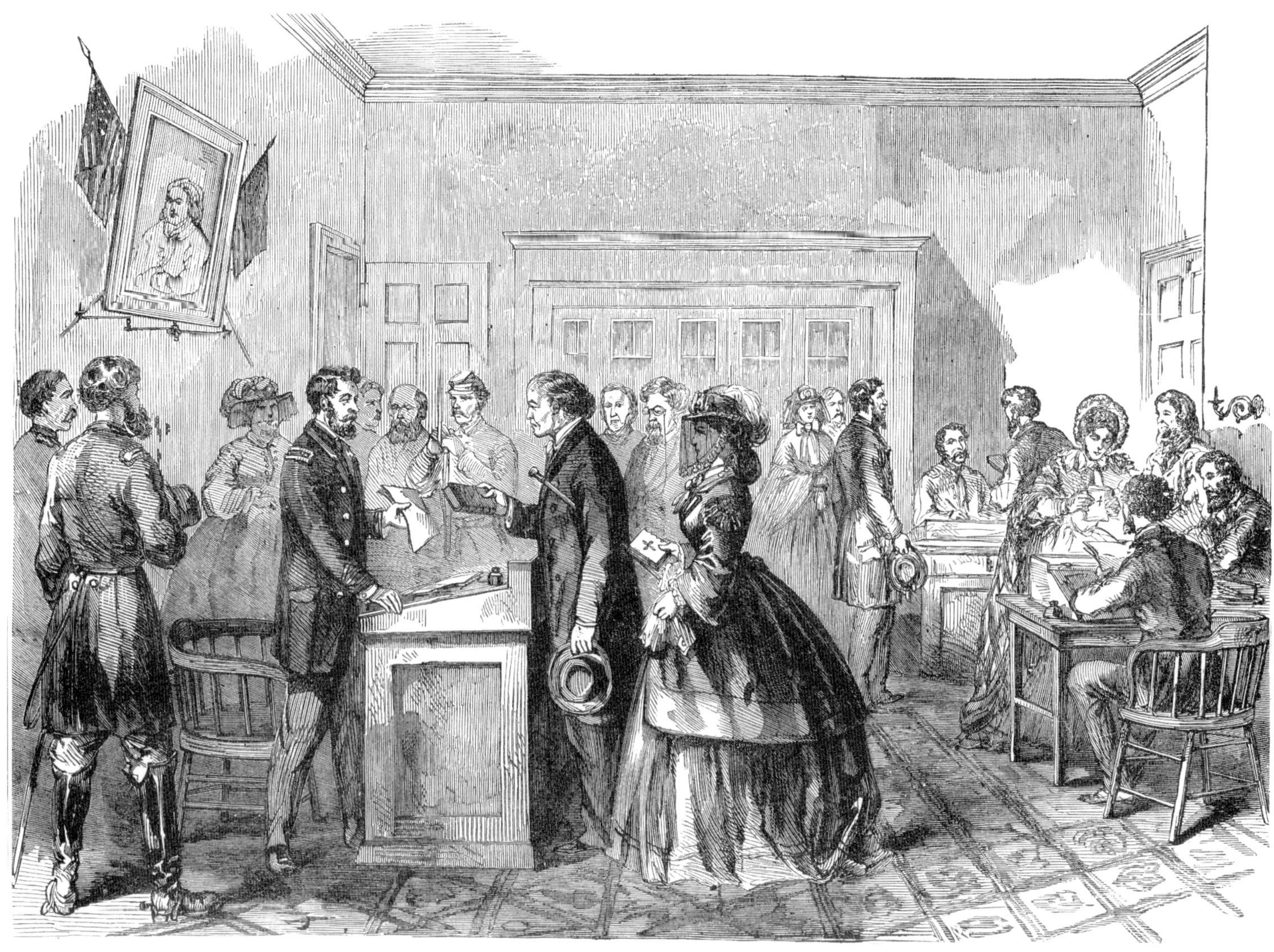

Taking the Oath of Allegiance

Artist: W. T. Crane
Frank Leslie's Illustrated Newspaper

After federal forces occupied Charleston, the city was placed under martial law, under Brig.-Gen. Alexander Schimmelfennig. Schimmelfennig established his headquarters at the Miles Brewton House at 27 King Street, which coincidentally served as the headquarters for the British army occupying Charleston during the Revolution.

On Feb. 28, Schimmelfennig issued General Order No. 8, requiring citizens of Charleston to take the Oath of Allegiance to the United States. Those who refused to take the oath had necessary passes refused to them. Additionally, Schimmelfennig ordered that anyone plundering a home flying the United States flag would be punished. The inference, naturally, was that homes not loyal to or swearing the Oath of Allegiance would be vulnerable to looting.

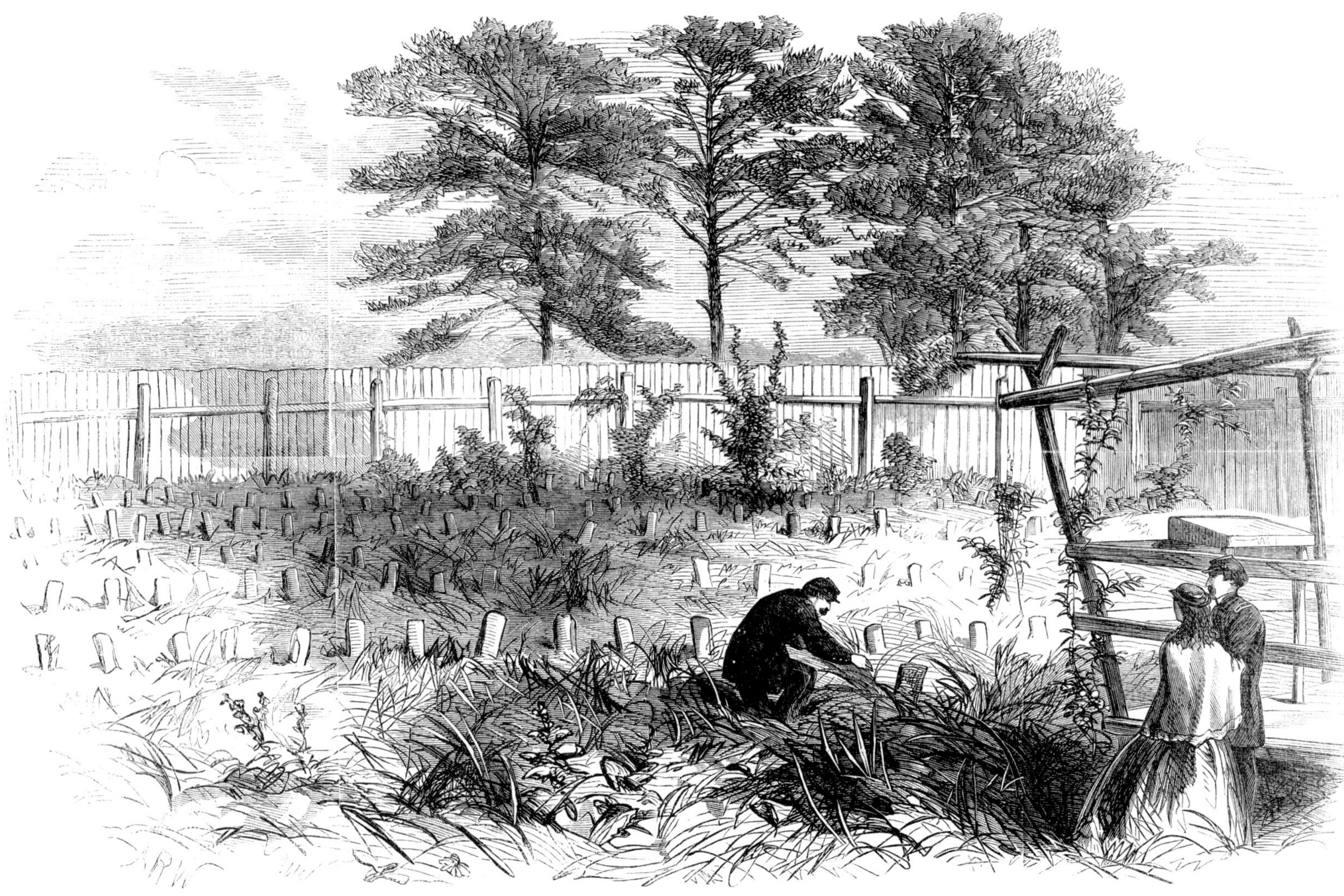

Martyrs of the Race Course

Artist: A. R. Waud
Harper's Weekly

Through the course of the war, the large number of Union prisoners required the establishment of many prison sites to contain them. One such prison was known as the "prison-pen," established at the race course just outside the city. Union soldiers who died while in captivity were buried in an open field next to the prison.

Harper's Weekly artist A. R. Waud visited the cemetery in 1867. In his report to the newspaper, he notes a sign hanging over the gate to the field with the inscription, "The Martyrs of the Race-Course." Of the cemetery, Waud offers this description: "There is a crude desk from which the service for the dead was sometimes read. At this time, a mass of tangled grass and herbage nearly hides from sight the little head-boards which mark the graves."

All of the men buried there were later moved to the National Cemetery established in Beaufort, S.C., also the final resting place of the Union soldiers recovered from Morris Island.

The site of the race-course cemetery is, today, Hampton Park. Prior to the Civil War, this site was used both for local horse racing and as a fair grounds.

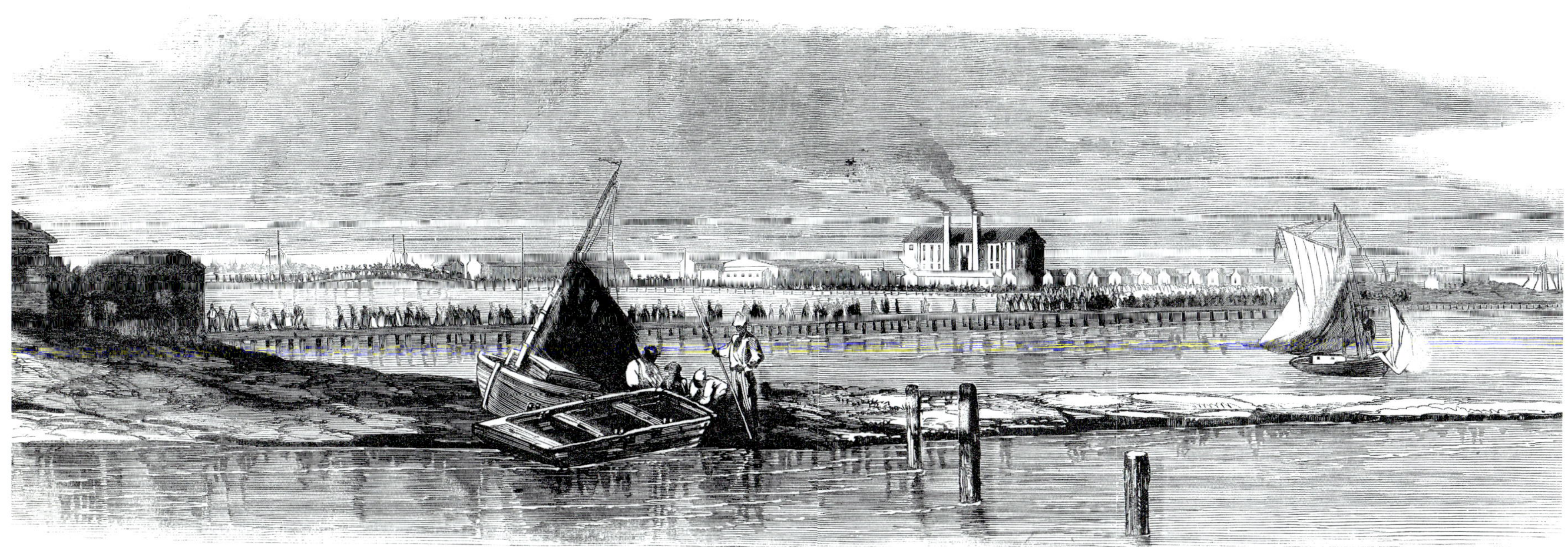

Feeding the Thousands

Artist: W. T. Crane
Frank Leslie's Illustrated Newspaper

Many wealthy Charlestonians fled the city prior to its occupation by Union forces. By the spring of 1865, those who remained in the city were poorer whites and freed slaves looking for opportunity.

Col. Augustus G. Bennett led the effort to secure the city and extinguish the many fires set by Confederates to prevent supplies from falling into Union hands. Next came the job of removing debris and feeding the thousands of homeless and starving people. Bennett appointed a citizen's committee to handle the critical task of distributing rice, corn meal and salt seized by the army in town.

The committee set up food distribution points around the city, one of which is depicted here at West Point Mills on the Ashley River. Separate days were appointed for whites and blacks to receive their food allotments – an effort to maintain order. To prevent people receiving more than one allotment per day, soldiers monitored the crowds entering the mill by one route and exiting by another. By June 1865, the committee had fed more than 20,000 people, depleting their supplies. The Freedman's Bureau, set up to distribute food and clothing to freed slaves, also had insufficient stores.

As if poor living conditions, a collapsed economy and exhausted food supplies were not enough of a challenge, at the end of 1865, both smallpox and "break-bone fever" spread to the city's struggling citizens.

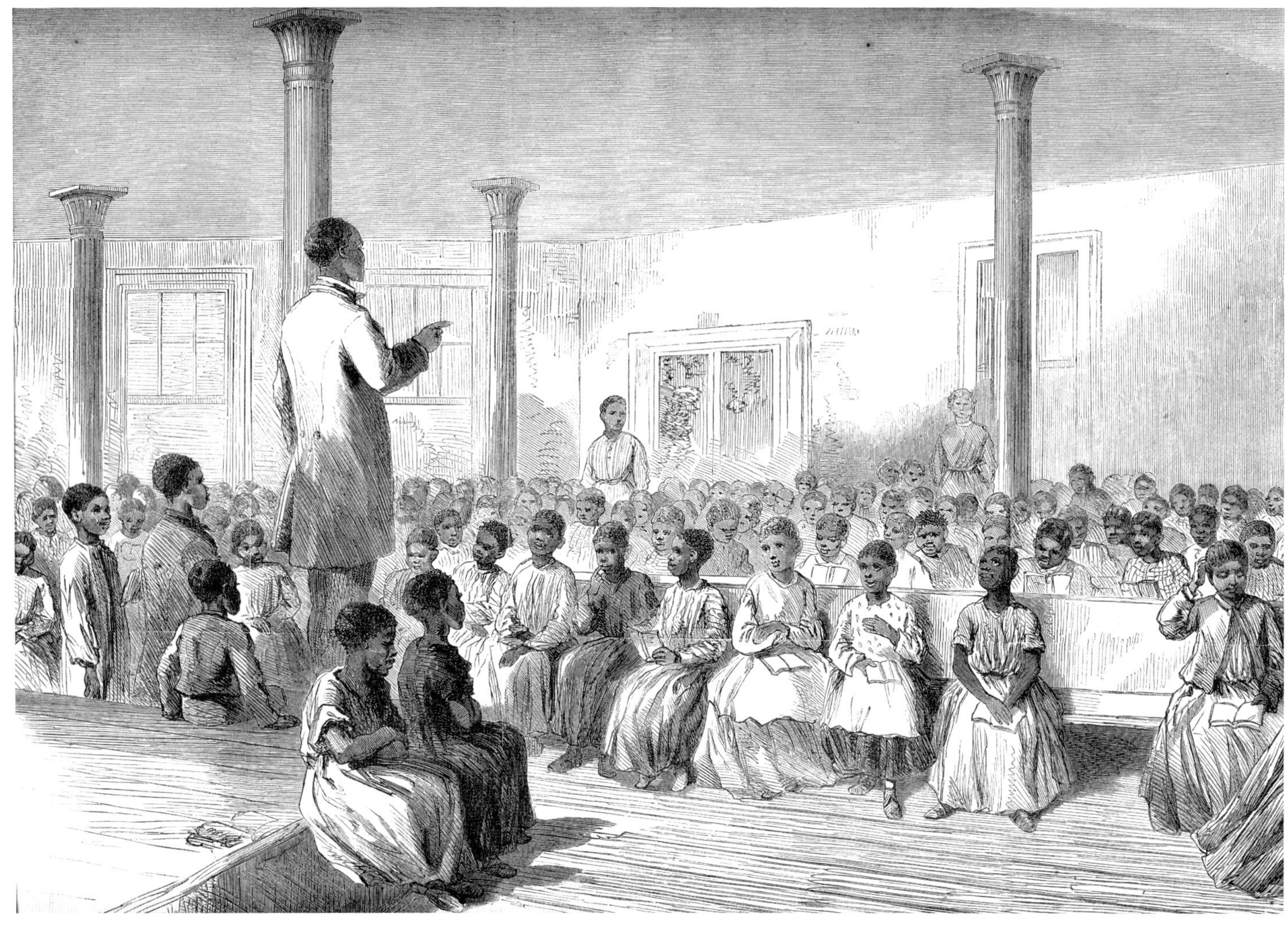

Zion School for Colored Children

Artist: A. R. Waud
Harper's Weekly

After the war, many missionaries and teachers moved South to work with the freedmen. In most cases, the missionaries and teachers were Northern whites. *Harper's* correspondent A. R. Waud sketched a picture of the Zion School, a Charleston school for black children. He notes the Zion School was unusual in that the entire staff was black. The school was organized by the Old School Presbyterian Church in December 1865.

Zion School, the last of the Charleston area schools opened and maintained by Northern philanthropists, had 850 black children enrolled and an average attendance of 720. The staff of teachers numbered 13. Shown in the illustration is the school principal and teacher, Mr. Van Horn of New Jersey.

In his report to *Harper's*, Waud writes, "Although the Southern people seem generally opposed to the education of the negroes, still, if they must have it, they prefer to see colored people in charge of their own race to having Northern whites as teachers."

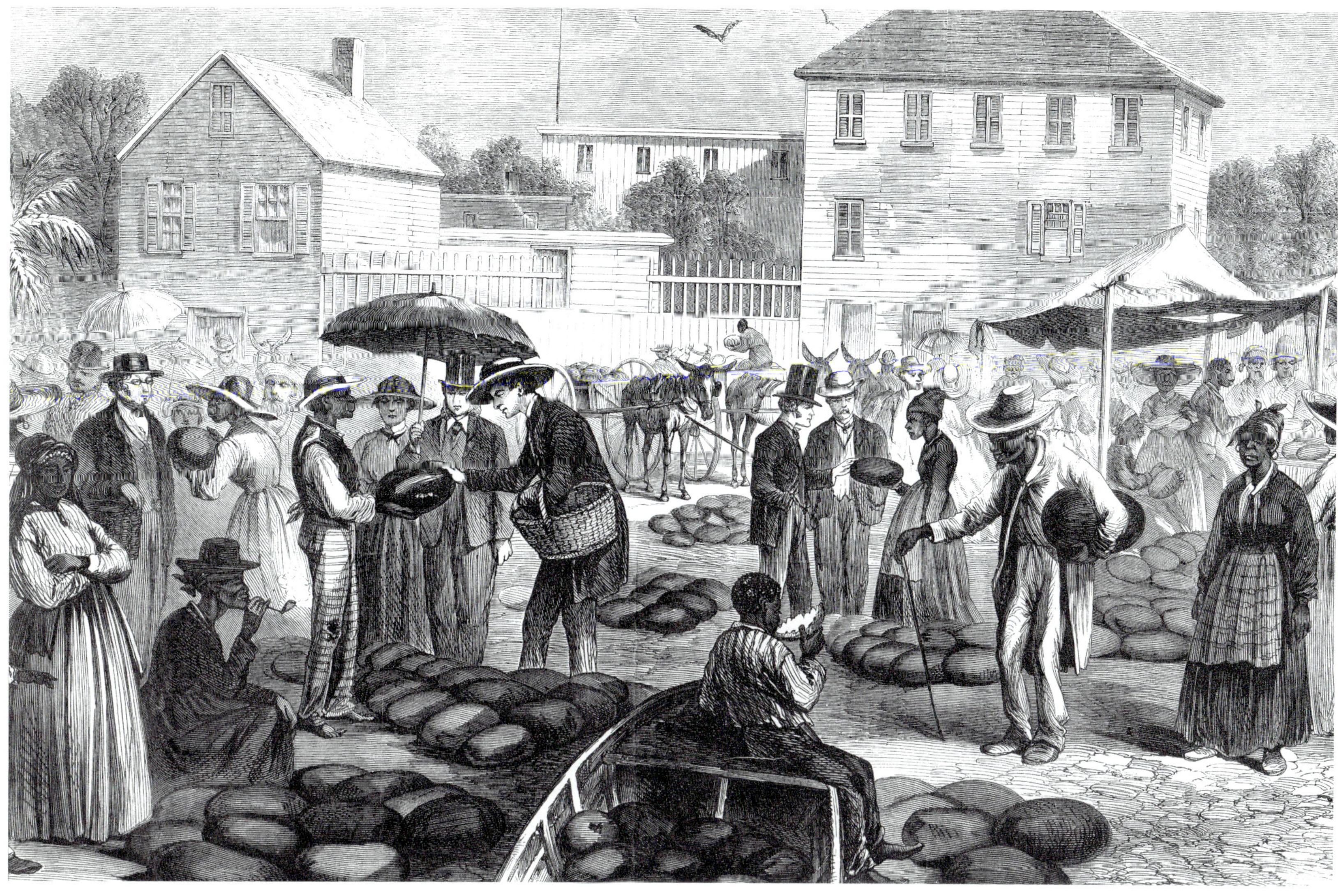

The Watermelon Market

Artist: James E. Taylor
Frank Leslie's Illustrated Newspaper

Occupation forces focused on policing and cleaning up the city throughout 1865. Along with the troops, several hundred laborers were hired to haul garbage and debris out of the city. Thousands of freedmen left farms and plantations, and flocked to Charleston seeking opportunity. Opportunities, however, were scant.

By 1866, Charleston was starting to get back on her feet. Pres. Andrew Johnson appointed native South Carolinian George W. Williams to oversee the customs operation in the state. A group of Charleston businessmen organized the Board of Trade to stimulate business in the city. The aim was to restore Charleston's place as the center of Southern trade and commerce.

As depicted in this illustration, food markets sprung up, offering fresh produce. The artist's rendering shows no change in the relationship of whites and blacks – all blacks are shown in subservient roles no different than during antebellum times. In other regards, however, with a struggling economy and dramatic changes to the city's social order, Charleston in 1866 resembled anything but the antebellum age.

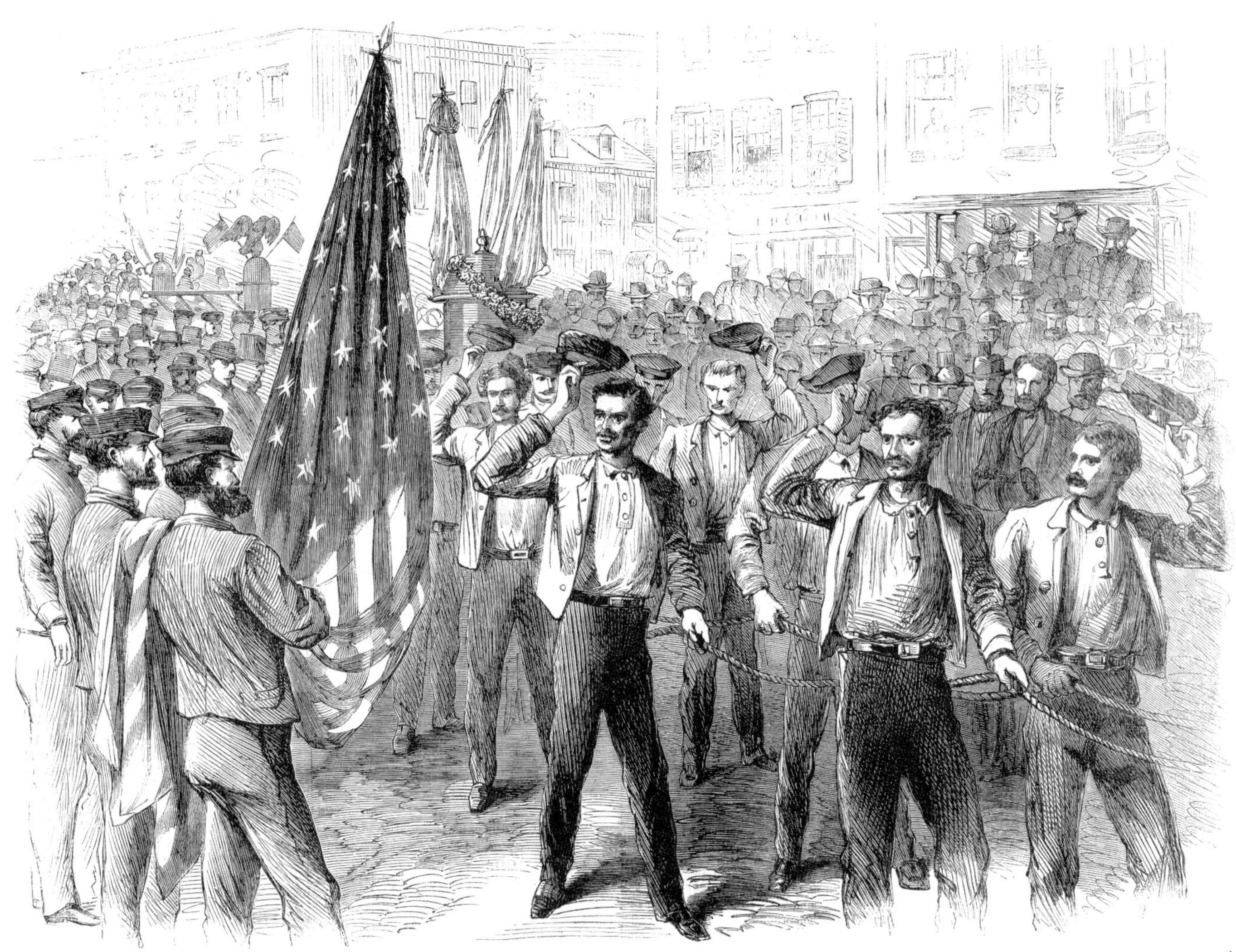

Saluting the Old Flag

Artist: A. R. Waud
Harper's Weekly

Charleston had a long tradition of volunteer fire companies. Each year, the city's volunteers would don their uniforms and parade ahead of their engines, passing for review by the Board of Firemasters, the mayor and local dignitaries. Major-Gen. Daniel Sickles, the military commander of South Carolina overseeing martial law, was quite put out that during the 1866 parade no United States flag was displayed on the reviewing stand. Fire Chief Nathan insisted it was a simple oversight.

The following year, as the review stand was assembled again for the annual parade, Sickles made a point to look for the United States flag. Again, no flag was displayed. He halted the parade, ordering Chief Nathan to secure a United States flag and place it on the street opposite the reviewing stand. He further ordered every man in the parade to salute the flag by lifting his hat while passing, forcing them literally to turn their eyes away from the review stand.

One fireman removed a star from the flag, a symbolic gesture that indicated South Carolina wanted no part of the Union. He was arrested promptly and imprisoned for 30 days.

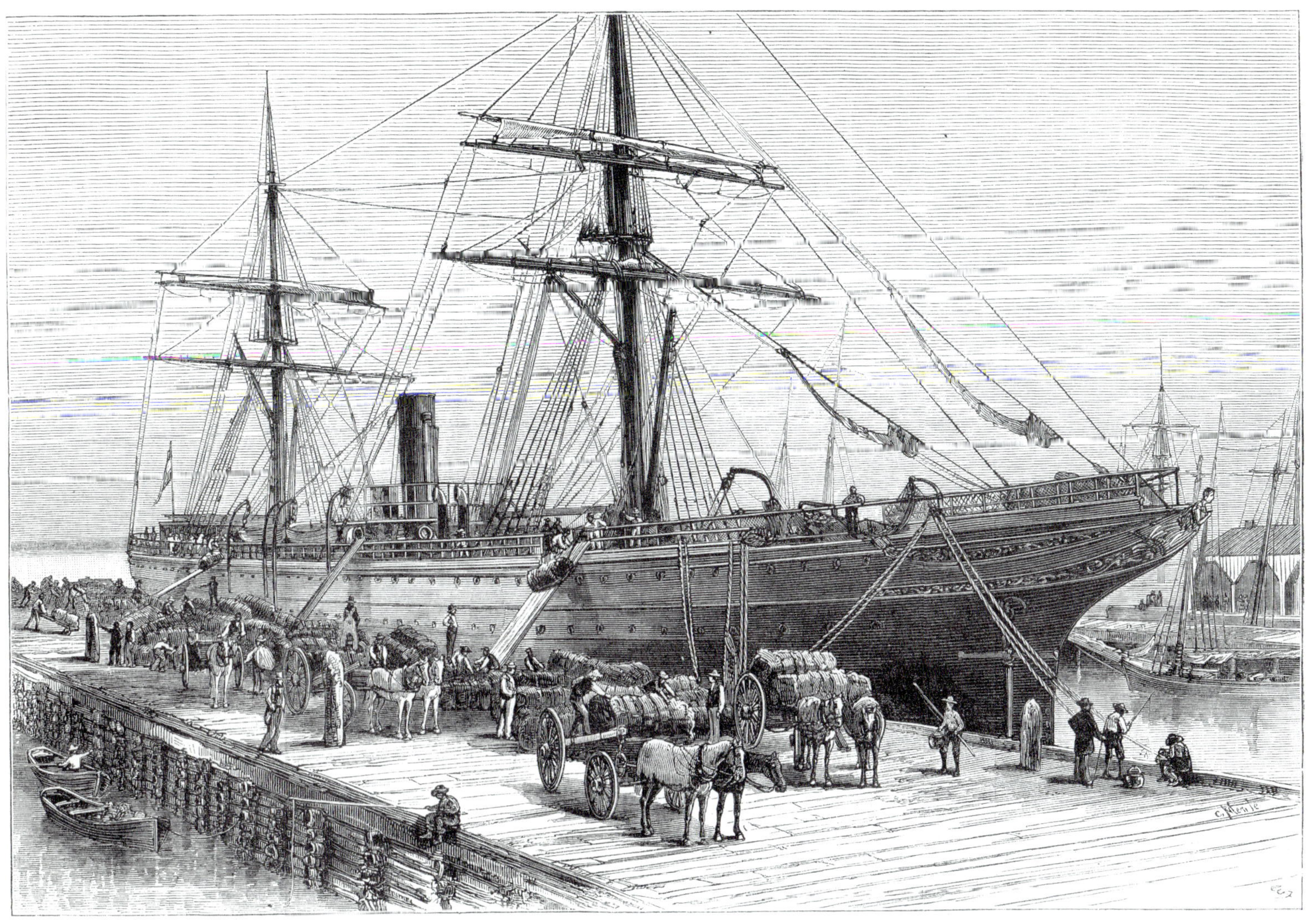

Loading Cotton

From a photograph by George N. Barnard
Harper's Weekly

Cotton and rice had created the enormous wealth of the aristocrat planter class in South Carolina. Both cash crops required prodigious labor forces, economically possible under the structure of slavery. After the war, with slavery formally gone, Charlestonians, white and black, had significant adjustments to make merely to survive.

Many white planters were either absent or dead following the war, often leaving children struggling with the responsibility of maintaining family plantation properties. They had no cash, few assets to obtain credit and no experience negotiating for labor in a manner never experienced by their forefathers.

Freedmen, though no longer enslaved, were severely compromised. While most had farming skills, they had neither cash nor experience negotiating for seed and credit.

RECOMMENDED READING

There are many excellent books that focus on the Civil War in Charleston. The following books are still in print and can be obtained for further reading:

For overviews of the war in Charleston, look for Milby Burton's, *The Siege of Charleston: 1861-1865* (Columbia, S.C.: University of South Carolina Press, 1970) and Robert Rosen's *Confederate Charleston: An Illustrated History of the City and People During the Civil War* (Columbia, S.C.: University of South Carolina Press, 1994). Both works are excellent studies that merit reading. *Confederate Charleston*, as an illustrated work, includes many notable paintings and portraits as well as some of the illustrations provided in this text. In *Confederate Charleston*, Rosen offers valuable insights about the lives of some key people involved in the war.

To examine the beginning of the war and the firing on Fort Sumter, consult David Detzer's *Allegiance: Fort Sumter, Charleston, and the Beginning of the Civil War* (New York: Harcourt, Inc., 2001). Detzer does an excellent job of presenting the personal lives of the many people caught up in the drama of Charleston in early 1861, which culminates with the Confederate firing on Fort Sumter.

The Battle of Secessionville was a short engagement early in the war that is often overlooked in Civil War books and documentaries. Patrick Brennan's book *Secessionville: Assault on Charleston* (Campbell, Calif.: Savas Publishing Company, 1996) not only brings the action to life through his detailed account, but puts the events on James Island into their proper place in the understanding of the early war.

Stephen Wise's *Gate of Hell: Campaign for Charleston Harbor, 1863*, (Columbia, S.C.: University of South Carolina Press, 1994) provides a splendid overview of the fierce and bloody campaign on Morris Island in 1863. Wise demonstrates his in-depth understanding of the strategies, ordinance and men involved on this sun-drenched sandy island that played such a key role in the siege of Charleston.

BIBLIOGRAPHY

Bradshaw Jr., Timothy Eugene. *Battery Wagner: The Siege, The Men Who Fought and the Casualties*. Columbia, S.C.: Palmetto Historical Works, 1993.

Brennan, Patrick. *Secessionville: Assault on Charleston*. Campbell, Calif.: Savas Publishing Company, 1996.

Brown, Joshua. *Beyond the Lines: Pictorial Reporting, Everyday Life, and the Crisis of Gilded Age America*. Berkeley, Calif.: University of California Press, 2002.

Burton, E. Milby. *The Siege of Charleston: 1861-1865*. Columbia, S.C.: University of South Carolina Press, 1970.

Castel, Albert. *Fort Sumter: 1861*. Harrisburg, Penn.: Eastern Acorn Press, 1981.

Charleston Courier. Charleston, S.C., 1860-1865.

Chesnut, Mary Boykin. *A Diary From Dixie*. Ed. Ben Amos Williams. Boston: Houghton Mifflin Company, 1949.

Cohen, David L. *The Life and Times of King Cotton*. New York: Oxford University Press, 1956.

Detzer, David. Allegiance: *Fort Sumter, Charleston, and the Beginning of the Civil War.* New York: Harcourt, Inc., 2001.

Doubleday, Abner. *Reminiscences of Forts Sumter and Moultrie in 1860-61*. Charleston, S.C.: The Nautical and Aviation Publishing Company of America, 1998.

Duncan, Russell, ed. *Blue-Eyed Child of Fortune: The Civil War Letters of Col. Robert Gould Shaw*. Athens, Ga.: University of Georgia Press, 1992.

Eaton, Clement. *A History of the Southern Confederacy*. New York: The Free Press, 1954.

Emilio, Luis F. *A Brave Black Regiment: The History of the Fifty-Fourth Regiment of the Massachusetts Volunteer Infantry, 1863-1865*. New York: Da Capo Press, 1995.

Fort Sumter: Anvil of War. Washington: U.S. Department of the Interior, 1984.

Flood, Charles Bracelen. *Lee: The Last Years*. Boston: Houghton Mifflin Company, 1981.

Frank Leslie's Illustrated Newspaper. New York, 1860-1867.

Fraser Jr., Walter J. *Charleston! Charleston!: The History of a Southern City*. Columbia, S.C.: University of South Carolina Press, 1989.

Harleston, John. "Battery Wagner on Morris Island 1863." *South Carolina Historical Magazine* 57 (1956): 1-13.

Harper's Weekly Journal of Civilization. New York, 1860-1878.

Harris, Brayton. *Blue and Gray in Black and White: Newspapers in the Civil War*. Washington: Batsford Brassey, Inc., 1999.

Hunter, Alvah Folson. *A Year on a Monitor and the Destruction of Fort Sumter*. Columbia, S.C.: University of South Carolina Press, 1987

Illustrated London News. London, 1860-1864.

Johnson, John. *The Defense of Charleston Harbor*. Charleston, S.C.: Walker, Evans and Cogswell Co., 1890.

Leslie's Illustrated Civil War. London: University of Mississippi Press, 1992.

Mercury. Charleston, S.C., 1860-1865

Neely Jr., Mark E., Harold Holzer and Gabor S. Boritt. *The Confederate Image: Prints of the Lost Cause*. Chapel Hill, N.C.: University of North Carolina Press, 1987.

Neely Jr., Mark E., and Harold Holzer. *The Union Image: Popular Prints of the Civil War North*. Chapel Hill, N.C.: University of North Carolina Press, 2000.

New York Illustrated News. New York, 1860-1864.

Perkins, Howard Cecil, ed. *Northern Editorials on Secession*. Gloucester, Mass.: Peter Smith, 1964.

Porter, D. D., A. Toomer. *Led On! Step by Step*. New York: G. P. Putnam and Sons, 1898.

Ripley, Warren, ed. *Siege Train: The Journal of a Confederate Artilleryman in the Defense of Charleston*. Columbia, S.C.: University of South Carolina Press, 1986.

Rosen, Robert N., *Confederate Charleston: An Illustrated History of the City and People During the Civil War*. Columbia, S.C.: University of South Carolina Press, 1994.

Sherman, Gen. W. T. *Memoirs of General W. T. Sherman*. New York: Charles L. Webster & Company, 1891.

Simpson, Marc. *Winslow Homer: Paintings of the Civil War*. San Francisco: The Fine Arts Museum of San Francisco, 1988.

Southern Illustrated News. Richmond, Va., 1862-1864.

Stokeley, Jim. *Fort Moultrie: Constant Defender*. Washington: U.S. Department of the Interior, 1985.

Storey, Graham. *The Letters of Charles Dickens*. Oxford: Clarendon Press, 1998.

Symonds, Craig L. *Charleston Blockade: The Journals of John B. Marchland, US Navy, 1861-1862*. Newport, R.I.: Naval War College Press, 1976.

Thompson, William F. The *Image of War: The Pictorial Reporting of the American Civil War*. Baton Rouge, La.: Louisiana State University Press, 1994.

War of the Rebellion: A Compilation of the Official Records of the Union and Confederate Armies, The. Washington: Government Printing Office, 1880-1901.

Wise, Stephen R. *Gate of Hell: Campaign for Charleston Harbor, 1863*. Columbia, S.C.: University of South Carolina Press, 1994.

Woodhead, Henry, ed. *Voices of the Civil War: Charleston*. Alexandria, Va.: Time-Life Books, 1997.

Young, Rogers W. "Castle Pinckney, Silent Sentinel of Charleston Harbor." *The South Carolina Historical and Genealogical Magazine* 39 (1938) 1-67.

INDEX

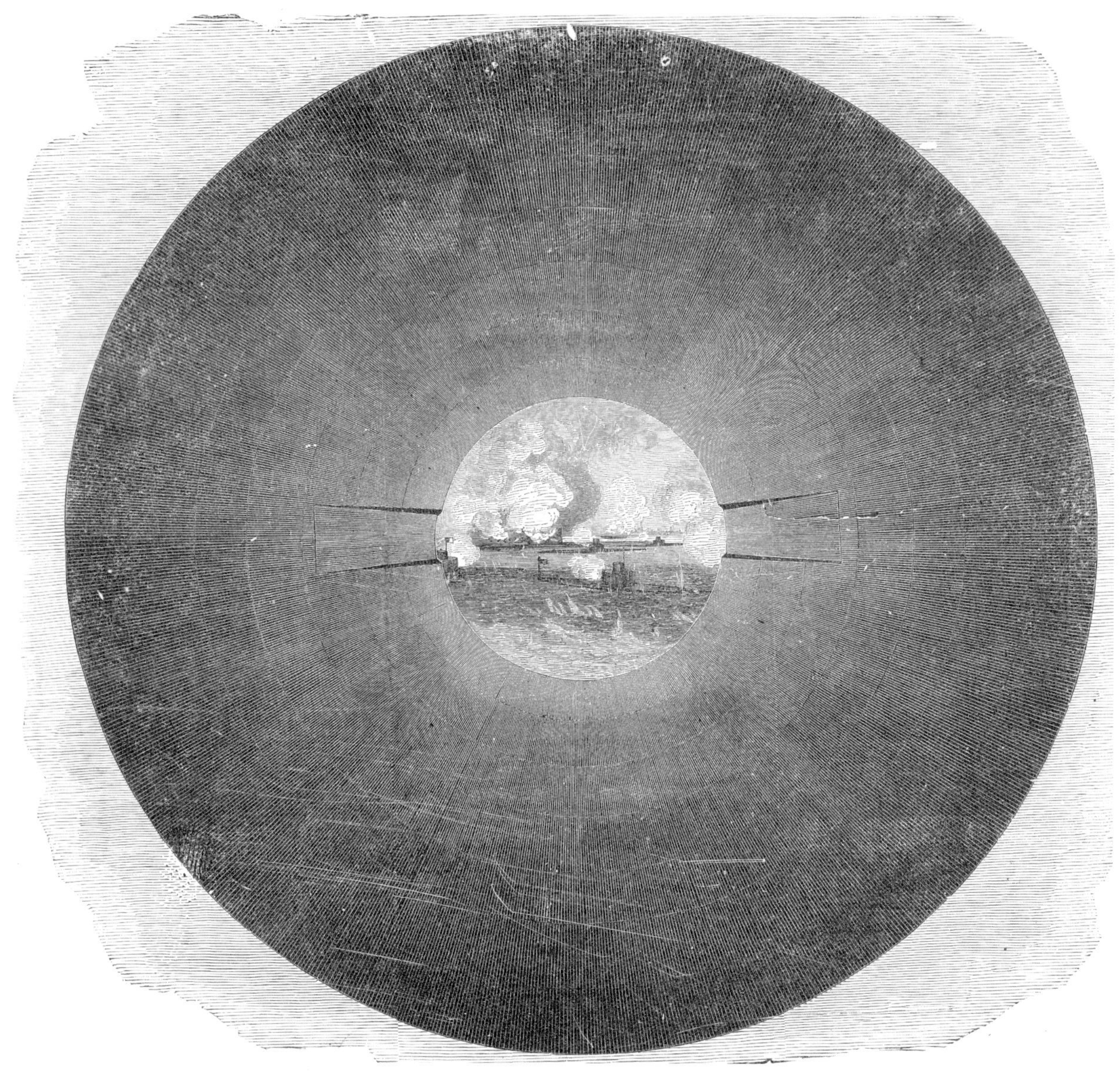

The bombardment of Fort Sumter as seen from the lookout of the turret of the *Weehawken*.

Attention corporations, universities, colleges and professional organizations: Quantity discounts are available for bulk purchases of this book for educational or gift purposes and as premiums for increasing magazine subscriptions or renewals. For information, please contact Joggling Board Press, LLC, P.O.Box 13029, Charleston, S.C., 29422. Ph. (843) 225-6009, www.jogglingboardpress.com.